Envision It! | Visual Skills Handbook

Author's Purpose

Categorize and Classify

Cause and Effect

Compare and Contrast

Draw Conclusions

Fact and Opinion

Generalize

Graphic Sources

Literary Elements

Main Idea and Details

Sequence

Author's Purpose

An author writes for many purposes, some of which are to inform, entertain, persuade, or express a mood or feeling. An author may have more than one purpose for writing. Sometimes the author's purpose is directly stated, but other times you have to figure it out on your own.

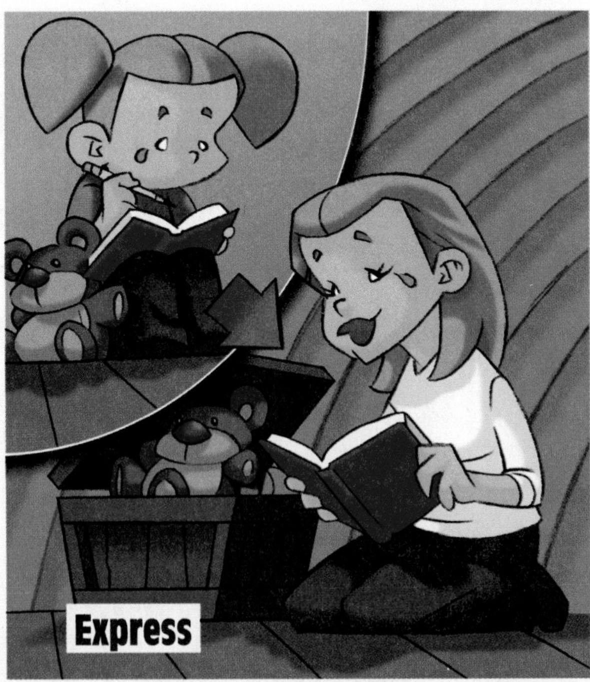

Categorize and Classify

When we categorize and classify, we look at how people or things are related based on their characteristics.

Cause and Effect

A cause is why something happened.

An effect is what happened.

An effect can have more than one cause.

A cause can have more than one effect.

Compare and Contrast

To compare and contrast is to look for similarities and differences in things.

Draw Conclusions

When we draw conclusions, we think about facts and details and then decide something about them.

Fact and Opinion

A fact is something that can be proved true or false. An opinion can't be proved.

Fact
Wow, you blew the tuba for 45 seconds straight!
Opinion
But I think it sounds HORRIBLE!

Generalize

To generalize is to make a broad statement or rule that applies to many examples.

Batteries never last very long.

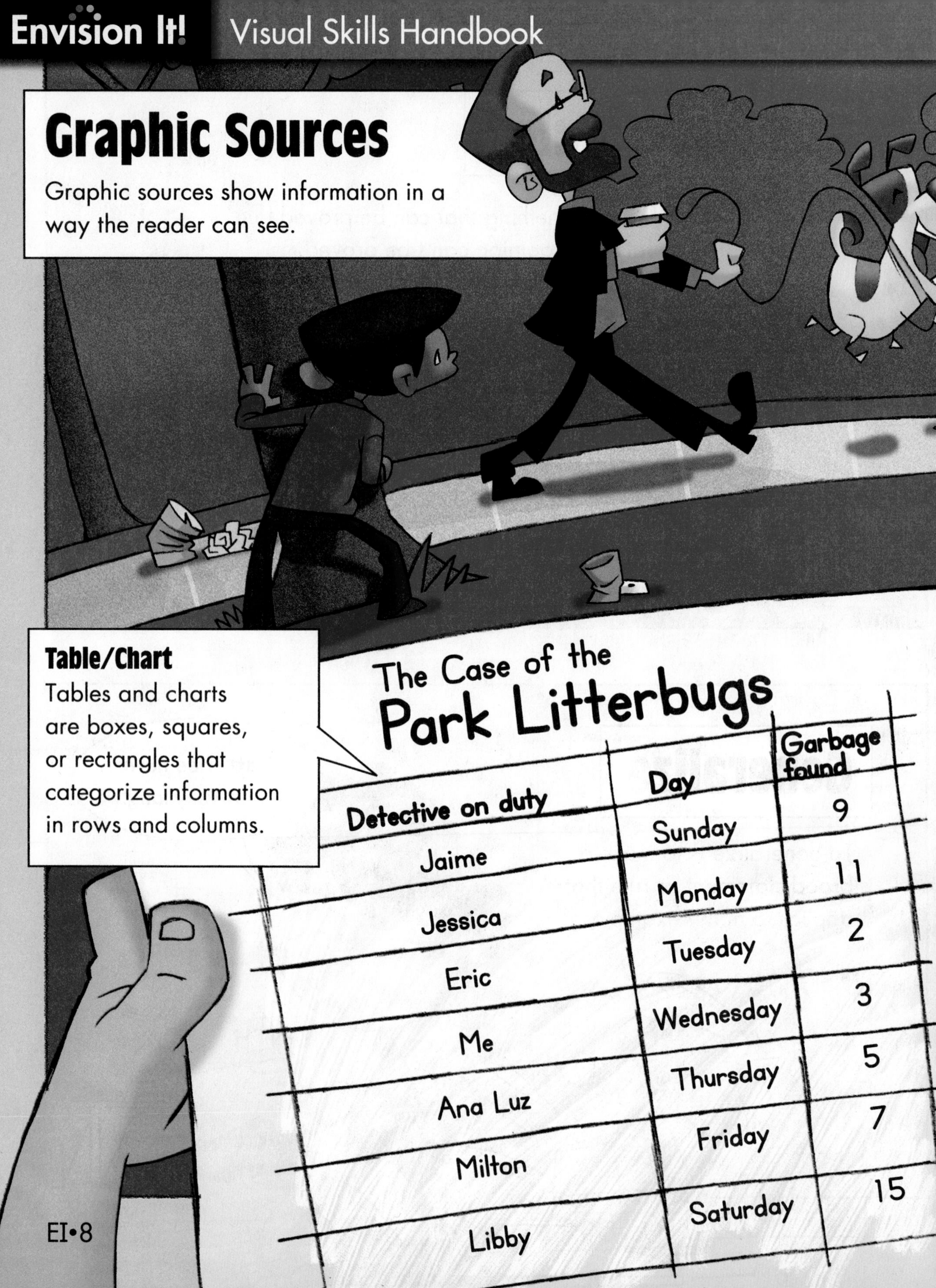

Graphic Sources

Graphic sources show information in a way the reader can see.

Table/Chart
Tables and charts are boxes, squares, or rectangles that categorize information in rows and columns.

The Case of the
Park Litterbugs

Detective on duty	Day	Garbage found
Jaime	Sunday	9
Jessica	Monday	11
Eric	Tuesday	2
Me	Wednesday	3
Ana Luz	Thursday	5
Milton	Friday	7
Libby	Saturday	15

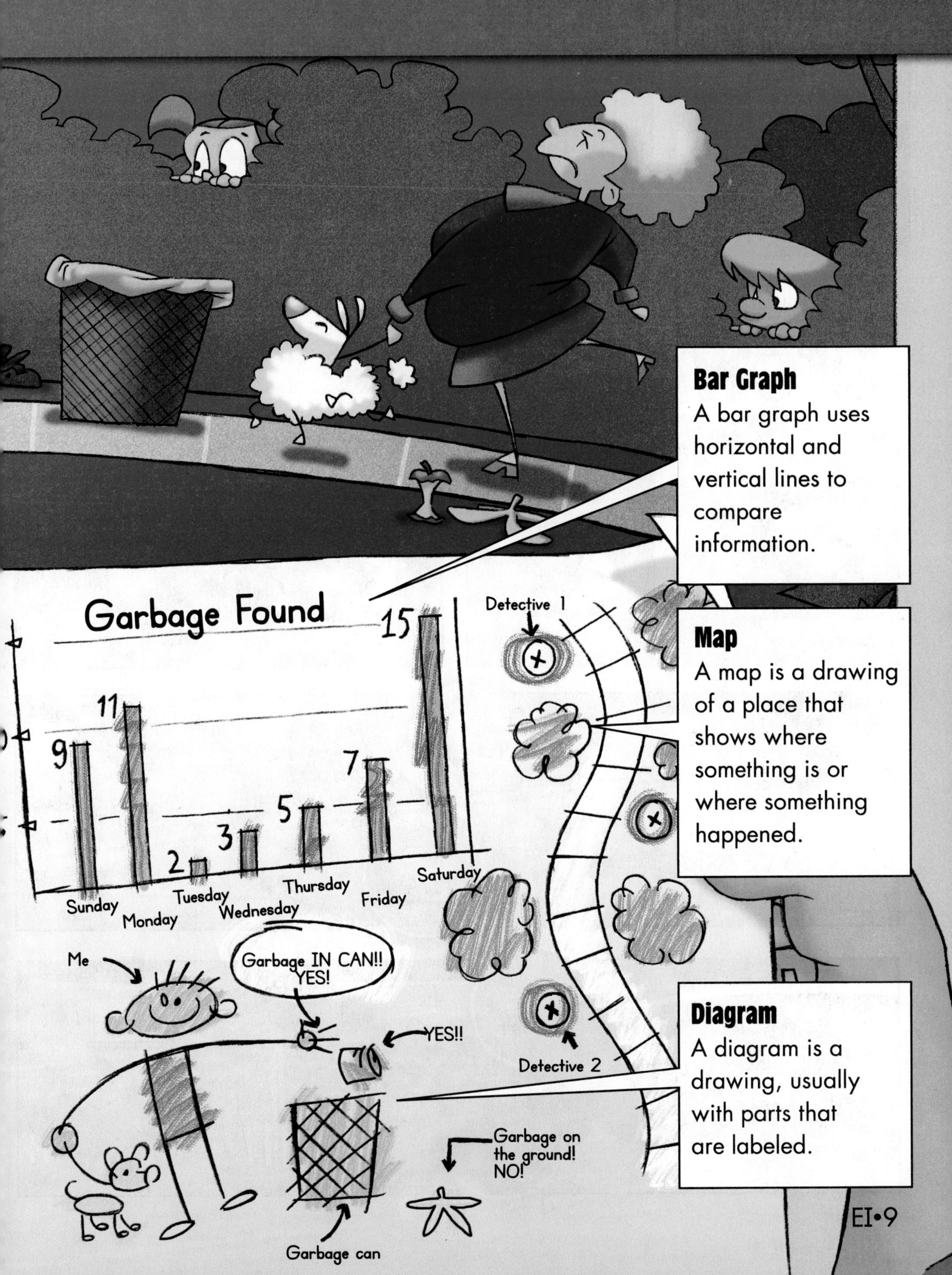
Bar Graph
A bar graph uses horizontal and vertical lines to compare information.
Garbage Found
15
11
9
7
5
3
2
Sunday
Monday
Tuesday
Wednesday
Thursday
Friday
Saturday
Detective 1
Map
A map is a drawing of a place that shows where something is or where something happened.
Me
Garbage IN CAN!! YES!
YES!!
Detective 2
Diagram
A diagram is a drawing, usually with parts that are labeled.
Garbage on the ground! NO!
Garbage can

Room To Grow

Literary Elements

Stories are made up of four main elements: character, setting, plot, and theme. Each of these parts gives you an overall understanding of the story.

Characters

A character is a person or an animal in a story.

Setting

The setting is the time and place in which a story happens.

Plot

The plot is the pattern of events in a story.

The plot starts with a problem or goal and builds toward a climax. The plot ends with a resolution or outcome.

Theme

The theme is the big idea of a story. We look at the plot, setting, or characters to determine the theme of a story.

Main Idea and Details

Main idea is the most important idea about a topic. Details support the main idea.

Sequence

Sequence refers to the order of events in text. We also use sequence when we list the steps in a process.

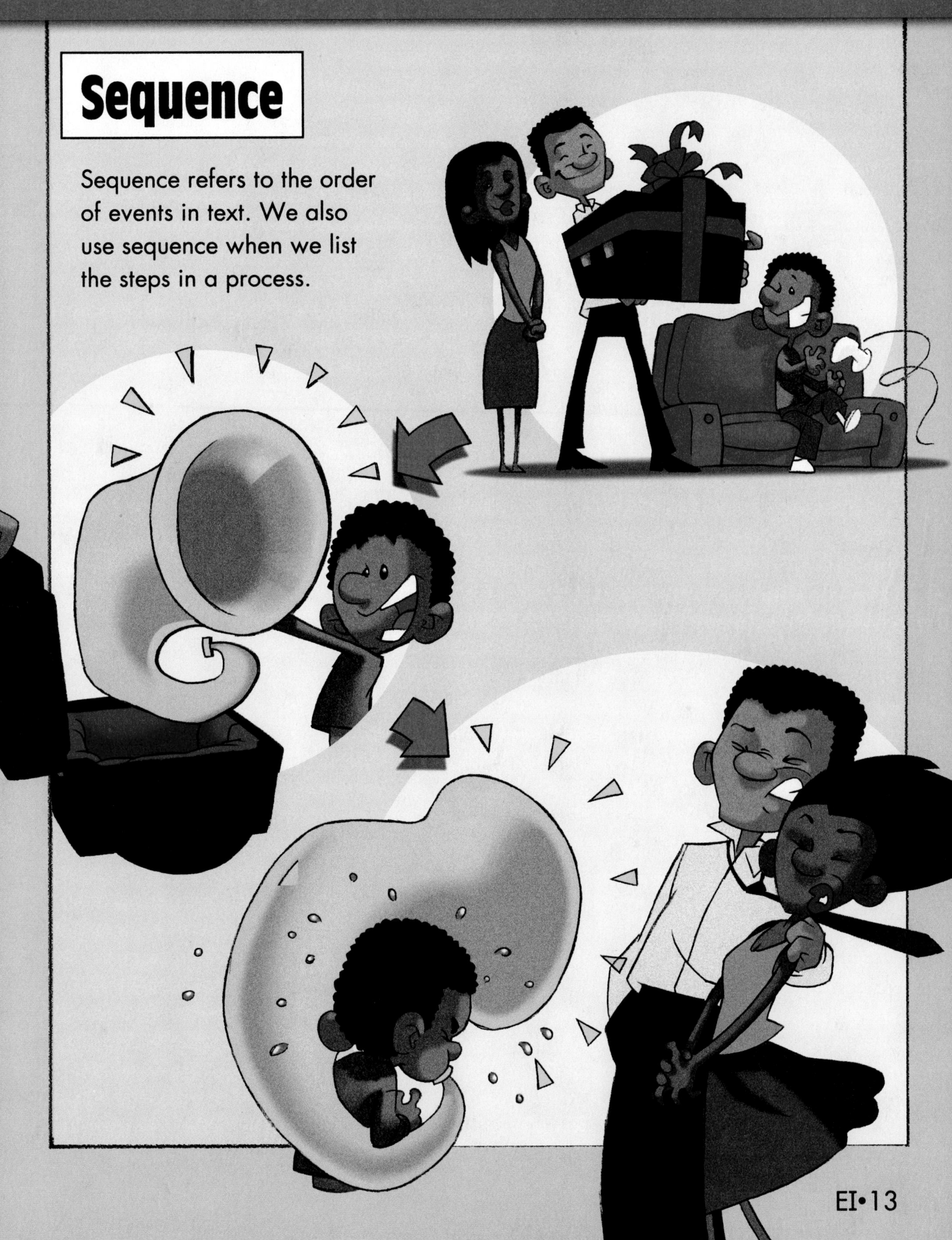

Envision It! | Visual Strategies Handbook

Background Knowledge

Important Ideas

Inferring

Monitor and Clarify

Predict and Set Purpose

Questioning

Story Structure

Summarize

Text Structure

Visualize

Background Knowledge

Background knowledge is what you already know about a topic based on your reading and personal experience. Make connections to people, places, and things. Use background knowledge before, during, and after reading to monitor comprehension.

To use background knowledge

- with fiction, preview the title, author's name, and illustrations
- with nonfiction, preview chapter titles, headings, graphics, and other text features
- think about what you already know

Officer Lee and Freckles remind me of characters in a fantastic book I am reading about working dogs.
WORKING DOGS
POLICE DOGS
POLICE

Let's Think About Reading!

When I use background knowledge, I ask myself

- Does this character remind me of someone?
- How is this story or text similar to others I have read?
- What else do I know about this topic from what I've read or seen?

Important Ideas

Important ideas are essential ideas in a nonfiction selection. Important ideas include information that provide clues to the author's purpose.

To identify important ideas

- read all titles, headings, and captions
- look for words in italics, boldface print, or bulleted lists
- look for signal words and phrases: *for example, most important,* and others
- use any photos, illustrations, diagrams or maps
- note how the text is organized—cause and effect, problem and solution, or other ways

Wow! The lettering is in bold type.
It must be an important idea.
Types of Clouds

Let's Think About Reading!

When I identify important ideas, I ask myself

- What information is included in bold, italics or other special lettering?
- What details support important ideas?
- Are there signal words and phrases?
- What do illustrations, photos, diagrams, and charts show?
- How is the text organized?
- Why did the author write this?

Inferring

When we **infer** we use background knowledge with clues in the text to come up with our own ideas about what the author is trying to present.

To infer

- identify what you already know
- combine what you know with text clues to come up with your own ideas

Brianna wore herself out before she reached the finish line.
Since you said Brianna wore herself out, that must mean you won the race!

Let's Think About Reading!

When I infer, I ask myself

- What do I already know?
- Which text clues are important?
- What is the author trying to present?

Monitor and Clarify

We **monitor comprehension** to check our understanding of what we've read. We **clarify** to find out why we haven't understood what we've read and to adjust comprehension.

To monitor and clarify

- use background knowledge as you read
- try different strategies: reread, ask questions, or use text features and illustrations

Aren't all deserts hot?
Antarctica: The Cold Desert!
I think the caption will help clarify your understanding.

Let's Think About Reading!

When I monitor and clarify, I ask myself

- Do I understand what I'm reading?
- What doesn't make sense?
- What fix-up strategies can I use?

Predict and Set Purpose

We **predict** to tell what might happen next in a story or article. The prediction is based on what has already happened. We **set a purpose** to guide our reading.

To predict and set a purpose

- preview the title, author's name, and illustrations or graphics
- identify why you're reading
- use what you already know to make predictions
- look back at your predictions to confirm them

I predict you'll find out about Ellen Ochoa's space travels in this "Missions" section.
Ellen Ochoa
Training
Missions
NASA
SPACE
Space Travel
Astronauts
REPORT

Let's Think About Reading!

When I predict and set a purpose, I ask myself

- What do I already know?
- What do I think will happen?
- What is my purpose for reading?

Questioning

Questioning is asking good questions about important text information. Questioning takes place before, during, and after reading.

To question

- read with a question in mind
- stop, think, and record your questions as you read
- make notes when you find information
- check your understanding and ask questions to clarify

Let's Think About Reading!

When I question, I ask myself

- Have I asked a good question with a question word?
- What questions help me make sense of my reading?
- What does the author mean?

Story Structure

Story structure is the arrangement of a story from beginning to end. You can use this information to summarize the plot.

To identify story structure

- note the conflict, or problem, at the beginning of a story
- track the rising action as conflict builds in the middle
- recognize the climax when the characters face the conflict
- identify how the conflict gets resolved and the story ends

Problem/Conflict

Rising Action

Resolution

Let's Think About Reading!

When I identify story structure, I ask myself

- What is the story's conflict or problem?
- How does the conflict build throughout the story?
- How is the conflict resolved in the end?
- How might this affect future events?

Summarize

We **summarize**, or retell, to check our understanding of what we've read. A summary is a brief statement—no more than a few sentences—and maintains a logical order.

To summarize fiction

- tell what happens in the story
- include the goals of the characters, how they try to reach them, and whether or not they succeed

To summarize nonfiction

- tell the main idea
- think about text structure and how the selection is organized

Let's Think About Reading!

When I summarize, I ask myself

- What is the story or selection mainly about?
- In fiction, what are the characters' goals? Are they successful?
- In nonfiction, how is the information organized?

Text Structure

We use **text structure** to look for the way the author has organized the text. For example, the author may have used cause and effect, problem and solution, sequence, or compare and contrast. Analyze text structure before, during, and after reading to locate information.

To identify text structure
- before reading: preview titles, headings, and illustrations
- during reading: notice the organization
- after reading: recall the organization and summarize the text

Let's Think About Reading!

When I identify text structure, I ask myself
- What clues do titles, headings, and illustrations provide?
- How is information organized?
- How does the organization help my understanding?

Visualize

We **visualize** to create a picture or pictures in our mind as we read. This helps us monitor our comprehension.

To visualize

- combine what you already know with details from the text to make pictures in your mind
- use all your senses to put yourself in the story or text

TODAY:
Pineapple pizza with cheese:
spicy sauce and sweet pineapple sprinkled on top

Let's Think About Reading!

When I visualize, I ask myself

- What do I already know?
- Which details create pictures in my mind?
- How can my senses put me in the story?

Program Authors

Peter Afflerbach
Camille Blachowicz
Candy Dawson Boyd
Elena Izquierdo
Connie Juel
Edward Kame'enui
Donald Leu
Jeanne R. Paratore
P. David Pearson
Sam Sebesta
Deborah Simmons
Alfred Tatum
Sharon Vaughn
Susan Watts Taffe
Karen Kring Wixson

PEARSON

Glenview, Illinois • Boston, Massachusetts • Chandler, Arizona • Upper Saddle River, New Jersey

We dedicate Reading Street to
Peter Jovanovich.

His wisdom, courage,
and passion for education
are an inspiration to us all.

About the Cover Artist
Tim Jessell draws and paints in Stillwater, Oklahoma. He and his wife are raising three great children, whom he coaches in many sports. When not playing catch or illustrating, Tim trains falcons for the sport of falconry. Occasionally, he can still be found making a racket behind his drum set, with kids dancing around.

Acknowledgments appear on pages 488–491, which constitute an extension of this copyright page.

ISBN-13: 978-0-328-45565-2
ISBN-10: 0-328-45565-2
5 6 7 8 9 10 V063 14 13 12 11
CC1

Dear Reader,

You are about to take a trip along a famous street—*Scott Foresman Reading Street.* During this trip you will meet exciting people, such as the famous code talkers of World War II, an astronaut who actually saw the "invisible" side of the moon, and the amazing detective team of Doyle and Fossey. You will visit exotic places, such as the Amazon, Antarctica, and Machu Picchu.

As you read selections about mysterious pink dolphins, the person who learned to decode hieroglyphics, and people who chase storms for a living, you will gain exciting new information that will help you in science and social studies.

While you're enjoying these exciting pieces of literature, you'll find that something else is going on—you are becoming a better reader, gaining new skills, and polishing old ones.

Have a great trip—and send us a postcard!

Sincerely,
The Authors

Puzzles and Mysteries

Is there an explanation for everything?

Week 1

Week 2

Week 3

Unit 4 Contents

Week 4

Week 5

Week 6

Unit 4

Envision It! A Comprehension Handbook

What makes an adventure?

Week 1

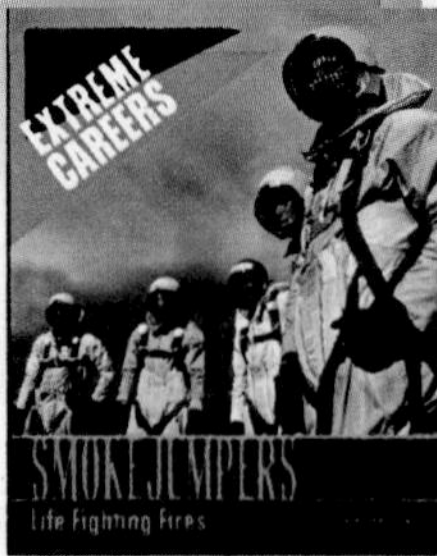

Let's Think About Reading!

Week 2

Week 3

Week 4

Week 5

Week 6

Unit 5

Envision It! A Comprehension Handbook

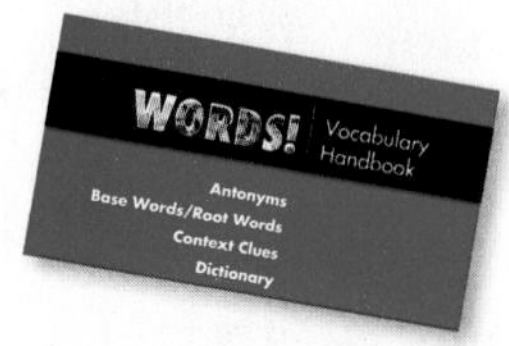

Reaching for Goals

THE BIG ? What does it take to achieve our goals and dreams?

Week 1

Week 2

Week 3

Unit 6 Contents

Week 4

Week 5

Week 6

Unit 6

Envision It! A Comprehension Handbook

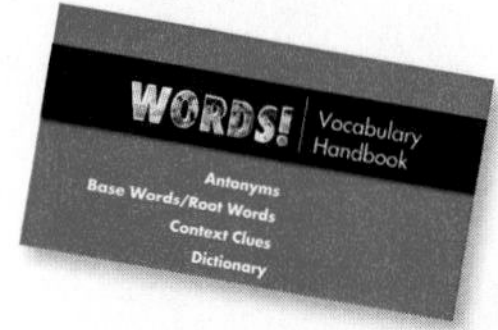

Don Leu
The Internet Guy

Right before our eyes, the nature of reading and learning is changing. The Internet and other technologies create new opportunities, new solutions, and new literacies. New reading comprehension skills are required online. They are increasingly important to our students and our society.

Those of us on the Reading Street team are here to help you on this new, and very exciting, journey.

See It!

- **Big Question Video**

- **Concept Talk Video**
- **Envision It! Animations**
- **eReaders**

Hear It!

- **eSelections**
- **Grammar Jammer**

- **Vocabulary Activities**

Concept Talk Video

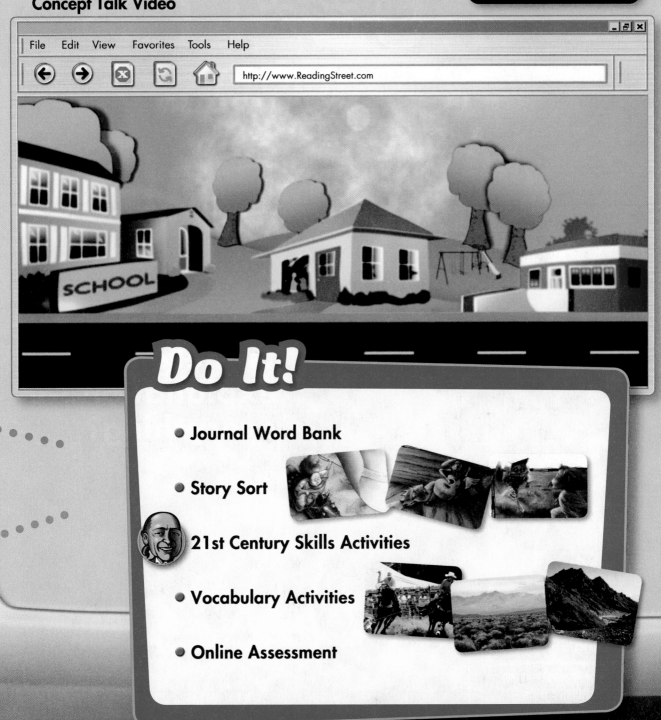

File Edit View Favorites Tools Help

http://www.ReadingStreet.com

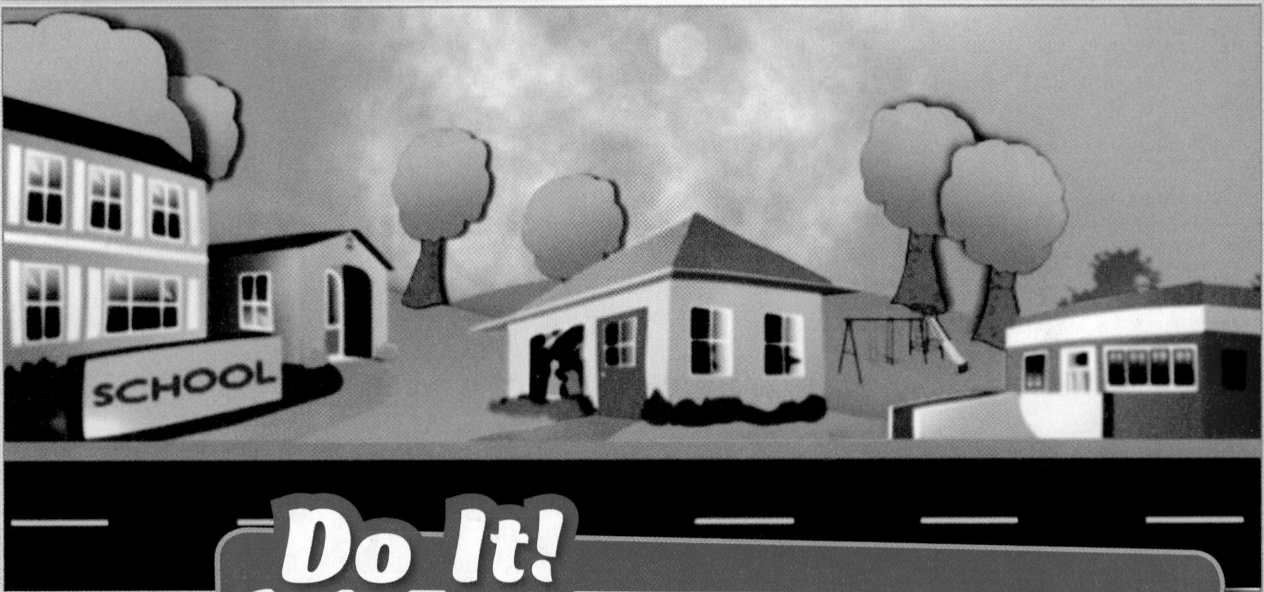

SCHOOL

Do It!

- Journal Word Bank
- Story Sort 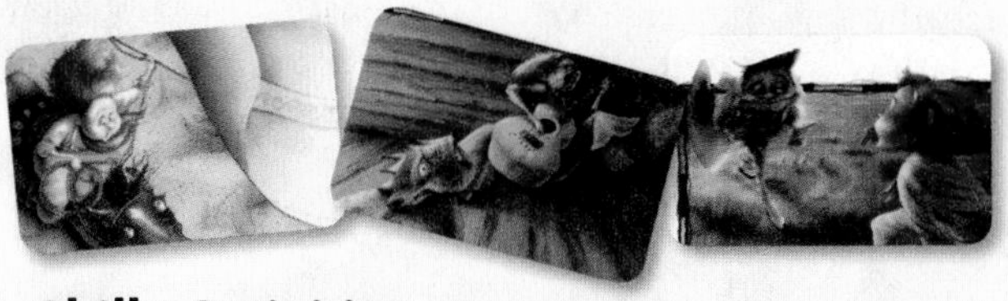 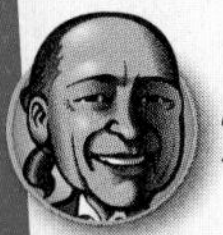
- 21st Century Skills Activities
- Vocabulary Activities 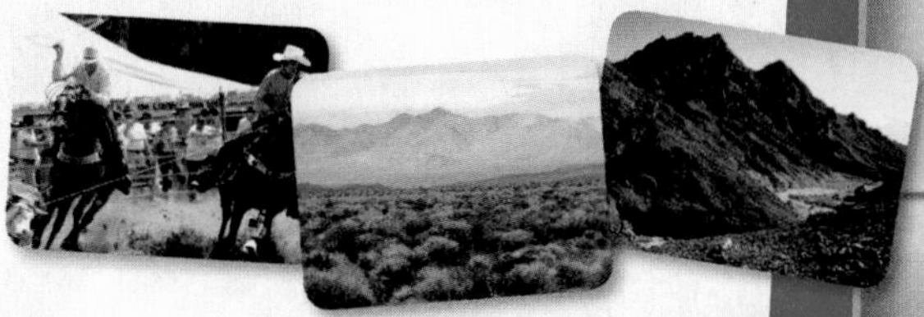
- Online Assessment

Puzzles and Mysteries

Is there an explanation for everything?

Reading Street Online

www.ReadingStreet.com

- Big Question Video
- eSelections
- Envision It! Animations
- Story Sort

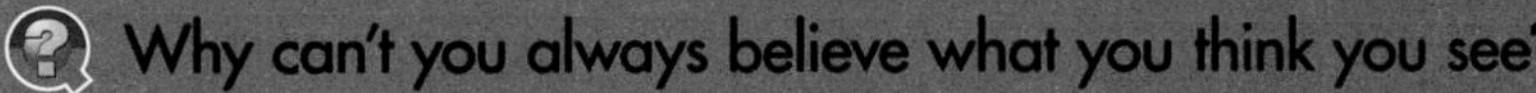

The Case of the Gasping Garbage REALISTIC FICTION

Why can't you always believe what you think you see?

Paired Selection
Mr. Talberg's Famous Bread Recipe RECIPE

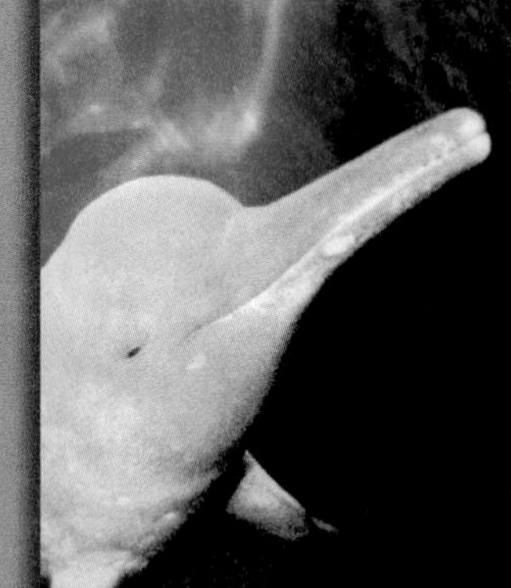

Encantado: Pink Dolphin of the Amazon EXPOSITORY TEXT

Why do animals behave the way they do?

Paired Selection
Mysterious Animals EXPOSITORY TEXT

Navajo Code Talkers EXPOSITORY TEXT

Why are secret codes necessary?

Paired Selection
Your Own Secret Language HOW-TO ARTICLE

Seeker of Knowledge BIOGRAPHY

How can knowing another language create understanding?

Paired Selection
Making Mummies SEARCH ENGINES

Encyclopedia Brown and the Case of the Slippery Salamander REALISTIC FICTION

How can attention to detail help solve a problem?

Paired Selection
Young Detectives of Potterville Middle School EXPOSITORY TEXT

Objectives

- Listen closely to speakers and ask questions about and comment on the topic.
- Speak clearly and to the point, give an opinion and support it with correct information. Make eye contact, change how fast, loud, and clearly you speak, and get your ideas across clearly.

Oral Vocabulary

Let's Talk About

Perception

- Describe seeing or hearing something that was not what it appeared to be.
- Ask questions about how the mystery was solved.
- Speak so everyone can hear you.

READING STREET ONLINE
CONCEPT TALK VIDEO
www.ReadingStreet.com

You've learned

1 5 0

Amazing Words

so far this year!

Objectives

- Compare and contrast the actions of characters in traditional and classic stories. • Monitor your comprehension of a text and adjust your reading based on how well you understand what you are reading.

Envision It! | **Skill Strategy**

Skill

Compare and Contrast
To compare and contrast is to look for similarities and differences in things.
SPEAKS 5 DIFFERENT LANGUAGES

Strategy

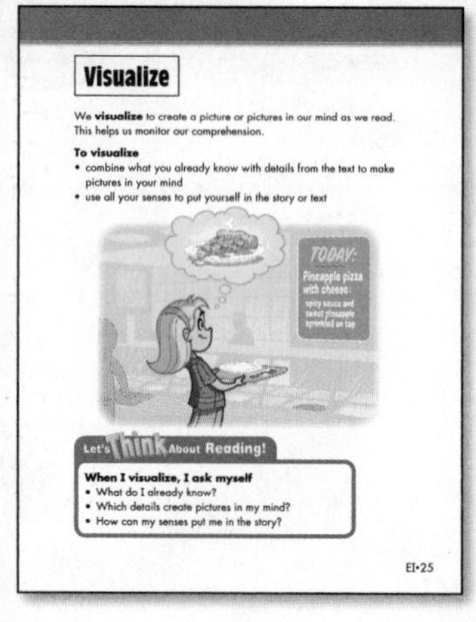

Visualize
We visualize to create a picture or pictures in our mind as we read. This helps us monitor our comprehension.
To visualize
• combine what you already know with details from the text to make pictures in your mind
• use all your senses to put yourself in the story or text
TODAY:
Let's Think About Reading!
When I visualize, I ask myself
• What do I already know?
• Which details create pictures in my mind?
• How can my senses put me in the story?

READING STREET ONLINE
ENVISION IT! ANIMATIONS
www.ReadingStreet.com

Comprehension Skill

Compare and Contrast

- When you compare and contrast, you tell how two or more things are alike and different.
- You can compare and contrast two or more things you read about or compare something you read about with something you already know.
- Use the graphic organizer below to compare and contrast Encyclopedia Brown and Nancy Drew as you read "Detective Techniques."

	Alike	Different
Two things in the text		
One thing in the text with something I already know		

Comprehension Strategy

Visualize

Good readers visualize as they read. Visualizing helps readers form mental pictures of what they are reading to help them understand ideas and information. Try to picture in your mind what the author has written to help the story come to life.

Detective Techniques

Kim and Tomas were talking about books they liked to read. "I really enjoy a good, suspenseful, detective mystery story," Kim said.

"Me too!" said Tomas. "Who's your favorite?"

"I think Encyclopedia Brown is great," Kim said. "I love when he closes his eyes and pieces the clues together."

"Really? I get bored when he does that," Tomas answered. "I like the way he listens to all the facts about a crime, and then tells about all the ways it might have been committed. Sometimes he's got the mystery figured out before he goes to the crime scene!"

"Then there's Nancy Drew," said Kim. "She really jumps right in and starts snooping around. She's always exploring the crime scene—going into spooky old houses and deserted castles searching for a clue. I get the shivers when the story gets dark and creepy—but I still have to keep reading!"

"That's what I love about mysteries!" Tomas said. "That suspenseful feeling—knowing *something* is going to happen, but you don't know what."

"Me too," Kim said. "But I *really* look forward to the end when the mystery is solved and the detective lets us know what clues led to solving the crime."

Skill Contrast Kim's and Tomas's reactions to Encyclopedia Brown. How are their reactions different?

Strategy If you visualize the spooky houses and empty castles, you will understand the suspenseful feeling Kim experiences.

Skill Compare what both Kim and Tomas love about mysteries. How are they the same?

Your Turn!

Need a Review? See the *Envision It! Handbook* for help with comparing and contrasting and visualizing.

Let's Think About...

Ready to Try It? Use what you've learned about comparing and contrasting as you read *The Case of the Gasping Garbage.*

Objectives

- Determine the meanings of unfamiliar words or multiple-meaning words by using the context of the sentence. • Complete analogies based on knowledge of synonyms and antonyms.

Envision It! Words to Know

beakers

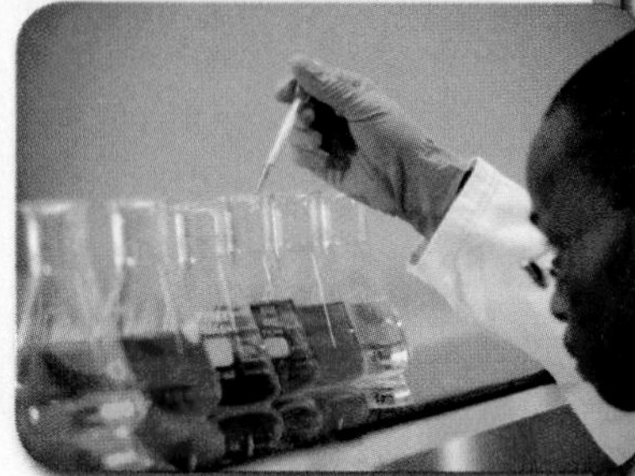

lecture

microscope

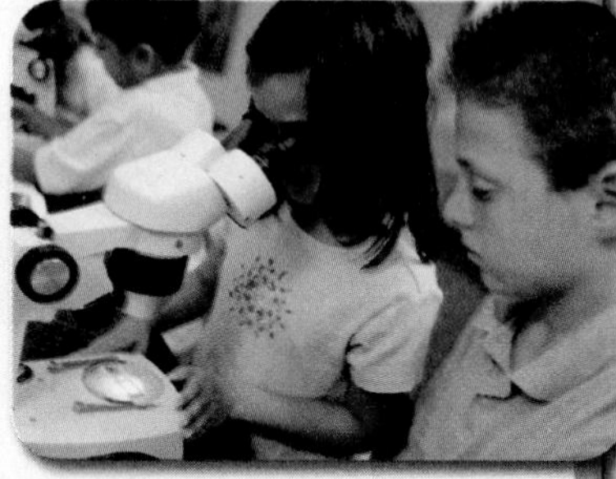

analysis
hollow
identity
precise
relentless

READING STREET ONLINE
VOCABULARY ACTIVITIES
www.ReadingStreet.com

Vocabulary Strategy for

Synonyms and Antonyms

Context Clues Sometimes an author will use a synonym or an antonym as a clue to help you determine the meaning of a word. Synonyms are words that have almost the same meaning. Antonyms are words with opposite meanings.

1. Think about synonyms and antonyms to complete this analogy using one of the vocabulary words from *Words to Know: excited* is to *calm* as *solid* is to ______.
2. When you read a word you don't know, reread the sentence with the unfamiliar word. Read the words and sentences around it. Look for a synonym or an antonym.
3. If you find a synonym or an antonym, try using it in place of the unfamiliar word. Does the synonym or antonym help you or clarify the meaning of the unfamiliar word?

As you read "A Scientist's Journal," check the context of words you don't know. Look for a synonym or an antonym to help you figure out an unfamiliar word.

Words to Write Reread "A Scientist's Journal." Imagine that you are writing in your journal about an experiment you performed. Use words from the *Words to Know* list.

A Scientist's Journal

Day 1. I'm about ready to perform my experiment. After listening to Professor Wilson's lecture, I got inspired. His speech made me eager and excited about testing a theory I have about some seeds.

Day 2. Yesterday, I examined the seeds in question with my microscope. I looked at the seeds up close and saw that none of them had decayed; instead, they all seemed to be healthy.

Day 3. I emptied the beakers of seeds into a pan. I have made sure my measurements of the pan were not just a guess but that they were very precise. I rechecked my theory so I could give it my final analysis before completing the experiment tomorrow.

Day 4. I am relentless; I won't give up. I put a lid on the pan and began to heat the seeds on the warming device. Soon, a crackling noise began inside the pan. Then it reached a peak and suddenly stopped. I tapped the pan. It once sounded empty and hollow, but it now sounded full. I opened the lid and proved my theory. The seeds were popcorn seeds! I like my new identity as a scientist—being a scientist can be delicious!

Your Turn!

Need a Review? For help with context clues and working with synonyms and antonyms, see *Words!*

Let's Think About...

Ready to Try It? Read *The Case of the Gasping Garbage* on pp. 26–41.

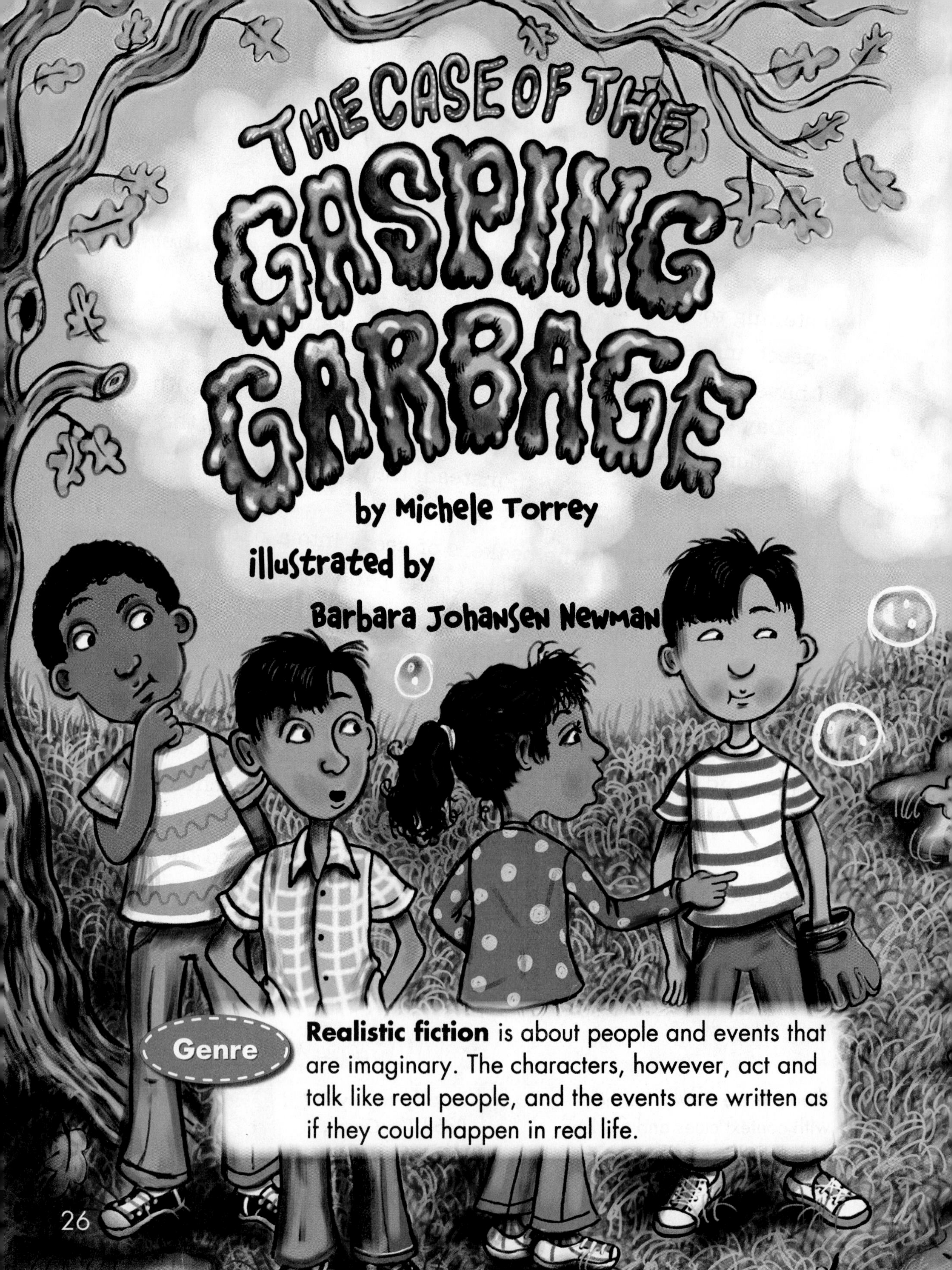

Genre

Realistic fiction is about people and events that are imaginary. The characters, however, act and talk like real people, and the events are written as if they could happen in real life.

DOYLE
BURP
GASP
BURP
Question of the Week
Why can't you always believe what you think you see?
Let's Think About Reading!

Monster Mission

Introducing Doyle and Fossey, Science Detectives.

Known throughout the fifth grade for their relentless pursuit of answers. And not just any answers. The right answers.

On a damp, drizzly day, in an attic not too far away, Drake Doyle worked alone in his homemade laboratory. The laboratory was filled with the latest scientific equipment: a chalkboard, racks of test tubes, flasks and beakers, dozens of sharpened pencils, and a lab coat with his name on it.

Drake's hair was quite wild (some would say it stuck straight up) and the color of toast. Cinnamon toast, that is. And perched on the end of his nose was a pair of round glasses, making him look very scientific indeed. Which, of course, he was. On this damp, drizzly day, an experiment was under way. A very important experiment.

Picture Drake and his laboratory. What do you think he looks like?
Visualize

The solution in the test tube fizzed and popped.

Drake Doyle glanced at his watch, then scribbled the results in his lab notebook.

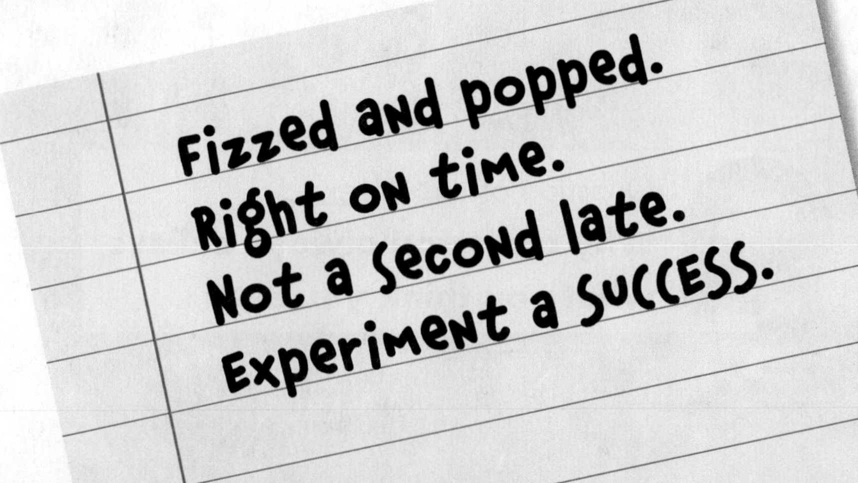

Fizzed and popped.
Right on time.
Not a second late.
Experiment a SUCCESS.

Drake slapped his notebook shut. (Serious scientists always slap their notebooks shut.) He shoved his pencil behind his ear just as the phone rang. "Doyle and Fossey," he answered, speaking in his best scientific voice. Nell Fossey was Drake's lab partner. They were in business together. Serious business. Their business card read:

DOYLE AND FOSSEY
Science detectives
CALL US. ANYTIME.
555-7822

"Hurry! Hurry! It's a major emergency!" someone screamed on the other end of the phone. "There's a monster in my garbage can!"

Drake pushed up his glasses with his finger. Obviously, this was an important phone call. Very important. And important phone calls were more important than important experiments. He set his test tubes aside. "Who is this?" he asked.

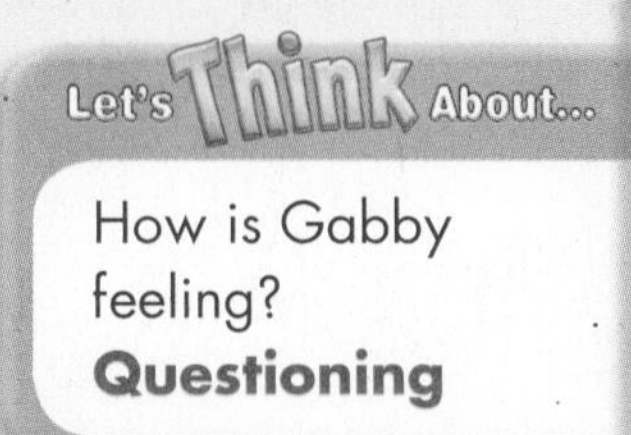

How is Gabby feeling?
Questioning

"Gabby Talberg," she shrieked. "Hurry! Hurry!"

"Oh, hi, Gabby." Gabby Talberg was in Drake's fifth-grade class at school. She was a nice girl, even if she did talk too much. "Now, calm down and speak slowly. What seems to be the problem?"

"Speak-slowly?-Are-you-nuts?-I-said-there's-a-huge-giant-bloodsucking-monster-in-my-garbage-can-and-it's-growing-bigger-and-bigger-every-second-and-I'm-alone-in-the-house-and-it's-going-to-gobble-me-up-and-I-don't-want-to-be-someone's-dinner!" Gabby gasped for breath.

Drake was excited. This could prove to be a great day for Doyle and Fossey, Science Detectives. They'd never had a monster assignment before. And, of course, it would be a great day for the small town of Mossy Lake. They'd publish their findings in the local newspaper. GARBAGE-EATING MONSTER DISCOVERED! MOSSY LAKE'S GARBAGE PROBLEMS SOLVED! Maybe they'd even lecture at Mossy Lake University!

But Drake couldn't allow his excitement to overwhelm his good scientific sense. That was the first rule of science. And Drake was a stickler about rules of science.

He cleared his throat and forced himself to speak calmly. "What makes you think there's a monster?" he asked.

"All kinds of weird gasping noises are coming from my garbage can. Something's inside. Hurry, Drake, you have to come over immediately and get rid of it. Because if you don't, I'll just have to call James Frisco."

Great Scott! thought Drake, horrified. Not James Frisco! Frisco was in their fifth-grade class at school. Frisco was a competitor. Frisco was a scientist, but he was a bad scientist. A very bad scientist. A mad scientist, you might say.

Frisco's business card read:

> FRISCO
> ~~BAD~~ MAD SCIENTIST
> (Better than Doyle and Fossey)
> Call me. Day or night.
> 555-6190

Why was Frisco such a ~~bad~~ mad scientist? Because if Frisco didn't like a number, he erased it. Because if an experiment asked for pink, Frisco used blue. Because if an experiment called for two, Frisco used one. (Or three.) But most especially, because if an experiment said "Adult Supervision Required, OR ELSE!" Frisco did it anyway. Alone.

How are Frisco's views about following rules different from Drake's views? **Monitor and Clarify**

Drake knew that if Gabby hired Frisco, there was no telling what could happen. Knowing Frisco's sloppy scientific techniques, Frisco might let the monster out of the can, and he and Gabby would never be seen again! Gobbled in the blink of an eye!

"Drake," said Gabby, "Drake, are you there? I said you have to come over immediately and get rid of it or else I'll call Frisco!"

"Check. I'll be right there."

Click.

Drake phoned Nell. She was the most fabulous partner an amateur scientist and detective genius could have. Whenever they had a serious case, Nell dropped everything and reported for duty.

"Doyle and Fossey," she answered, picking up the phone on its first ring.

"Drake here. Meet me at Gabby's house right away. Gabby's garbage is gasping."

"Right."

Click.

Nell was already waiting on Gabby's porch by the time Drake arrived. He wasn't surprised, as she was the fastest runner in the fifth grade. With her coffee-colored hair pulled back in a no-nonsense ponytail, her scientist cap shoved atop her head, and her mouth set in a firm line, she looked ready to take on this most difficult case.

"Afternoon, Scientist Nell."

"Afternoon, Detective Doyle." And so saying, Nell rapped sharply on the door.

Inside Gabby's house, Gabby pointed to a dark corner of the garage. "There," she whispered. "There's the bloodsucking monster. Inside that garbage can. Hurry, get rid of it before it eats us all."

Suddenly, the garbage can gasped.

It trembled.

It burped and yurped.

It belched and yelched.

Let's Think About...

Can you visualize Nell? What kind of person do you think she is?

Visualize

All in all, it was very scary indeed.

Drake and Nell immediately went to work. They pulled on surgical gloves.

Snap!

Gabby edged toward the door. "You're not going to take off the lid, are you?"

"If there's a monster inside," Drake replied, "removing the lid would be most foolish. Now, stand back, we'll take it from here."

They tapped the sides of the can. "Sounds hollow," whispered Nell. She scribbled in her lab notebook and tapped again.

Drake sniffed the air. "Smells like fresh-baked bread," he observed. "Hmm. That reminds me. Ms. Talberg, isn't your dad a baker?"

"The best baker there is," answered Gabby. "He won the blue ribbon last year at the county fair. Why?"

What details give you an idea of the type of scientists Drake and Nell are? **Inferring**

"Just wondering," Drake muttered as he recorded his findings in his lab notebook.

Meanwhile, Nell peered at the garbage can with her magnifying glass. She checked its temperature. She drew diagrams and charts. She was a most efficient scientist.

Finally, Drake and Nell stood back and removed their surgical gloves.

Snap!

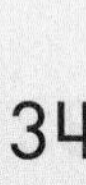

"Well?" asked Gabby.

"Puzzling," said Drake.

"Fascinating," said Nell.

Drake pushed up his glasses. "Tell me, Ms. Talberg. Does your garbage can always sit here next to the furnace?"

Gabby shook her head. "My dad moved it a few days ago. Why?"

"It's very warm next to the furnace, that's all," said Drake.

"Eighty-seven degrees, to be precise," added Nell.

"Curious. Very curious," mumbled Drake. He jotted a note to himself in his notebook.

"What are you going to do now?" asked Gabby.

"Nell and I will take the garbage can back to the lab for further analysis. Expect our report within twenty-four hours."

Let's **Think** About...

Will the noises from the garbage have something to do with the temperature? **Predict**

Great Gasping Garbage!

How does the author's description help you experience moving the garbage can?
Visualize

Drake and Nell slogged through mud puddles, lugging the garbage can between them. For a monster, it wasn't very heavy. Even so, Drake slipped and almost fell because his glasses had fogged. Nell helped him up and brushed him off. She was a great partner. (And besides, she was his best friend.)

Finally, they pushed the garbage can through Drake's back door, dragged it up two flights of stairs, and into the attic lab. They set the garbage can in a corner next to a heater. "We must simulate the same environment," said Drake.

"Eighty-seven degrees, to be precise," said Nell.

Drake cleaned his glasses and put on his white lab coat. Nell did, too, except she didn't have any glasses to clean. They stuck sharpened pencils behind their ears, sat on stools, and opened their lab notebooks. Drake pulled a book off the shelf and shuffled through it until he found the right page. It read: "Monster Analysis: What to do when your garbage is gasping."

Just then, Drake's mom poked her head in the lab. Kate Doyle was a fine cook and ran her own catering company from home. Blueberry muffins were her specialty. Now Mrs. Doyle asked if they wanted any hot chocolate with their muffins, seeing that it was such a damp, drizzly day.

"No thanks," Drake said politely. "Just muffins."

(Real scientists don't drink hot chocolate. Ditto for real detectives. And they were both.)

"Let's go over the facts again," said Nell.

Drake nodded. "Just the facts, ma'am."

Together they pored over their observations.

After a while, Drake's dad stuck his head in the lab. Sam Doyle owned a science-equipment and supply company. He regularly brought home used equipment for the lab: computers, microscopes, telescopes, glassware, Bunsen burners—even an old sink that he plumbed with hot and cold water. If either Drake or Nell needed equipment, Mr. Doyle was the man.

How does Mr. Doyle's job help Drake? What evidence in the text makes you think so? **Inferring**

Now Mr. Doyle glanced at the rumbling garbage can and told them to be careful.

"We will," said Drake and Nell.

Mr. Doyle rolled his eyes and closed the door. "What's he think we're going to do?" asked Drake. "Blow up the lab?"

"You did last time," reminded Nell.

"That's beside the point. Now, where were we? Ah, yes. Based on our observations, Scientist Nell, I have formulated a hypothesis. . . ."

All through the evening they worked. Later Mrs. Doyle brought them tomato soup and grilled cheese sandwiches with a pickle on the side. (Mrs.

Doyle always cooked from her vegetarian menu whenever Nell was around, because Nell was a vegetarian.) Drake and Nell washed their hands and sat at Drake's desk, knowing they should never eat or drink while conducting experiments. They were top-notch scientists.

After supper, Nell called her mother and asked if she could stay extra late, given that there was no school tomorrow and that they were swamped with experiments and under a deadline. Ann Fossey was a biology professor at Mossy Lake University. Her specialty was wildlife biology. "Goodness gracious sakes alive," exclaimed Professor Fossey. "Sounds like you're a busy scientist. Now, don't you worry about a thing, my dear. I'll be sure to feed your rats and lizards."

"And don't forget my snakes and bugs."

"Of course, dear," said Professor Fossey. "I'll leave the light on for you."

Finally, after midnight, they had their answer.

In the morning, Nell hurried back to Drake's house. They called Gabby first thing. "Meet us in

Let's Think About...

What can you learn about Nell from her conversation with her mother?
Inferring

the lab," said Nell. "We've discovered the identity of the monster."

After Gabby arrived, Drake paced the floor while Nell sat on a stool. "You see, Ms. Talberg," Drake was saying, "it's really quite simple. Nell?"

"Thank you, Detective Doyle. First of all," said Nell, "the garbage can sounded hollow when we tapped on it. Second, the garbage can wasn't too heavy."

"You see, Ms. Talberg," said Drake, "most monsters are quite heavy."

"In addition," added Nell, "the garbage can was stored in a very warm environment. We copied that environment in our lab by setting the can next to the heater and checking its temperature. But most important, the garbage can smelled like bread."

"Remember, your dad is a baker," said Drake. "The best baker around, to be exact. Therefore, based on the clues and our observations, I developed an educated guess—what we scientists call a hypothesis. I believed that the monster lurking inside your garbage can was not really a monster at all, but . . ."

> **Let's Think About...**
>
> How do you know that the problem in the story is close to being solved?
> **Story Structure**

Let's Think About...

Good readers ask evaluative questions of text as they read. For example, "How does knowing the clues help me solve the case?" What questions can you ask yourself to evaluate this text as you read? **Inferring**

Let's Think About...

Do you think the information Drake wrote in his notebook helped solve the case? **Questioning**

"Yes?" asked Gabby, her eyes wide.

"Yeast," said Drake. "Pure and simple yeast."

"Yeast?"

"Yes, yeast. Allow Scientist Nell to explain."

Nell pointed to a chalkboard with her long, wooden pointer. "As I said, the smell of fresh-baked bread was our biggest clue. You see, yeast is used in making bread. Yeasts are tiny plants that eat starches and sugars. They then turn the starches and sugars into alcohol and carbon dioxide gas."

GARBAGE CAN CLUES

1. Sounded Hollow
2. Wasn't Heavy
3. Warm Environment
4. Smelled Like Bread
5. Gabby's Dad a Baker

"The tiny bubbles in bread," said Drake, "are the result of carbon dioxide gas."

Nell tapped the chalkboard with her pointer. "You see, Gabby, your dad must have thrown away a combination of yeast and flour. Ingredients used in baking bread. Easily purchased at any grocery store."

Drake pushed up his glasses. "With the right amount of moisture—"

"And a warm environment—" added Nell.

"The yeast was able to grow and multiply by feeding on the flour inside the can," finished Drake. "Quite harmless, really. But the yeast produced so much carbon dioxide gas that the garbage can simply had to 'burp' to release some of the gas."

"We tested our hypothesis," said Nell, "with a thorough set of experiments. We examined the yeast under the microscope and grew it in several different mediums. We've positively identified yeast as your culprit. You can be certain there is no monster inside your garbage can."

Naturally, Gabby was a little disappointed. After all, yeast was not as exciting as a bloodsucking monster. She shook their hands anyway for a job well done. "I knew you could do it," she said. "I can't wait to tell all my friends."

Nell handed Gabby their business card. "Call us. Anytime."

Later that day, Drake wrote in his lab notebook:

Let's Think About...

How would you summarize *The Case of the Gasping Garbage?* **Summarize**

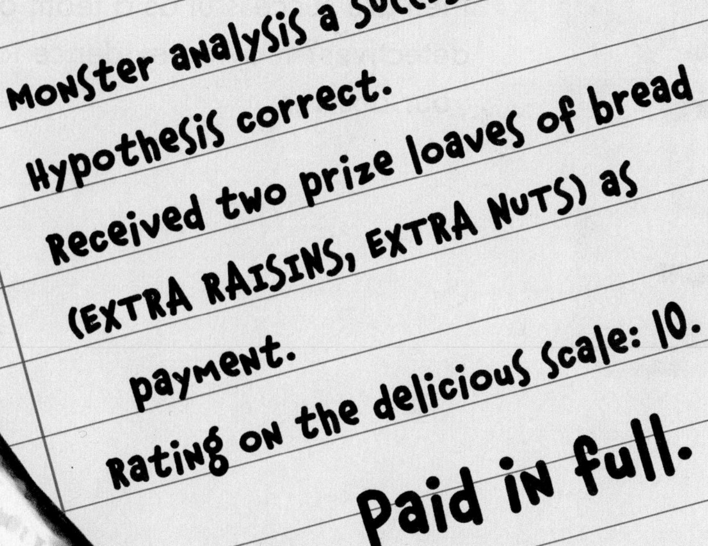

Monster analysis a SUCCESS.
Hypothesis correct.
Received two prize loaves of bread
(EXTRA RAISINS, EXTRA NUTS) as
payment.
Rating on the delicious scale: 10.
Paid in full.

Objectives
- Read independently for long periods of time and paraphrase the reading, including the order in which events occur.
- Write responses to texts using details to show understanding.

Envision It! Retell

READING STREET ONLINE
STORY SORT
www.ReadingStreet.com

Think Critically

1. Gabby was afraid of the noises coming from the garbage can. Have you ever been afraid of a noise? Did you react the same way Gabby did? **Text to Self**

2. On pages 34 and 35, the author gives readers several clues about what is causing the problem inside the garbage can. Why do you think the author chose to provide these clues? **Think Like an Author**

3. James Frisco is a competitor of science detectives Drake Doyle and Nell Fossey. How are the methods used by the two sets of detectives similar? How are they different? **Compare and Contrast**

4. On page 30, the author describes what the monster in the garbage can is like. How does the author's description help you visualize the monster and feel the suspense rising in the story? **Visualize**

5. **Look Back and Write** Look back at pages 39–40. Why do you think Drake and Nell are successful as a team of science detectives? Provide evidence to support your answer.

Meet the Author and the Illustrator

Michele Torrey

Michele Torrey wrote a story about a dinosaur egg popping out of the kitchen sink when she was in the fifth grade. The teacher liked the story and read it aloud to the class. Michele knew she'd be a writer some day.

When she was young, Michele's father, a high school science teacher, brought home a bag of gadgets for her to play with. She became hooked on science. As an adult, she earned a degree in microbiology, taught in college, and worked in several laboratories. Unlike Drake Doyle, however, she never blew one up.

Barbara Johansen Newman

Barbara Johansen Newman has been illustrating for more than twenty years. Before she became an illustrator, she worked with puppets and created sculptures. As a young girl, Barbara was encouraged by her mother to draw on the walls. This is when Barbara believes she became an artist. Ms. Newman and her family live in Massachusetts.

Here are other books by Michele Torrey.

The Case of the Mossy Lake Monster

The Case of the Barfy Birthday

Use the Reading Log in the *Reader's and Writer's Notebook* to record your independent reading.

Objectives

- Write creative stories that build to an ending and contain details about the characters and setting.
- Use and understand reflexive pronouns.

Key Features of a Mystery

- story includes a problem or puzzling situation that needs a solution
- characters often include detectives, suspects, and witnesses
- suspense often controls the plot
- setting may include unusual or ordinary places

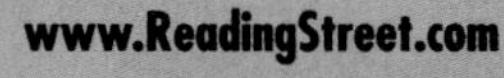

READING STREET ONLINE
GRAMMAR JAMMER
www.ReadingStreet.com

Mystery

Mysteries are fictional stories built around a problem that needs solving, with one part hidden until the end. The student model on the next page is an example of a mystery story.

Writing Prompt Write your own mystery story about something that seems unexplainable.

Writer's Checklist

Remember, you should ...

- ✓ introduce a problem early.
- ✓ describe possible suspects.
- ✓ provide clues and details about characters and setting.
- ✓ build the suspense to a climax.
- ✓ tell how the main character used clues to solve the mystery.
- ✓ use reflexive pronouns correctly.

Student Model

The Case of the Missing Cat

"I can solve this case," Marcia said. "Just calm down and give **me** the facts."

Toby explained, "Patches didn't come home last night. **She** never stays outside at night. **She** must be hurt somewhere. Unless someone has taken her!"

Toby explained how **his** new neighbor, Amy, had been trying to buy Patches. "Amy said **she** always wanted a calico cat, and Patches was perfect for **her**. **She** was pretty upset when I refused. Maybe I should call the police."

"**We** can find Patches **ourselves**," Marcia said. "We'll hide in the bushes in front of Amy's house and keep watch. If Patches is there, **we** will find her. Let's go!"

Marcia and Toby hid under the bushes. Suddenly **they** heard faint meowing sounds at the side of the house. Carefully scanning the surrounding shrubbery, Marcia saw two big yellow eyes staring at **her**. It was Patches! But Patches wasn't alone—curled up next to **her** were four tiny newborn kittens. "That's why Patches didn't come home, Toby," said Marcia. "**She** couldn't leave **her** kittens!"

Writing Trait Word Choice The dialogue between characters sounds realistic.

Genre Mysteries include suspects and clues.

Singular and plural pronouns are used correctly.

Conventions

Singular and Plural Pronouns

Remember A **singular pronoun** refers to one person or thing. A **plural pronoun** refers to more than one person or thing. A **reflexive pronoun** is used to refer back to the person or people mentioned earlier in the sentence.

Objectives

• Determine the sequence needed to follow a procedure. • Explain information that is shown in graphics. • Make connections between literary and informational texts with similar ideas and support your ideas with details from the texts.

Science in Reading

Genre

Recipe

- Procedural texts explain how to do or make something. A recipe is an example of procedural text. A recipe tells you how to make a type of food.
- Procedural texts, like recipes, contain a sequence of activities needed to carry out a procedure.
- Some procedural texts use charts, diagrams, graphs, or illustrations to explain information.
- Read "Mr. Talberg's Famous Bread Recipe." Look for elements that make this text a procedural text.

Mr. Talberg's Famous Bread Recipe

(and one not-so-famous bread recipe)

Michele Torrey

That's right! Here's Mr. Talberg's recipe, famous all over Mossy Lake; soon to be famous in your town too.

TOP SECRET: This is also a top-secret operation, but it's so cleverly disguised that your poor unsuspecting family *won't even know it.*

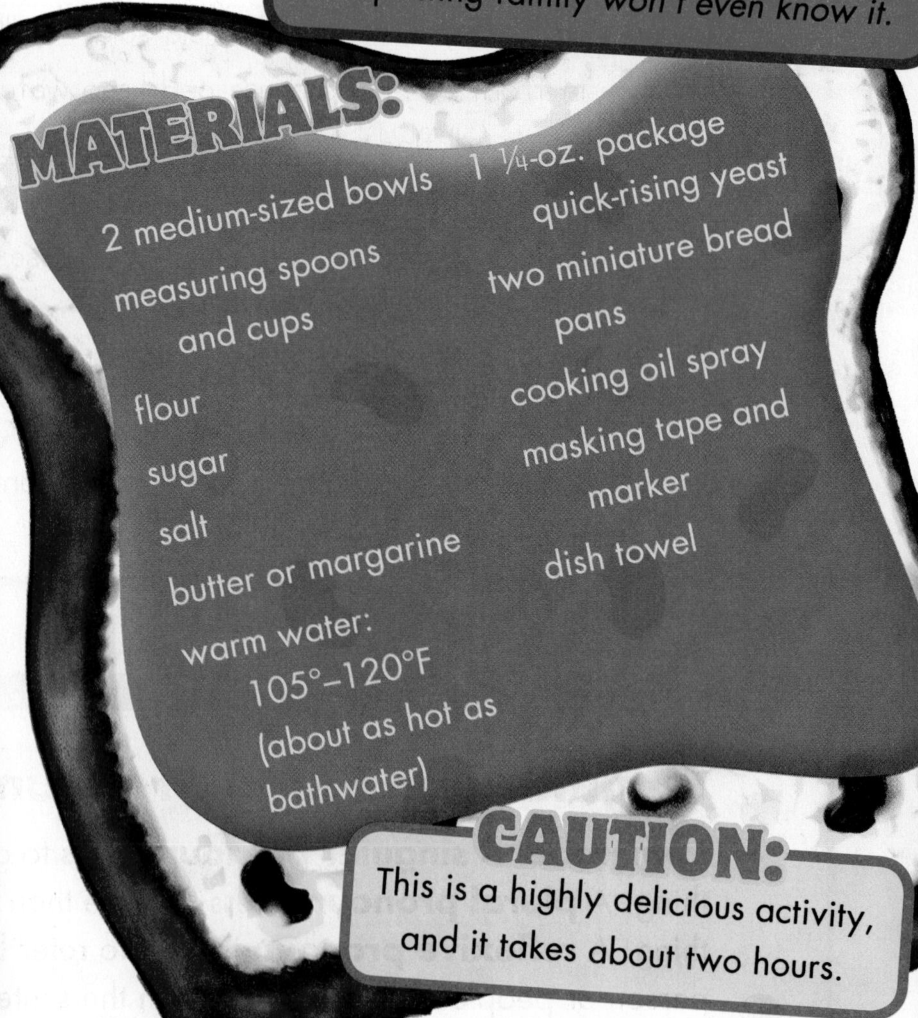

MATERIALS:

2 medium-sized bowls
measuring spoons and cups
flour
sugar
salt
butter or margarine
warm water: 105°–120°F (about as hot as bathwater)
1 ¼-oz. package quick-rising yeast
two miniature bread pans
cooking oil spray
masking tape and marker
dish towel

CAUTION: This is a highly delicious activity, and it takes about two hours.

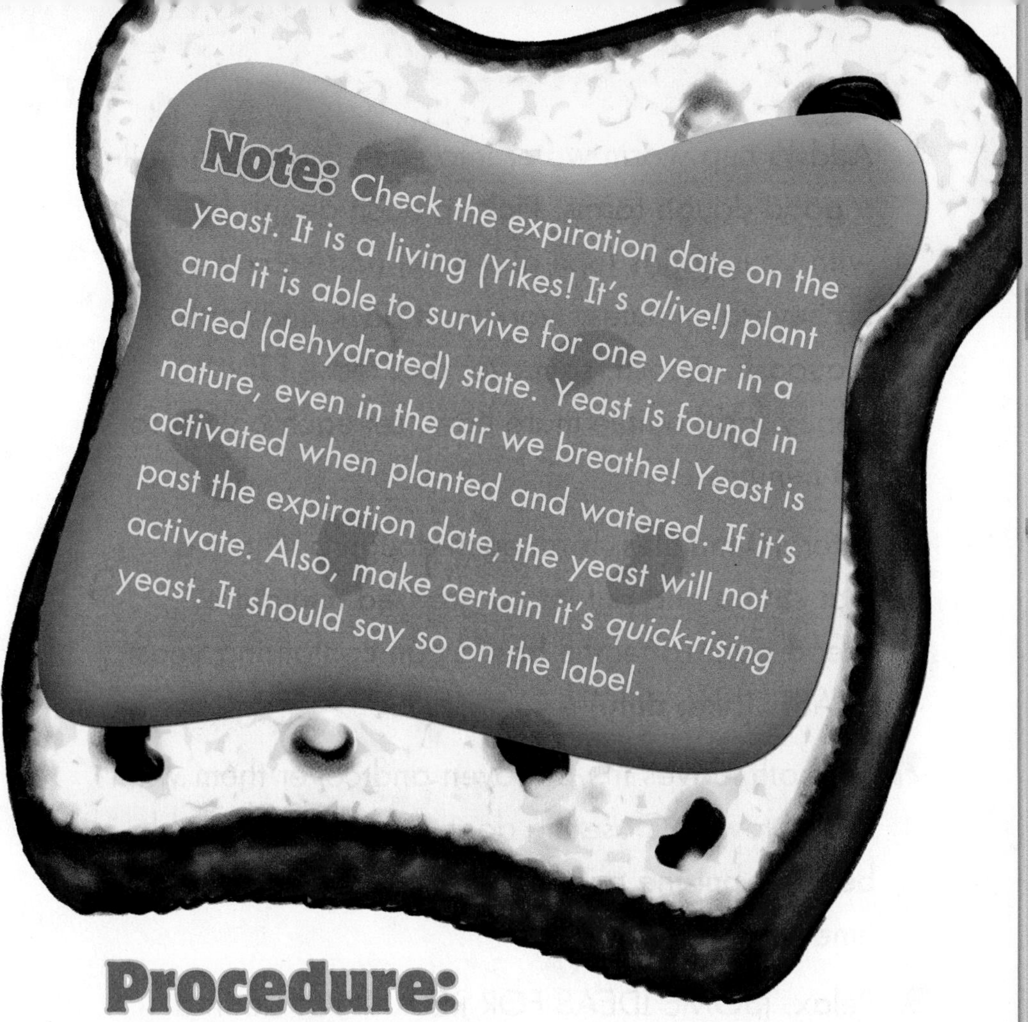

Note: Check the expiration date on the yeast. It is a living (Yikes! It's alive!) plant and it is able to survive for one year in a dried (dehydrated) state. Yeast is found in nature, even in the air we breathe! Yeast is activated when planted and watered. If it's past the expiration date, the yeast will not activate. Also, make certain it's quick-rising yeast. It should say so on the label.

Procedure:

1. Turn on your oven light and close the oven door. This will create a warm environment for the yeast to grow. (Oven should be OFF. Light should be ON.)
2. Wash your hands. (All good scientists wash their hands.)
3. Into each bowl, measure 1 ½ cups flour, 1 tablespoon sugar, ½ teaspoon salt, and 1 teaspoon butter or margarine.
4. Add ½ teaspoon yeast to *one* of the bowls containing the flour mixture. Label the bowl YEAST. Mix well.

Let's Think About...

How does this recipe present a sequence of activities? **Recipe**

Let's Think About...

Explain how the illustrations help you find the ingredients. **Recipe**

5. Add ½ cup warm water into each bowl. Stir until a good dough forms. Pick up each dough ball with your hands (one at a time) and squeeze it for several minutes, working it back and forth. (Squoosh, moosh, squeeze, and tease.) If it's gooey, add a little more flour. Let each ball sit for 10 minutes.

6. After 10 minutes, form each dough ball into a loaf shape and put into a greased miniature bread pan. Label the bread pan containing yeast, YEAST. (Like, duh.)

7. Set both loaves in your oven and cover them with a dish towel. Close the door. (Your oven should be OFF, but the oven light should be ON.) Set the timer for one hour.

8. Relax. (SOME IDEAS FOR RELAXING: Lie in a hammock, pester your mother, call your best friend, play solitaire, jog in place, study Einstein's theory of relativity.)

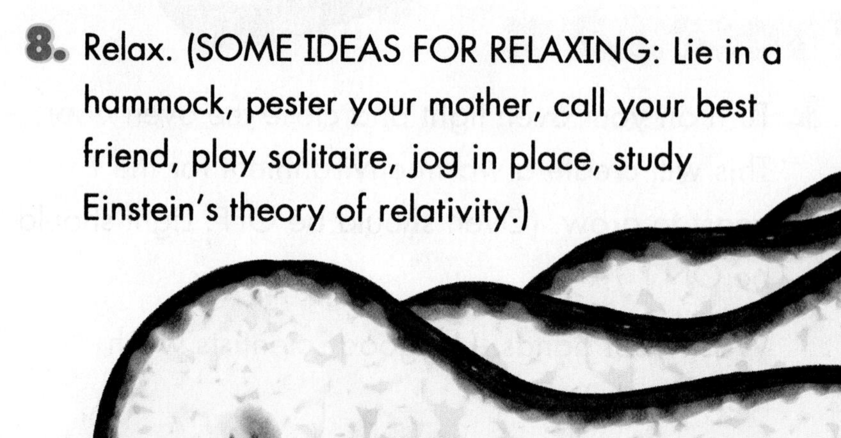

Let's Think About...

How do the illustrations help you understand the information presented in the recipe? **Recipe**

9. Once the timer goes off, remove dish towel from the loaves. Now turn on the oven and bake loaves at 350°F for 40–45 minutes, or until golden brown. (The one without the yeast may be pale, hard, and ugly, but that's the way it goes.)

10. Serve your unsuspecting family both loaves of bread. Pretend you don't notice the difference. Later, write down their reactions in your lab notebook and draw your conclusions regarding yeast. (EXAMPLES OF REACTIONS: Amazing! Delicious! Mouthwatering! Three cheers for the cook! OR: Disgusting! Ow, I broke my tooth! Who made that stuff anyway?)

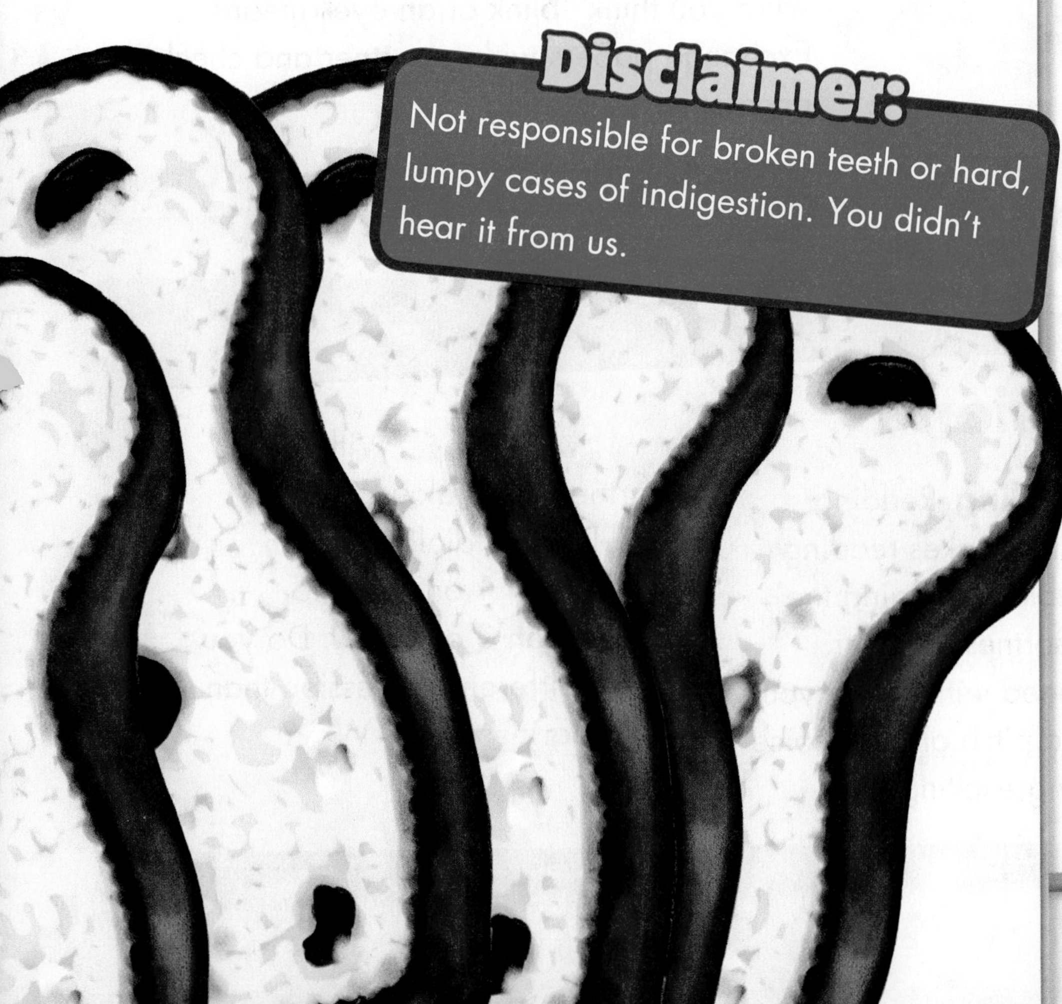

Disclaimer:

Not responsible for broken teeth or hard, lumpy cases of indigestion. You didn't hear it from us.

Let's Think About...

Reading Across Texts Reread the last two pages of *The Case of the Gasping Garbage.* Then reread "Mr. Talberg's Famous Bread Recipe." What information do both texts present about yeast?

Writing Across Texts Write a paragraph that explains why yeast is important for baking bread. Include information that describes what happens when yeast is not used as an ingredient in bread.

Objectives

• Read aloud grade-level texts and understand what is read. • Identify the meaning of common idioms. • Explain the positive and negative effects of advertising and how it influences what people buy and do. • Listen closely to speakers and ask questions about and comment on the topic. • Speak clearly and to the point, give an opinion and support it with correct information. Make eye contact, change how fast, loud, and clearly you speak, and get your ideas across clearly.

READING STREET ONLINE
ONLINE STUDENT EDITION
www.ReadingStreet.com

Vocabulary

Idioms

Context Clues An idiom is a phrase or expression whose meaning cannot be understood from its literal definition. Context clues give hints about what an idiom means. When you come across an idiom, try to figure out its meaning from context.

Practice It! Look at the phrase "Gobbled in the blink of an eye" in *The Case of the Gasping Garbage* on page 32. Write what you think "blink of an eye" means. Exchange papers with a partner and check each other's meaning.

Fluency

Expression

Partner Reading Reading with expression makes reading more enjoyable. Changing the loudness or softness of your voice, the speed with which you read, and the pitch of your voice makes reading exciting.

Practice It! With a partner, read aloud Gabby and Drake's dialogue from paragraph 1 on p. 29 to paragraph 3 on p. 30. Do you use a different expression than your partner does? Why?

Listening and Speaking

Get Ready For Middle School

When you give a presentation, speak clearly so that your audience can understand your ideas.

Advertisement

An advertisement promotes a product, a service, or an event. Advertisers use many techniques to influence consumers. Using a celebrity to sell a product is one technique. Does doing this have a positive impact on consumers? You decide. Express and support your opinion with accurate information, such as "I think people listen to celebrities that they admire."

Practice It! With a partner, create a newspaper ad for Doyle and Fossey's science detective agency. Use pictures and words in your ad. Include testimonials from happy customers in your ad. Present your ad to the class.

Tips

Listening . . .

- Listen for the main points and important details in the context of the advertisement to help you understand what is familiar to you and unfamiliar.
- Be ready to make pertinent comments.

Speaking . . .

- Speak loudly to effectively communicate your ideas.
- Express an opinion supported by conventions of language.

Teamwork . . .

- Provide suggestions that build upon the ideas of others.
- Share with a partner familiar and unfamiliar points you heard in the advertisement.

Objectives

- Speak clearly and to the point, give an opinion and support it with correct information. Make eye contact, change how fast, loud, and clearly you speak, and get your ideas across clearly.

Oral Vocabulary

Let's Talk About

Animal Behavior

- Describe with specificity and detail the mystifying behavior of a dog or cat or bird. For example, instead of saying, "The dog ran," say, "The dog raced around the tree chasing a squirrel."
- Express opinions about why animals behave the way they do.
- Speak at a rate that helps everyone understand your ideas.

READING STREET ONLINE
CONCEPT TALK VIDEO
www.ReadingStreet.com

You've learned
1 6 0
Amazing Words
so far this year!

Objectives

- Describe how ideas are related in texts whether the ideas are directly stated or not. • Summarize information in a text.

Envision It! | **Skill Strategy**

Skill

Strategy

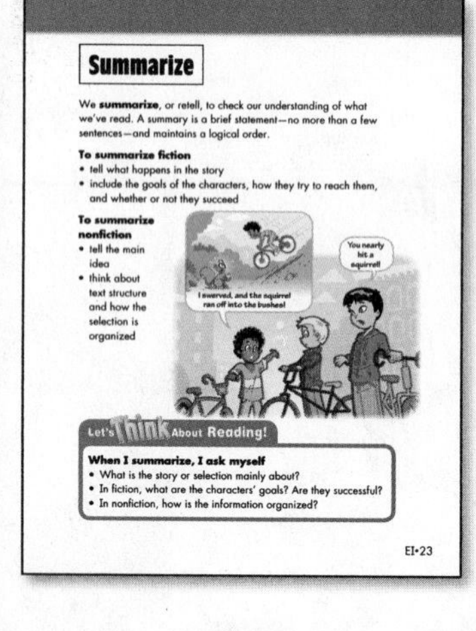

READING STREET ONLINE
ENVISION IT! ANIMATIONS
www.ReadingStreet.com

Comprehension Skill

Compare and Contrast

- To compare and contrast is to tell how two or more things are alike and different. These relationships may be explicit or implicit.
- Clue words such as *like* and *as* show explicitly how two things are alike. Clue words such as *but, instead,* and *unlike* show explicitly how they are different.
- Implicit comparisons don't use clue words. The reader has to figure out for him- or herself that two or more things are alike or different.
- Use this graphic organizer and what you know about explicit and implicit comparisons as you read "It's a Jungle Out There."

Comprehension Strategy

Summarize

Good readers summarize information in texts, while maintaining meaning. As you read, decide which are the main ideas and important details. Then put these important ideas together into a short statement, or summary. As you summarize information, keep your important ideas in logical order.

IT'S A JUNGLE OUT THERE!

Well, actually, it's a tropical rain forest out there. It's easy to confuse the terms *rain forest* and *jungle,* but they don't mean exactly the same thing. A jungle is a particular part of the rain forest.

In the rain forest, thousands and thousands of huge trees grow so close together that the tops overlap to form a kind of roof high above the forest floor. This leafy roof is called the canopy.

Strategy Summarize how the canopy in a rain forest is formed.

You can walk around fairly well on the forest floor under the canopy. That's because the tops of the tall trees grow so thickly together that they shut out most of the sunlight. Plants need sunlight to grow, but there's not enough light for them to grow under the canopy.

The jungle is another matter. In the rain forest there are clearings (for example, on the banks of rivers) where there are not as many gigantic trees. Here the sunlight can reach the ground, so smaller trees and plants can grow. And do they ever! This wild, thick tangle of plants is the jungle. You would need a big, sharp knife called a machete to hack your way through it. Good luck!

Skill The topic is shifting to the jungle. Pay attention to how it is both like and unlike the rain forest.

Skill Ask yourself how the jungle is different from the rain forest.

Your Turn!

Need a Review? See the *Envision It! Handbook* for help with comparing and contrasting and summarizing.

Ready to Try It? Use what you've learned about comparing and contrasting as you read *Encantado*.

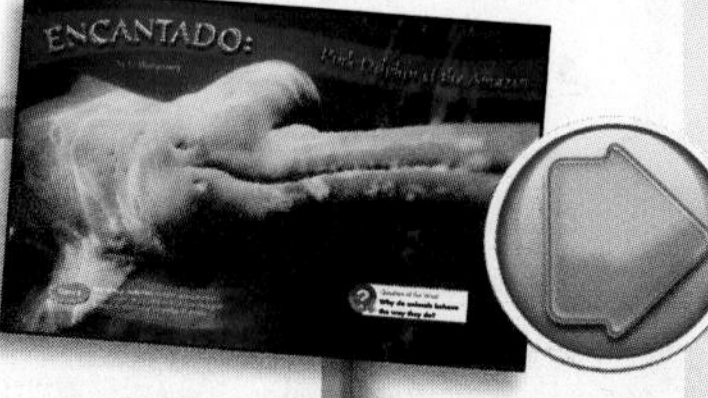

Objectives

- Determine the meanings of unfamiliar words or multiple-meaning words by using the context of the sentence.

Envision It! | **Words to Know**

aquarium

dolphins

flexible

enchanted

glimpses

pulses

surface

READING STREET ONLINE
VOCABULARY ACTIVITIES
www.ReadingStreet.com

Vocabulary Strategy for

Multiple-Meaning Words

Context Clues When you read, you may find that the meaning of a word you know does not make sense in a sentence. This may be because the word has more than one meaning. Sometimes the definition of the multiple-meaning word will be given in a nearby sentence. But often you will have to use context to determine the correct meaning of a multiple-meaning word.

1. Examine the word and try the meaning you know. Does it make sense in the sentence?
2. If it does not make sense, is there a definition of the word nearby? You can use it to figure out the word.
3. Try the meaning in the sentence and see if it makes sense.

As you read "Dolphins," use context clues to figure out multiple-meaning words. There may be a definition of the multiple-meaning word in a nearby sentence. Or there may be an example of the word in the same sentence.

Words to Write Reread "Dolphins." Imagine that you have an aquarium. What would you put in it? Describe your aquarium in a paragraph. Use the *Words to Know* in your description.

Dolphins

Dolphins are animals that live in the sea. Unlike many sea animals, they are mammals, not fish.

Dolphins have long, smooth bodies and flippers instead of fins. When they swim, dolphins move their tails up and down instead of side to side as fish do. Dolphins must go to the surface of the water to breathe. A dolphin breathes through a hole on top of its head.

Dolphins send out pulses or vibrations of sound to find things. The sound bounces off an object and back to the dolphin. The dolphin uses the sound to tell where the object is.

If you go to an aquarium or a zoo, you will most likely see bottle-nosed dolphins. They look like they are smiling. These animals are friendly and smart. They can be trained to jump through hoops, throw balls through nets, and "walk" backward on the water using their flexible tails.

People have long been enchanted by dolphins. The ancient Greeks drew pictures of them on pottery and walls. For centuries sailors have believed that catching glimpses of dolphins following their ships would bring them good luck.

Your Turn!

Need a Review? For help with multiple-meaning words, see *Words!*

Ready to Try It? Read *Encantado: Pink Dolphin of the Amazon* on pp. 58–71.

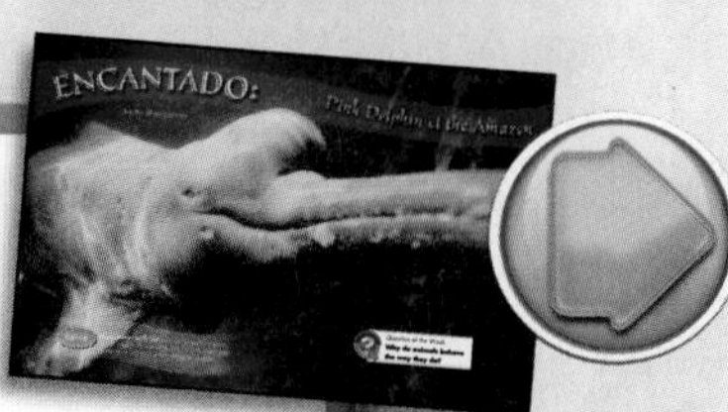

ENCANTADO:

by Sy Montgomery

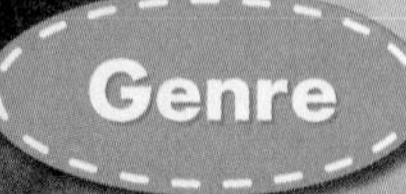

Expository Text provides factual information about a topic. As you read, look for facts about pink dolphins to add to your knowledge of animals.

Pink Dolphin of the Amazon

Question of the Week

Why do animals behave the way they do?

ENCOUNTERS with ENCANTADOS

You're traveling to a world that is full of water.

In the Amazon, the wet season lasts half the year. During the rainiest part of the wet season, from March through May, it rains every day. Not all day but every day. Sometimes the rain lasts less than an hour, and then the bright, hot sun comes out to burn your skin. But every day there is some kind of downpour.

The wet season is the best time of year to explore the Amazon. You'll soon see why. So bring a poncho. On your expedition, you will watch the rain remake this jungle world. Swollen with rainwater, the Amazon River and its many branches—smaller rivers called tributaries—overflow their dry-season banks. The rivers flood people's gardens. Water covers the village soccer fields. The school playgrounds are underwater. Instead of taking a school bus to class, the kids take a canoe.

The village school is like a treehouse, perched high on stilts. Many of the village houses are built on stilts too. Others float on the river, like rafts. People have to tie their floating houses to big trees so they don't drift away.

On your expedition, you'll sleep in a jungle lodge on stilts. You'll visit Amazon villages where the little girls play with real baby caimans (a kind of crocodile) the way girls at home play with dolls—and where the people will tell you stories about amazing creatures they call "encantados."

Encantado means the same thing in Portuguese (the language most people speak in Brazil) and in Spanish (which people speak in Peru and many other South American countries). It means "enchanted." And once you meet an encantado on the river, you'll know why.

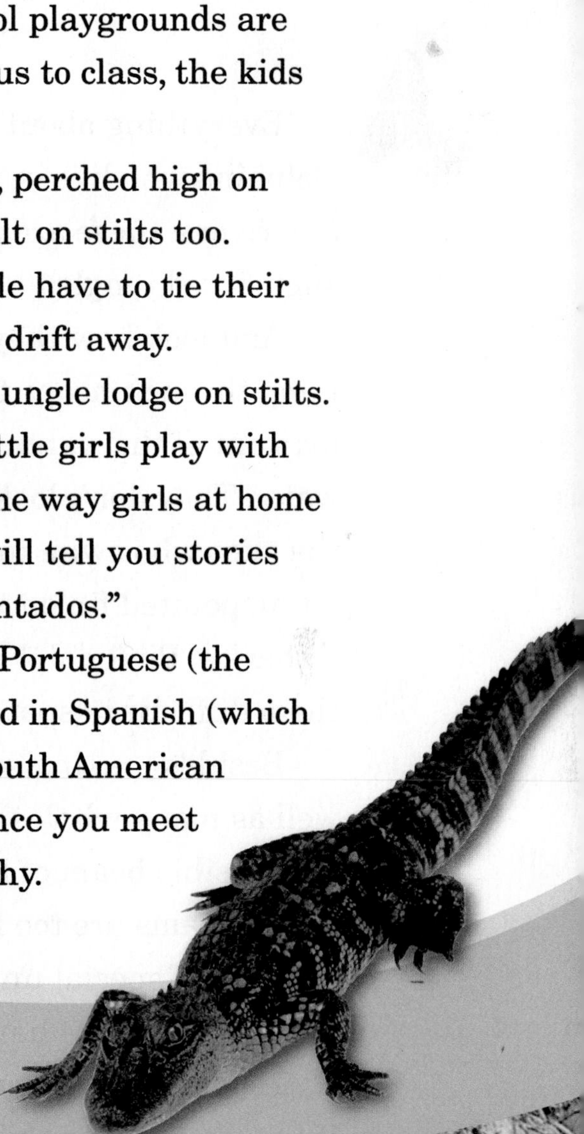

Some village houses float on the river.

WHALES of the AMAZON

Everything about them sounds impossible: pink dolphins! Dolphins who live in rivers, not in the ocean. And not just any rivers: these are rain-forest dolphins, who swim in a submerged jungle.

And look how they do it. Unlike the athletic dolphins who jump through hoops for aquarium shows, pink dolphins don't leap out of the water. Watch: they swim slowly, low in the water. They don't look like "regular" dolphins, either: Unlike the ones who swim in the sea, the pink dolphin doesn't have a tall, pointed fin on the back, sticking out of the water like a shark's. Pink dolphins just have a low ridge, which makes them difficult to spot.

Besides making sounds from their mouths, dolphins (as well as many whales) can also send out pulses of sound, like an invisible beam of light, from inside their foreheads. The sound beams are too high-pitched for our ears. Listening with the help of special underwater microphones and recording devices, scientists have learned that these sounds are a series of pulsed clicks. The clicks travel through the water. When they hit an object—a tree branch, a tasty fish, or even a swimming person—the sounds come bouncing back to the dolphin. That's right—it's an echo. Dolphins can locate objects by their echoes. That's why this sense is called echolocation. It's also sometimes called sonar, which ships and submarines use to probe the water too.

In fact, the echoes form a three-dimensional image in the dolphin's brain, allowing the animal to "see" not only the object's shape and size but also its insides.

Pink dolphins make sounds from their mouths. They also send out pulses of sound from inside their foreheads.

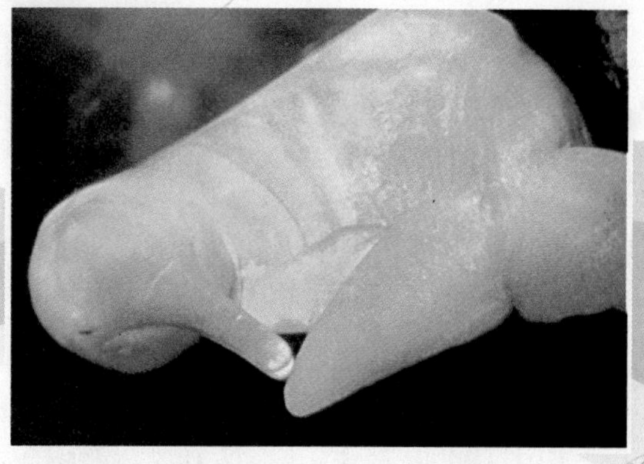

Dolphin doughnut: a pink dolphin touches its tail to its nose.

In addition to this super-sonar, pink dolphins have another special talent. Ocean dolphins' bodies don't bend very well. They'd never be able to get around all the branches in the Amazon. Pink dolphins can bend their bodies to twist gracefully through the underwater treetops. They are so flexible they can even touch their tail to their nose—like a dolphin doughnut.

Because of their unique flexibility, pink dolphins can also swim in shallow waters that ocean dolphins can't manage. Sometimes they get stuck—but not for long. You probably have already noticed that pink dolphins have really big front flippers—almost like wings. At moments like these, those flippers come in handy. Pink dolphins can use their front flippers not just to swim but also to crawl—both out of and back into the water!

Sometimes pink dolphins' behavior seems downright weird. Here's another example: sometimes they sleep upside down. Imagine finding a 300-pound dolphin floating upside down like a dead goldfish! Why do they do this? Why don't other dolphins?

No one knows. And that's just one of the mysteries about them.

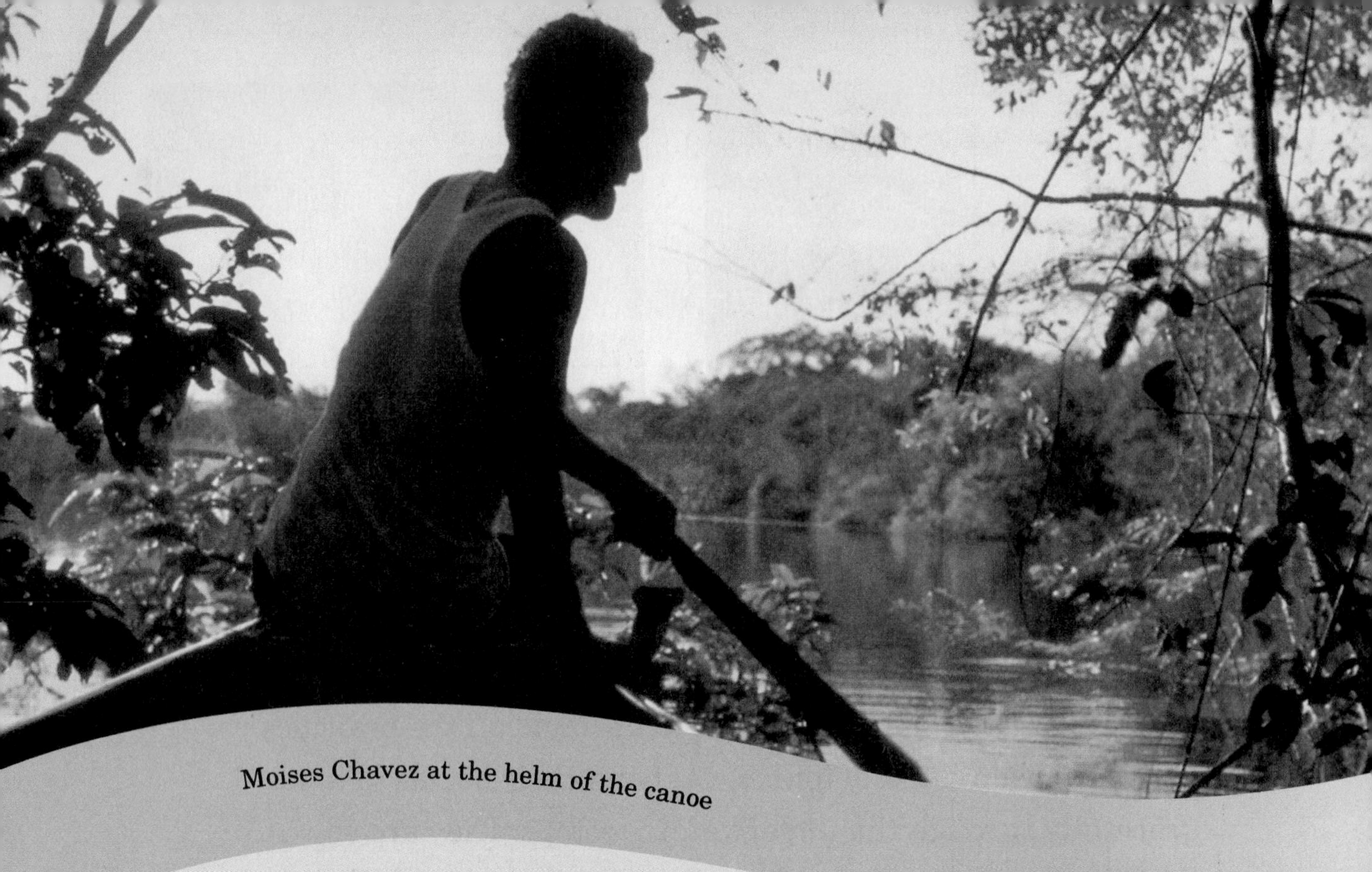

Moises Chavez at the helm of the canoe

NIGHTMARE DREAM WORLD

Canoeing through the flooded forest feels like a dream.

Strange lives cling to every tree. Fist-sized, hairy megalomorph spiders, who look like tarantulas, hunt for bugs in tree holes. The purselike nests of little birds called oropendulas hang from the tips of branches. Centipedes curl in the cracks of bark. Snails cling to the undersides of leaves.

"Duck!" Moises Chavez (MOY-sess SHAH-vez), your Peruvian guide, calls out from the front of the boat.

A duck? Where? But no—he motions you to get your head down, fast. You don't want to smack your head on a low branch as the canoe glides beneath it. Particularly this branch—because hanging down from it is a wasp nest the size of a pumpkin.

Fortunately, Moises knows these waterways well. He can warn you of the dangers. He grew up in the Amazon rain forest. His father was a teacher working in Amazonian Indian villages. Moises speaks some of the Indian languages, as well as Spanish and English. He has learned many of the jungle's secrets, including where to find the pink dolphins.

Today he's taking you to his favorite lake, where he knows you'll see pink dolphins. But to get there, you have to thread through twisting waterways, the heart of the Amazon rain forest.

Trees poke out of the water on all sides. Moises explains that it's important to keep your hands away from the sides of the boat. It's easy to see why. Some of the trees have spines growing out of their trunks. "They're sharp as needles," he says. "Don't touch the trees! See this guy"—he points to a tree with smooth bark—"this guy has sap that can burn your skin. And this guy," he says, pointing to a short tree with yellow flowers, "from its leaves you can make a tea to cure yellow fever. And this guy—"

Electric eels live in the Amazon River.

A centipede

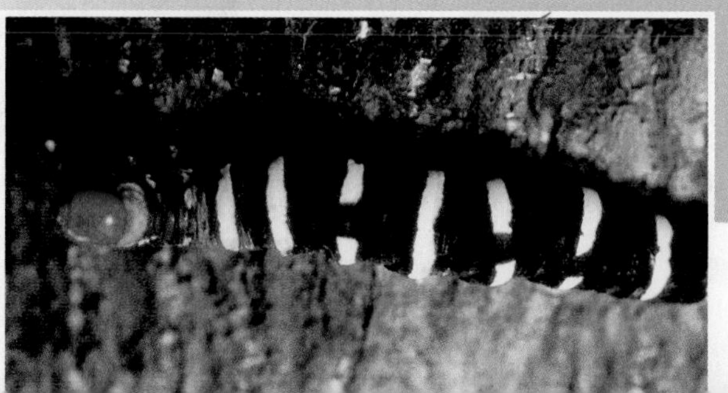

Hairy megalomorph spiders defend themselves with the hairs on their legs.

BANG!

Your canoe has come to an abrupt halt. The bottom is hung up on an underwater tree limb.

Your canoe is stuck in the treetops!

But Moises quickly gets the situation under control by pushing against a tree to free the canoe.

You're over the log, but you're not out of trouble.

"Watch out!" calls Moises. "Tangarana tree!"

Moises recognizes the tree's long, oval leaves right away. And he also knows that its hollow stems teem with thousands of stinging black tangarana ants. Each ant is more than an inch long. When something bumps against the tree, the ants think it's an attack on their home. Bravely, they'll rush to defend it. They'll even jump off branches into your canoe to sting you if they think their tree is threatened.

At the last minute, with some skilled paddling, Moises veers the canoe away from its dangerous path. You miss the ant tree by inches.

And then, pushing aside some branches like a curtain on a stage, Moises reveals your destination: the dolphin lake. You've made it.

During the dry season, the lake is little more than a puddle. But now, full of rainwater, it covers an area larger than a thousand football fields. It's shaped like a figure eight, with the crown of a mimosa tree poking up the middle.

Across the lake you can hear a dolphin blowing: "CHHHAAA!"

Some trees protect themselves with sharp spines.

The tangarana tree is home to thousands of stinging black tangarana ants.

REFLECTIONS on the WATER

You're surrounded.

At first, it seemed that you would see the dolphins only far away—just a pink shimmer on the water's surface. At first glance, you weren't sure whether you really saw one or just imagined it.

But Moises had a great idea. "Let's call them," he suggested. He leaned over the side of the canoe and, reaching underwater, banged on the side of the boat with his knuckles. The dolphins responded. And now they are all around you.

Right behind your canoe, you hear one blow. You twirl around, but all you see is the dolphin's wake, the wave it made when it dived just a split second ago. Then—"CHAAHHH!" A dolphin surfaces in front. "Look!" cries Moises—but you see only a trail of bubbles.

A diving dolphin leaves a wake and a trail of bubbles.

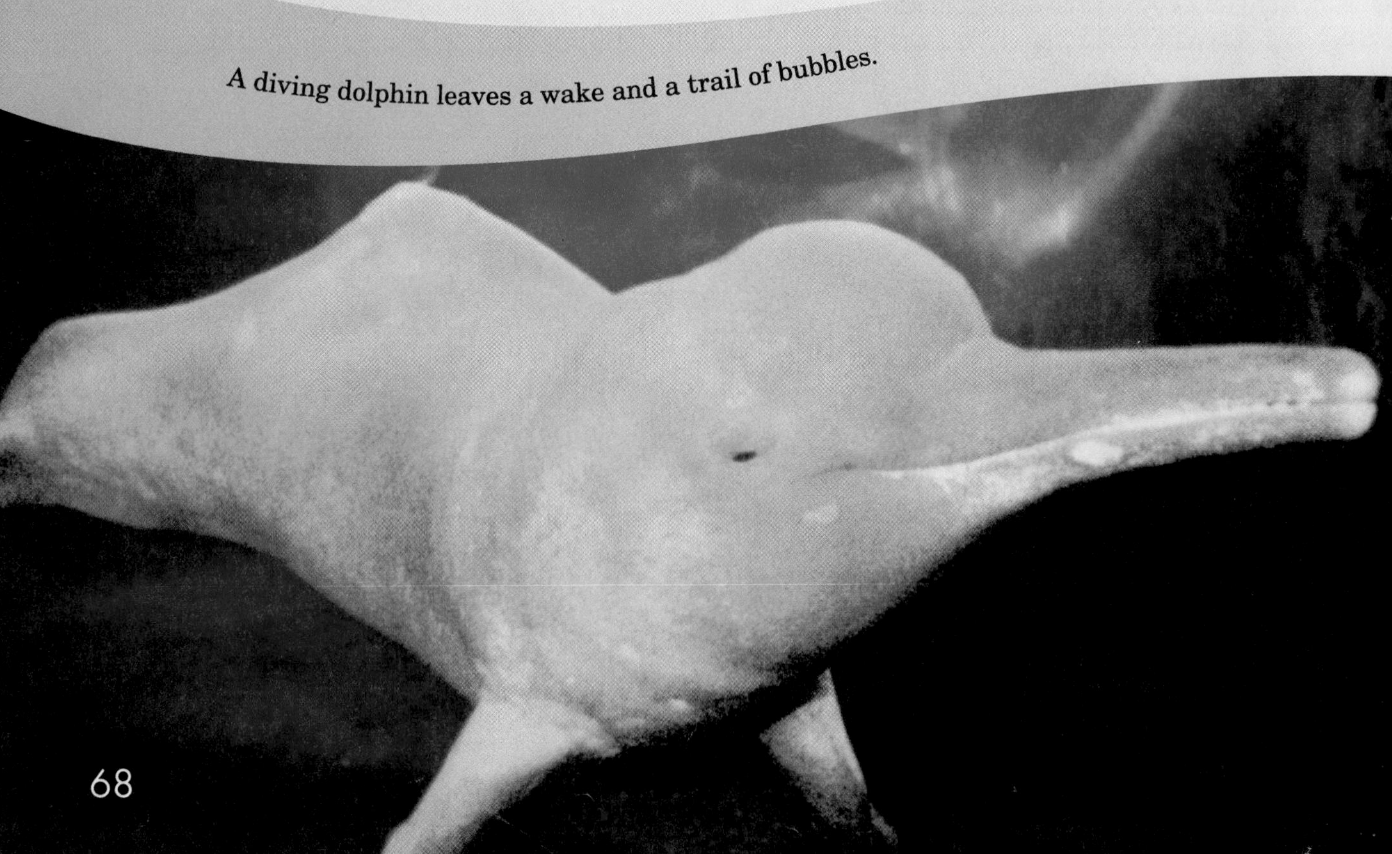

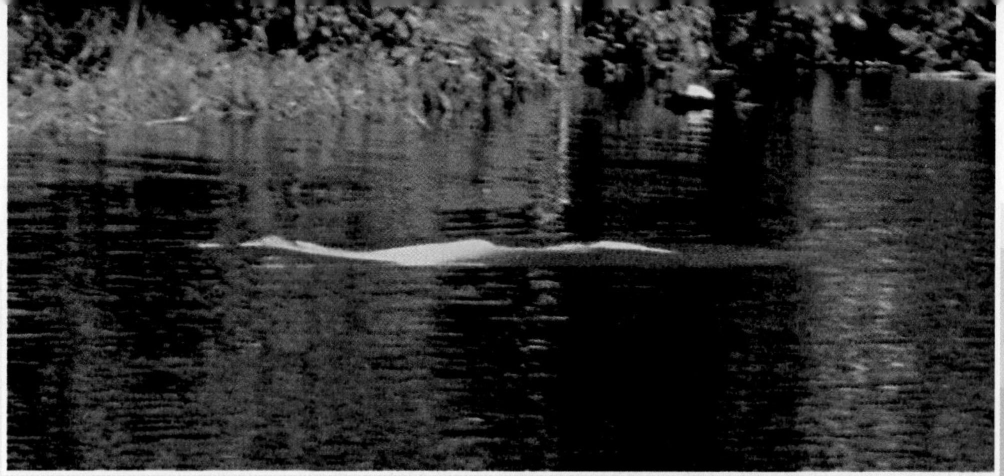

This pink dolphin looks almost like a reflection on the water.

SPLASH! Off to your left, a big pink form has surfaced. But by the time you turn, you see only a tail.

If the water were clear, as in an aquarium tank, you could see them swimming beneath the surface. But the water in the lake is as dark as night. It's not polluted; it's stained with natural chemicals from decaying rain-forest leaves.

Because of the dark water, it's impossible to count the dolphins. It certainly seems there are several. After all, one surfaced in back of the boat, then one in front of the boat. Another rose to the side. Does that mean there were three dolphins?

Maybe not. Remember that pink dolphins, with their bendy bodies, don't have to swim in a straight line. You can't predict where they might surface next. They can turn and twist beneath the water, even whirl around like a Ferris wheel. Maybe the three glimpses you had were all of the same dolphin.

How would you tell? Most animals, including dolphins, look as different from one another as people do. You just have to learn to see the differences. Some are bigger than the others, some are darker. One might have a notch or a scar on the back or head. One might have a bent snout.

But here's the problem: because pink dolphins don't leap out of the water, and because the lake water is so dark, you never see much of any individual dolphin at one time. You get only little glimpses: the glistening pink top of a head here, a tail there, a quick look at the low fin on the back here. And you can't identify them by color, because these dolphins grow pinker with exercise, just as people do.

For half an hour, the dolphins, whether one or several, continue to visit near your canoe. Could they be as curious about you as you are about them?

As you and Moises paddle back to the lodge for dinner, you're full of questions about the dolphins. How many of them visit the lake? Do they stay there all year, or do they move to other lakes and rivers? Are there mothers with babies among them? What kinds of fish do they like to eat?

Moises knows a lot about the wildlife in the Amazon. But even he doesn't know the answers to your questions. "The bufeo*, they are very mysterious," he says.

****Bufeo colorado*** (Boo-FEY-oh co-low-RAH-doe) is another name for the pink dolphin. *Bufeo* is the local word for *dolphin. Colorado* is a Spanish word that means "ruddy or reddish."

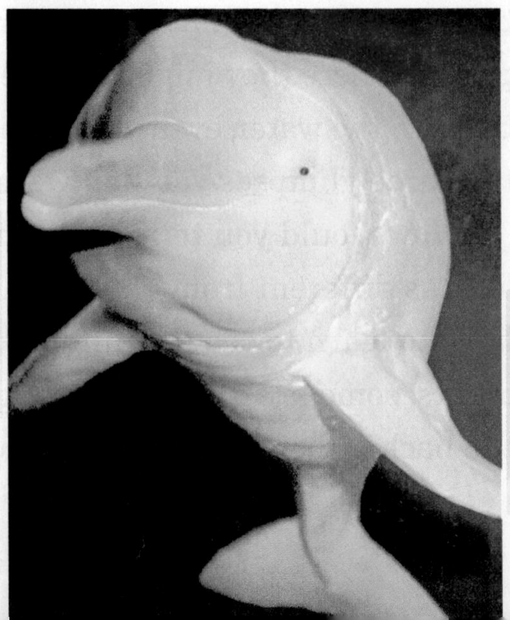

Because they are difficult to study in the wild, pink dolphins remain a mystery to scientists.

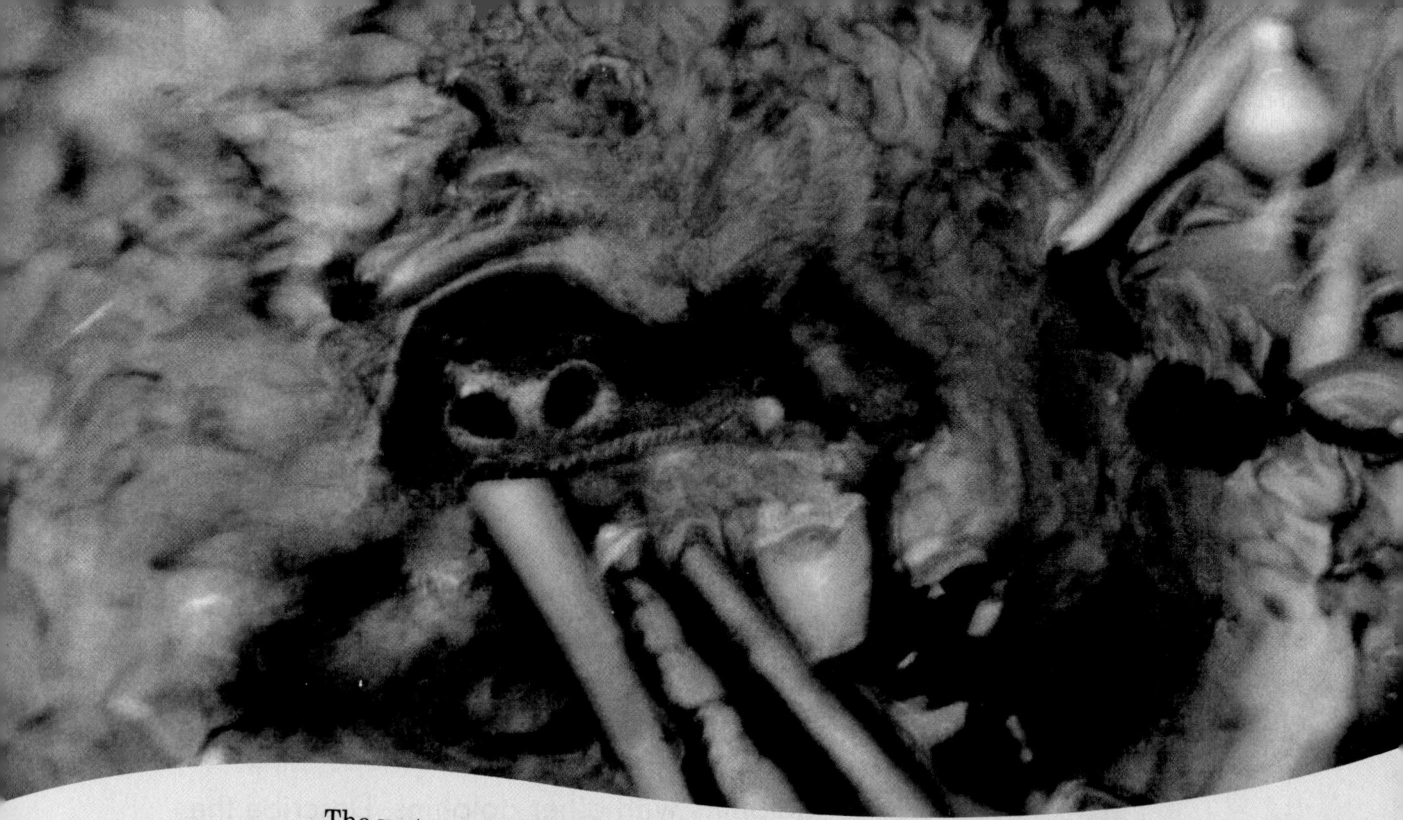

The water is so dark you can't tell who might be swimming in there with you! This nose (above) belongs to a huge Amazonian manatee.

Objectives

- Read independently for long periods of time and paraphrase the reading, including the order in which events occur. • Write responses to texts using details to show understanding.

Envision It! Retell

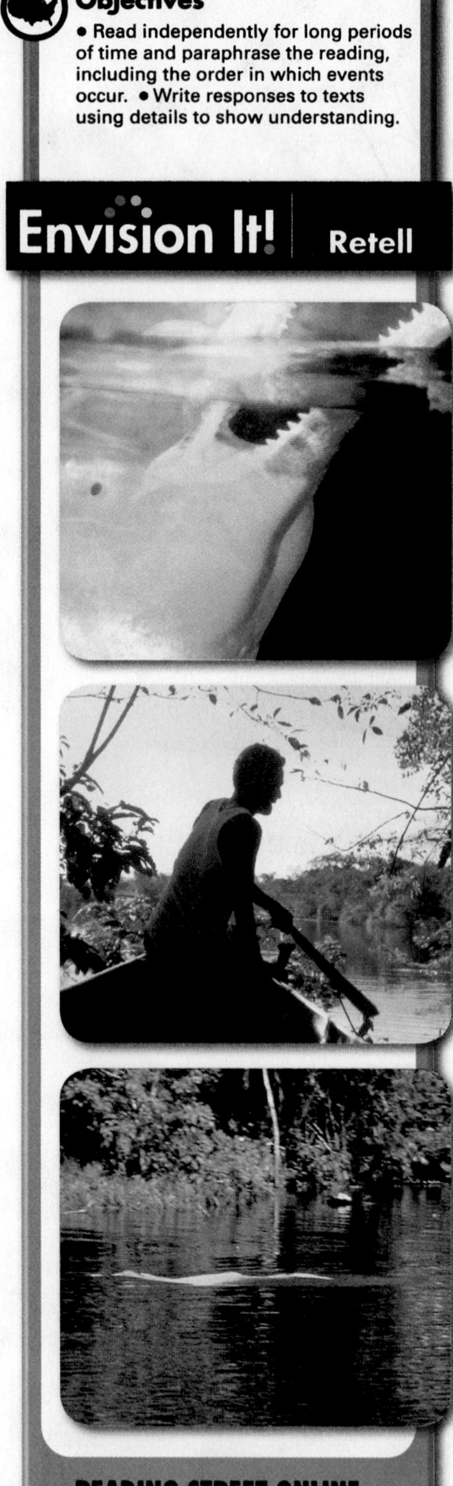

READING STREET ONLINE
STORY SORT
www.ReadingStreet.com

Think Critically

1. On pages 60 and 61, you read about the wet season and floating houses. How would you feel if you had to float down a river to get to school or go to the grocery store? What would you like about it? What would you dislike? **Text to Self**

2. How does the author involve you in her journey to the Amazon? Find sample sentences that show how she brings the reader along to the rain forest. **Think Like an Author**

3. Reread the section titled "Whales of the Amazon." Compare and contrast pink dolphins with other dolphins. Describe the special body structure of the pink dolphin. What does its body structure allow it to do? **Compare and Contrast**

4. Imagine you are canoeing through the Amazon rain forest. Use details from the selection to summarize what you see and hear as you glide through the rain forest. **Summarize**

5. **Look Back and Write** Look back at pages 62–63. Explain why pink dolphins are called *encantados*, or "enchanted." Provide evidence to support your answer.

Meet the Author

SY MONTGOMERY

Sy Montgomery really gets to know the animals she writes about. She traveled to Peru and Brazil to study and even swim with dolphins. She remembers, "They would sometimes swim underneath me and blow bubbles up at me. The bubbles sizzled on my skin. Researchers believe they blow bubbles to give each other a tickly, calming feeling—like a whirlpool bath or massage."

Ms. Montgomery has written many books about nature for both adults and children. She especially loves writing for children. "When we are young, we find in books hopes and dreams and futures we never would have found otherwise. It is my hope in writing for kids that my readers find we share the same dream: a world in which people, animals, land, plants, and water all are seen as precious and worthy of protection."

Here are other books by Sy Montgomery.

The Man-Eating Tigers of Sundarbans

The Snake Scientist

Use the Reading Log in the *Reader's and Writer's Notebook* to record your independent reading.

Objectives

- Use and understand adjectives and their special forms.
- Use and understand reflexive pronouns.

Key Features of a Song

- divided into lines
- set to a melody
- often uses rhyme

READING STREET ONLINE
GRAMMAR JAMMER
www.ReadingStreet.com

Narrative

Song

A **song** is a type of short composition set to music. The student model on the next page is an example of a song.

Writing Prompt Write a song about the pink dolphins of the Amazon.

Writer's Checklist

Remember, you should ...

- ✓ use vivid adjectives in your descriptions.
- ✓ create a regular rhythm and repeat it throughout the song.
- ✓ help the reader understand how you feel about the subject.
- ✓ use subject, object, and reflexive pronouns properly.

Student Model

Encantado, I long to see **you**,
Whirling free, out in the river.
Encantado, I long to see **you**,
A flash, a rosy light, in the dark, dark Amazon.

Encantado, I feel your presence,
You make **yourself** a fleeting shadow,
Encantado, I feel your presence,
That seems unreal, a flash, a whirl.

Encantado, **you** are a mystery,
Swimming low, through watery treetops.
Encantado, **you** are a mystery,
A smile, a splashing clown, in the dark, dark Amazon.

Genre
A **song** uses repetition to create rhythm.

Subject, object, and **reflexive** pronouns are used correctly.

Writing Trait Word Choice
Vivid nouns and adjectives create a "word picture."

Conventions

Kinds of Pronouns

Remember A **subject pronoun** performs the action in the sentence. An **object pronoun** is the recipient of the action. A **reflexive pronoun** refers to a person or animal mentioned earlier in the sentence.

Objectives

- Explain the difference between a stated purpose and an implied purpose in expository texts.
- Describe how ideas are related in texts whether the ideas are directly stated or not.

Science in Reading

Genre

Expository Text

- Expository text contains facts and information.
- Some authors of expository texts state their purpose for writing. Others do not. When a purpose is not stated, a reader needs to infer, or figure out, the purpose.
- This author organized information by comparison. Comparisons can be explicit (or stated, using words such as "like") or implicit (not directly stated).
- Read the article. Look for elements that make this expository text. Is the author's purpose for writing this text stated or implied?

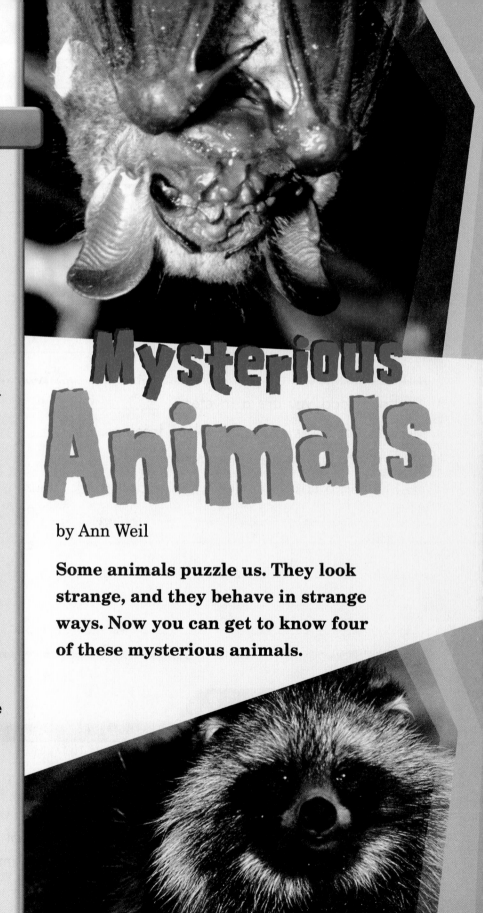

Mysterious Animals

by Ann Weil

Some animals puzzle us. They look strange, and they behave in strange ways. Now you can get to know four of these mysterious animals.

Wrinkle-Faced Bat

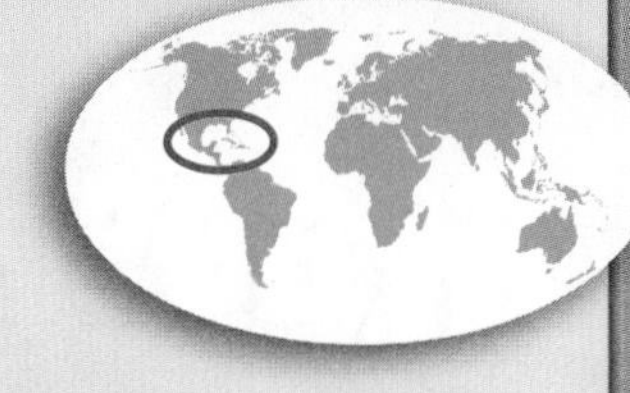

The wrinkle-faced bat sleeps during the day and goes out to look for food at night (like other bats). It does not look like other bats, however. Its face is covered with folds of skin. Why it has all that extra skin is still a mystery.

Where it lives: Mexico, Central America, and the West Indies

Favorite food: fruit

Weight: 1 ounce or less

Size: 2–3 inches

3 inches

3 inches

Raccoon Dog

This strange dog looks like a raccoon. It sleeps through the winter like a bear. Oddly, this dog does not bark. Hunters prize this animal for its fur.

Where it lives: northern Asia and parts of Europe

Favorite foods: plants, fruits, insects, fish, and small animals

Weight: 8–22 pounds

Size: head and body: 1.5–2 feet long; tail: 5–10 inches long

3 feet

Let's Think About...

Reread p. 76. Does the author state why she is writing this article? What is her purpose?
Expository Text

Let's Think About...

How does the wrinkle-faced bat compare to other bats?
Expository Text

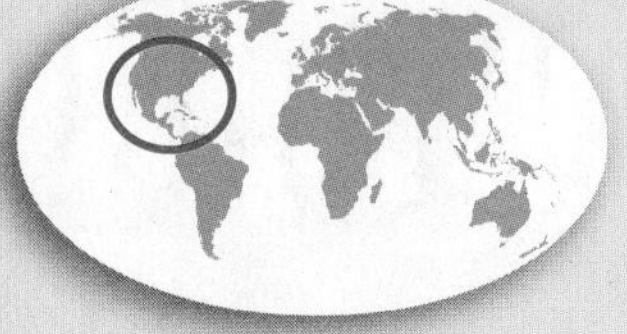

Grasshopper Mouse

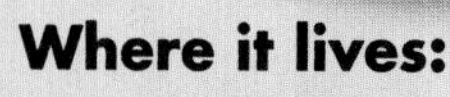

Where it lives: North America

Favorite foods: insects and small animals

Weight: 1–2 ounces

Size: 2 inches tall with a head-body length of 3–5 inches

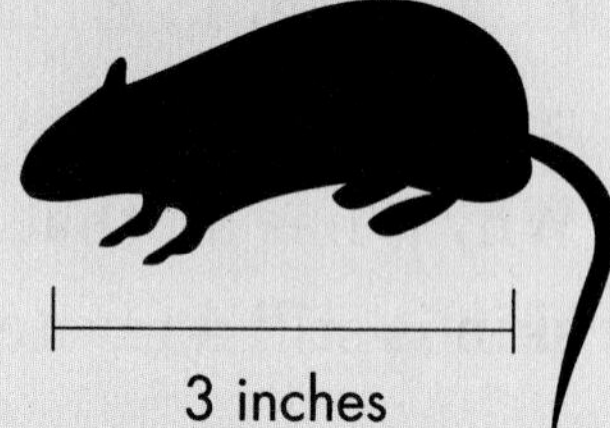

This small mouse is not timid or quiet. It has sharp teeth and big jaw muscles for killing and eating its prey. Unlike some other mice, it does not squeak softly. Instead, it stands on its back legs and roars! Its cry can be heard more than 100 yards away.

Let's Think About...

How does the sound that grasshopper mice make compare to the sound of other mice? **Expository Text**

Bush Dog

These dogs are equally at home on land and in the water. With their webbed feet, they can swim and dive underwater. Though they may swim like fish, these strange dogs sound like birds. Their "bark" resembles a whistle or chirp.

Where it lives: parts of Central and South America

Favorite foods: birds and rodents

Weight: 11–15 pounds

Size: head and body: 1.75–2.5 feet; tail: 4–6 inches

3 feet

Let's Think About...

Reading Across Texts *Encantado* takes place in Brazil, a country in South America. Which of the animals in "Mysterious Animals" also makes its home in South America?

Writing Across Texts Tell two ways in which pink dolphins and one of these animals are alike and two ways in which they are different.

Objectives

• Read aloud grade-level texts and understand what is read. • Determine the meanings of unfamiliar words or multiple-meaning words by using the context of the sentence. • Explain the positive and negative effects of advertising and how it influences what people buy and do. • Listen closely to speakers and ask questions about and comment on the topic.

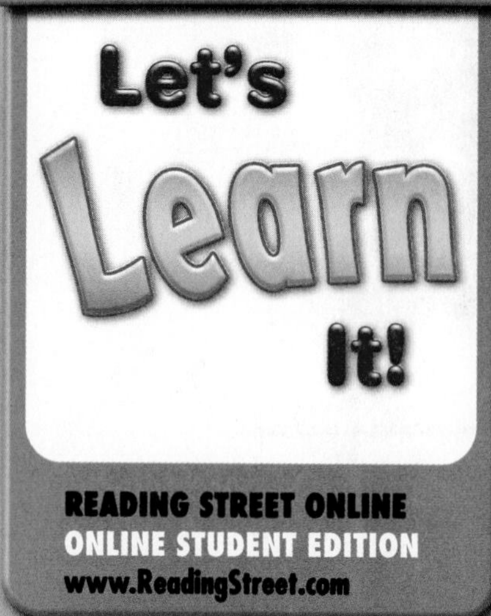

READING STREET ONLINE
ONLINE STUDENT EDITION
www.ReadingStreet.com

Vocabulary

Multiple-Meaning Words

Context Clues Some words have more than one meaning. You can use context clues to help you figure out which meaning of a multiple-meaning word is being used.

Practice It! In the story *Encantado: Pink Dolphin of the Amazon,* find the word *branches* on page 60. Use the context of the sentence to determine the meaning of the word. Write two definitions for *branches.* Then write two sentences, using a different meaning of *branches* in each sentence. Repeat for the word *duck* on page 64.

Fluency

Appropriate Phrasing

Partner Reading Punctuation cues help to guide your voice as you read. Paying attention to punctuation marks as you read helps you better understand a story's meaning.

Practice It! With a partner, identify the punctuation marks in the last four paragraphs of page 66 of *Encantado: Pink Dolphin of the Amazon*. Look for commas, periods, colons, exclamation points, and quotation marks. Then read each paragraph aloud to your partner, using the clues that the punctuation marks give you to help you read.

When you create a presentation, keep your purpose and your audience in mind.

Media Literacy

TV Commercial

A TV commercial uses words, visuals, and sounds to tell about a product, an event, or a place to visit. TV commercials use various techniques to impact consumer behavior. For example, commercials only focus on the positive aspects of a product. Be aware that commercials could have a negative impact on consumers. TV ads may convince people to buy a product they don't really need.

Practice It! With a partner, create a one-minute TV commercial that advertises tours to the Amazon region in South America. Use information from *Encantado: Pink Dolphin of the Amazon*. Choose important points that you want to emphasize for your audience and include music and visuals. Record your commercial and then present it to the class.

Tips

Listening . . .

- Listen attentively.
- Ask questions that are related to the topic.

Speaking . . .

- Express an opinion supported by accurate information.
- Enunciate clearly to effectively communicate your ideas.

Teamwork . . .

- Provide suggestions that build upon your partner's ideas.
- Answer questions from the audience with appropriate detail.

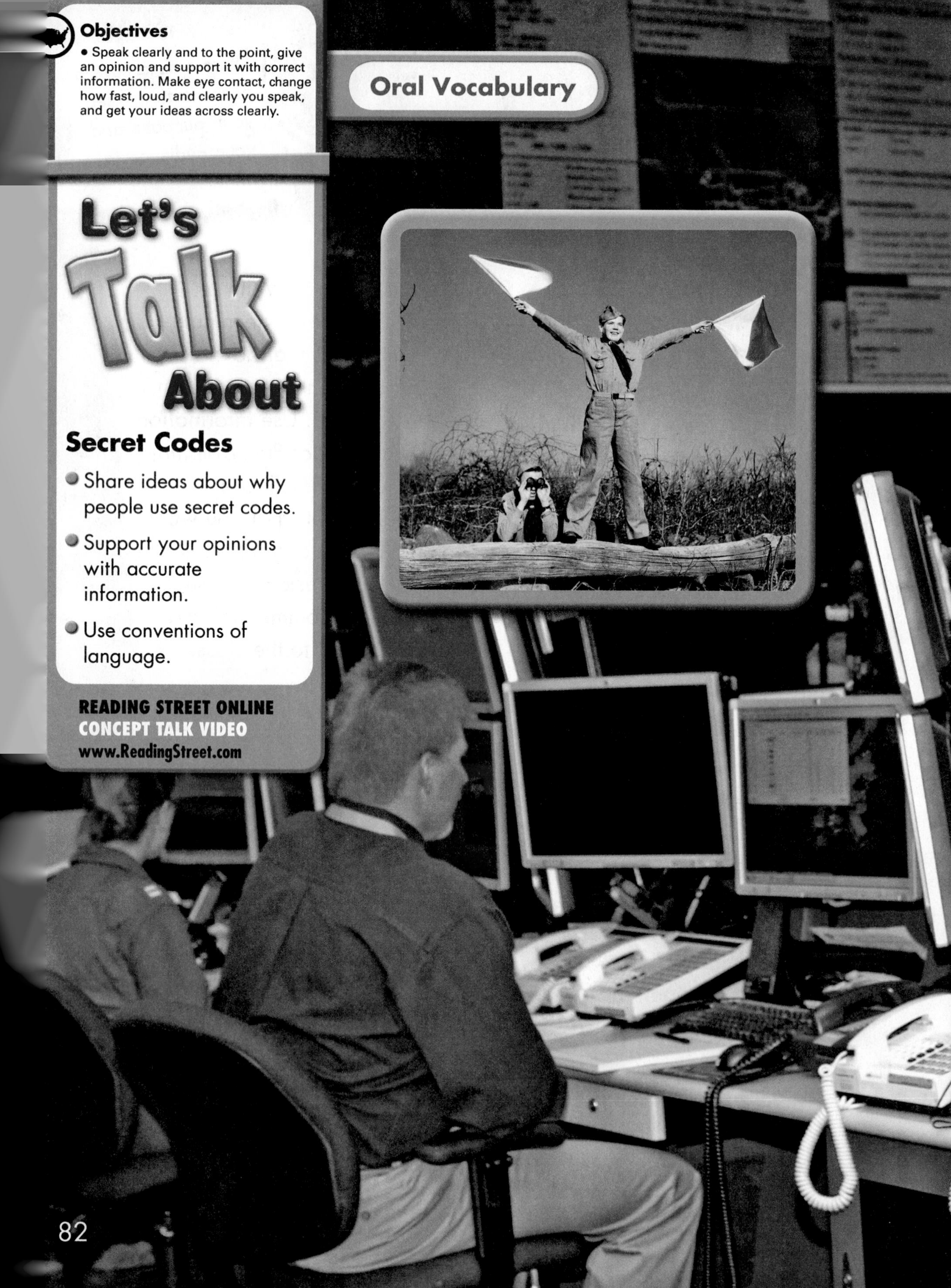

Objectives

- Speak clearly and to the point, give an opinion and support it with correct information. Make eye contact, change how fast, loud, and clearly you speak, and get your ideas across clearly.

Oral Vocabulary

Let's Talk About

Secret Codes

- Share ideas about why people use secret codes.
- Support your opinions with accurate information.
- Use conventions of language.

READING STREET ONLINE
CONCEPT TALK VIDEO
www.ReadingStreet.com

You've learned
1 7 0
Amazing Words
so far this year!
CANADA

Objectives

• Summarize the main idea and supporting details. • Describe how ideas are related in texts whether the ideas are directly stated or not.

Envision It! | **Skill Strategy**

Skill

Sequence

Sequence refers to the order of events in nonfiction. We also use sequence when we list the steps in a process.

EI•13

Strategy

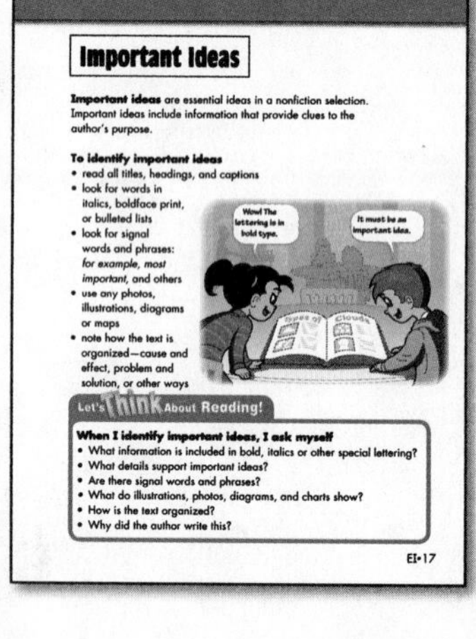

Important Ideas

Important ideas are essential ideas in a nonfiction selection. Important ideas include information that provide clues to the author's purpose.

To identify important ideas

- read all titles, headings, and captions
- look for words in italics, boldface print, or bulleted lists
- look for signal words and phrases: *for example, most important,* and others
- use any photos, illustrations, diagrams or maps
- note how the text is organized—cause and effect, problem and solution, or other ways

Let's Think About Reading!

When I identify important ideas, I ask myself

- What information is included in bold, italics or other special lettering?
- What details support important ideas?
- Are there signal words and phrases?
- What do illustrations, photos, diagrams, and charts show?
- How is the text organized?
- Why did the author write this?

EI•17

READING STREET ONLINE
ENVISION IT! ANIMATIONS
www.ReadingStreet.com

Comprehension Skill

Sequence

- Sequence is the order in which relationships among ideas happen in a text. Sequence can also mean the steps people follow to do something.
- You can identify explicit sequence relationships because clue words such as *first, then, next, after,* and *last* tell you the order of the events.
- If the sequence is implicit, there may not be any clue words. You will have to figure out the order of the events on your own.
- Words such as *while, meanwhile,* and *during* can show when events happen at the same time.
- Use this graphic organizer to figure out the explicit and implicit sequence of events in "Merril Sandoval: The Life of a Code Talker."

Comprehension Strategy

Important Ideas

Important ideas are the essential ideas in a text. While reading a nonfiction text, try to identify the most important ideas an author has to say about the topic. You can use the subheads, photographs, and illustrations to help you identify the important ideas. Then try to notice the difference between important ideas and interesting details.

Merril Sandoval: THE LIFE OF A CODE TALKER

Merril Sandoval was a freshman at Farmington Mission School in New Mexico when Marines visited his school. They were looking for young Navajo men to train as code talkers—Navajos who sent and received secret coded messages during World War II. Merril wanted to join, but he was only sixteen years old. Samuel, Merril's older brother, was able to join. So Merril stayed in school, and Samuel left with the Marines.

Skill Sometimes two events happen at the same time. What event took place while Merril was still in school?

In March 1943, during Merril's second year in high school, he was old enough to become a Marine. He was excited to be part of the Navajo code-talking program.

Strategy What important idea about the topic is in this paragraph?

From March through June, Merril attended boot camp in California for basic training. After boot camp, he went to communications school to learn how to use and fix radios.

On February 19, 1945, Merril was sent to Iwo Jima, Japan. While there, he translated reports from code talkers on the island. Then he sent back the important messages to the military in Hawaii.

After his discharge from the Marine Corps in March 1946, Merril finished high school.

Skill Which of the following events took place first? How do you know?
(a) Merril learned how to use a radio.
(b) Merril went to boot camp.
(c) Merril finished high school.

Your Turn!

Need a Review? See the *Envision It! Handbook* for help with sequence and important ideas.

Ready to Try It? Use what you've learned about sequence as you read *Navajo Code Talkers*.

Objectives

- Use a dictionary or glossary to find the meanings of unknown words, the syllable rules for these words, and how to pronounce them.

Envision It! | **Words to Know**

exhausting

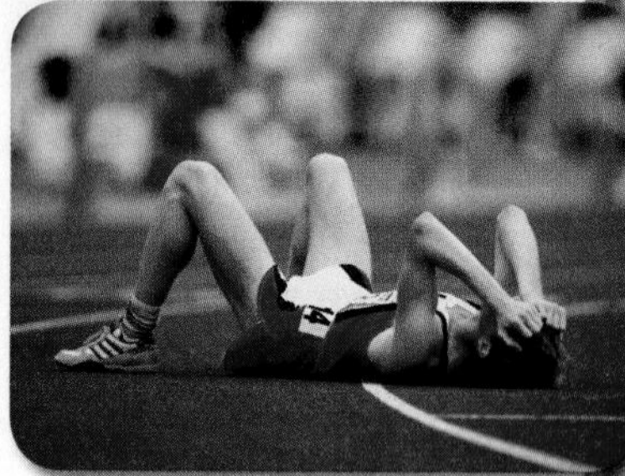

intense

messages

advance
developed
impossible
headquarters
reveal

READING STREET ONLINE
VOCABULARY ACTIVITIES
www.ReadingStreet.com

Vocabulary Strategy for

Unknown Words

Dictionary/Glossary When you read, you may come across a word you don't know. If you can't use the context, or words and sentences around the unknown word, to figure it out, you can use a dictionary or a glossary to help you.

Choose one of the *Words to Know* and follow these steps.

1. Look in the back of your book for the glossary.
2. Find the entry for the word. The entries are in alphabetical order.
3. Use the pronunciation key to pronounce the word.
4. Read all the meanings given for the word.
5. Choose the meaning that makes the best sense in the sentence.

As you read "A New Way to Win a War," use context clues to figure out the meanings of this week's *Words to Know*. If the context doesn't help, use a dictionary or the glossary to determine their meanings.

Words to Write Reread "A New Way to Win a War." Imagine you were in a place where no one spoke your language. Write about how you could try to communicate with another person. Use some of the *Words to Know* in your writing.

A New Way to Win a War

During World War II, a group of marines known as Navajo code talkers developed a special code to send and receive secret messages. A different Navajo word stood for each letter of the English alphabet. The code was impossible for the Japanese to figure out. It was based on the Navajo language, which is very difficult to learn.

To help advance the United States troops and their allies, code talkers were often in the areas with the most intense fighting. The code talkers would reveal the location of the enemy during battle and send the coded message back to their headquarters. Knowing this information, the United States and its allies were able to determine what to do next. Fighting during the war was exhausting, and the radios and equipment the code talkers had to carry made it even more difficult, but because of their hard work and sacrifice, Navajo code talkers helped the U.S. to victory in World War II.

Your Turn!

Need a Review? For help with using a dictionary to determine the meanings of unknown words, see *Words!*

Ready to Try It? Read *Navajo Code Talkers* on pp. 88–103.

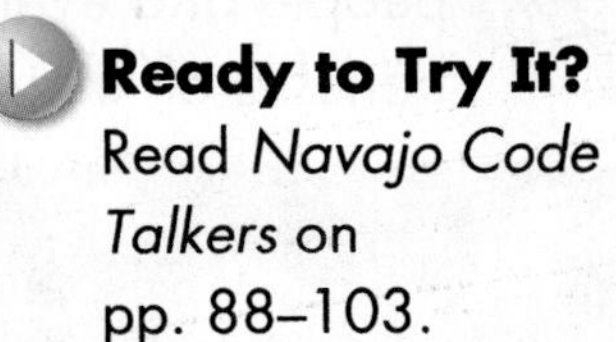

Navajo Code Talkers

by Andrew Santella

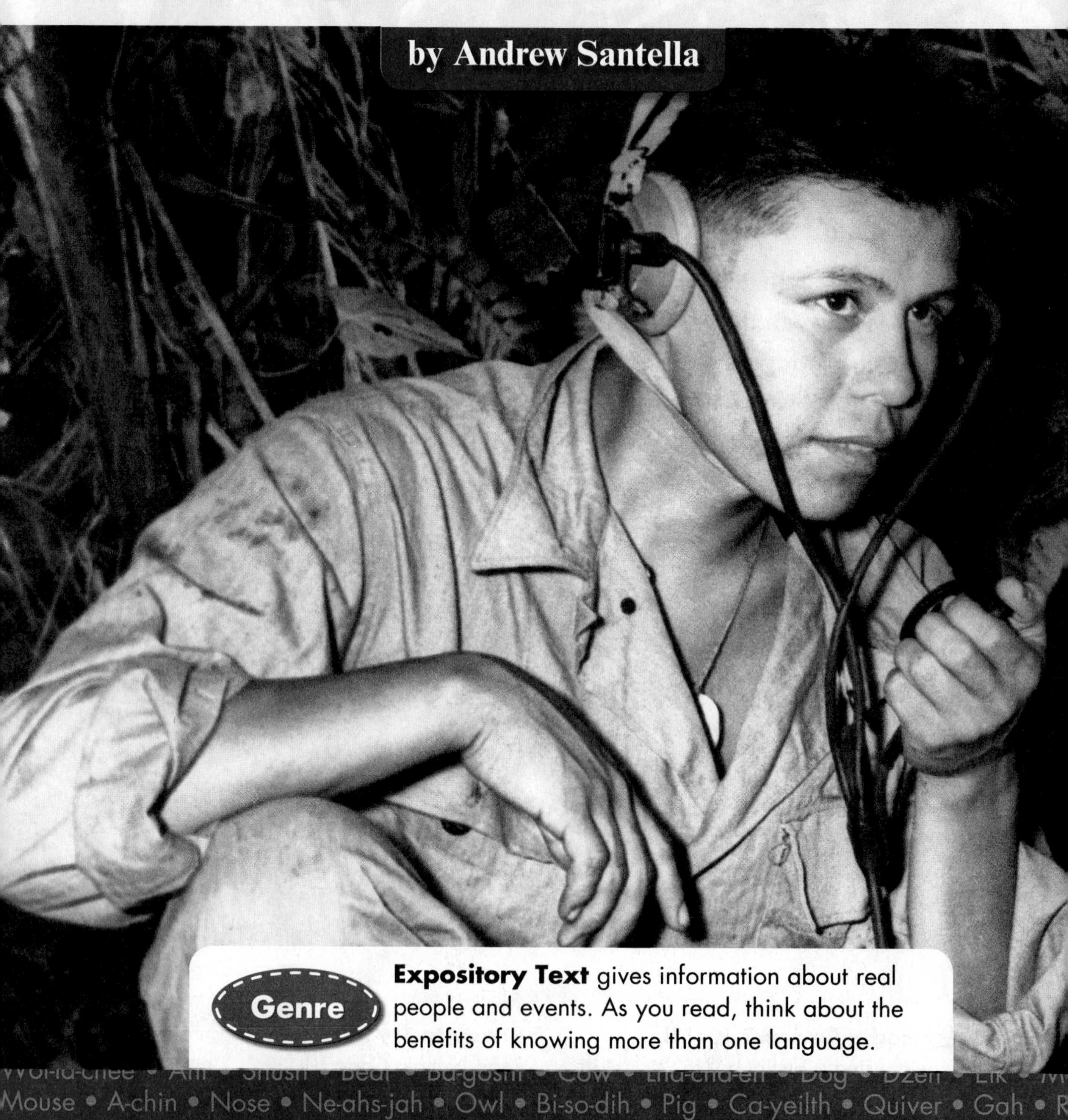

Genre

Expository Text gives information about real people and events. As you read, think about the benefits of knowing more than one language.

Mouse • A-chin • Nose • Ne-ahs-jah • Owl • Bi-so-dih • Pig • Ca-yeilth • Quiver • Gah • R
• Dog • Dzeh • Elk • Ma-e • Fox • Ah-tad • Girl • Lin • Horse • Tkin • Ice • Klizzie-yazzie •
• Quiver • Gah • Rabbit • Klesh • Snake • A-woh • Tooth • Wol-la-chee • Ant • Shush •
• Ice • Klizzie-yazzie • Kid • Ah-jad • Leg • Na-as-tso-si • Mouse • A-chin • Nose • Ne-
Wol-la-chee • Ant • Shush • Bear • Ba-goshi • Cow • Lha-cha-eh • Dog • Dzeh • Elk • M

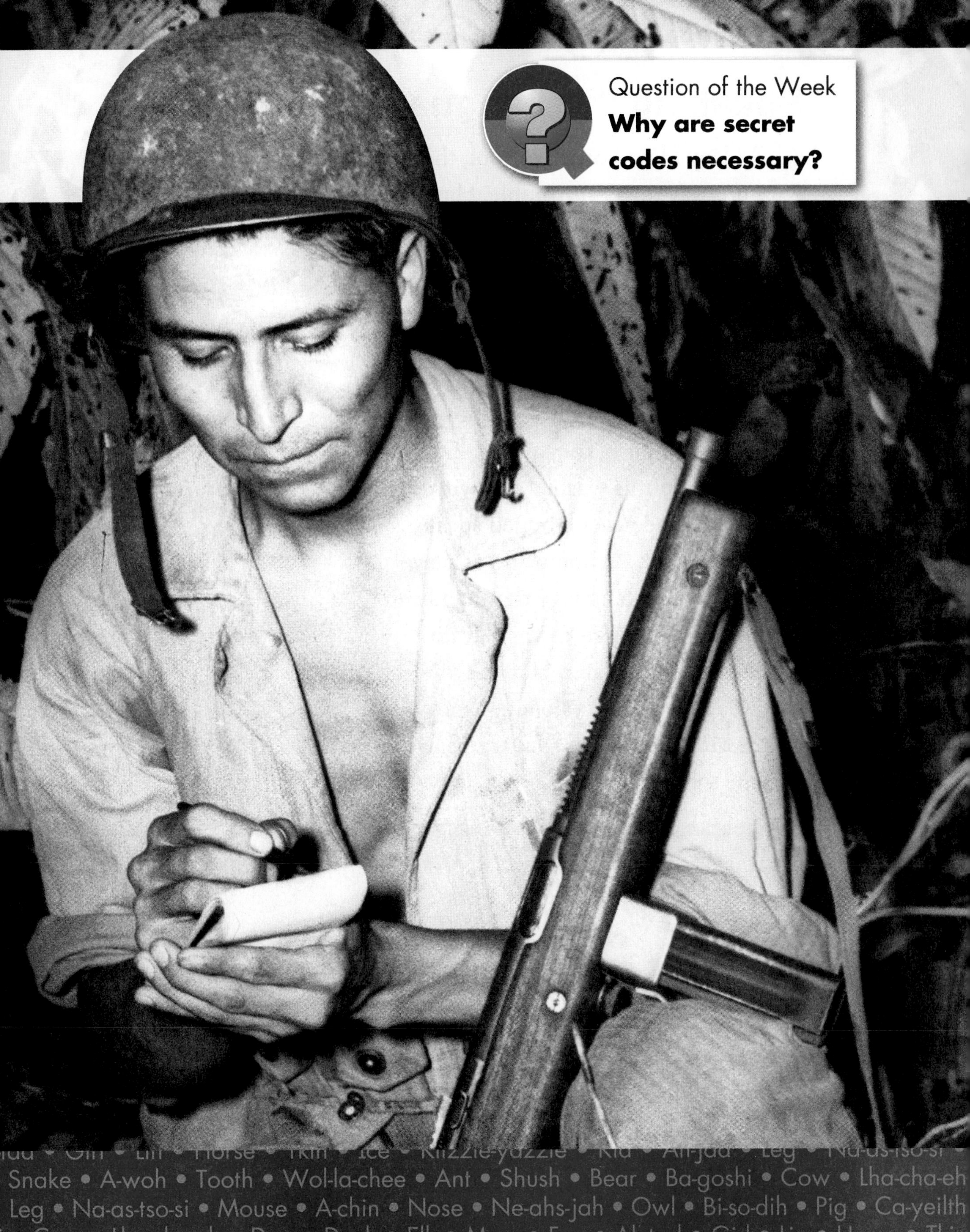

Question of the Week

Why are secret codes necessary?

Snake • A-woh • Tooth • Wol-la-chee • Ant • Shush • Bear • Ba-goshi • Cow • Lha-cha-eh

Leg • Na-as-tso-si • Mouse • A-chin • Nose • Ne-ahs-jah • Owl • Bi-so-dih • Pig • Ca-yeilth

Cow • Lha-cha-eh • Dog • Dzeh • Elk • Ma-e • Fox • Ah-tad • Girl • Lin • Horse • Tkin

Bi-so-dih • Pig • Ca-yeilth • Quiver • Gah • Rabbit • Klesh • Snake • A-woh • Tooth

Speaking the Language

At Roy Hawthorne's school, there was one sure way to get in trouble. Hawthorne lived on the Navajo reservation in New Mexico in the 1930s and attended a school run by the United States government. Students at the school were strictly forbidden to speak their native Navajo language. If they spoke anything other than English, they would likely have their mouths washed out with soap.

Former code talkers Roy Hawthorne (left) and John Brown Jr. attend the premiere of the 2002 movie *Windtalkers,* which tells their story.

Hawthorne never stopped speaking Navajo, though. At home and at play, he still used the language that had been passed down through many Navajo generations. Years later, Hawthorne's knowledge of the Navajo language paid off for him and for his country. Hawthorne became a code talker.

A Navajo family stands in front of their home in the mid-1930s.

The code talkers were a group of about 400 Navajos who served in the United States Marine Corps during World War II (1939-1945). Their job was to send and receive secret coded messages. The code talkers invented a code that was never broken by the enemy. The code helped the United States and its allies win the war. The code they invented was based on the Navajo language—the same language that once got Navajo children like Roy Hawthorne in trouble.

A World at War

On December 7, 1941, Japanese forces attacked the U.S. naval base at Pearl Harbor in Hawaii. The next day, the United States declared war on Japan, and U.S. forces were soon at war around the world.

Victory depended upon the ability to quickly communicate battle plans and other important information over long distances.

The Japanese attacked Pearl Harbor on December 7, 1941.

Top Code talkers Preston Toledo (left) and his cousin Frank Toledo send coded messages over a wireless radio.

Bottom Members of the Japanese Army listen in on radio broadcasts during a training session in World War II.

By the 1940s, the military had developed new wireless radios that could send and receive messages. They were bulky and heavy, but they allowed troops to stay in almost constant contact with other friendly forces. The trouble was, the enemy could hear these radio conversations too. The Japanese military used groups of English-speaking soldiers to listen in on American military radio messages.

The Japanese hoped to learn details about American defenses or troop movements. They hoped to get advance warning of American plans.

The U.S. military would develop codes to make it more difficult for the enemy to understand their messages. However, enemy code breakers would figure out these codes, and then new ones were needed.

What was needed was a simple, but unbreakable, code. The solution came not from the military, but from a Los Angeles engineer named Philip Johnston. He was the son of missionaries who had spent years working with the Navajos.

Though Johnston wasn't a Navajo himself, he had grown up on a Navajo reservation and knew the Navajo language well. Johnston had read about the military's efforts to develop secret codes. He believed that a code based on the Navajo language would be almost impossible to break.

Johnston was one of just a few non-Navajos who could speak and understand the Navajo language. He knew from personal experience how hard it was for non-Navajos to learn the language.

Philip Johnston's Idea

Johnston contacted Marine Corps offices in southern California and eventually arranged a meeting with Major James E. Jones. However, military leaders knew that even students from other countries, including Japan and Germany, had begun to study Native American languages.

In response to Jones's doubts, Johnston explained how the Navajo language could be used to create a code. He said the Navajo language was not as well understood as other Native American languages.

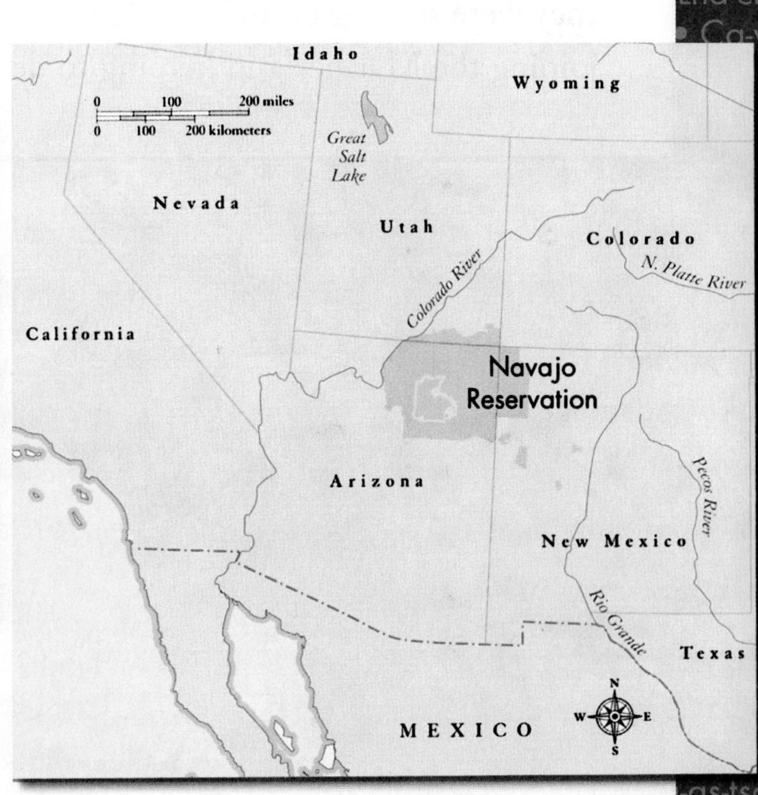

Above Philip Johnston (right) talks with a Navajo friend in 1941.

Right A map of the Navajo reservation and surrounding area

Even if enemy code breakers could understand other languages, they would likely be puzzled by Navajo.

Johnston's presentation convinced Jones. In March 1942, he arranged for Johnston to meet with Major General Clayton Vogel and Colonel Wethered Woodward from U.S. Marines headquarters in Washington, D.C. Johnston sold them on the idea, too, and the top leadership of the Marines agreed to give Johnston's plan a tryout. The Marines would recruit a group of Navajos, who would develop a code using their language.

To find Navajos to enlist in the Marines' code program, recruiters traveled to the Navajo reservation. The largest in the United States, the Navajo reservation stretches across parts of Utah, Arizona, and New Mexico.

The Navajo code project was top secret, so the Navajos didn't know they were signing up to be code talkers. They knew only that they were joining the Marines and helping to defend the United States.

New recruits stayed in barracks like these at Camp Elliott.

Military Training

In May 1942, the new Marines from the Navajo reservation were sent to the Marine Corps Recruit Training Depot in San Diego. For many, the trip marked their first time on a bus. Some had never left the reservation before. Most had never been in a big city. Like most Marines, they struggled to complete the seven exhausting weeks of training.

In some ways, the training course clashed with Navajo traditions. Many Navajos wore their hair in thick braids, but as Marine recruits they had to shave off their hair. Marine drill instructors insisted on looking directly into the eyes of recruits, but in the Navajo culture this is considered rude. Even wearing a military uniform seemed foreign to some of the Navajos. Despite the difficulties, the 29 Navajos completed boot camp and graduated to the next step in their training. They were about to become code talkers.

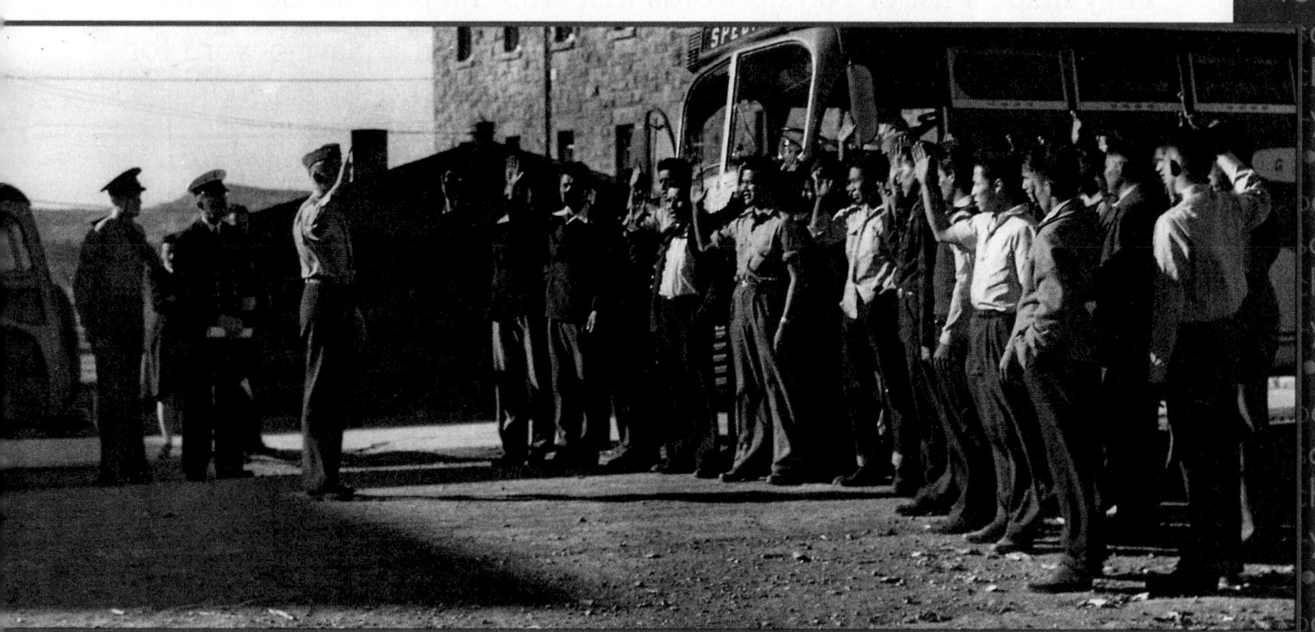

The original 29 code talkers were sworn in at Fort Wingate, New Mexico, in 1942.

Creating the Code

After boot camp, the Navajos were sent to Camp Elliott, a Marine Corps post in southern California. There they received training in radio communications and basic electronics. They learned to use, care for, and repair the radios that would send their coded messages. Only at Camp Elliott did it become clear to the Navajos what their special mission would be. Finally, it came time to create the unbreakable code.

A Navajo code talker named Chester Nez later recalled how the code came to be. "We were told to use our language to come up with words representing each letter, from A to Z," he explained. "And they also told us to come up with code words for military terms. They put us all in a room to work it out and at first everyone thought we'd never make it. It seemed impossible, because even among ourselves, we didn't agree on all the right words."

However, the Navajos devised a code that worked extremely well. They made a list of Navajo words that would represent each letter in the English language alphabet. For example, the Navajo word for apple (*be-la-sana*) stood for the letter A. The Navajo word for bear (*shush*) stood for the letter B, and the Navajo word for cat (*moasi*) stood for the letter C. The code talkers sent messages by using Navajo code words to spell out words in English. For example, to say "Navy," code talkers would say the Navajo words that stood for each letter: *Nesh-chee* (or nut, for N), *wol-la-chee* (or ant, for A), *a-keh-di-glini* (or victor, for V), and *tsah-as-zih* (or yucca, for Y).

Later, the Navajos made the code more difficult to crack by adding more code words. Some English letters could be represented by as many as three different Navajo words. For example, for the letter A, code talkers could use *wol-la-chee* (ant), *be-la-sana* (apple), or *tse-nill* (ax).

Sample of the Navajo Dictionary

English Letter	Navajo Word	Meaning
A	Wol-la-chee	Ant
B	Shush	Bear
C	Ba-goshi	Cow
D	Lha-cha-eh	Dog
E	Dzeh	Elk
F	Ma-e	Fox
G	Ah-tad	Girl
H	Lin	Horse
I	Tkin	Ice
J	Yil-doi	Jerk
K	Klizzie-yazzie	Kid
L	Ah-jad	Leg
M	Na-as-tso-si	Mouse
N	A-chin	Nose
O	Ne-ahs-jah	Owl
P	Bi-so-dih	Pig
Q	Ca-yeilth	Quiver
R	Gah	Rabbit
S	Klesh	Snake
T	A-woh	Tooth
U	Shi-da	Uncle
V	A-keh-di-glini	Victor
W	Gloe-ih	Weasel
X	Al-na-as-dzoh	Cross
Y	Tsah-as-zih	Yucca
Z	Besh-do-tliz	Zinc

English Word	Navajo Word	Meaning
Corps	Din-neh-ih	Clan
Switchboard	Ya-ih-e-tih-ih	Central
Dive bomber	Gini	Chicken hawk
Torpedo plane	Tas-chizzie	Swallow
Observation plane	Ne-as-jah	Owl
Fighter plane	Da-he-tih-hi	Hummingbird
Bomber	Jay-sho	Buzzard
Alaska	Beh-hga	With winter
America	Ne-he-mah	Our mother
Australia	Cha-yes-desi	Rolled hat
Germany	Besh-be-cha-he	Iron hat
Philippines	Ke-yah-da-na-lhe	Floating island

Not all words had to be spelled out letter by letter, however. The code talkers came up with a list of Navajo words or phrases that could be used to represent common military terms. Many of these code words came from the Navajo knowledge of the natural world. Fighter planes flew quickly and made a buzzing noise, so they were given the code name *da-he-tih-hi,* which is the Navajo word for hummingbird. Dive bombers were named for chicken hawks, or *gini.* The bombs they dropped were given the code name *a-ye-shi,* the Navajo word for eggs.

Battleships were called *lo-tso,* or whales in Navajo. Submarines were called *besh-lo,* which translates as iron fish. The code word for the United States was *ne-he-mah,* which means "our mother" in Navajo.

Jimmie King played a drum as he and three of his fellow Navajo Marines prepared to entertain other recruits at Camp Elliott in 1942.

Philip Johnston (right) with five Navajos who served as instructors at Camp Elliott. They are (from left) Johnny Manuelito, John Benally, Rex Knotz, Howard Billiman, and Peter Tracy.

To start with, the code had about 200 such words, but by the end of the war it had grown to include about 600 words. The code talkers had to memorize the entire code before being shipped out for active duty. To keep the code secret, no written lists were allowed outside Marine training centers. Code talkers also practiced sending and translating messages quickly. They practiced until they could send and translate a three-line message in just 20 seconds. Most important of all, they learned to send and translate messages without errors. The slightest mistake could change the meaning of a message and place troops in danger.

Marine Corps leaders were so pleased with the code that they expanded the code talker program. From the original 29 code talkers, the program grew to include about 400 Navajos.

Army Private Floyd Dann speaks in his native Hopi language to send messages in 1943.

On the Battlefield

By the summer of 1942, the first Navajo code talkers were ready to join troops at the front line. Between 1942 and 1945, code talkers took part in most of the major battles fought in the Pacific Ocean. United States and allied forces were able to stop Japanese advances.

Code talkers were often in the middle of the heaviest fighting. They were usually among the first wave of troops to storm enemy positions. They carried their bulky radios and set them up while under intense fire from the enemy. They reported the location of enemy forces, sent word on the progress of allied forces, and made requests for reinforcements. With bullets flying all around them, the code talkers worked calmly to send and receive the information that helped ensure victory. Often they worked in foxholes, or shallow trenches they dug for protection from enemy fire. At the key battle of Iwo Jima, six code talkers worked day and night to send more than 800 messages. They made not a single mistake. Later, Marine Major Howard Connor said, "Were it not for the Navajo, the Marines would never have taken Iwo Jima."

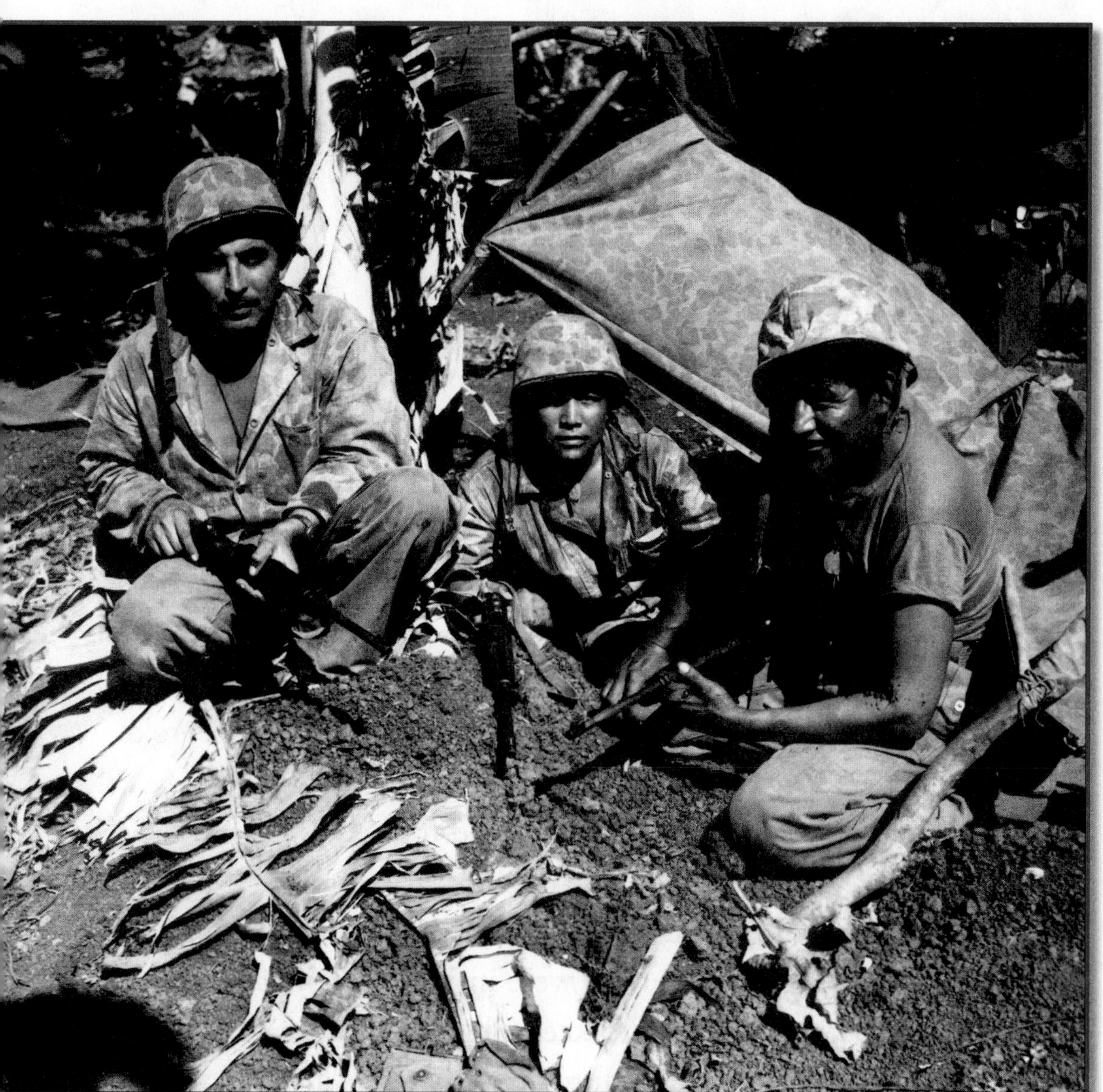

Navajo code talkers were among the first Marines to land on Saipan in June 1944.

Left Marines raised the flag at Iwo Jima on February 23, 1945.

Below John Brown Jr. receives a Congressional gold medal from President Bush at the Capitol in 2001.

Back Home

The code worked exactly as the Marines had hoped. When the enemy was able to listen in on American radio conversations, they failed to understand anything being said. All they heard were noises that sounded like no language they knew. The Japanese never broke the Navajo code.

Japan's surrender in 1945 brought an end to the fighting in the Pacific Ocean. The work of the code talkers was complete. Of the 400 or so Navajos who served as code talkers, 13 had died in action. At the end of the war, the survivors were instructed not to talk about their jobs. The Marines wanted to keep the Navajo code a secret, in case it had to be used again in future conflicts. As a result, very few people knew of the remarkable role the code talkers had played in World War II. They received no special recognition or honors. Instead, they quietly resumed their lives on the reservation.

Not until 1969 did military officials reveal the secret of the Navajo code talkers. Slowly, interest in the story of the code talkers grew.

Finally, in 2000, an act was signed into law officially honoring the original 29 Navajo code talkers. In 2001, the President of the United States awarded the code talkers and their families with Congressional gold medals. As Senator Nighthorse Campbell of Colorado said, "All Americans owe these great men a debt of gratitude."

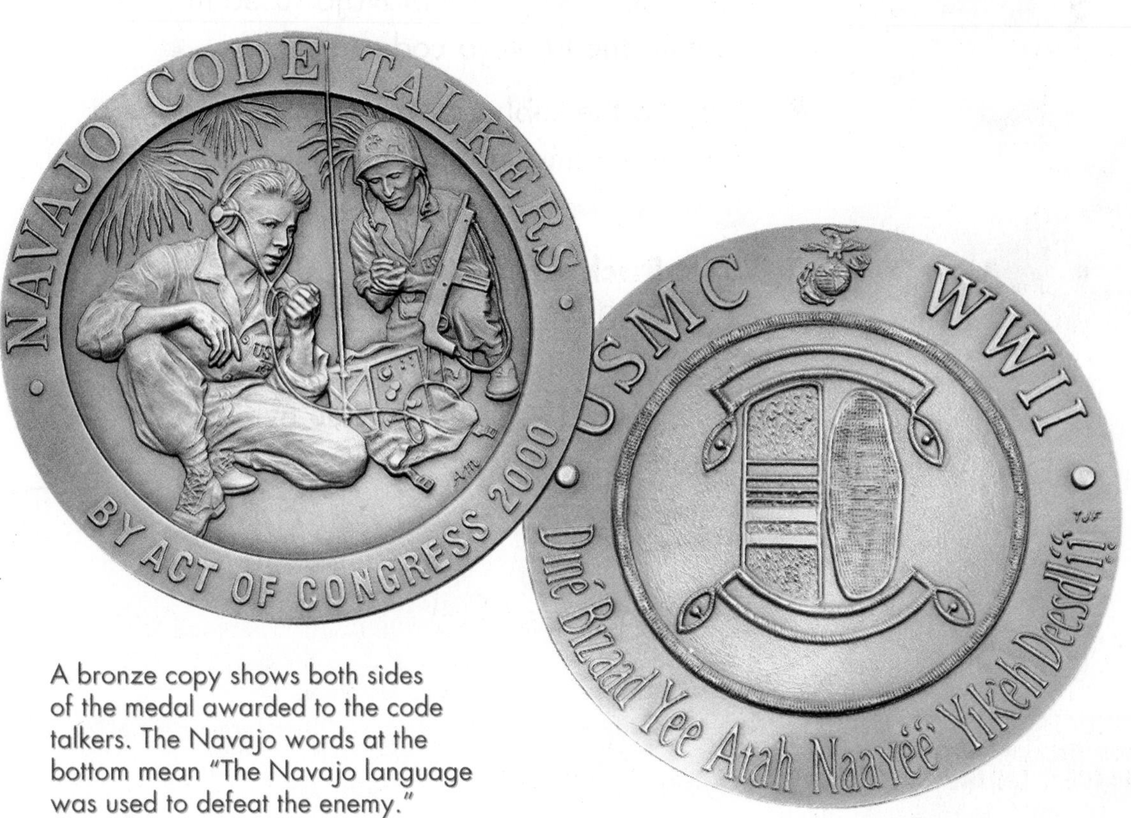

A bronze copy shows both sides of the medal awarded to the code talkers. The Navajo words at the bottom mean "The Navajo language was used to defeat the enemy."

Objectives

• Read independently for long periods of time and paraphrase the reading, including the order in which events occur. • Write responses to texts using details to show understanding.

Envision It! Retell

READING STREET ONLINE
STORY SORT
www.ReadingStreet.com

Think Critically

1. The Navajo code talkers bravely served their country during World War II. There are many heroes in the world today. Think of a hero you read about recently. Why do you think that person chose to act heroically? **Text to World**

2. Why do you think the author included a section titled "Philip Johnston's Idea"? What information does it provide to readers? **Think Like an Author**

3. Look back at page 96. Describe the explicit sequence of steps the Navajos used in creating the Navajo code. **Sequence**

4. How did the subheads in the article help you identify the important ideas in the selection? **Important Ideas**

5. **Look Back and Write** Look back at pages 100–101. How would you describe the character of the Navajo code talkers during World War II? Provide evidence to support your answer.

TEST PRACTICE **Extended Response**

Andrew Santella

Andrew Santella has written more than 75 nonfiction books for children. He often writes about major figures in American history, such as Daniel Boone, Martin Luther King Jr., and James Madison. One of his favorite topics is Native American culture. He has written several books on Native American cultures.

When Mr. Santella is not busy editing and writing books, he frequently writes articles for many popular magazines such as *Chicago Magazine, New York Times Magazine,* and *Nickelodeon*. He also keeps a blog of his daily life on his Web site. Mr. Santella lives in the Chicago area with his wife and son.

Reading Log

Use the Reading Log in the *Reader's and Writer's Notebook* to record your independent reading.

Objectives

- Write brief texts that establish a main idea in a topic sentence.
- Use and understand reflexive pronouns.

Let's Write It!

Key Features of Instructions

- explain each step in a process
- often use time-order words such as *first, next,* and *last*
- often written in list form

READING STREET ONLINE
GRAMMAR JAMMER
www.ReadingStreet.com

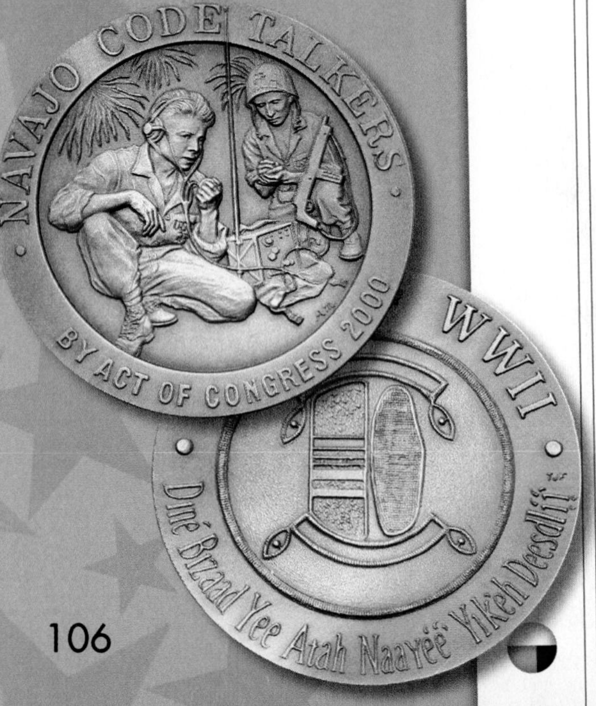

Expository

Instructions

Instructions explain how to do something in an easy-to-follow way. The student model on the next page is an example of a list of instructions.

Writing Prompt Codes have been used in military conflicts, in game playing, and in identifying many of the products we buy every day. Think about a code you are familiar with, or create your own. Then write a list of instructions to explain the code to someone who is not familiar with it.

Writer's Checklist

Remember, you should ...

- ✓ organize the information in a logical way, such as in a list.
- ✓ use time-order transition words to help organize the steps.
- ✓ review the steps to make sure nothing has been left out.
- ✓ tell a friend the steps so that he or she can restate and follow them.

Student Model

The Navajo code was developed during World War II to send secret radio messages to the troops. Navajo **speakers** developed the code **themselves.** These steps explain how the Navajo code works:

1. First, a different Navajo word was chosen to represent each letter of the English alphabet. For example, the Navajo word for "girl" (ah-tad) stands for the letter "g."
2. Then, to create a coded message, each English word is "translated" into a combination of Navajo words. For example, the English word "go" is represented by the Navajo word "ah-tad," which stands for the letter "g," and "ne-ahs-jah," which means "owl" and stands for the letter "o."
3. The person who receives the message must know the English word that each Navajo word represents. Only the first letter of the English word is used to spell out the message.

Pronouns and antecedents are used correctly.

Writing Trait Organization Instructions are given in step-by-step order.

Genre Instructions often use numbers to organize steps.

Conventions

Pronouns and Antecedents

Remember In a sentence, a **pronoun** takes the place of a noun. An **antecedent** is the word, phrase, or clause to which a pronoun refers. The antecedent usually comes before the pronoun.

Objectives

- Determine the sequence needed to follow a procedure. • Explain information that is shown in graphics. • Make connections between literary and informational texts with similar ideas and support your ideas with details from the texts.

Social Studies in Reading

Genre

How-to Article

- Like other procedural texts, how-to articles explain how to do or make something.
- Most procedural texts contain a sequence of activities needed to carry out a procedure.
- Some procedural texts explain information using charts or diagrams.
- Read "Your Own Secret Language." Look for elements that make this article a procedural text.

Your Own Secret Language

by Darius Johnson

Want to send secret messages in a language that only you and a friend can understand? Try using a cipher. A cipher is a message written in a secret language.

Spies use ciphers to send secret messages safely. Only the sender and receiver know this secret language. To everyone else, it looks like nonsense. Here's how to make your own personal cipher.

Step One Write down all 26 letters of the alphabet.

Step Two Below each letter, write a different letter or a number. Be sure to use each alphabet letter or number only once. This is your cipher.

Step Three Give a copy to a friend.

Step Four Write a message using the letters and numbers in your secret language. Now only you and your friend can read it.

Here is an example:

A	B	C	D	E	F	G	H	I	J	K	L	M	N
Z	6	2	B	X	C	W	4	V	E	8	F	T	G

O	P	Q	R	S	T	U	V	W	X	Y	Z
S	9	R	I	3	J	P	5	O	L	7	M

Here is a message in the secret language of the cipher above.

TXXJ TX VG J4X W7T ZJ GSSG

Can you figure out what it says?

MEET ME IN THE GYM AT NOON

Let's Think About...

Where can you determine the sequence of activities needed to complete your own personal cipher? **Procedural Text**

Let's Think About...

How does the graphic example on this page help you complete your own cipher? **Procedural Text**

Let's Think About...

Reading Across Texts How is the Navajo code like a cipher? Use a Venn diagram to list your ideas.

Writing Across Texts Choose two ideas from your diagram and explain them in a paragraph.

Objectives

• Read aloud grade-level texts and understand what is read. • Use a dictionary or glossary to find the meanings of unknown words, the syllable rules for these words, and how to pronounce them. • Speak clearly and to the point, give an opinion and support it with correct information. Make eye contact, change how fast, loud, and clearly you speak, and get your ideas across clearly.

READING STREET ONLINE
ONLINE STUDENT EDITION
www.ReadingStreet.com

Vocabulary

Unknown Words

Dictionary/Glossary Turn to the glossary on page 478. It gives the part of speech along with the definition of each word. Knowing what part of speech a word is can help you understand its meaning as you read.

Practice It! Choose two unknown words from the glossary. For each word, write the part of speech and definition. Exchange papers with a partner. Write sentences using each of your partner's words.

Fluency

Expression

Partner Reading
Expression is the way that your voice rises and falls as you speak. Placing more emphasis on some words and less stress on others makes a story more meaningful as you read.

Practice It! With a partner, take turns reading aloud the section "Back Home" on pages 102–103 in *Navajo Code Talkers*. First read the section with no intonation or expression. Then read it with intonation and expression. Which way helps you better understand the story?

Listening and Speaking

Get Ready For Middle School

When you participate in a discussion, include details as you ask and answer questions.

Interview

During an interview, one person asks another person questions. The purpose is to learn what the person being interviewed knows about something.

Practice It! With a partner, conduct an interview. One person can be Roy Hawthorne and the other person can be a newspaper reporter. As the reporter, you should write Hawthorne's answers to your questions in a notebook. Then partners switch roles.

Tips

Listening . . .

- Ask relevant questions.
- Listen to the main points of each interview to help you understand the language that is familiar and unfamiliar to you. Discuss it with a partner.

Speaking . . .

- Make eye contact with your partner when you speak.
- Use reflexive pronouns correctly.
- Express an opinion supported by accurate information.

Teamwork . . .

- Ask and answer questions with appropriate detail.
- If a question isn't fully answered, ask a follow-up question.

Objectives

- Listen closely to speakers and ask questions about and comment on the topic.
- Speak clearly and to the point, give an opinion and support it with correct information. Make eye contact, change how fast, loud, and clearly you speak, and get your ideas across clearly.

Oral Vocabulary

Let's Talk About

Communication

- Describe with specificity and detail different ways to communicate. For example, you can communicate with others by using a cell phone, a text message, or an instant message.
- Make eye contact when you share your ideas with others.
- Express your ideas with the conventions of language.

READING STREET ONLINE
CONCEPT TALK VIDEO
www.ReadingStreet.com

You've learned
180
Amazing Words
so far this year!

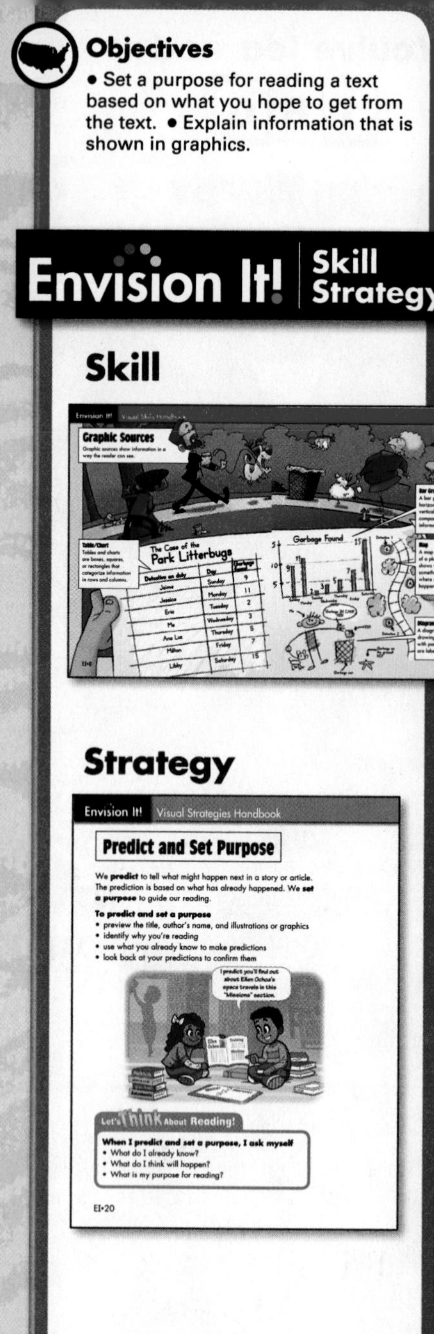

READING STREET ONLINE
ENVISION IT! ANIMATIONS
www.ReadingStreet.com

Comprehension Skill

Graphic Sources

- A graphic, such as a chart, diagram, graph, or illustration, can help you organize factual information.
- As you read, use graphic sources to help you understand information. Compare information in the text with information in the graphic.
- Use what you learned about graphic sources as you read "Picture This." Then draw this Egyptian cartouche. Write your first name in the cartouche in hieroglyphics. Place your name and all of your classmates' names in a box. Pick one and use the chart on page 115 to discover whose cartouche you have.

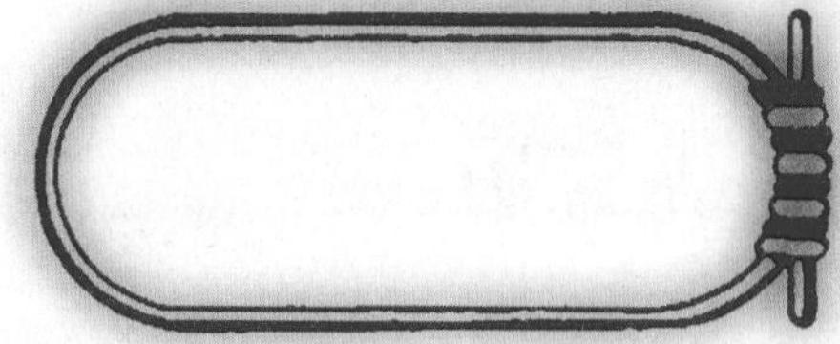

Comprehension Strategy

Predict and Set Purpose

Before they read, good readers look over an article to predict what it is about. Predicting helps good readers set a purpose for reading, such as to be entertained or to be informed. Setting a purpose helps readers determine how they should read the text.

Picture This

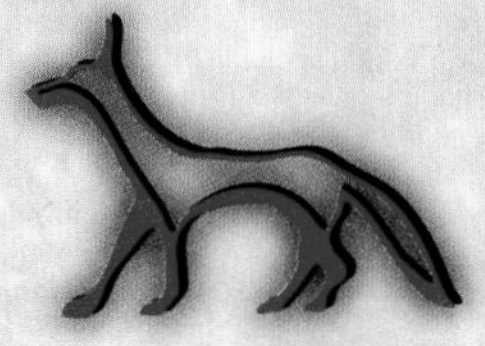

In ancient Egypt, people used a form of picture writing known as **hieroglyphics.** This word means "sacred writing." Hieroglyphics were carved on the walls of temples, tombs, and cartouches—oval figures that contained the names of rulers in hieroglyphics.

English writing is made up of letters. The letters represent the sounds of the language. Hieroglyphics were just pictures—no letters at all! Sometimes a picture stood for the thing it showed. For example, sometimes meant "water." Other times stood for the sound /nnn/ from the Egyptian word for *water.* This chart shows hieroglyphics that can be used for English letters.

Strategy Look at the chart below. Predict what the passage will be about. Consider the purpose of the chart and how it will help you understand the text.

Skill How does this information relate to the chart below?

Skill Which hieroglyphic can be used for the letter *d*? Which letters have the same hieroglyphic?

Your Turn!

Need a Review? See the *Envision It! Handbook* for help with graphic sources and predicting and setting purpose.

Ready to Try It? Use what you've learned about graphic sources as you read *Seeker of Knowledge.*

Objectives

- Determine the meaning of English words with roots from Greek, Latin, and other languages.

Envision It! | **Words to Know**

scholars

temple

uncover

ancient

link

seeker

translate

triumph

READING STREET ONLINE
VOCABULARY ACTIVITIES
www.ReadingStreet.com

Vocabulary Strategy for

Greek and Latin Roots

Word Structure Many words in English, especially academic vocabulary, have Greek and Latin roots. For example, the Latin *trans* in *translation* means "across, through, or beyond." The academic word *hieroglyphics* is made up of the Greek word parts *hieros,* meaning "holy," and *gluphe*, meaning "carving."

1. When you read an academic word you don't know, check the word for any Greek or Latin roots whose meanings you already know.
2. Use the meaning of the root to help you figure out the meaning of the unknown word.
3. Try the meaning in a sentence to see if it makes sense.

As you read "The Rosetta Stone," use Greek and Latin roots to help you figure out academic words, such as *scholars* and *archaeologists.*

Words to Write Reread "The Rosetta Stone." Imagine you've been asked by your school newspaper to interview Jean-François Champollion. Prepare a list of questions you will ask him about his life and his work on the Rosetta Stone. Use words from the *Words to Know* list as you write your questions.

The Rosetta Stone

In 1799, a French army officer found a stone slab near the city of Rosetta in Egypt. On the stone was the same announcement in three different languages. At the top was hieroglyphics, a writing that uses pictures or symbols to stand for ideas and sounds. This writing was used in ancient Egypt. In the middle was an Egyptian language called demotic. At the bottom was the Greek language.

For more than three thousand years, the ancient Egyptians used hieroglyphics on their temple walls and monuments. But over time the language was forgotten. For hundreds of years, scholars were unable to figure out how to read hieroglyphics.

Jean-François Champollion was a French scholar who wanted to be the first to read hieroglyphics. He studied the language his whole life. He was a true seeker of knowledge. He used the Greek part of the Rosetta Stone to translate the Egyptian part. The Rosetta Stone gave him a link between the known and the unknown.

Champollion's work was a triumph. It allowed other scholars and archaeologists to uncover the history of ancient Egypt.

Your Turn!

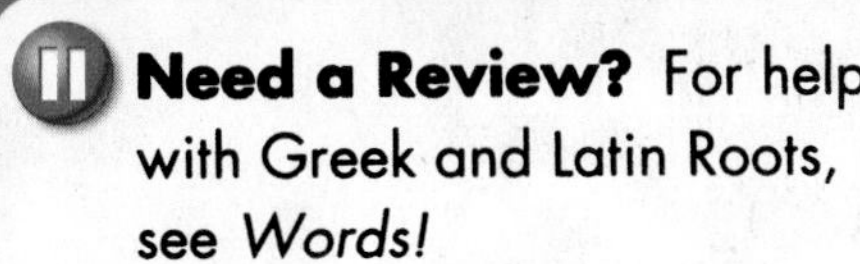

Need a Review? For help with Greek and Latin Roots, see *Words!*

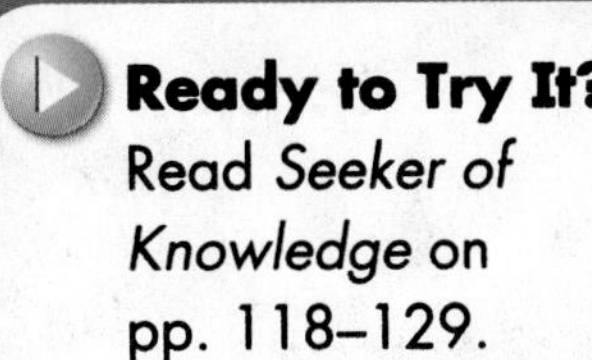

Ready to Try It? Read *Seeker of Knowledge* on pp. 118–129.

SEEKER OF KNOWLEDGE

THE MAN WHO DECIPHERED EGYPTIAN HIEROGLYPHS

text and illustrations
by James Rumford

A **biography** is the story of a real person's life as told by another person. As you read this biography, notice how the author uses words and images to tell his story.

Question of the Week

How can knowing another language create understanding?

There is a jumping, free-spirited kid goat in the Egyptian word "imagine."

There is a sharp-eyed ibis bird in the word "discover."

There is a long-necked, far-seeing giraffe in "predict."

In 1790, a French boy named Jean-François Champollion was born.

When he was seven, his older brother told him about General Napoleon, the great leader of France, who was in Egypt uncovering the past.

"Someday I'll go to Egypt too!" Jean-François told his brother as he sat spellbound, imagining himself with Napoleon, making his own discoveries.

When Jean-François was eleven, he went to school in the city of Grenoble. There, his brother took him to meet a famous scientist who had been in Egypt with Napoleon.

The scientist's house was filled with Egyptian treasures. Each one captured the boy's imagination.

"Can anyone read their writing?" asked Jean-François.

"No. No one," the scientist replied.

"Then I will one day," said Jean-François, and he left the house full of enthusiasm, sure that he would be the first to discover the key to Egyptian hieroglyphs.

Back home, his brother helped him get down all the books they had on Egypt. On moonlit nights, Jean-François stayed up reading long after he should have been asleep.

His brother nicknamed him "the Egyptian" and bought him notebooks. Jean-François filled them with hieroglyphs. There were prowling lions, angry monkeys, trumpeting elephants, and sharp-eyed ibis birds with their long, curved bills. He could not read the Egyptian words, but he dreamed that one day he would, as he sailed up the Nile.

Jean-François had a favorite animal. It was the lion because there was one in his name:
JEAN-FRANÇOIS CHAMPOL**LION.**

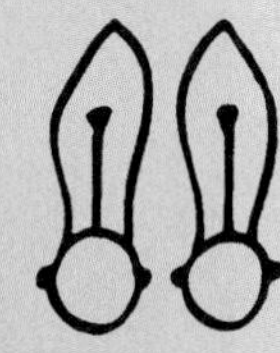

There are strongly woven sandals firmly planted on the ground in "never give up."

When Jean-François finished school at sixteen, his brother took him to Paris to meet the scholars who were studying a black stone from Rosetta, Egypt. The stone was covered with Egyptian and Greek words and told of a king of Egypt named Ptolemy. By reading the Greek, the scholars hoped to decipher the Egyptian. But the work was difficult—certainly too difficult for a boy—and the scholars turned Jean-François away.

They did not see the fire burning bright in his eyes. They did not recognize the genius who

had already learned all the known ancient languages. They did not know that he was a seeker of knowledge, one who would not rest until he had found the answer.

Jean-François gathered his notebooks and returned to Grenoble. There he taught school. His students often came to hear him talk about Egypt—her pharaohs and gods and the mysterious writing.

Once, even Napoleon came to Grenoble and sat up all night, listening spellbound as Jean-François told the great man of his dreams.

Napoleon promised to send Jean-François to Egypt when he conquered the world. Napoleon dreamed of glory. Jean-François dreamed of discovery.

There are two regal, heads-up-high leopards in the word "glory."

Thoth, one of the ancient gods

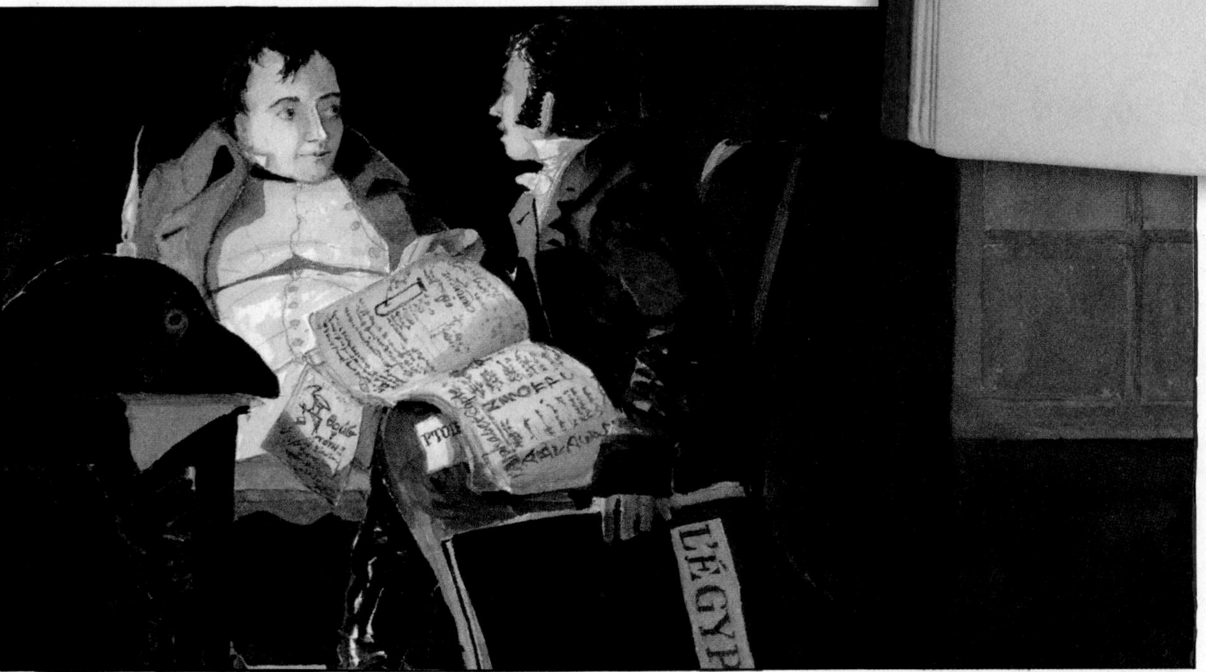

There is a roaming, black-as-night jackal in the word "mystery."

There is an unblinking crocodile lurking in the word "trouble."

But a few months later, Napoleon was defeated at the Battle of Waterloo. France was now defenseless. Her enemies poured in. They surrounded Grenoble and in the early morning bombarded the city. Jean-François ran to save his notebooks from the flames.

The people were angry with Napoleon and anyone who knew him. They pointed fingers at Jean-François and called him a traitor. He fled into the woods, leaving his notebooks behind. There he lived like a hunted dog. It was weeks before it was safe to come out and months before he saw his notebooks again.

During these troubled times, scholars everywhere were racing to solve the mystery of Egyptian writing. Unbelievable things were said. Ridiculous books were written. No one had the answer. Then an Englishman discovered that a few of the hieroglyphs on the Rosetta Stone were letters, and he deciphered King Ptolemy's name. Everyone said that the Englishman would be the first to unlock the door to Egypt's past—everyone except Jean-François .

When Jean-François was thirty, he gathered up his notebooks and left Grenoble. He made his way back to Paris—to his brother.

The letter **P** *in Ptolemy's name*

The letter **T** *in Ptolemy's name*

To Jean-François, this was the letter **A.**

The letter **W**

In Paris, Jean-François studied the Rosetta Stone and other inscriptions. He compared the Greek letters with the Egyptian hieroglyphs and herded together his own alphabet of eagles 𓄿 and lions 𓃭 and dark-eyed chicks 𓅱. But this wonderful list of letters was no help in reading the language. There were too many pictures he did not understand. What to make of a fish with legs, a jackal with wings, or an ibis god with a long, curved bill? There had to be a link between the pictures and the Egyptian letters. But what was it? Jean-François slept little. He ate almost nothing.

Then, on a September morning in 1822, Jean-François found a small package on his doorstep—from a friend in Egypt! In it were the names of pharaohs copied from a

temple wall. Each name was a jigsaw puzzle of letters and pictures. Jean-François studied the names and saw the link! The pictures were sounds too. Not single letters, but syllables, even whole words!

One of the names drew him. It began with the hieroglyph of an old, silent friend perched on a sacred staff. This was a picture of the god of writing, Thoth, followed by the letters *m* and *s*.

"Thothmes!" Jean-François suddenly exclaimed, and the rushing sound of the pharaoh's name, as if carried on wings across the centuries, filled the room.

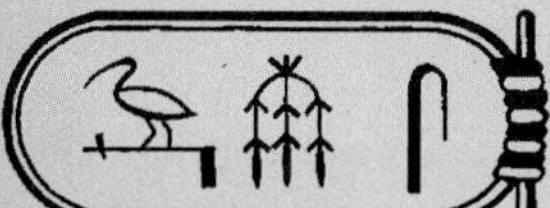

The royal cartouche, *or ring of rope, encircling Thothmes's name*

Thothmes (also written Thutmose *or* Thutmosis), *one of the ancient pharaohs*

There is a blue lotus, its center as bright as the yellow sun, in the word "joy."

There are rippling river waves in the word "Nile."

Jean-François raced down the street to his brother's office. He burst through the door, exclaiming, "I have the key!"

Then he collapsed . He had not eaten. He had not slept. For five days, he lay near death.

On the fifth day, he awoke. "Pen and paper," he whispered, and he wrote of his discovery to the world.

People all over France celebrated his triumph as Jean-François became the first to translate the ancient writing and open the door to Egypt's past.

A few years later, the people of France sent Jean-François to Egypt on an expedition to uncover more secrets. He knew Egypt so well in his mind that he felt he was going home. As Jean-François had imagined a thousand times in his dreams, he sailed up the Nile.

Once ashore, he entered the ruins of a temple. A magnificent flock of ibis suddenly rose up from the reeds and took flight.

Below, the ibis saw the seeker of knowledge touch the stone walls.

His fingers dipped into the carved pictures. He pressed his ear to the stone and listened to the ancient voices.

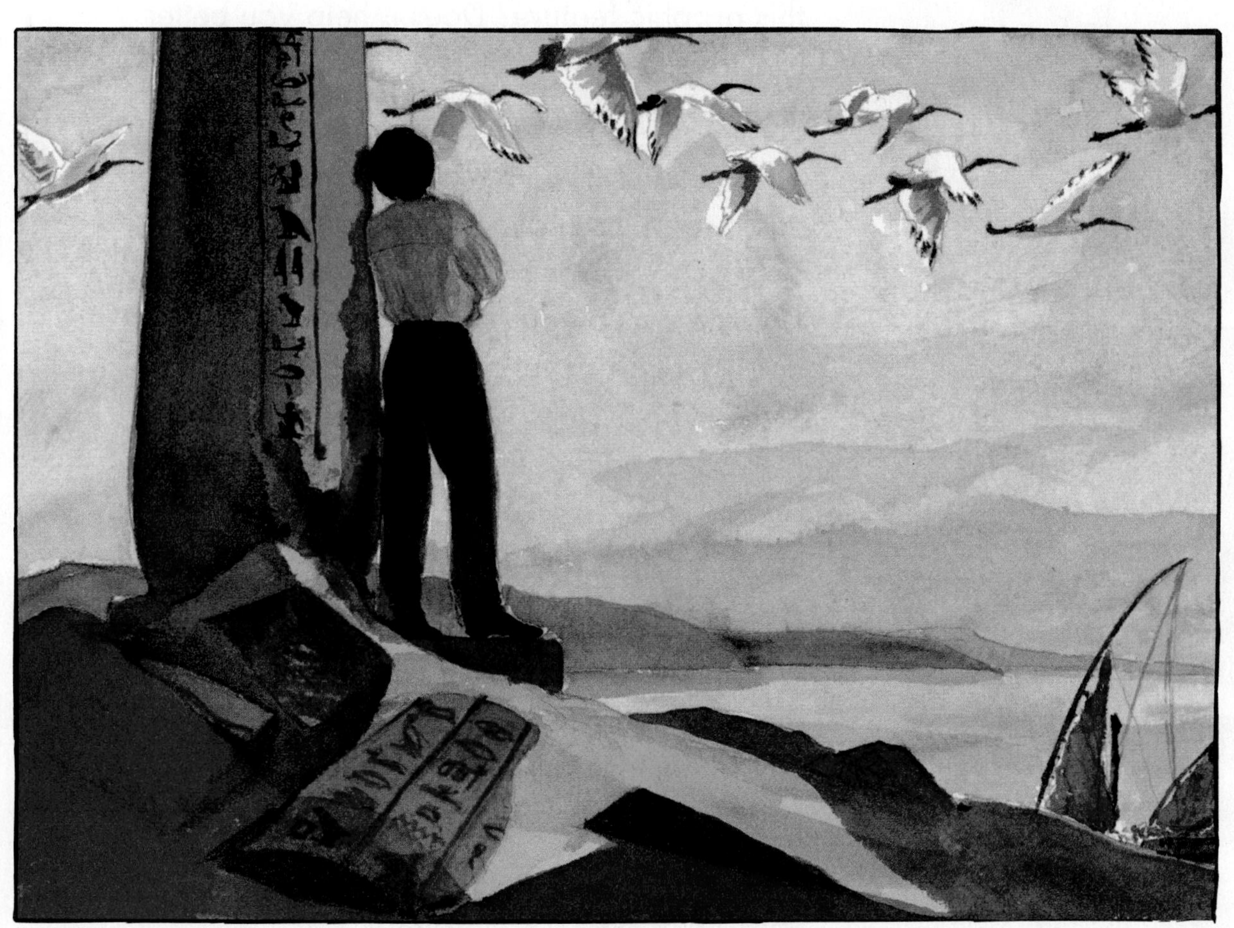

Objectives

• Read independently for long periods of time and paraphrase the reading, including the order in which events occur. • Write responses to texts using details to show understanding.

Envision It! | **Retell**

READING STREET ONLINE
STORY SORT
www.ReadingStreet.com

Think Critically

1. Both Jean-François and the Navajo code talkers worked in the world of codes. Do you think Jean-François would have been able to break the Navajo's code? Tell why or why not. Support your answer with information from the selections. **Text to Text**

2. The author placed pictures throughout the text. Choose one of the pictures and explain why you think the author included it. **Think Like an Author**

3. On many pages of the selection, part of a notebook appears. What is the purpose of this graphic feature? Does it help you better understand the text? If so, how? **Graphic Sources**

4. When Jean-François was told that no one could read the writing on Egyptian treasures, he replied, "Then I will one day." Does his statement help you predict whether or not he will discover the key to Egyptian hieroglyphs? Does it help you set a purpose for your reading? Explain your thinking. **Predict and Set Purpose**

5. **Look Back and Write** Look back at pages 120–123. Based on what you read, write about what young Jean-François did that enabled him, as an adult, to unlock the key to ancient Egyptian writing. Provide evidence from the selection to support your answer.

TEST PRACTICE **Extended Response**

Meet the Author

JAMES RUMFORD

James Rumford began writing books in his forties. Before that, he worked for the Peace Corps and taught English all over the world, including in Africa, the Middle East, and Asia. He currently lives in Hawaii, where he runs a small publishing company. He handles every step of the book-making process, from making his own paper to setting type to printing pages on a hand press. He even binds his books—one at a time. The books he prints contain both Hawaiian and English.

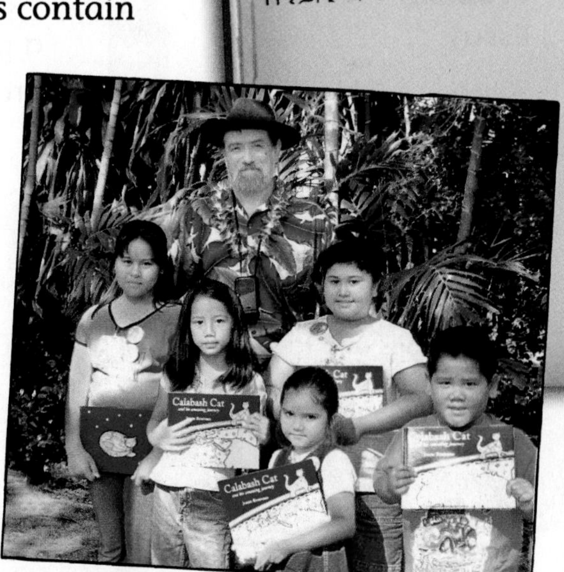

Mr. Rumford can speak or translate many languages. For *Seeker of Knowledge,* he taught himself hieroglyphics.

"I think all kids are like Jean-François Champollion," says Mr. Rumford. "When they're 10, 11, 12 years old, most of them have a clear picture of what they want to do." Mr. Rumford wants kids to know that dreams can come true with hard work.

Here are other books by James Rumford.

Traveling Man: The Journey of Ibn Battuta, 1325–1354

The Island-below-the-Star

Use the Reading Log in the *Reader's and Writer's Notebook* to record your independent reading.

Objectives

- Write brief texts that establish a main idea in a topic sentence.
- Write brief texts that include sentences that support your ideas with simple facts, details, and explanations.

Key Features of a Problem-Solution Essay

- clearly establishes the problem.
- includes opinions supported by details and facts.
- uses solutions supported by details and facts.

READING STREET ONLINE
GRAMMAR JAMMER
www.ReadingStreet.com

There is a roaming, black-as-night jackal in the word "mystery."

There is an unblinking crocodile lurking in the word "trouble."

Problem-Solution Essay

A **problem-solution essay** describes a problem that needs to be solved and gives one or more solutions to the problem. The student model on the next page is an example of a problem-solution essay.

Writing Prompt Jean-François Champollion solved a problem by figuring out the meanings of hieroglyphs. Think of a problem you want to solve. Now write a problem-solution essay telling how to solve it.

Writer's Checklist

Remember, you should . . .

- ✓ establish a position about the problem raised in the topic sentence.
- ✓ write for an appropriate audience.
- ✓ use facts, details, and explanations to support your solution.
- ✓ use a persuasive tone.
- ✓ conclude with a call to action.

Student Model

Reducing Garbage

Have you ever noticed how many garbage bags line the streets on trash pick-up day? Experts estimate that each person produces about five pounds of garbage every day. This means that one person creates more than 1,800 pounds of garbage in just one year! In order to save our environment from becoming a huge garbage dump, we must reduce the amount of garbage we produce.

Many cities and towns encourage residents to recycle their paper, glass, metal, and plastics. Recycling greatly reduces the volume of garbage that must be hauled to land-fills. Some people say that recycling is too difficult, but all it takes is a little thought and organization. Every time you decide to throw something in the trash, stop and ask your-self, "Can this item be reused for something else? I know it's mine, and I'm done with it—but can it be recycled?" Soon, recycling will become second nature, and you'll be doing your part to save our environment from being filled up with garbage dumps!

Writing Trait Focus/Ideas The introductory paragraph states the problem clearly and with details.

Genre A **problem-solution essay** answers possible objections to the solution.

Possessive pronouns are used correctly.

Conventions

Possessive Pronouns

Remember A **possessive pronoun** shows ownership. Some forms, such as *my, our,* and *your*, are used with nouns. Other forms, such as *mine, hers,* and *theirs*, can be used alone. *His* can be used alone or with nouns.

Objectives

- Compare how different writing styles are used to communicate different kinds of information on the Internet.

21st Century Skills
INTERNET GUY

Search Engines Use quotes in a search engine. "King Tut" only finds pages with all the words together. King Tut finds every page with at least one word.

- Search engines can direct you to Web sites. Each search engine has a window in which you can type key words. Key words are the main words you would find in your research topic.
- A list below the search window displays the results of the search. You can also click on a link—an underlined word or phrase—to get more information.
- Read "Making Mummies." Compare Web-based expository writing with writing in e-mails. Notice how they are different.

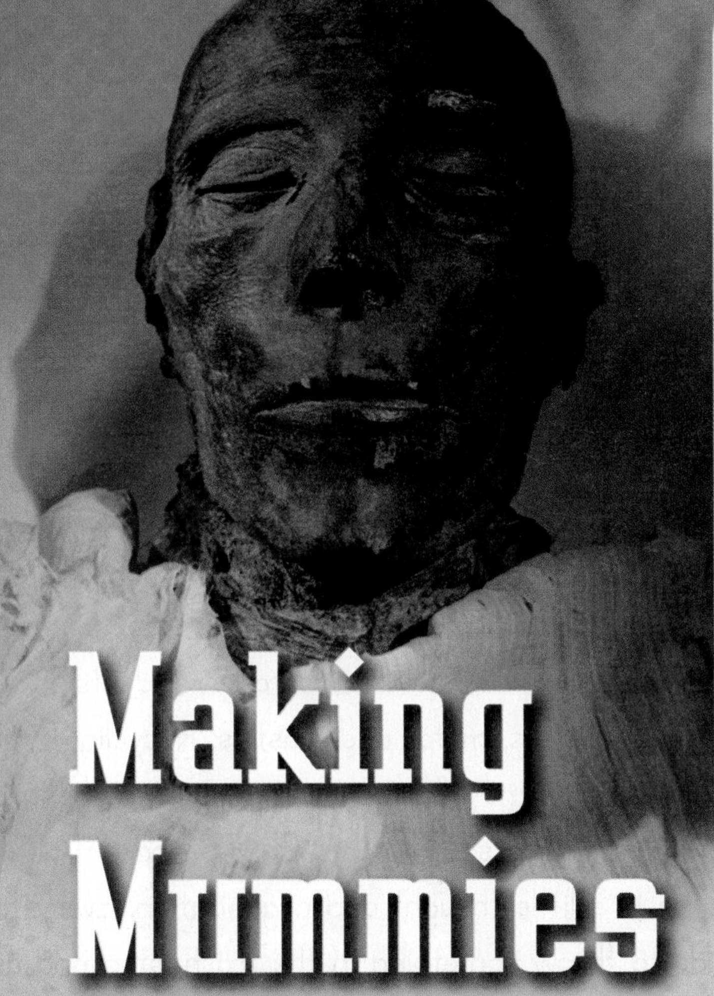

Making Mummies

Jean-François Champollion revealed secrets about Egyptian culture and the lives of pharaohs by decoding hieroglyphics. If you wanted to know more about the pharaohs and why they were made into mummies, you could type "mummies" into a search engine window and click the search button.

The search engine might come up with a long list of Web sites about mummies. You might find results such as these:

1. **Mummies.** Free encyclopedia: A **mummy** is a dead body preserved from decay. Egyptian **mummies** have lasted more than 3,000 years. **Mummies** have also been discovered in places such as China, Greenland, and South America. Check out the Web links and other . . .

2. **Mummification.** The practice of treating a body to keep it from rotting is called embalming, and it is common throughout the world. The ancient Egyptian way of making **mummies** has been discovered through reading hieroglyphics. For pictures, hieroglyphics, and how **mummies** were made . . .

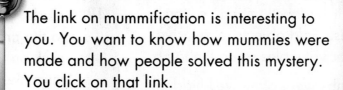

The link on mummification is interesting to you. You want to know how mummies were made and how people solved this mystery. You click on that link.

The link takes you to the Mummies of Ancient Egypt Web site. This is what you see:

Mummies of Ancient Egypt

What is a mummy? Have you ever seen a mummy movie? Often these scary films have a bandaged monster that has come back from the dead. This kind of Hollywood fun does not give mummies a very good name. Real mummies are nothing to fear. They are just dead bodies that have dried out so bacteria cannot make them rot.

Find out more about mummies from these Web pages:

Where do mummies go? **How are mummies made?**

Each underlined phrase is a link to a Web page. You decide you want to see the story "Where do mummies go?" so you click on that link.

Favorites Tools Help

http://www.url.here

The Pharaohs' Tombs

Where do mummies go? The pharaohs and other wealthy Egyptians worried about grave robbers. They worried with good reason. Inside their burial chambers, or tombs, lay heaps of riches. Gold objects, expensive furniture, and other valuables sat in the tomb.

The pharaohs' tombs were often well hidden, but many people still found them. Many mummies fell apart when robbers unwrapped them. Most of the mummies wore valuable jewels and other trinkets.

This Web page talks about what you would find inside a burial tomb. If you wanted to find out more about how the mummies were made, you could go back to the previous page and click on the link about how mummies were made.

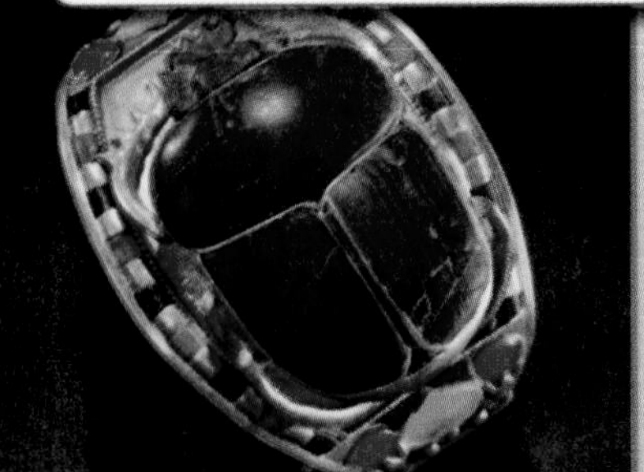

File Edit View Favorites Tools Help

http://www.url.here

The Pharaohs' Tombs

Making a Mummy There were three different ways that the body could be taken care of after death. The hardest way of making a mummy also took a long time. It cost the most money, but it was the best way to make sure the body was preserved for the afterlife.

First, the body was washed. The washing water contained natron, a kind of salt that soaks up water. Natron also kept the body from becoming infected before it was mummified.

After washing, vital organs were removed from the body. The kidneys and heart were left in the body. The Egyptians believed the heart was needed in the afterlife.

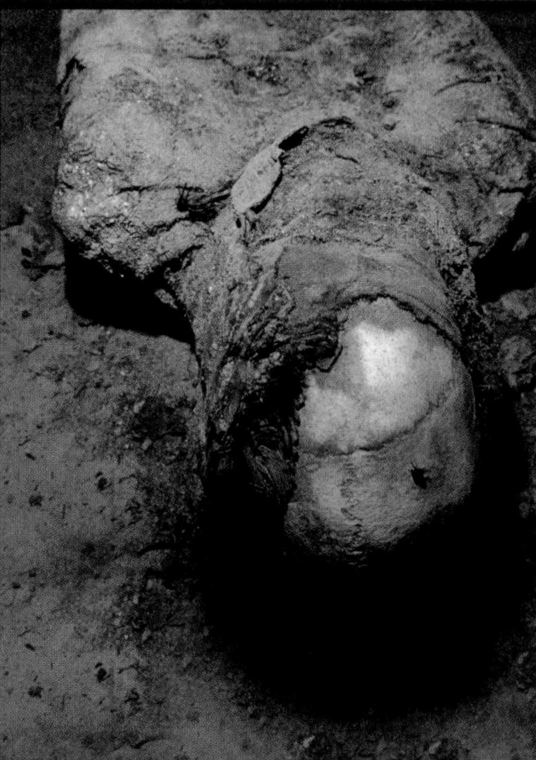

for more practice

www.ReadingStreet.com

Use a search engine to find information about mummies.

21st Century Skills Online Activity

Log on and follow the step-by-step directions for using a search engine to find more information about mummies.

Objectives

• Read aloud grade-level texts and understand what is read. • Determine the meaning of English words with roots from Greek, Latin, and other languages. • Listen closely to speakers and ask questions about and comment on the topic. • Take part in discussions led by teachers or other students, ask and answer questions, and offer ideas that build on the ideas of other people.

READING STREET ONLINE
ONLINE STUDENT EDITION
www.ReadingStreet.com

Vocabulary

Greek and Latin Roots

Word Structure Many English words contain roots, or word parts, from Greek or Latin. Use the meaning of a root to help you determine a word's meaning.

Practice It! The Latin roots *scrib* and *script* mean "to write." Reread page 126 in *Seeker of Knowledge* to find a word that contains the root *script*. Write the word and its meaning. Check the meaning in a dictionary. Then write other words that contain the root *scrib* or *script*.

Fluency

Appropriate Phrasing

Partner Reading When you group together certain words and phrases as you read, the story flows more freely.

Practice It! With a partner, practice reading aloud paragraphs 4 and 5 of page 121 of *Seeker of Knowledge*. Do you and your partner group some words and phrases differently? Which way helps you better understand the story?

Listening and Speaking

It is important to narrate a retelling with specificity and detail.

Retelling

Retelling a story means to tell what happened in the story using your own words. A retelling includes the most important events of the story.

Practice It! Reread *Seeker of Knowledge,* and list the events in sequence, or the order in which they happen. Use your list to plan a retelling. Rehearse in front of a small group. Ask the group of listeners to restate the sequence of action. Use their comments to improve. Then retell the story to the class.

Tips

Listening . . .

- Ask the speaker to restate any series of related sequences of action that are unclear, such as "Please restate what happened when Jean-Francois went back to Grenoble."
- Be ready to make pertinent comments.

Speaking . . .

- Express an opinion supported by accurate information.
- Narrate with specificity and detail.
- Restate any sequences of action that are unclear.

Teamwork . . .

- Answer questions with appropriate detail.

Objectives

- Speak clearly and to the point, give an opinion and support it with correct information. Make eye contact, change how fast, loud, and clearly you speak, and get your ideas across clearly.

Oral Vocabulary

Let's Talk About

Inquiry

- Describe an inquiry you would like to conduct of something puzzling.
- Ask questions about how to go about the inquiry.
- Maintain eye contact when describing the inquiry.

READING STREET ONLINE
CONCEPT TALK VIDEO
www.ReadingStreet.com

You've learned
190
Amazing Words
so far this year!
ELECTION
VOTE BEN
VOTE DEREK
VOTE DANA

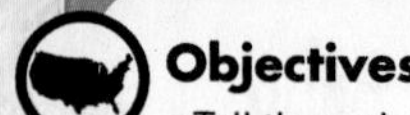

Objectives

- Tell the order of events in a story, summarize the events, and explain how they will influence future events in the story.
- Describe how characters relate to each other and the changes that happen to them.

Envision It! Skill Strategy

Skill

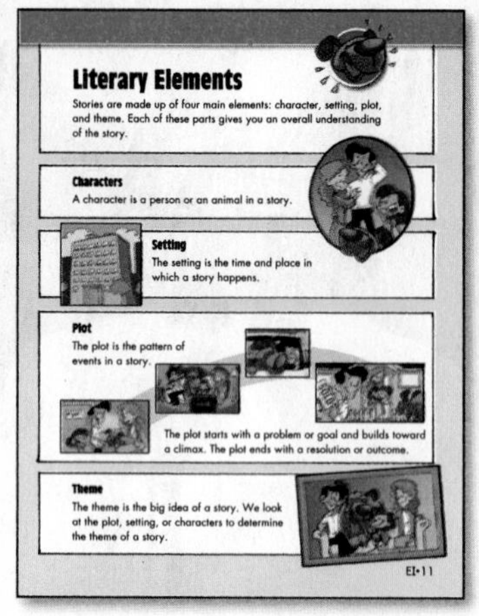

Literary Elements

Stories are made up of four main elements: character, setting, plot, and theme. Each of these parts gives you an overall understanding of the story.

Characters

A character is a person or an animal in a story.

Setting

The setting is the time and place in which a story happens.

Plot

The plot is the pattern of events in a story.

The plot starts with a problem or goal and builds toward a climax. The plot ends with a resolution or outcome.

Theme

The theme is the big idea of a story. We look at the plot, setting, or characters to determine the theme of a story.

EI•11

Strategy

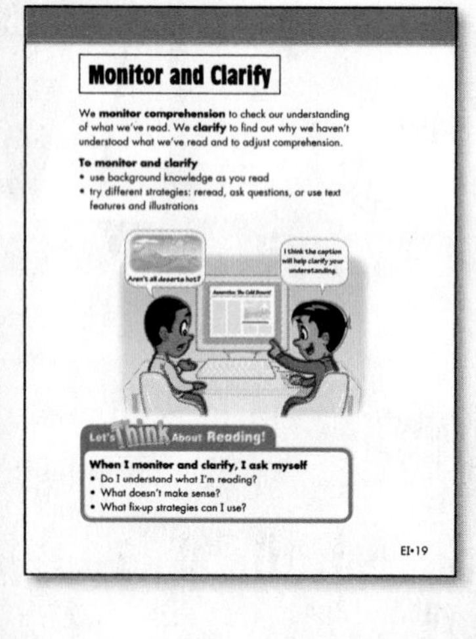

Monitor and Clarify

We **monitor comprehension** to check our understanding of what we've read. We **clarify** to find out why we haven't understood what we've read and to adjust comprehension.

To monitor and clarify

- use background knowledge as you read
- try different strategies: reread, ask questions, or use text features and illustrations

Aren't all deserts hot?
I think the caption will help clarify your understanding.

Let's Think About Reading!

When I monitor and clarify, I ask myself

- Do I understand what I'm reading?
- What doesn't make sense?
- What fix-up strategies can I use?

EI•19

READING STREET ONLINE
ENVISION IT! ANIMATIONS
www.ReadingStreet.com

Comprehension Skill

Character and Plot

- A character is a person or animal who takes part in a story. You can learn about a character through the character's words and thoughts. You can also learn about a character through the author's description of the character's relationships.
- A plot is the series of sequenced, related events in a story. The plot includes the conflict, or problem; the rising action; the climax; and the resolution, or outcome.
- Use a graphic organizer like this one to identify the events of the plot in "Oh, No!"

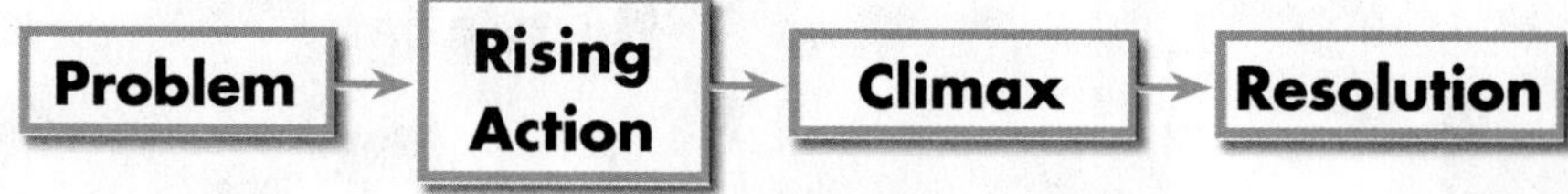
Problem
Rising Action
Climax
Resolution

Comprehension Strategy

Monitor and Clarify

When you are reading, it's important for you to monitor when you understand something and when you don't. If you are confused, stop and reread the section aloud. Looking back and rereading is one way to clarify, or "adjust," your understanding. Asking an interpretive question of text is another way. An interpretive question is answered by using information in the text to figure out the answer on your own.

Catherine was very excited when she learned that both she and her friend Shelly had gotten parts in the play. She had always wanted to act. Mr. Kiley, the director, explained that it was important for everyone to attend each rehearsal.

Skill What do you think Catherine's problem is going to be?

On Day 4 of rehearsals, Catherine felt feverish. That night her fever was high, and the next day she stayed in bed.

The doctor told Catherine that she would probably miss a week of school. "Oh, *no!* I can't miss that much!" she cried. "I'll be replaced in the class play."

Strategy Why does Catherine think Mr. Kiley will replace her in the play? Stop and reread aloud the beginning of the selection to clarify why Catherine thinks this.

That evening Catherine heard the telephone ring. Several minutes later her mother came into her bedroom.

"That was Mr. Kiley on the telephone," she said.

"He called to tell me I've been replaced, no doubt," Catherine moaned, suddenly feeling worse.

"No," said her mother. "He asked if Shelly could visit you after each rehearsal to keep you informed. Then you'll be able to catch up when you get back next week."

"Oh, *yes!*" Catherine screamed excitedly and jumped up.

"Hey!" laughed her mother. "Do you want your fever to *ever* go down?"

Skill The problem is resolved here. How has Catherine changed from the beginning of the story?

Your Turn!

Need a Review? See the *Envision It! Handbook* for additional help with character and plot and monitoring and clarifying.

Ready to Try It? Think about character and plot as you read *Encyclopedia Brown and the Case of the Slippery Salamander*.

Objectives

• Determine the meanings of unfamiliar words or multiple-meaning words by using the context of the sentence. • Complete analogies based on knowledge of synonyms and antonyms.

Envision It! Words to Know

lizards

reptiles

salamanders

amphibians

crime

exhibit

reference

stumped

READING STREET ONLINE
VOCABULARY ACTIVITIES
www.ReadingStreet.com

Vocabulary Strategy for

Synonyms and Antonyms

Context Clues You can use the context of a sentence to help determine the meaning of an unfamiliar word. The clue may be a synonym or an antonym. Synonyms are words that have the same meaning. Antonyms have the opposite meanings.

1. Complete this analogy using a word from the *Words to Know* and your knowledge of synonyms and antonyms: *big* is to *large* as *confused* is to ______.
2. Reread the sentence with the unfamiliar word. Look for a synonym or an antonym. Does the synonym make sense in the sentence? Does the antonym help you figure out the unfamiliar word's definition?
3. If there is not a synonym or an antonym in the same sentence, check the sentences around it. If you find a synonym or an antonym there, try it in the sentence.

As you read "It Is Not All in the Family," use context clues or synonyms and antonyms to help you figure out any unfamiliar words.

Words to Write Reread "It Is Not All in the Family." Imagine you are a zoo worker who will explain the differences between reptiles and amphibians. Write the points that you will make about each. Use words from *Words to Know*.

IT IS NOT ALL IN THE FAMILY

Are you interested in the world of snakes, frogs, turtles, lizards, toads, and salamanders? You probably think of all of these animals as one big creepy family. In fact, they are not. Snakes, turtles, and lizards are all reptiles. Frogs, toads, and salamanders are all amphibians. Read on to discover the differences. If you are stumped, read on.

Amphibians have skin that must be kept wet. If you touch the skin, it feels slimy. This is because amphibians live near water. They lay their eggs in water because the eggs have no shell. Reptiles, on the other hand, have dry skin that is covered with scales. Their eggs have a tough covering. These eggs can be laid on land.

If you are still baffled or confused about these animals, read about them in a reference book, such as an encyclopedia. The next time you are at a zoo, look them up. A zoo exhibit has live animals that you can see up close. The display gives facts about the animals. And remember, it is not a crime to ask questions! Zoo workers like to share what they know.

Your Turn!

Need a Review? For help with using context clues to determine the meaning of unfamiliar words, see *Words!*

Ready to Try It? Read *Encyclopedia Brown and the Case of the Slippery Salamander* on pp. 146–154.

ENCYCLOPEDIA

written by DONALD J. SOBOL

Realistic fiction tells about events that could really happen. As you read, think about how the events in this story are similar to events in real life.

BROWN and the Case of the Slippery Salamander

illustrated by BRETT HELQUIST

Question of the Week

How can attention to detail help solve a problem?

To a visitor, Idaville looked like an ordinary seaside town. It had churches, two car washes, and three movie theaters. It had bike paths, sparkling white beaches, a synagogue, and plenty of good fishing spots.

But there was something out of the ordinary about Idaville: For more than a year, no child or grown-up had gotten away with breaking a law.

People wanted to know: How did Idaville do it?

The secret resided in a red-brick house at 13 Rover Avenue. That was where Idaville's police chief lived with his wife and son.

Chief Brown was a smart, kind, and brave man. But he wasn't the one who kept crooks from getting away with their crimes. No, the brains behind it all was his ten-year-old son, Encyclopedia.

Encyclopedia's real name was Leroy. But only his parents and teachers called him that. Everyone else called him "Encyclopedia" because his brain was filled with more facts than a reference book.

Sometimes the Brown family was tempted to tell the world about Encyclopedia's amazing talent as a crime-solver. But so far they hadn't leaked a word. For one thing, the Browns didn't like to boast. For another, who would believe that Idaville's top detective was a fifth-grader?

One Monday night Chief Brown sat at the dinner table, staring at his plate of spaghetti. So far he hadn't slurped up a single strand. Encyclopedia and his mother knew the reason.

The chief wasn't eating because he had come up against a crime that he couldn't solve.

Encyclopedia waited for his dad to tell him about the case. Whenever Chief Brown was stumped, Encyclopedia cracked the case for him, usually by asking just one question.

At last Chief Brown looked up. "There was a theft at the aquarium today," he said, rubbing his forehead.

Last summer an aquarium had opened near the beach. The most popular attractions were the giant shark tanks, the dolphin shows, and the Den of Darkness.

The Den of Darkness was a huge indoor exhibit of reptiles and amphibians. Encyclopedia especially liked visiting the frogs and salamanders in the amphibian section.

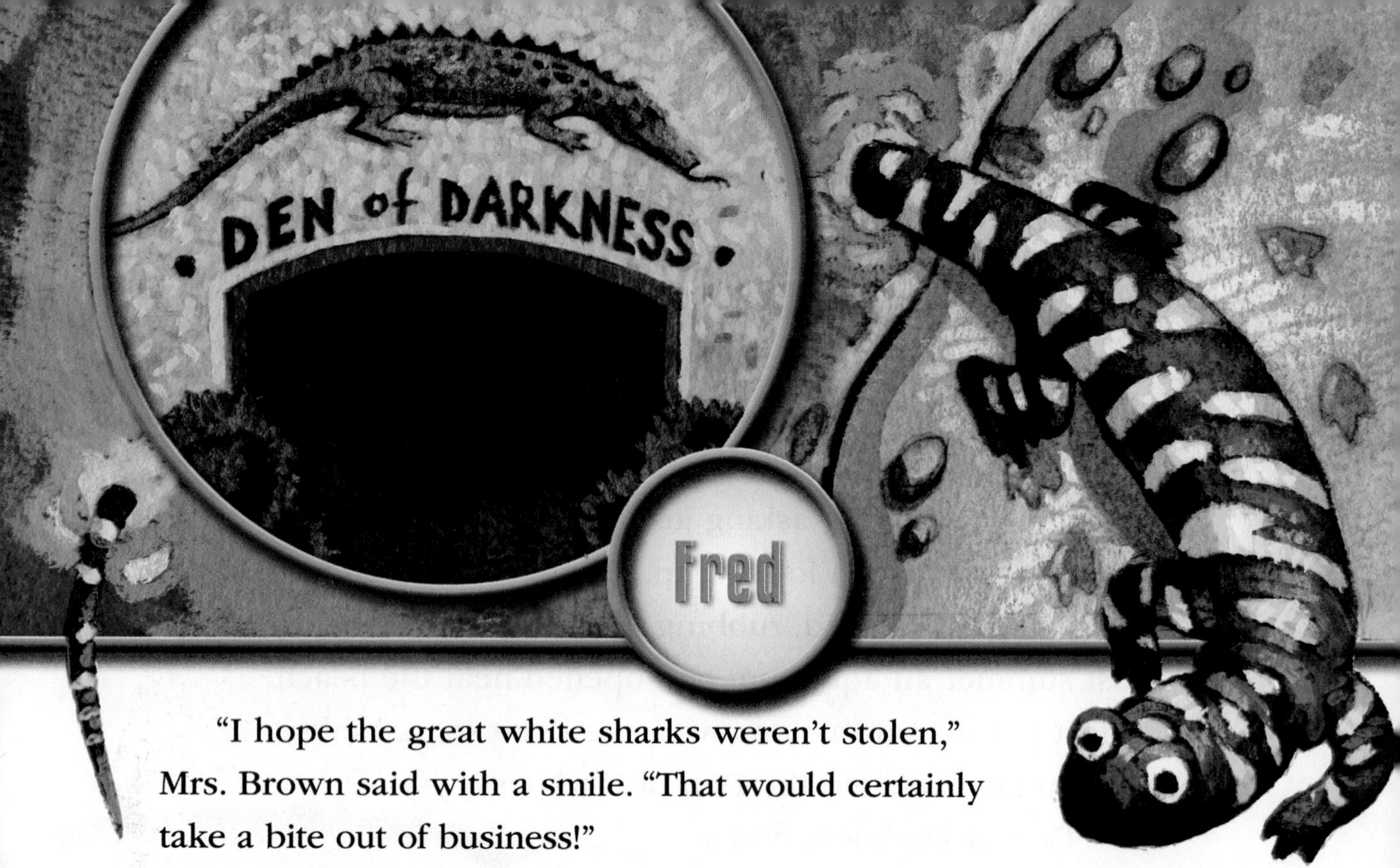

"I hope the great white sharks weren't stolen," Mrs. Brown said with a smile. "That would certainly take a bite out of business!"

Chief Brown shook his head. "It wasn't the sharks."

Encyclopedia put down his fork and listened carefully as his father explained that Fred, a tiger salamander, had been stolen.

"Fred was shipped to the aquarium only two days ago," Chief Brown said. "He was being kept apart from the other animals until the officials were sure he was healthy. If he got a clean bill of health, he was to go on display next month."

"Do you have any clues, dear?" Mrs. Brown asked.

The chief frowned. "Not many. All we know is that the salamander disappeared this morning, sometime between ten-thirty and eleven forty-five."

"Why would someone steal a salamander?" Mrs. Brown wondered.

"Fred is the aquarium's only tiger salamander," her husband explained. "From what the director of the aquarium told me, someone could sell him for a lot of money."

"Really?" Mrs. Brown's eyes widened. "Do you think a visitor might have stolen him?"

"It's very unlikely," Chief Brown replied. "Employees and volunteers are the only ones who have access to the back room in the Den of Darkness where Fred was being kept."

Chief Brown told Encyclopedia and Mrs. Brown that three people had been working at the exhibit that morning: Mrs. King, who volunteered at the aquarium every Monday; Sam Maine, the man in charge of cleaning and maintaining the exhibits; and Dr. O'Donnell, an expert on reptiles and amphibians.

"Did you question the three of them?" Mrs. Brown asked.

The chief nodded. "Dr. O'Donnell spent the morning examining a new crocodile from Australia. Sam Maine told me he was busy cleaning out exhibits and feeding some of the lizards. Several people saw him working," Chief Brown added, "so it looks like he's telling the truth."

"What about Mrs. King?" his wife prodded.

Chief Brown frowned. “Actually, Sam Maine seems very suspicious of Mrs. King,” he confided. “And after talking with her I can see why. Mrs. King is fascinated with salamanders.”

“Fascinated with salamanders?” Mrs. Brown echoed.

The chief nodded again. “She told me she has dozens of them at home as pets, and that Fred is the first tiger salamander she’s ever seen.” He shook his head. “Mrs. King does seem odd—she thinks salamanders are sacred creatures with magical powers.”

Encyclopedia spoke up. “In ancient times, people used salamanders for medicine. They also believed that salamanders could eat fire and live in flames.”

“Maybe Fred wasn’t stolen for money,” Mrs. Brown said thoughtfully. “Maybe Mrs. King took Fred just because she thinks he’s a special specimen!”

“That’s exactly what I’ve been thinking,” Chief Brown admitted. “But there’s no proof that Mrs. King had the opportunity to steal Fred. She was with a group of schoolchildren from ten-thirty to eleven-fifteen. After that she went over to the cafeteria for a coffee break. One of the cashiers said he saw her there.”

Chief Brown sighed with frustration. "I hate to admit it, but this case has me baffled!"

Encyclopedia closed his eyes. His parents watched him hopefully. They knew that when Encyclopedia closed his eyes, it meant he was doing his deepest thinking.

A moment later Encyclopedia was ready. He opened his eyes and asked his one question:

"Has Sam Maine been working at the aquarium long, Dad?"

"Actually, he was hired only two weeks ago," Chief Brown answered. "But he has a lot of experience. Sam told me he's been taking care of salamanders and other lizards for more than nineteen years."

That was all Encyclopedia needed to hear.

"Oh no, he hasn't!" Encyclopedia declared with a satisfied smile. "If he's a lizard expert, then I'm the queen of England! Sam Maine is lying, and I can prove it!"

How does Encyclopedia know?

SOLUTION to the Case of the Slippery Salamander

Encyclopedia knew that Sam Maine was lying because he told Chief Brown he'd been taking care of "salamanders and other lizards for more than nineteen years." Anyone who'd been taking care of salamanders for that long would know that salamanders are not lizards. They are classified as amphibians. Lizards are classified as reptiles.

Sam Maine admitted stealing the valuable new tiger salamander that morning. After he returned Fred to the aquarium, he was fired from his job as caretaker.

SALAMANDER FACT SHEET

Class: Members of the amphibian class, salamanders have to live in wet environments. All amphibians are cold-blooded animals with a backbone (vertebrae) that spend part of their time on land and part in water. Salamanders need to breathe air and drink water through their skin.

Size: Salamanders are measured from their heads to the end of their tails. Most are small, ranging from 1 to 5 inches (2.54 to 12.7 centimeters) long. The pygmy salamander can be as small as 1½ inches (3.8 centimeters). The Chinese giant salamander can grow to be over 5 feet (1.8 meters) long.

Habitat: Salamanders inhabit every continent except Australia and Antarctica.

Range: They live in any damp area—ponds, swamps, forests, in holes, and under rocks.

Appearance: Their skin is smooth, with spots or stripes. They are usually dark-colored, but some are red or orange. They do not have scales, ears, or claws.

Life Span: Most live for 8 to 20 years. Some live more than 50 years.

Red-backed Salamander

Chinese Giant Salamander

Objectives

- Read independently for long periods of time and paraphrase the reading, including the order in which events occur.
- Write responses to texts using details to show understanding.

Envision It! | **Retell**

READING STREET ONLINE
STORY SORT
www.ReadingStreet.com

Think Critically

1. *Encyclopedia Brown* is a detective story. The main character is a child detective. Think of another story you read about child detectives. Tell what the detectives do to solve the mystery in the story. **Text to Text**

2. Idaville is not a real place, but the author includes details to make it seem real. Find at least three details that the author uses to make Idaville seem like a real town. **Think Like an Author**

3. As the plot develops, you meet several different characters. Which character is the main character? How do you know? What is the problem in the story and how is it resolved? **Character and Plot**

4. Reread page 154 aloud to clarify how Encyclopedia Brown knew that Sam Maine stole the tiger salamander. What is the clue word that helps Encyclopedia crack the case? How did it help? **Monitor and Clarify**

5. **Look Back and Write** Look back at pages 151–152. Why does Chief Brown suspect Mrs. King of stealing the salamander? Provide evidence to support your answers.

TEST PRACTICE **Extended Response**

Meet the Author and the Illustrator

Donald J. Sobol

Donald J. Sobol was born in New York City in 1924. *Encyclopedia Brown: Boy Detective*, his first story about this famous character, was published in 1963. Since then, he has written more than twenty books about Encyclopedia Brown. In most of these books, there are ten mysteries, with the solutions to the mysteries at the back of the book. Leroy "Encyclopedia" Brown is the ten-year-old sleuth who solves the mysteries—even though his father is the town's police chief!

Mr. Sobol once said, "Readers constantly ask me if Encyclopedia Brown is a real boy. The answer is no. He is, perhaps, the boy I wanted to be—doing the things I wanted to read about but could not find in any book when I was ten." Now in his eighties, Mr. Sobol lives in Florida, where he continues to write Encyclopedia Brown stories for a new generation of fans.

Here are other books by Donald Sobol.

Encyclopedia Brown Sets the Pace

Encyclopedia Brown and the Case of the Jumping Frogs

Brett Helquist

Brett Helquist is best known as the illustrator of the Lemony Snicket books, *A Series of Unfortunate Events*. While illustrating those books might seem like enough danger for one man, Mr. Helquist has also illustrated many other children's books, as well as many newspapers and magazines, including *The New York Times*, *Time for Kids*, and *Cricket*.

Use the Reading Log in the *Reader's and Writer's Notebook* to record your independent reading.

Objectives

- Write creative stories that build to an ending and contain details about the characters and setting.
- Recognize and use quotation marks.

Let's Write It!

Key Features of an Adventure Story

- often takes place in an interesting setting
- is built around a quest or problem
- includes unusual and exciting situations

READING STREET ONLINE
GRAMMAR JAMMER
www.ReadingStreet.com

Adventure Story

Adventure stories are imaginative stories that describe a dangerous or exciting quest, or search. They often include a fast-paced plot and physical action. The student model on the next page is an example of the beginning of an adventure story.

Writing Prompt Write an adventure story that takes place in another country.

Writer's Checklist

Remember, you should . . .

- ✓ include details that describe the characters and foreign setting.
- ✓ build the plot to a climax around a quest or problem.
- ✓ introduce an element of excitement.
- ✓ use quotation marks to show characters' dialogue.

Student Model

Danger at Dun Angus

Clouds shot swiftly across the skies above Inish Island. Pushed by strong winds off the Atlantic, Liam and Rachel climbed up the rock-strewn hill, using shovels as walking sticks. Perched at the edge of a 300-foot cliff, the ancient stone fort known as Dun Angus loomed ahead.

"I wish you **hadn't** lost Uncle Pat's letter," grumbled Liam. "How do we know this is really the place he buried his treasure?"

"I **didn't** lose the letter!" Rachel replied, blue eyes flashing. "Those shifty-looking men back there at the restaurant stole it from my bag. But **don't** worry, I remember all the clues. The clues are all in code, so **I'm** pretty sure those guys **won't** be able to beat us to the treasure."

"Wow!" exclaimed Liam, passing through a doorway to the inside of the fort. "**There's** no wall along the cliff! Stay away from the edge, Rachel. **It's** a sheer drop."

"**He's** right, Rachel," growled a menacing voice to their right. "**It's** a sheer drop."

Writing Trait Word Choice Strong active verbs add excitement and paint a picture in the reader's mind.

Genre Adventure story plots are built around quests.

Contractions and negatives are used correctly.

Conventions

Contractions and Negatives

Remember A **contraction** is a shortened form of two words that uses an apostrophe where a letter or letters have been dropped. A **double negative** is the incorrect use of two or more negatives in a sentence.

Objectives

• Explain the difference between a stated purpose and an implied purpose in expository texts. • Use text features to understand the text and to locate information.

Science in Reading

Genre
Expository Text

- An expository text contains facts and information about a subject.
- Some authors of expository texts state their purpose for writing. Other authors do not. They imply what their purpose is, and the reader has to figure it out for him- or herself.
- Some expository texts use text features, such as topic sentences and concluding sentences, to organize information.
- Read "Young Detectives of Potterville Middle School." Look for elements that make this article an expository text.

The

Crime scene investigation: Students use tools, such as a microscope, to evaluate evidence at the scene of a "crime."

aily Journa

Young Detectives

of Potterville Middle School

by Bonnie Kepplinger

Sixth graders in a Michigan middle school solve crimes during one class period each day. Their classroom has become a crime lab. Their tools are microscopes, rubber gloves, goggles, and fingerprinting brushes and powder. These students work together to evaluate evidence at a "crime" scene. Hair and fiber analysis can answer questions that identify criminals. *Does this hair belong to a dog, a cat, or a human? What kinds of fibers were found on the victim's clothes? What do clues tell us about anyone else present at the scene of the crime?*

Let's Think About...

Does the author state her purpose for writing this article? Or does she imply what the purpose is? Provide evidence for your answer. **Expository Text**

Let's Think About...

What is the topic sentence on this page? **Expository Text**

Let's Think About...

What is a good example of a topic sentence on this page? Why is it a good example? **Expository Text**

Let's Think About...

Good readers ask interpretive questions of text as they read. For example, "What skills from this class might translate to a real job?" What questions can you ask yourself to help you interpret this text? **Expository Text**

A young detective analyzes "blood" samples.

"We rush to this class," said one student. "No one's ever really tardy because we like to come."

"I don't want to leave this class," added another student. "We get to solve crimes. It's fun because we get to find out by ourselves instead of having someone else tell us or show us."

Several high schools in mid-Michigan offer forensic science classes. (*Forensic* refers to science that can be used in legal courts.) However, Potterville Middle School is believed to be the first in the area to bring such classes to younger students. These classes teach students how to think, question, and solve problems. Young Potterville detectives enjoy improving their science skills through investigation.

During the nine weeks of classes, students have several projects. One week they were given a burglary scene with four possible suspects. Their job was to analyze fake blood samples. Then they matched one suspect's blood type with the sample found at the crime scene.

Teachers say that this is a way to get students interested in and excited about science. "We have never seen kids this excited about science as we have this year," said sixth-grade teacher Maureen Dykstra. "They have become close observers and careful recorders of data."

Like all good detectives, students learn how to collect and weigh information. They even draw pictures of the crime scene. Students also have a place to stage the crimes. This is a portable unit outside the school that used to be a music room.

Guest speakers visit the class to talk about careers. Visitors have included a forensic scientist, a police officer, and a detective. Jeff Hudak is a crime investigator for the local police department. He knows that working with young students encourages them to think about future jobs. "It lets them know what they have to do to get involved in crime scene investigation," he said. "It's never too early to get them interested."

SPECIAL POLICE

Let's Think About...

Reread the last sentence on this page. Is this a good example of a concluding sentence? Why or why not? **Expository Text**

Let's Think About...

Reading Across Texts Do you think that the forensics class at Potterville Middle School would make Encyclopedia Brown a better detective? Make a list of traits that good detectives have.

Writing Across Texts Look at your list of traits. Write a short paragraph explaining why you would or wouldn't make a good detective.

Objectives

• Read aloud grade-level texts and understand what is read. • Identify the meaning of common idioms. • Explain how the different methods used in media affect the message that is being communicated. • Listen closely to speakers and ask questions about and comment on the topic. • Speak clearly and to the point, give an opinion and support it with correct information. Make eye contact, change how fast, loud, and clearly you speak, and get your ideas across clearly.

READING STREET ONLINE
ONLINE STUDENT EDITION
www.ReadingStreet.com

Vocabulary

Idioms

Context Clues An idiom is a phrase whose meaning is something other than the literal meaning of its words. Context clues give clues about an idiom's meaning. When you come across an idiom, try to figure out its meaning from context.

Practice It! Look at the phrase "Encyclopedia cracked the case" on page 149 of *Encyclopedia Brown*. Write what you think "cracked the case" means and exchange papers with a partner.

Fluency

Expression

Reading with varied expression makes it easier to understand what you are reading. Raising and lowering your voice as you read helps make the events and the people in the story come alive.

Practice It! With a partner, take turns reading aloud page 150 and the first paragraph of page 151. Change the tone of your voice as you read the dialogue. Does the story sound more interesting when you read it this way? Do the characters "sound" different from one another?

Media Literacy

When you talk in front of an audience, speak clearly, loudly, and slowly.

Newscast

In a newscast, TV reporters tell news stories. The purpose of a newscast is to inform people about important events that have happened. Camera work is important in newscasts. The camera can zoom in to show a close-up of a speaker. Other times the camera shoots a wide-angle view.

Practice It! With a partner, create a newscast about the events that occurred in *Encyclopedia Brown*. Take turns acting as newscaster and director. Keep your news stories brief, including the most important ideas and details. Decide which shots will be close up or wide angle. Deliver your newscast to the class. Then explain why you filmed the camera angles you did.

Tips

- News directors use different camera angles to convey the emotional messages of their stories and influence their viewers.
- A close-up is when the camera shows only the face or any small area of who or what is being filmed. This shot focuses the viewer's attention on the subject.
- A wide-angle view shows a landscape. It sets the scene of the story or report.

Objectives

- Explain how different poems use elements of poetry, such as rhyme and meter.
- Identify how an author uses similes and metaphors to create imagery.
- Set a purpose for reading a text based on what you hope to get from the text.

Poetry

- A **simile** compares two things using the words *like* or *as*. *My love is like a rose* is a simile.
- **Lyrical poetry** rhymes, uses meter, and is made up of stanzas. It sounds like a song.
- **Free verse** may not rhyme or have regular meter. The lines may not begin with capital letters. Some have line breaks that don't look like stanzas.
- Read "The Seed" and "Carolyn's Cat." Look for similes. Explain what kind of poem each is.

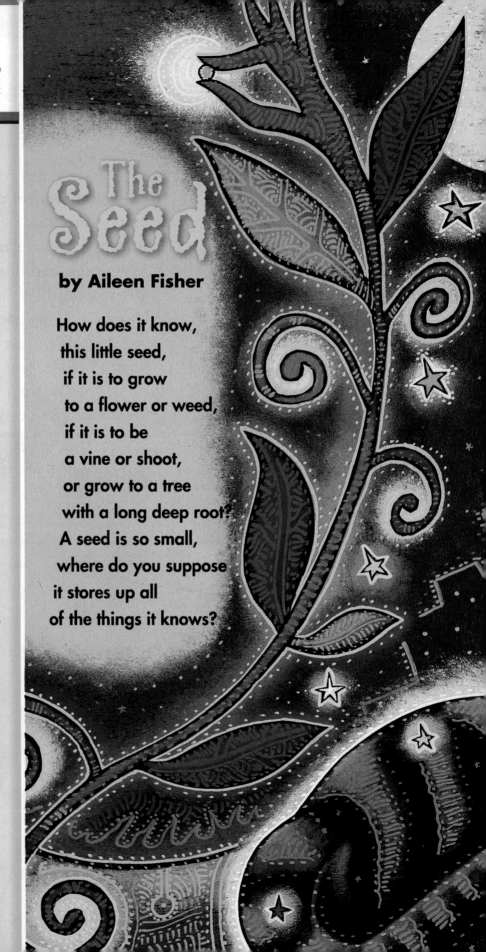

The Seed

by Aileen Fisher

How does it know,
this little seed,
if it is to grow
to a flower or weed,
if it is to be
a vine or shoot,
or grow to a tree
with a long deep root?
A seed is so small,
where do you suppose
it stores up all
of the things it knows?

Carolyn's Cat

by Constance Kling Levy

She's a house cat
pampered like a child,
cuddled and petted
and very well fed,
a stranger
to the wild
outside.
(She's the kind of cat
you'd invite to tea.)

Her life, it seems,
is peaceful and good
with only her house
for a neighborhood:
the plump pillows,
the soft chairs,
the smooth wood.

But I saw her one night
posed perfectly still,
like a china cat,
on the windowsill,
meeting, with moonlike eyes,
the full moon's glow.

And I think
there are things
about Carolyn's cat
that even Carolyn
doesn't know.

Let's Think About...

Which poem is a lyrical poem? Which is free verse? Explain how you know.

Let's Think About...

Find two similes in "Carolyn's Cat." Explain what these similes tell you about the cat.

Who Knows?

by Fatou Ndiaye Sow

Who knows
How many stars
Are in the roof of the sky?
How many fishes
In the deep seas?
How many people
In the whole wide world?
Who knows
Where, every evening
The sun flees to?
Where the moon lights up?
Where dawn starts,
Where the endless horizon ends,
Who knows? . . . Who knows?

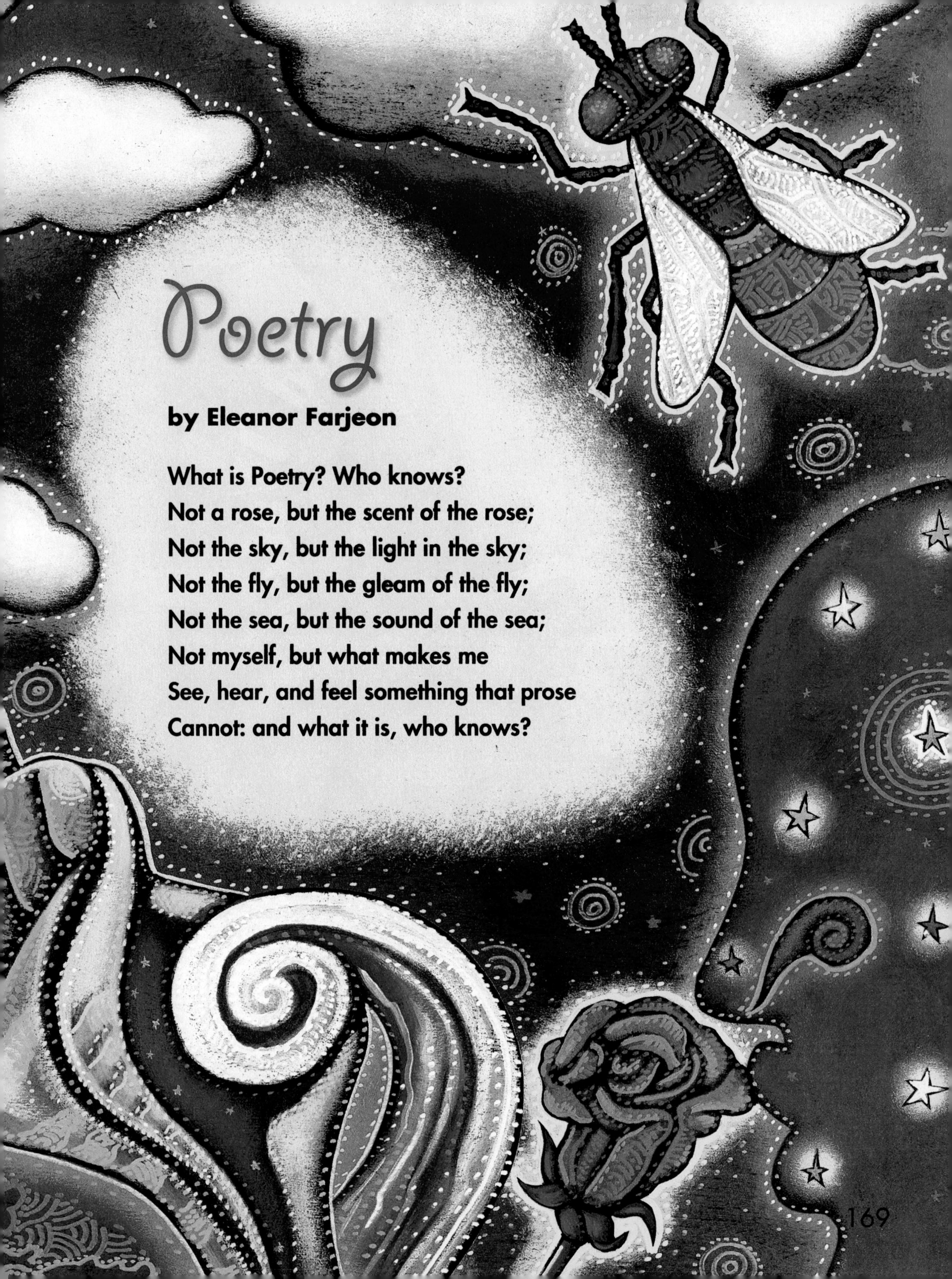

Poetry

by Eleanor Farjeon

What is Poetry? Who knows?
Not a rose, but the scent of the rose;
Not the sky, but the light in the sky;
Not the fly, but the gleam of the fly;
Not the sea, but the sound of the sea;
Not myself, but what makes me
See, hear, and feel something that prose
Cannot: and what it is, who knows?

Unit 5

Adventures by Land, Air, and Water

What makes an adventure?

Reading Street Online

www.ReadingStreet.com

- Big Question Video
- eSelections
- Envision It! Animations
- Story Sort

Smokejumpers: Life Fighting Fires
EXPOSITORY TEXT

connect to SCIENCE

How can we prepare for emergencies?

Paired Selection
Camp with Care PERSUASIVE ESSAY

Lost City: The Discovery of Machu Picchu
BIOGRAPHY

connect to SOCIAL STUDIES

What surprises can happen on an expedition?

Paired Selection
Riding the Rails to Machu Picchu PERSONAL ESSAY

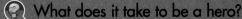

Cliff Hanger REALISTIC FICTION

connect to SOCIAL STUDIES

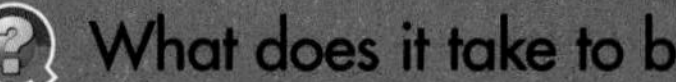

What does it take to be a hero?

Paired Selection
Rock Climbing ONLINE SOURCES

Antarctic Journal JOURNAL

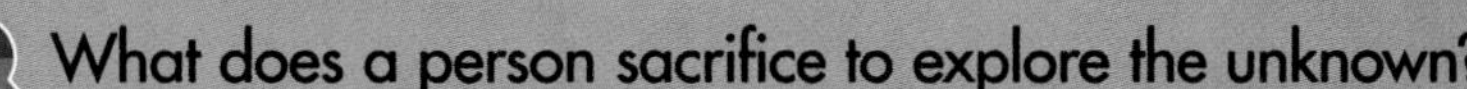

What does a person sacrifice to explore the unknown?

connect to SCIENCE

Paired Selection
Swimming Towards Ice BIOGRAPHY

connect to SCIENCE

Moonwalk SCIENCE FICTION

What are the risks when walking on the moon?

Paired Selection
A Walk on the Moon EXPOSITORY TEXT

Objectives

- Speak clearly and to the point, give an opinion and support it with correct information.
- Take part in discussions led by teachers or other students, ask and answer questions, and offer ideas that build on the ideas of other people.

Oral Vocabulary

Let's Talk About

Emergencies

- Share opinions about what an emergency is.
- Tell how to act, and include information in your description.
- Build upon the ideas of others.

READING STREET ONLINE
CONCEPT TALK VIDEO
www.ReadingStreet.com

You've learned
200
Amazing Words
so far this year!

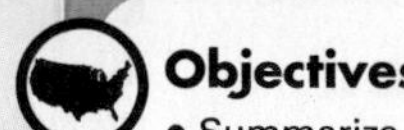

Objectives
• Summarize the main idea and supporting details. • Set a purpose for reading a text based on what you hope to get from the text.

Envision It! Skill Strategy

Skill

Envision It! Visual Skills Handbook

Author's Purpose

Inform

Entertain

An author writes for many purposes, some of which are to inform, entertain, persuade, or express a mood or feeling. An author may have more than one purpose for writing. Sometimes the author's purpose is directly stated, but other times you have to figure it out on your own.

BUY

BUY ME!

Persuade

Express

EI•2

Strategy

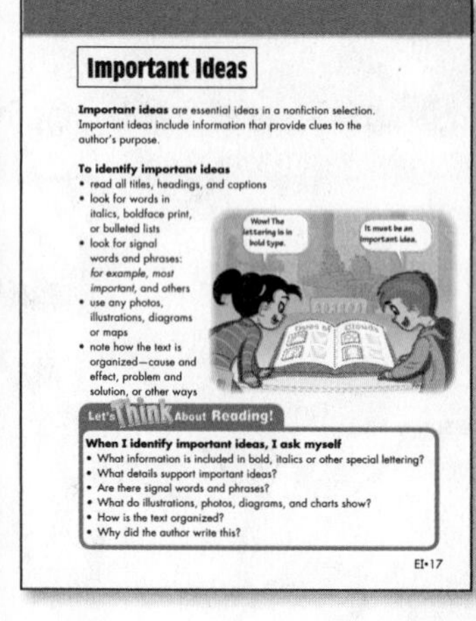
Important Ideas

Important ideas are essential ideas in a nonfiction selection. Important ideas include information that provide clues to the author's purpose.

To identify important ideas
- read all titles, headings, and captions
- look for words in italics, boldface print, or bulleted lists
- look for signal words and phrases: *for example, most important,* and others
- use any photos, illustrations, diagrams or maps
- note how the text is organized—cause and effect, problem and solution, or other ways

Wow! The lettering is in bold type.

It must be an important idea.

Let's Think About Reading!

When I identify important ideas, I ask myself
- What information is included in bold, italics or other special lettering?
- What details support important ideas?
- Are there signal words and phrases?
- What do illustrations, photos, diagrams, and charts show?
- How is the text organized?
- Why did the author write this?

EI•17

READING STREET ONLINE
ENVISION IT! ANIMATIONS
www.ReadingStreet.com

Comprehension Skill

Author's Purpose

- Four common reasons authors have for writing are to persuade, to inform, to express ideas or feelings, or to entertain.
- Authors often have more than one purpose for writing. An author may write to both inform and entertain.
- When you figure out an author's purpose, you can adjust the way you read. You might read a funny story faster than a news article.
- Use the graphic organizer to identify author's purpose as you read "Parachutes All over the World."

Ideas	→	**Genre**	←	**Author's Purpose**
What are they? How are they expressed?		Nonfiction? Fiction?		Persuade? Inform? Entertain? Express?

Comprehension Strategy

Important Ideas

Good readers try to identify the important, or main, ideas presented in a selection to help them determine an author's purpose for writing. The important or main ideas can help you understand the topic of a selection. Details in the text can support the important ideas, but you need to know the difference between important ideas and interesting ideas.

Parachutes All over the World

One of the first pictures of a parachute was drawn by Leonardo da Vinci in 1480! Da Vinci was a gifted Italian artist. People wonder how he ever thought of a parachute in the first place, because it was about four hundred years before the Wright brothers flew their plane at Kitty Hawk.

A French scientist, Louis-Sébastien Lenormand, who lived in the 1700s, is thought to have been the first person to use a parachute successfully. He named the parachute using the French words *parasol* (sun shield) and *chute* (fall). Lenormand tested it by jumping out of a very tall tree.

Many have contributed to the modern parachute. In San Francisco in 1885, Thomas Scott Baldwin became the first American to fall from a hot-air balloon with a parachute. In 1911, Gleb Kotelnikov, a Russian, had the idea of putting a parachute inside a knapsack. Before that, parachutes were held close to the body with both hands, very tightly.

Skill Look at the title, photograph, and diagram. What do you think is the author's purpose for writing the article?

Strategy Summarize two important or main ideas the author wants you to know about the role Lenormand played in the development of the parachute.

Strategy Summarize the most important idea of this paragraph. Summarize the details supporting it.

Your Turn!

Need a Review? See the *Envision It! Handbook* for help with author's purpose and important ideas.

Let's Think About...

Ready to Try It? Use what you've learned about author's purpose as you read *Smokejumpers*.

Objectives

- Determine the meanings of unfamiliar or multiple-meaning words by using the context of the sentence.
- Use a dictionary or glossary to find the meanings of unknown words, the syllable rules for these words, and how to pronounce them.

Envision It! Words to Know

concentrating

parachute

underbrush

dedication

essential

method

steer

wind

READING STREET ONLINE
VOCABULARY ACTIVITIES
www.ReadingStreet.com

Vocabulary Strategy for

Homographs

Dictionary/Glossary Homographs are words that are spelled the same but have different meanings and sometimes different pronunciations. For example, *dove* is a homograph. *Dove* (duv) means "a kind of bird." *Dove* (long /o/ sound) means "jumped headfirst into water."

1. When you read a homograph, read the words and sentences around it.
2. Is there an example or definition of the word in the context? Put that meaning into the sentence and see if it makes sense.
3. If the word still doesn't make sense, use a dictionary or glossary to find the meaning.

As you read "Remembering Firefighting Heroes," use a dictionary or glossary to figure out the meanings of *wind* and *steer.*

Words to Write Reread "Remembering Firefighting Heroes." Figure out the meanings of the homographs in the passage. Write what you think each word means. Use a dictionary or glossary to check your work.

Remembering Firefighting Heroes

Smokejumpers are firefighters who parachute into remote areas and use the parachute to steer themselves near deadly fires. The U.S. Forest Service began using smokejumpers in 1940. They have become an essential part of protecting our country's national forests.

On August 5, 1949, a wildfire raged at Mann Gulch in Montana. A bolt of lightning had probably set fire to some underbrush near the Missouri River. At the same time, the wind picked up, feeding the fire even more.

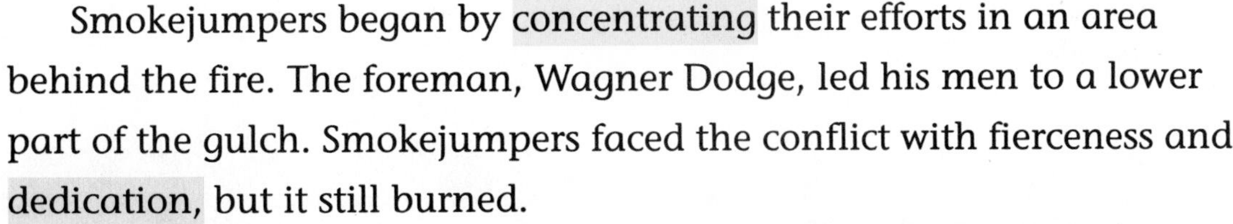

Smokejumpers began by concentrating their efforts in an area behind the fire. The foreman, Wagner Dodge, led his men to a lower part of the gulch. Smokejumpers faced the conflict with fierceness and dedication, but it still burned.

Dodge realized that his method wasn't working. The fire was getting worse, so he ordered his men to run up the slope of the gulch to escape. At about the same time, the wind began blowing in the same direction, essentially chasing the firefighters up the hill. Fifteen men lost their lives.

In 1999, a dedication ceremony was held on the fiftieth anniversary of the fire. Smokejumpers landed in Mann Gulch to remember the sacrifice of those who had died.

Your Turn!

Need a Review? For help with homographs, see *Words!*

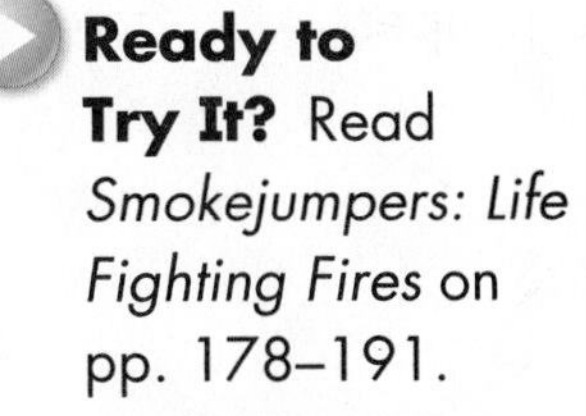

Ready to Try It? Read *Smokejumpers: Life Fighting Fires* on pp. 178–191.

Mark Beyer

SMOKEJUMPERS
Life Fighting Fires

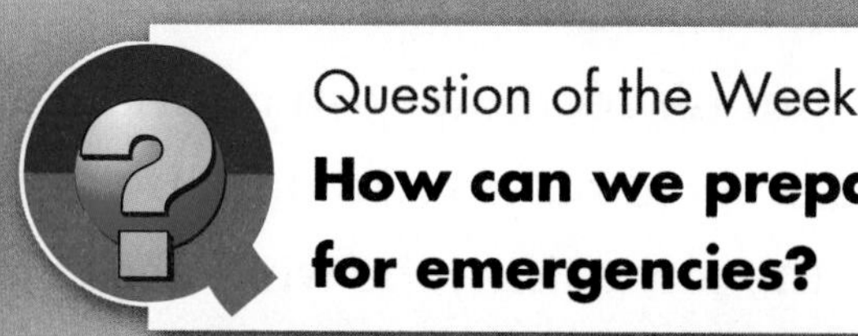

Question of the Week
How can we prepare for emergencies?

Expository Text gives information about real people and events. As you read, think about the skills needed to become a smokejumper.

PALMER
Let's Think About Reading!

Extreme Risk

Let's Think About...

How can you figure out what the important idea of this section will be? Do the title and pictures help?
Important Ideas

Fighting forest wildfires is a dangerous business. Some wildfires, however, are easier to get to than others. They can begin to burn near roads, or they can move through low-lying forests, on flat ground or gentle slopes. These wildfires are fought bravely by ground crews of "hot shots." Hot shots can be a line of five, eighteen, or seventy men and women who are working very close to a blazing wall of fire.

Other wildfires burn in far-off, remote areas of a forest. These wildfires can start in a deep gulch or high on a mountainside. These places are often far from roads. The only way to get to these blazes quickly is by dropping firefighters from planes. So what do you get when you cross a wildfire firefighter with a parachutist? That's right: a smokejumper.

When a wildfire occurs in a remote area, parachuting firefighters called smokejumpers are called in to battle the blaze.

Smokejumpers and hot shots are equally dedicated to putting out wildfires. Their mission is the same: stop wildfires before their destructive energy destroys the forest, kills the animals, or threatens human life. Smokejumpers have an added task, however. Before they even hit the ground, smokejumpers are hard at work tracking the fire, finding the right place to jump, and concentrating on landing safely.

Once on the ground, smokejumpers work the same way any forest firefighter does. They cut down trees and drag them from the wildfire's path. They dig up stumps. They chop away the underbrush. Then they turn the soil over and over until just dirt remains. All of this work is done while the fire creeps closer to them.

Let's Think About...

How does using what you know about firefighters help you understand what a smokejumper does when on the ground? **Background Knowledge**

A firebreak is a wide dirt barrier created by firefighters to contain a forest fire.

The firefighters create a firebreak, a wide dirt barrier, which is essential in helping to stop the spread of a wildfire. Sometimes, though, even fifty feet of dirt is not enough to keep sparks from drifting over to another dry forest area. Little sparks can create raging fires. Smokejumpers can work for days against a large wildfire. They might work eighteen hours with only breaks for food. Their dedication has stopped the destruction of millions of acres of forests all over the world.

Jumping into a Fire

Every summer seems drier than the last up in the Rocky Mountains. Underbrush is like a tinderbox. A careless hiker or a flash of lightning could cause the area to quickly go up in flames. And then it happens. Lightning hits in the high gulch. Smoke is spotted from miles off. There are no roads nearby, and before long the wildfire may get out of control. This is a job for smokejumpers.

Danger lurks all around the smokejumpers. The airplane fights high winds caused by the rush of air from the blaze below. The plane must get the smoke-jumpers to the drop zone. There is no large clearing. Rocks line the mountainside. The area is remote. If the fire rages out of control, rescuing the smokejumpers will be difficult and dangerous. What is the plan?

Situations like this are almost a daily routine for smokejumpers. However, they trust that their training will help them overcome the obstacles that make fighting wildfires so difficult. Special uniforms, equipment, and tools also help smokejumpers fight wildfires as well as provide them with protection while they battle those blazes. Most of all, smokejumpers work together and help one another to make it through a long day—or days—of wildfire firefighting.

Let's Think About...

What are some of the ways smoke-jumpers overcome the dangers of their jobs?

Important Ideas

Jumpsuit and Safety Gear

Let's Think About...

Use multiple text features to locate information and important ideas. How do the heading and the photo help you predict what this section will be about? **Predict**

You don't go to the beach without your swimsuit, do you? Of course not. Well, smokejumpers don't jump from an airplane into a firestorm without the right clothing either. Smokejumpers wear lightweight jumpsuits made of fire-retardant material. The jumpsuits help keep them cool during the long workday digging a firebreak. Jumpsuits are either bright orange, white, or yellow. These colors can be easily seen from the air and through the trees. If a smokejumper gets separated from his or her crew, or stick, during a jump or while fighting a blaze, a plane has a better chance of spotting the bright-colored suit.

Jumpsuits are padded to break the fall of a parachute jump. This is important in the rocky areas of a drop zone. Each jumpsuit has several large pockets for carrying small tools and the all-important safety line ladder. Smokejumpers also wear gloves while fighting wildfires. Gloves, however, are not worn during the jump because controlling a parachute is easier with bare hands.

Let's Think About...

Read the text and look at the photo. What details did the author provide about the smokejumpers' jumpsuits and safety gear? **Important Ideas**

A helmet and goggles are supplied to each smokejumper. The helmet is made of aluminum because this metal is lightweight and strong. Also, metal does not burn, so smokejumpers don't have to worry about burning embers floating around while they work. Attached to the helmet is a face mask, somewhat like the one on a football helmet. The face mask protects a smokejumper from branches when he or she lands in a tree. Goggles protect the eyes from wind, flying embers, branches, and smoke.

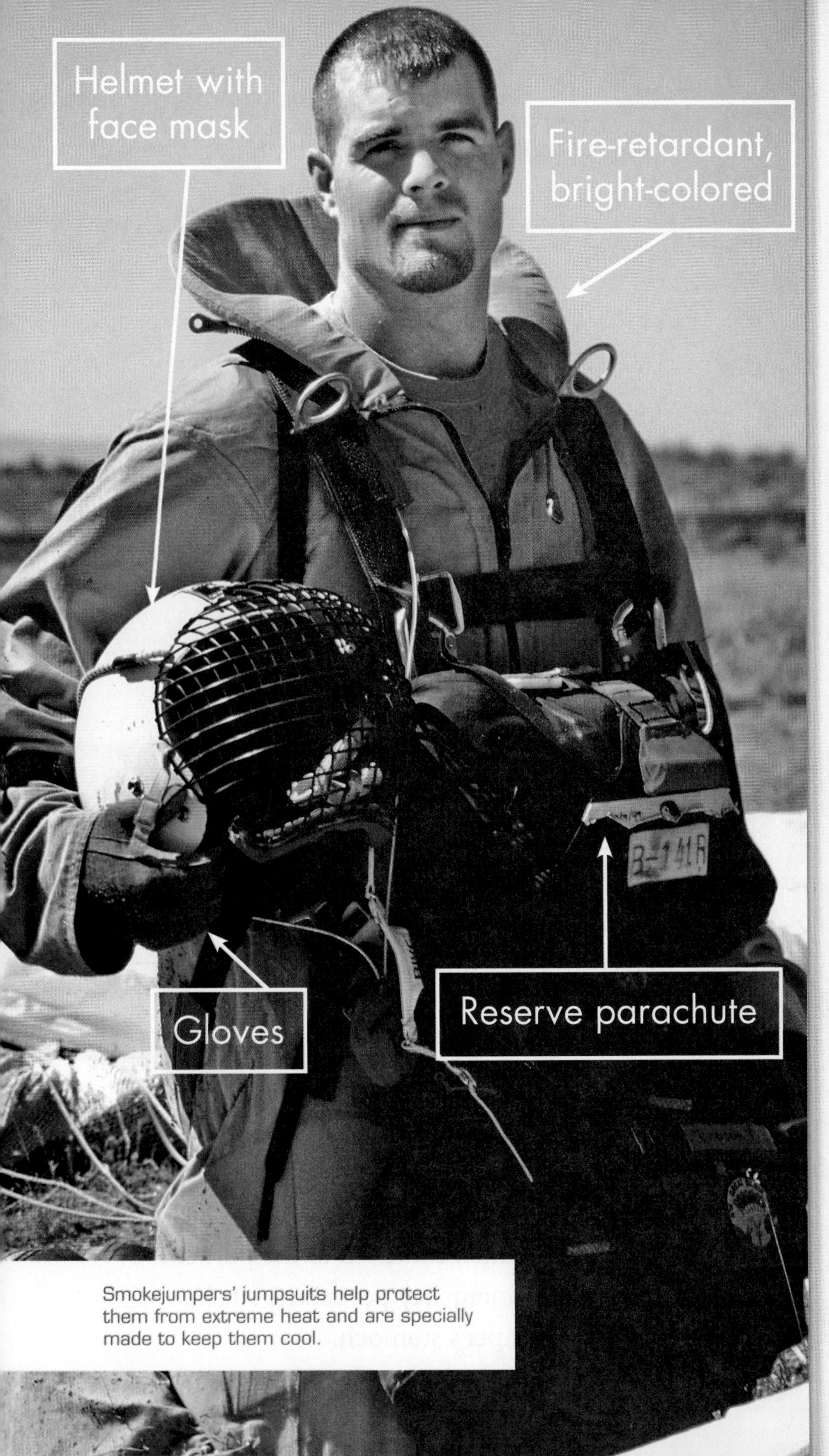

Smokejumpers' jumpsuits help protect them from extreme heat and are specially made to keep them cool.

Smokejumpers hook their parachutes to a static line, which causes their chutes to open automatically when they jump.

The Parachute

The master parachute rigger is in charge of packing each smokejumper's parachute. Parachutes must be packed in a certain way for them to unfold properly during a jump. A poorly packed parachute could tangle in its own ropes and send the smokejumper crashing to the ground.

As the plane carrying the smokejumpers nears the drop zone, the smokejumpers check their parachutes and gear. The parachute is attached to their backs by a harness. The harness is strapped around a jumper's shoulders, across the chest, and between the legs. The harness keeps the jumper attached to the parachute during the fall. An emergency parachute sits in a pack against the jumper's stomach.

Let's Think About...

What clues in the text help you infer what a "drop zone" is? **Inferring**

The Jumpmaster

The jumpmaster does not jump with the smoke-jumpers. The jumpmaster's job is to make sure that the smokejumpers are jumping from the right place in the air so that they will land safely near the fire. The jumpmaster does this with the help of the airplane pilot. They both spot areas on the ground that could serve as the landing zone. Before the jumpmaster gives the signal to jump, however, he or she must be sure that the plane is in the right position. To do this, the jumpmaster drops crepe paper streamers out of the plane from 1,500 feet. This is the proper height for smokejumpers to jump from. The jumpmaster watches the streamers fall toward the ground, and their path tells the jumpmaster if the wind direction is right for the smokejumpers to drop safely to the ground.

Let's Think About...

What important idea have you learned about the jumpmaster's job? **Important Ideas**

The jumpmaster makes sure that smokejumpers are jumping from the right spot to land safely near a fire.

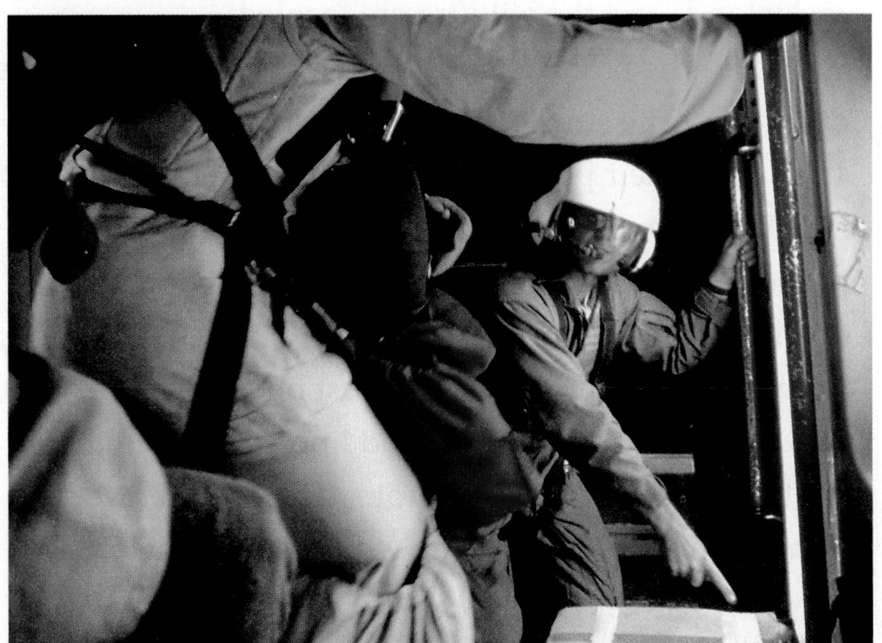

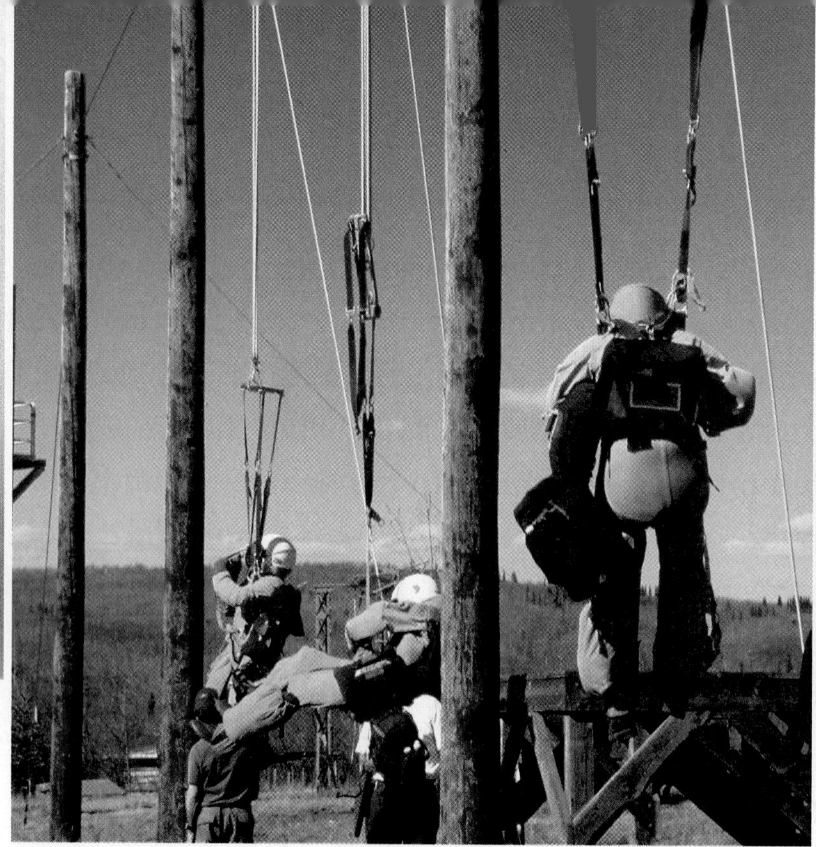

During tower training, smokejumper recruits learn what it feels like to land with a parachute.

While the jumpmaster and the pilot spot for landing zones, the smokejumpers look out the window at the land below. They study the ground and the area near the fire. They need to know where clearings, rocky land, and the wildfire are located.

When the plane is positioned correctly, it circles the drop zone. The smokejumpers then prepare to jump. They hook their parachutes to a static line, which is a thick wire attached inside the plane that holds parachute release cords so that smokejumpers' chutes open automatically when they jump. When the chutes open, the smokejumpers don't just float down. Instead, they use the parachute "shroud lines" attached to the chute to steer toward the landing zone—and away from the fire. When the smokejumpers hit the ground,

Let's Think About...

How does the smokejumper steer with the "shroud lines"?
Questioning

they roll to absorb the hard impact. They quickly pull their chutes onto the ground and gather them to make sure no wind pulls the chutes and drags their bodies along the ground.

Sometimes smokejumpers actually aim for trees if there is no clearing. Once caught on a tree, they drop themselves to the ground with their safety line. Smokejumpers get out of trees quickly. They don't want to be caught dangling from a branch when fire is nearby.

Bundled Tools

Let's Think About...

How do the heading and photo help predict what this section will be about? **Predict**

Once the smokejumpers have gathered themselves on the ground, they need their tools. The plane circles the area and drops more parachutes. These chutes hold packages containing tools, food supplies, or other equipment. If a stream, pond, or lake is near the fire, hoses and water pumps will be packed too.

The parachutes are colored to identify what they are carrying. A red parachute's bundle might include shovels and saws. A yellow parachute might carry food supplies. Color-coded supply parachutes save smokejumpers valuable time. The last thing a smokejumper needs is to find sandwiches when he or she is looking for a shovel!

The pulaski, a combination of an ax and a hoe, is the tool of choice for smokejumpers.

Ready to Move Out

Once the supplies are gathered, the smokejumpers head toward the fire with all their gear on their backs. Now the real work begins. But before they can get to the fire's edge, the smokejumpers must determine where the fire is, where it might be heading, and the best way to tackle the blaze.

Getting Home Safely

Putting out a wildfire may be the job that smokejumpers are sent to do, but the first order of business is to keep everyone safe. Over the many years smokejumpers have been fighting wildfires, very few of them have died. This is because safety precautions are taken before, during, and after a fire is fought. As crazy as these men and women who work as smokejumpers may seem, they have no death wish. The opposite is true. They love the environment and want to help keep it safe for animals and humans. Their job is extremely dangerous, but they are professionals. They understand the risks, and know what to do to avoid death.

Let's Think About...

Do you understand why smokejumpers choose to do such a dangerous job? How has the author explained this idea? **Important Ideas**

When the fire has been smothered and all the work is done, it's time for the smokejumpers to return to base. But since they dropped from the skies into this remote area, how will they get out? Often by the same method they got in. The team radios its base and calls for a helicopter to come pick the smokejumpers up. Sometimes the team must walk a long way to get to a clearing where a helicopter can land. This walk is a victory march. The success the team has achieved by putting out a destructive fire is well worth the few hours that smokejumpers must hike to get to the rescue area. When all are aboard, a cheer goes up. They're going home.

If you are not clear on how the smoke-jumpers got into the remote areas, what can you do? **Monitor and Clarify**

Objectives

- Read independently for long periods of time and paraphrase the reading, including the order in which events occur.
- Write responses to texts using details to show understanding.

Envision It! | Retell

READING STREET ONLINE
STORY SORT
www.ReadingStreet.com

Think Critically

1. Many firefighters perform heroic deeds to save the lives and property of others. What makes these brave men and women willing to risk their own lives in the line of duty? **Text to World**
2. The author describes what it's like to be a smokejumper. How does he help you understand the dangers and excitement of being a smokejumper? Find sentences that help you understand. **Think Like an Author**
3. The author goes into great detail about the training smokejumpers receive and the equipment they use. Why do you think the author provided this information to his readers? **Author's Purpose**
4. In the last section of the article, "Getting Home Safely," the author provides readers with several important ideas as well as interesting details. Identify the ideas you think are important and the details you found to be interesting. **Important Ideas**
5. **Look Back and Write** Look back at pages 180–182, the section titled "Extreme Risk." After reading about the life of a smokejumper, do you think the title "Extreme Risk" would have been a better title for the whole article? Why or why not? Provide evidence to support your answer.

TEST PRACTICE **Extended Response**

Meet the Author

Mark Beyer

Mark T. Beyer is a writer and educator who lives in Florida. He has written books for young people on a variety of subjects, but most often on technology.

These books focus on the future and past effects of technology. His books about the future typically deal with robotics and space exploration. In them, he imagines the consequences of technological advances on human life. His books about past technologies explore the different ways people transported themselves: by bicycle, motorcycle, and train.

Mr. Beyer also likes to write about people who have daring, interesting jobs, such as smokejumpers and those who work for the secret service.

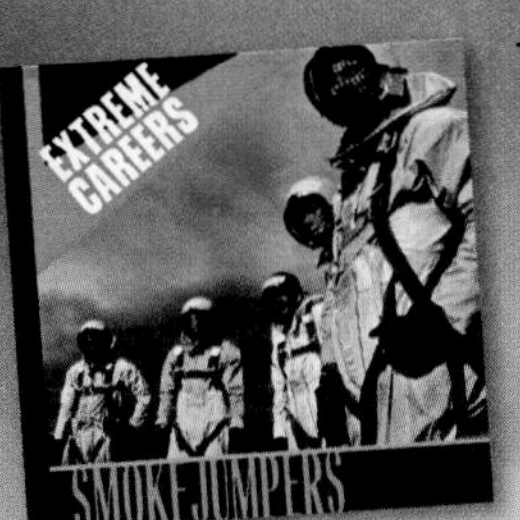

Select a book for independent reading from the library. Then establish a purpose for reading your selected text based on your own desired outcome to enhance comprehension. Write your purpose for reading in your log.

Objectives

• Write creative stories that build to an ending and contain details about the characters and setting. • Use and understand adjectives and their special forms.

Let's Write It!

Key Features of a Fantasy

- characters seem believable but could not be real
- setting is often imaginary and unusual
- events may be unrealistic but make sense

READING STREET ONLINE
GRAMMAR JAMMER
www.ReadingStreet.com

Narrative

Fantasy

Fantasy stories are made up of imaginary elements. The student model on the next page is an example of a fantasy story.

Writing Prompt Write a fantasy story about fighting a fire.

Writer's Checklist

Remember, you should ...

- ✓ create an imaginative story and build the plot to a climax.
- ✓ invent characters and a setting and use creative details to describe them.
- ✓ make sure the plot makes sense, even if it isn't realistic.
- ✓ use descriptive adjectives.

Student Model

Rainmaker

One hot, humid day, Shira Gamsee was imagining a cool rain pouring down her face. Suddenly she was drenched! That was the moment she discovered she could make rain! By focusing her complete attention on something, she could cause a gentle shower or a teeming downpour to occur.

Walking through the woods one day, Shira wondered about what she could do with her newly discovered ability. Suddenly **a young** man came running toward her, shouting, "Turn around! The woods are on fire! The fire is out of control!"

Shira turned her complete focus to **the crimson** flames filling the skies above. "Come on!" shouted the man, but Shira couldn't move. Within minutes, the fire was out.

"What was that?" exclaimed the man. "It was like you had a superpower!" With a little grin, Shira turned to the man and calmly said, "Come on, we'd better go tell the fire department."

Genre Fantasy stories contain unreal elements.

Descriptive adjectives and articles are used correctly.

Writing Trait Sentences are complete.

Conventions

Adjectives and Articles

Remember An **adjective** describes a person, place, or thing in the sentence. The adjectives *a, an,* and *the,* called **articles,** stand before the words they modify.

Objectives

- Explain the effects of an author's use of language on the reader.
- Make connections between literary and informational texts with similar ideas and support your ideas with details from the texts.

Science in Reading

Genre

Persuasive Essay

- A persuasive essay is a type of persuasive text. It tries to influence a reader to do something or to think about something in a certain way.
- In persuasive text, authors use language to present information. They use this information to influence their readers.
- Persuasive text contains facts. It also contains opinions that can be supported by facts.
- Read the persuasive essay "Camp with Care." Think about the language the author uses. What does he want you to do? What does he want you to think?

CAMP WITH CARE

BY JEFF WILSON

When you go camping, you must camp with care. When you leave a campsite, take your garbage with you. Litter pollutes the air, land, and water.

Think about it. You toss an empty cup on the ground. What happens next? An animal may try to taste the inside of the cup. The animal may get stuck. Or the animal may eat the cup and get very sick. If the cup floats into a stream, it can cause even more damage. Fish and birds may eat it, and they will get sick. The cup will pollute the water in the stream.

And think about other campers. They have come a long way to look at a beautiful countryside. They do not want to see garbage. So leave your campsite just the way you found it. It takes a little effort, but it makes a big difference.

PREVENT FOREST FIRES

By camping with care, you can be a firefighter. You can stop fires before they start. Every year more than 100,000 forest fires burn in the U.S. Millions of trees burn to the ground. Sometimes homes are even destroyed. And here's the really bad news. Most of these fires are started by careless people. But here's the good news. All it takes is a little care to help prevent forest fires.

When campers start a fire, they should keep a close eye on it. If the fire gets too big, they should put it out.

Many do just the opposite. They start a fire and then they do something else. They may go for a swim. When they come back, the fire is too big. This is how forest fires start. Campers, NEVER leave a fire unattended.

It is also important to put out a fire properly. Just because the flames have died down does not mean that the fire is dead. The ashes may still be burning. A breeze can bring the fire back. So, campers need to put a lot of water on their campfire. They should check that the ash is fully drenched with water.

It is up to all of us to protect nature. By camping with care, we'll all enjoy our campgrounds for a long time.

Let's Think About...

What language does the author use to influence the reader? What does the author want the reader to do? **Persuasive Essay**

Let's Think About...

Reading Across Texts Look back at *Smokejumpers* and ask yourself what the smokejumpers would think about this persuasive essay. Do you think they would agree with the essay? Why or why not?

Writing Across Texts Use what you have learned from *Smokejumpers* and "Camp with Care" to write a story about a forest fire. Include details about how a careless camper starts the fire and how smokejumpers put it out.

Objectives

- Read aloud grade-level texts and understand what is read.
- Use a dictionary or glossary to find the meanings of unknown words, the syllable rules for these words, and how to pronounce them.
- Listen closely to speakers and ask questions about and comment on the topic.
- Take part in discussions led by teachers or other students, ask and answer questions, and offer ideas that build on the ideas of other people.
- Use and understand adjectives and their special forms.

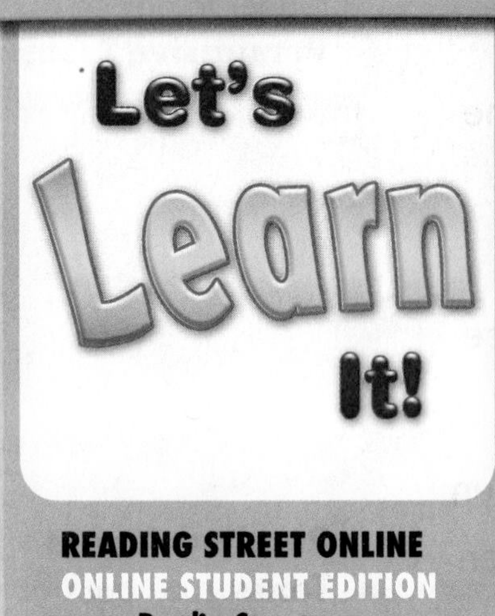

READING STREET ONLINE
ONLINE STUDENT EDITION
www.ReadingStreet.com

Vocabulary

Homographs

Dictionary/Glossary Some words have the same spelling but have different meanings and sometimes different pronunciations. For example, someone who *tears* his or her favorite shirt may shed *tears*.

Practice It! Work with a partner. Find the word *winds* in *Smokejumpers: Life Fighting Fires*, page 183. Read aloud that sentence, paying attention to how you pronounce *winds*. Explain to your partner the meaning of *winds*. Then think of another pronunciation and meaning for *winds*. Check your pronunciations and definitions in the glossary.

Fluency

Rate and Accuracy

When you read too quickly or too slowly, you may not understand what you are reading. Reading smoothly and at the right speed helps you make sense of what you read.

Practice It! With your partner, take turns reading aloud *Smokejumpers: Life Fighting Fires*, page 183. Begin by reading slowly and then read more quickly. Decide which pace works best with the story. Practice reading aloud at the pace you choose.

Listening and Speaking

Get Ready For Middle School

When you participate in a performance, speak loudly and clearly to your audience.

Dramatization

In a dramatization, people act out scenes from a story. A dramatization may show one or more events in the story. Often you need to use your background knowledge to understand implicit, or unstated, ideas and information.

Practice It! Work with a small group. Use information from *Smokejumpers: Life Fighting Fires* to create a dramatic scene. Assign roles to each group member. Include a beginning, middle, and end in your scene. Decide whether to write a script or to make up dialogue as you act out the scene. Present your dramatization to the class. Then discuss it.

Tips

Listening . . .

- Be prepared to make pertinent comments.
- Listen for implicit ideas and information.

Speaking . . .

- Adjust your speaking rate to match the pace of the scene.
- Share implicit ideas and information.

Teamwork . . .

- Discuss the performance with other students, and provide suggestions that help improve the performance and that build upon the ideas of others. For example, if someone comments on the end of the scene, tell what you think about the end of the scene.

Objectives

- Take part in discussions led by teachers or other students, ask and answer questions, and offer ideas that build on the ideas of other people.

Oral Vocabulary

Let's Talk About

Ancient Cities

- Tell what you would like about exploring an ancient city.
- Maintain eye contact when you speak.
- Answer questions with appropriate detail by including descriptions of size, color, and shape in your response.

READING STREET ONLINE
CONCEPT TALK VIDEO
www.ReadingStreet.com

You've learned
2 1 0
Amazing Words
so far this year!

Objectives

- Monitor your comprehension of a text and adjust your reading based on how well you understand what you are reading.
- Describe how ideas are related in texts and whether the ideas are directly stated or not.

Envision It! | **Skill Strategy**

Skill

Compare and Contrast
To compare and contrast is to look for similarities and differences in things.
SPEAKS 5 DIFFERENT LANGUAGES
$23.95
$19.95
20% OFF
EI•5

Strategy

Visualize
We visualize to create a picture or pictures in our mind as we read. This helps us monitor our comprehension.
To visualize
• combine what you already know with details from the text to make pictures in your mind
• use all your senses to put yourself in the story or text
TODAY:
Let's Think About Reading!
When I visualize, I ask myself
• What do I already know?
• Which details create pictures in my mind?
• How can my senses put me in the story?
EI•25

READING STREET ONLINE
ENVISION IT! ANIMATIONS
www.ReadingStreet.com

Comprehension Skill

Compare and Contrast

- To compare and contrast means to tell how two or more things are alike and different.
- Authors may use clue words such as *like, as,* and *same* to show explicit similarities. They may use words such as *but, unlike,* and *different* to show explicit differences.
- Authors may not use clue words when making comparisons. The reader has to figure out these implicit relationships for him- or herself.
- Use this graphic organizer to identify ideas the author compares and contrasts as you read "Archaeology: Dig It."

Similarities	Differences

Comprehension Strategy

Visualize

Active readers transform the words on the page into mental images. Visualizing similarities and differences between two people or things that are being compared helps you understand what you read.

Archaeology: Dig It

Archaeology is the study of things left by people who lived in the past. Some archaeologists study people who left behind things and written records. Others study people who had no written language.

With the passing of time, ancient places often are covered with layers of earth. The archaeologist has to dig down to find the things people left behind. These things give clues to how those people lived.

All people have certain things in common. We all need to eat and a place to live. So archaeologists look for things such as dishes, cooking pots, arrowheads, and hunting knives. They hope to find things people built, such as houses and roads. They study these things to understand how people lived in the past.

The way we live today is different from how people lived long ago. Most of us don't hunt our food. We don't make our own cooking pots or dishes. But we do live in homes and travel on roads, and we do keep written records. We will leave behind these records for other people to read in the future.

Skill What does one type of archaeologist do that the other does not? Is this an explicit or implicit comparison?

Strategy What might people in the future discover about the way we live today? Visualize and describe things they might find that will tell them about us.

Skill Compare and contrast the way people live today with how people lived long ago.

Your Turn!

Need a Review? See *Envision It! Handbook* for help with comparing and contrasting and visualizing.

Ready to Try It? Use what you've learned about comparing and contrasting as you read *Lost City*.

Objectives

- Determine the meaning of English words with roots from Greek, Latin, and other languages.

Envision It! | **Words to Know**

ruins

terraced

thickets

curiosity

glorious

granite

torrent

READING STREET ONLINE
VOCABULARY ACTIVITIES
www.ReadingStreet.com

Vocabulary Strategy for

Greek and Latin Roots

Word Structure Many words, particularly academic vocabulary words, have Latin or Greek roots. The Latin root *terra* means "earth" or "land." It appears in *terrain* (surface of the ground) and *territory* (an area of land). The Greek root *graphikos* means "of writing" and *arkhaiologia* means "the study of ancient things." Knowing Latin and Greek roots can help you figure out unknown words.

1. Look at the unknown word. Try to identify a Greek or Latin root that you know.
2. Does the meaning of the Greek or Latin root give you a clue to the unknown word?
3. Try the meaning in the sentence to be sure it makes sense.

As you read "Looking for the Past," use what you know about Greek and Latin roots to help you figure out the meanings of *archaeologists, terraced,* and *graphics.*

Words to Write Reread "Looking for the Past." Imagine that you are a scientist looking for the past in a faraway land. Write a journal entry describing the sights you see and discoveries you make. Use words from the *Words to Know* list in your journal.

Looking for the Past

Some scientists called archaeologists study the past. They look at objects and buildings from past civilizations. They have curiosity about people who lived long ago. How did they live? What did they eat? What did they do every day? Did they read and write? Thanks to these scientists, we have learned a great deal about people who lived long ago.

These scientists have ventured into places that few others would go. They have cut their way through jungles with thickets full of dangerous animals. They have climbed steep mountains. They have crossed mountain rivers that fall in a raging torrent. They have found ruins of places people built long ago. These may look like nothing more than rocks to us, but they are glorious to these scientists.

Imagine a team of scientists as they discover terraced fields on the side of a mountain. These show that people long ago were clever farmers. Think of the scientists as they look at beautiful temples made of granite or marble. These show that people long ago had beliefs. Watch as the scientists carefully uncover clay pots decorated with unknown graphics. These show that people long ago were artistic and loved beauty.

Your Turn!

Need a Review? For help with Greek and Latin roots, see *Words!*

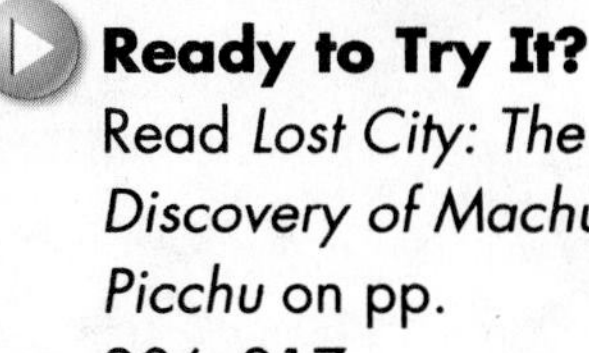

Ready to Try It? Read *Lost City: The Discovery of Machu Picchu* on pp. 206–217.

LOST

The Discovery of Machu Picchu

BY TED LEWIN

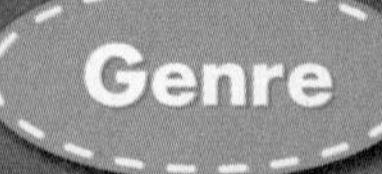

A **biography** is a kind of literary nonfiction that tells about a real person and the events of his or her life. The details of these events are often presented in sequence. Look for the sequence of the events leading to the discovery of this lost city as you read.

CITY

Question of the Week
What surprises can happen on an expedition?

In his first journey to South America, Yale professor Hiram Bingham longed to explore the hidden lands that lay beyond the snowcapped peaks of the Andes. Legend had it that the lost city of the Inca, Vilcapampa, lay there. Bingham was determined to discover it. So in 1910, the Yale Peruvian Expedition was organized. Finally, in July 1911, Bingham and his fellow adventurers arrived in Cusco, the first capital city of the Inca. What lay ahead for them was far from what they had expected. And more amazing. Our story begins high in the mountains of Peru. . . .

The boy looked out at the cloud-covered peaks all around him. Already his papa was working in the terraced fields. But last night he had dreamed of a tall stranger carrying a small black box. He could not get the dream out of his mind.

Suddenly, the clouds burned off and the mountains were bathed in glorious light. The dream foretold of something wonderful, he was sure.

Sixty miles south, in Cusco, Hiram Bingham gazed thoughtfully at the old Incan stone wall. He had come to Peru in search of Vilcapampa, the lost city of the Inca. But right here was the most beautiful stonework he had ever seen—huge stones cut so perfectly that not even a razor blade could be slipped between them.

The Inca had no iron tools to carve them, no wheel or draft animals to move them. The wall had withstood time and earthquakes. How had the Inca built it?

It was a mystery.

He walked through the cobbled streets of the old capital. The Spanish had come to this city, conquered the Inca, taken their gold, and built churches over their temples. Suddenly, he stopped. Before him was the famous Temple of the Sun. He placed his hands on the sun-warmed stones so beautifully carved, as if they had grown together.

Hidden in the mountains, the lost city would be built of stones like these. Would it hold gold and fabulous riches like the Spanish had found in Cusco?

More than ever he was determined to find that city.

The next day Bingham began his search. He would look for ruins–that might be the key.

He and his party, accompanied by military escort Sergeant Carrasco, left by mule train for the sacred valley of the Urubamba River.

They came to the sleepy old village of Ollantaytambo, long ago an important city. Its ancient stone terraces stepped up into the clouds.

"Are there any ruins nearby?" Bingham asked. He went door to door. He sat for hours in the cantina. "Are there any ruins near here?" he asked anyone who came in. "Do you know of the lost city of Vilcapampa?" No one knew of it.

Traveling north, the adventurers came upon a remote and wild canyon. Granite cliffs rose thousands of feet above the roaring rapids of the Urubamba River. In the distance were snowcapped mountains over three miles high. Bingham's

determination to find the lost city grew with each turn of the increasingly wild trail.

Meanwhile, high on one of these granite ridges, the boy tried to help his papa on the terraces. But he couldn't shake the dream from his mind. Who was this stranger with the black box? When would he come? What was in the black box? Anxiously, he searched the mountains for a sign.

Far below in the valley, Bingham's party camped on a sandy beach alongside the thundering rapids of the Urubamba. Days had gone by. He was tired and discouraged. No one knew of any ruins.

But now the travelers aroused the curiosity of a local farmer named Arteaga.

"Are there ruins nearby?" Bingham asked when Arteaga ventured into camp.

This time, through the interpreter, the farmer said, "Yes. There are very good ruins on top of the mountain called Machu Picchu."

The farmer pointed straight up.

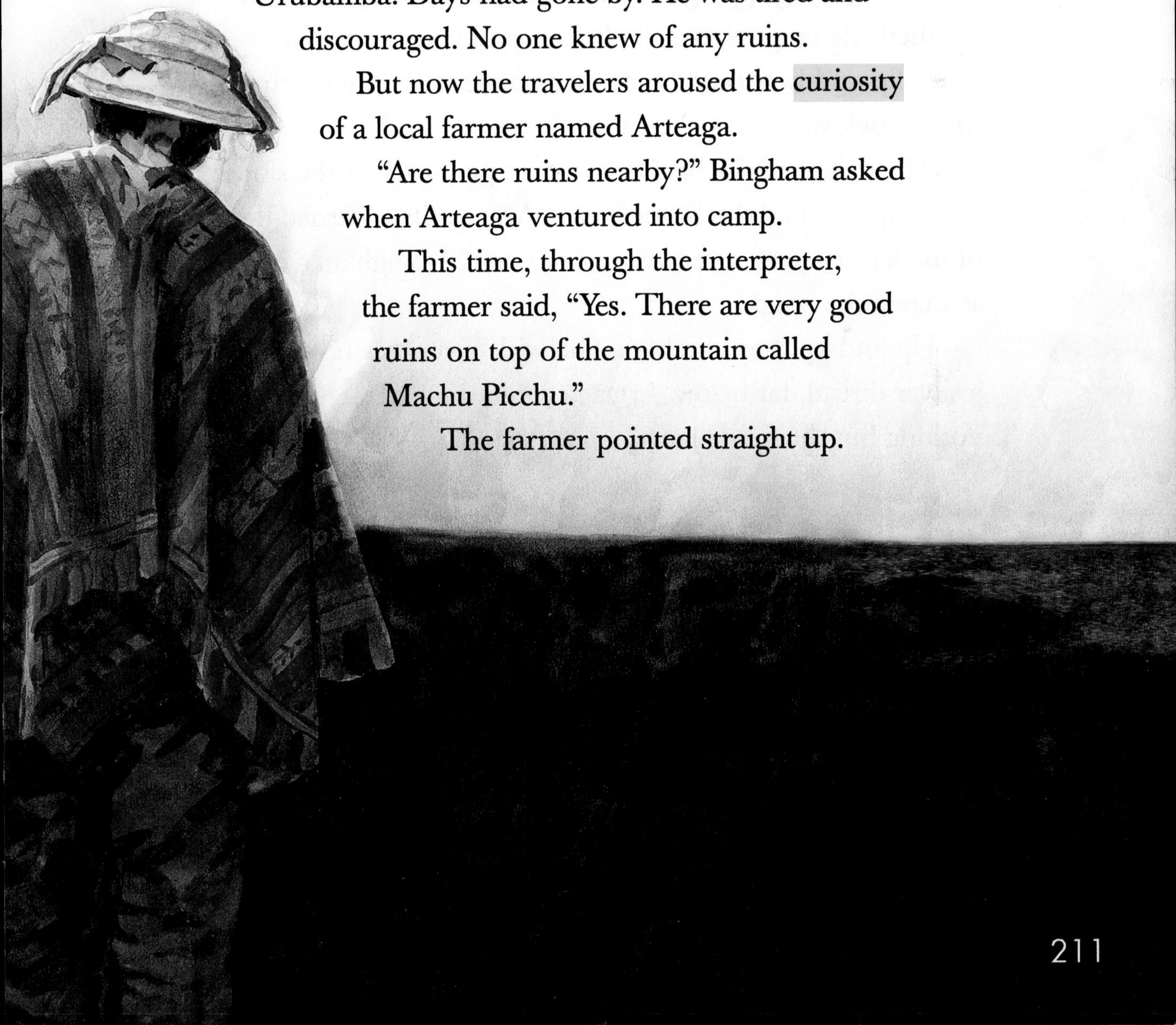

"Can you take us there?" Bingham asked.

"No," said Arteaga. "It is a very hard climb and there are many snakes." Bingham offered him coins. Arteaga nodded–he would show them the way.

Arteaga led them down the river trail. Suddenly, he plunged into the jungle. Bingham and the sergeant followed Arteaga through dense undergrowth down to the very edge of the river to a flimsy bridge made of slim logs. What was he getting himself into!

Sergeant Carrasco and Arteaga took off their shoes and crossed easily, gripping with their bare feet. Bingham was terrified–he crept across the bridge on hands and knees. One slip and he would be dashed to pieces in the roaring torrent below.

They climbed the bank into dense jungle. Now the slopes were slippery and the heat terrible. Arteaga had warned them of the fer-de-lance, a very venomous snake. Bingham's eyes searched the jungle.

Up and up they climbed. The wide river was now but a silver thread, far below. Arteaga could think of nothing but the fer-de-lance;

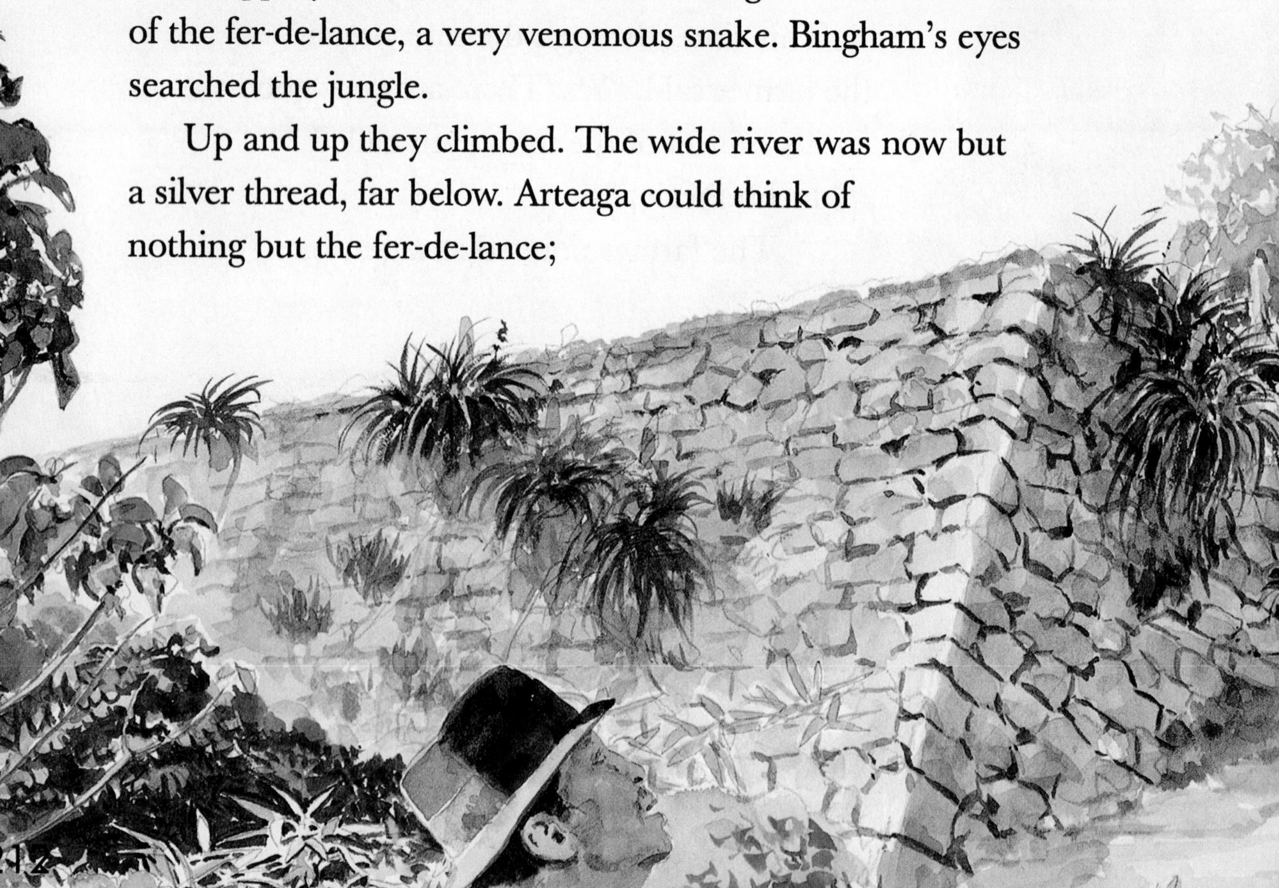

Sergeant Carrasco thought about his good, sturdy shoes; Bingham thought of nothing but the lost city. They cut their way through tangled thickets. Up and up they climbed.

Had an hour passed? Two? Three? Now they crept on all fours. They slipped and slid. In some places, they held on by their fingertips.

Finally, thirsty and exhausted, they broke through the jungle into sunlight. Above them stood a little Quechua boy beside a stone hut. What could he be doing at the top of this mountain?

"Ama llulla, ama quella, ama su'a" (Don't lie, don't be lazy, don't steal), the boy called out in the traditional Quechua greeting.

It was the tall stranger from his dream. Carrying the black box!

The boy's whole family crowded around to greet the exhausted travelers, then brought gourds of cool water and boiled sweet potatoes.

Bingham, still gasping for breath, asked, "Where are the ruins?" The boy said, *"Amuy, amuy!"* (Come, come!)

Bingham and the sergeant left Arteaga behind and followed at the boy's urging. *"Amuy, amuy!"* he kept saying.

At first they saw only stone terraces like the ones they had seen at Ollantaytambo. They looked as if they had been recently cleared of jungle and the vegetation burned off in order to plant crops.

But there were no ruins. Just more jungle beyond. Bingham had climbed this mountain and found–no lost city.

"Amuy, amuy!" Still, the boy beckoned him into the jungle beyond. Weary and discouraged, Bingham followed. At first all he saw were bamboo thickets and more tangled vines. Then he looked closer. Through the vines, he saw–stones. Inca stones. Then walls, beautiful stone walls! They were covered with mosses. And trees.

"Jaway, jaway!" (See, see!) the boy whispered, pointing ahead to a curved stone wall. Bingham pushed his way to it and placed his hands on the fine granite stones. A sun temple. More beautiful even than the one in Cusco.

They came to a grand stone staircase. Where could this lead? What else was here?

"Jaway, jaway," the boy called.

At the top of the staircase was a clearing. A small vegetable garden, and then . . . a temple built of enormous stones. Grander than any Bingham had ever seen. It stole his breath away.

Something was going on here, he could sense it.

Something just beyond his eyes. What was it?

He followed the boy to another temple. As magnificent. This one had three windows. But now he looked across the countryside. He looked past the thickets, past the vines. He began to see the outlines of stone streets and stone cottages. He began to see the outlines of a city!

"Here, boy," he said as he opened the black box that he had been carrying, extended the bellows and focused his camera.

The first picture would be of the boy. The boy who had led him to Vilcapampa, lost city of the Inca.

But about this Bingham was wrong. When the vines were removed and the tales told, he had discovered not Vilcapampa, but a place even more amazing.

He had stumbled on Machu Picchu, a city lost in time, a city lost in the clouds.

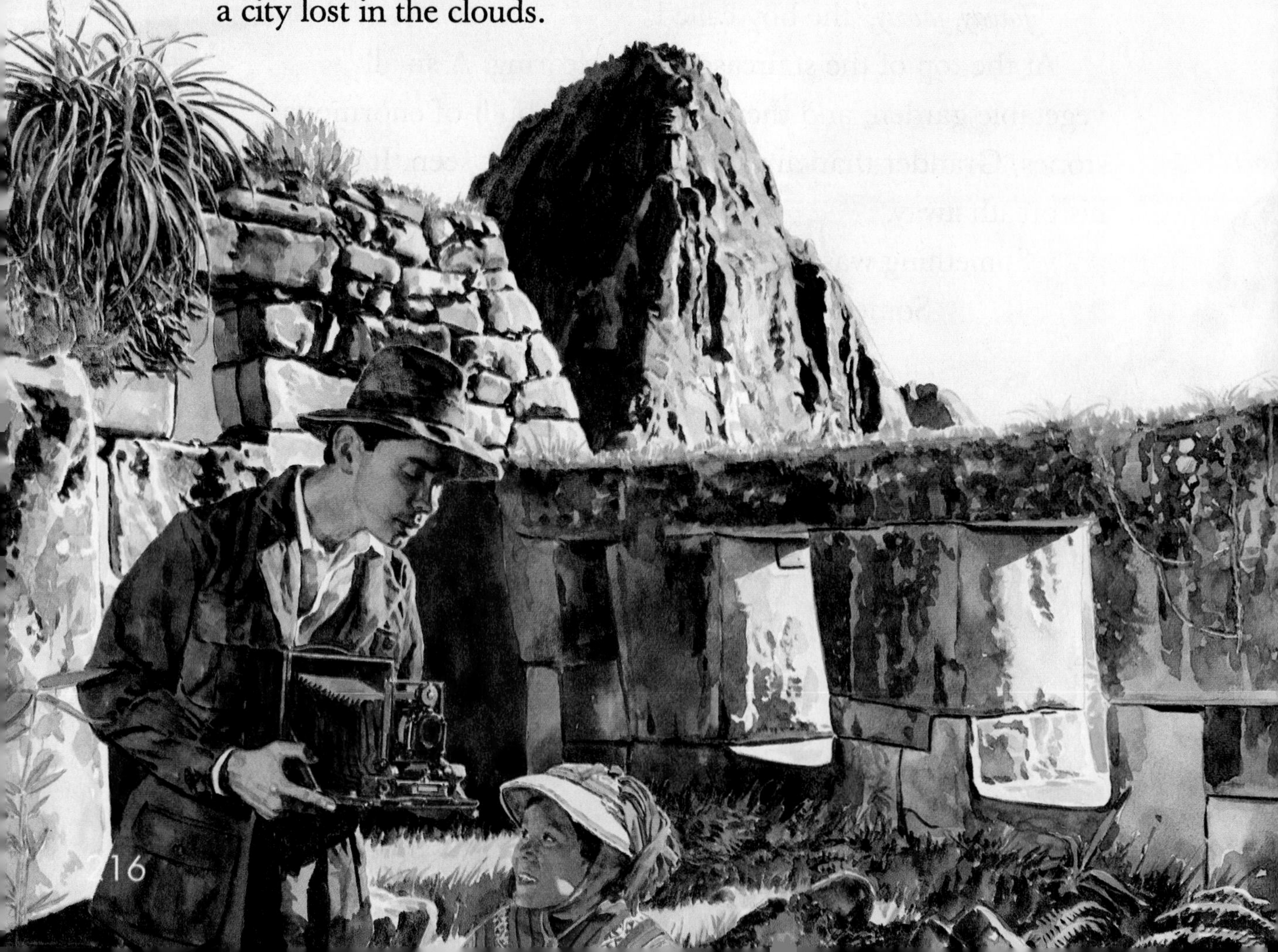

AUTHOR'S NOTE

To research this book on the discovery of Machu Picchu, I first read Hiram Bingham's journal. In it he tells how a little Quechua boy led him to the site in the jungle. Then I traveled to Peru and followed in Hiram's footsteps as closely as I could.

I traveled to Ollantaytambo, as Hiram did, climbed the ancient terraces there, and sat in a little cantina, maybe the very one in which Hiram sat. I walked part of the rugged Inca trail to Pisac, and finally arrived at the Sun Gate above Machu Picchu.

I also journeyed through the sacred valley of the Urubamba River to Machu Picchu, and spent a week exploring and photographing the site and its surrounding cloud forest. And from the high pastures, I witnessed the magical sunset that I tried to capture on the jacket painting.

But the day the story began to come alive in my mind was the day I saw a young Quechua boy who raced our bus 2,500 feet down the mountain from Machu Picchu to the valley below—and won. As he stood, dripping with perspiration and chest heaving with exertion, I thought that Hiram's young guide must have looked just like this boy.

The most exciting part of working on the paintings was re-creating the way Machu Picchu must have looked when Hiram Bingham discovered it, hidden by five hundred years of jungle growth.

—Ted Lewin

Objectives

- Read independently for long periods of time and paraphrase the reading, including the order in which events occur.
- Write responses to texts using details to show understanding.

Envision It! Retell

READING STREET ONLINE
STORY SORT
www.ReadingStreet.com

Think Critically

1. In several ways, this selection is similar to the Unit 4 selection, *Encantado: Pink Dolphin of the Amazon.* Skim the earlier selection found on pages 58–71 in this book. Then discuss what the two selections have in common. **Text to Text**

2. The illustrations in this selection are big and bold, and run across two pages. Why do you think the author used the illustrations in this way? **Think Like an Author**

3. In what ways were Hiram Bingham and the stranger in the boy's dream alike? **Compare and Contrast**

4. The author describes the moment Hiram Bingham first sees Machu Picchu on page 215. Visualize as you reread that part of the selection. Describe what you see, hear, smell, and feel. **Visualize**

5. **Look Back and Write** Look back at pages 208–209. Why do you think Hiram Bingham considered the old stone wall in Cusco to be such a mystery? Provide evidence to support your answer. **TEST PRACTICE** **Extended Response**

Meet the Author

TED LEWIN

Ted Lewin loves to travel. He writes and illustrates books about his trips. For *Lost City*, he hiked the jungle trail to Machu Picchu in Peru. He has also photographed gorillas in Uganda and rhinos in Nepal. He has watched a tiger from an elephant's back in India. And he has been much too close to grizzly bears, rattlesnakes, and bison.

When he travels, Mr. Lewin uses a journal, a sketchbook, photographs, and recordings to help him remember what he sees. His wife, Betsy, comes with him. She is also an artist, and they sometimes write books together.

Mr. Lewin grew up in Buffalo, New York, where he says he had "two brothers, one sister, two parents, a lion, an iguana, a chimpanzee, and an assortment of more conventional pets." The lion stayed only a short time—his mother donated it to the Buffalo Zoo.

Here are other books by Ted and Betsy Lewin.

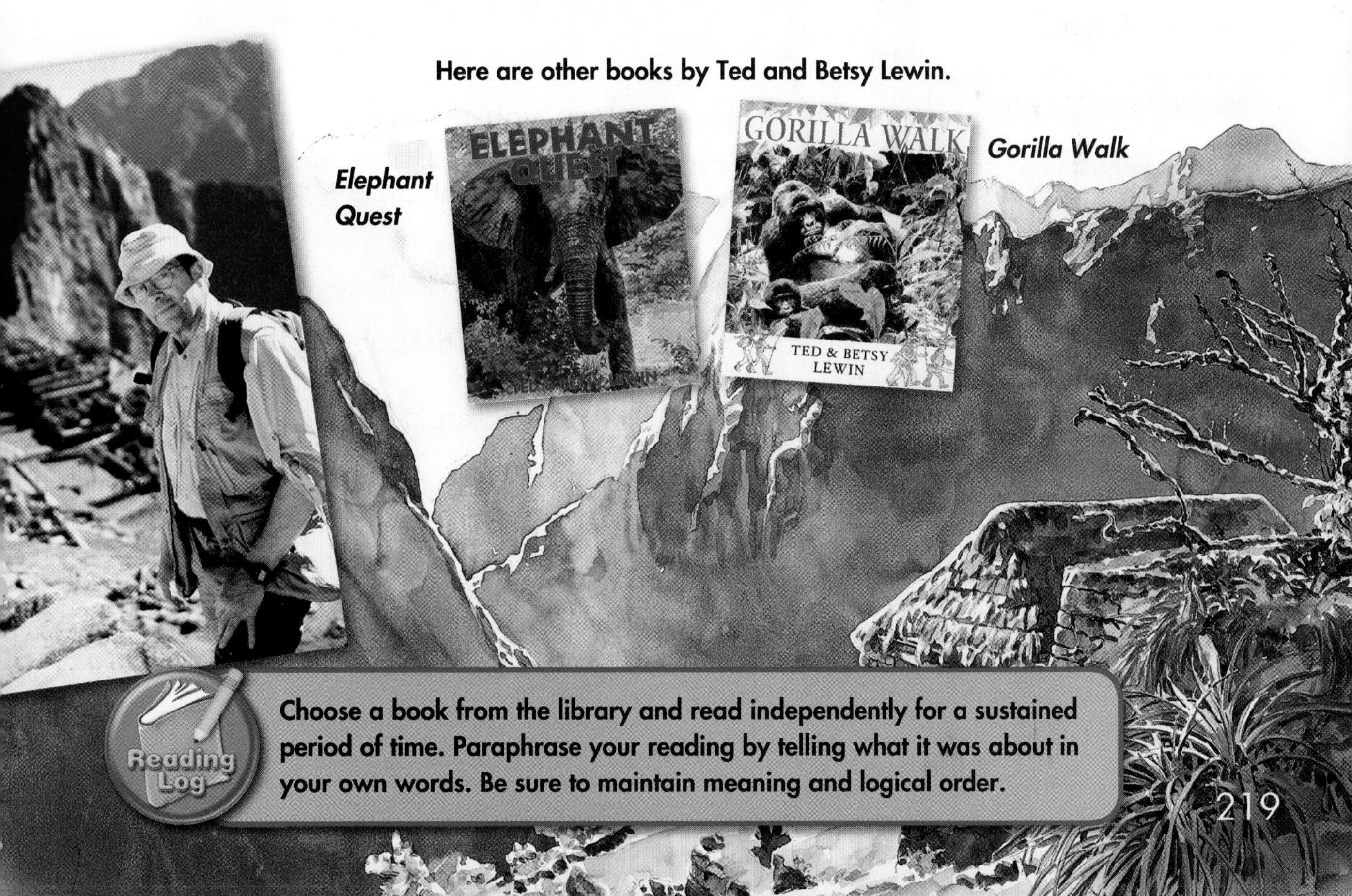

Elephant Quest

Gorilla Walk

Choose a book from the library and read independently for a sustained period of time. Paraphrase your reading by telling what it was about in your own words. Be sure to maintain meaning and logical order.

Objectives
- Write creative stories that build to an ending and contain details about the characters and setting.
- Use and understand adverbs.

Key Features of a Legend

- tells about the great deeds of a hero
- invents or exaggerates the character traits of the hero
- story is often part fact and part fiction

Narrative

Legend

A **legend** is a story about a hero or heroes that may be based on historical events. Legends often put historical figures in fictional situations or give them fictional traits. The student model on the next page is an example of a legend.

Writing Prompt Write a legend about Hiram Bingham and the discovery of Machu Picchu.

Writer's Checklist

Remember, you should . . .

- ✓ create an imaginative story based on historical events.
- ✓ use details to describe fictional traits of a heroic character.
- ✓ include details about the historical setting.
- ✓ build the plot to a climax.
- ✓ use adverbs correctly.

Student Model

The Legend of Hiram Bingham

Tales of Hiram Bingham's daring adventures in Peru are still told throughout the land. Bingham was an explorer who went on a search to find ancient Inca ruins. He traveled hundreds of miles on his quest, climbing steep cliffs, swimming dangerous waters, and hacking his way through thick jungles. Once he fell into a pit of poisonous snakes, but he stayed calm. It is said that Hiram Bingham stopped the snakes from striking just by **threateningly** staring at them. Nothing could stop him.

One day Bingham needed to cross a deep gorge. There was a 1,900-foot drop to a raging river, so Bingham cut down a tree and laid it across the gorge to form a bridge. Then he **casually** strolled across the unsteady tree trunk.

After Bingham had **finally** climbed high in the Andes mountains, he met a young boy who led him to an ancient ruin. There, **completely** covered by jungle vegetation, was the lost city of the Incas—Machu Picchu. At last, Bingham had reached the end of his quest.

Genre Legends often describe historical characters.

Writing Trait Sentences Short, choppy sentences are combined.

Adverbs are used correctly.

Conventions

Adverbs

Remember An **adverb** is a word that modifies a verb, an adjective, or another adverb. Adverbs often tell how, when, where, why, how often, and to what extent.

Objectives

- Explain the difference between a stated and an implied purpose in expository texts.
- Explain information in graphics.
- Make connections between literary and informational texts with similar ideas and support your ideas with details.

Social Studies in Reading

Genre

Personal Essay

- A personal essay is an example of literary nonfiction.
- A personal essay is an account of an individual's experience and is written in the first person.
- The author's purpose is to inform readers, as well as to entertain them. The author may state why he or she is writing the essay or he or she may not state the purpose.
- Read the essay "Riding the Rails to Machu Picchu." Look for elements that make this text a personal essay. What do you think is the author's purpose for writing this essay?

Riding the Rails to Machu Picchu

by Katacha Díaz

High atop one of the Andes Mountains in Peru is one of the greatest human-made wonders of the world—Machu Picchu, the lost city of the Incas. Every year about 400,000 people from around the world make the journey to see this amazing site. Several years ago I was one of them.

Anyone who visits Machu Picchu begins in the city of Cusco. Cusco itself is historic. Founded in the twelfth century by the Incas, it was conquered by an army from Spain in 1533.

There are three ways to get to Machu Picchu from Cusco. You can hike the old Inca Trail, a hard four-day journey. Guides will take you. Tents, food supplies, and anything other than your backpack will be carried by llamas. You can whisk from Cusco to Machu Picchu by helicopter. On this 25-minute trip you will quickly see glorious scenery. Finally, you can take a daily three-hour train ride. I am adventuresome. However, I didn't feel like making the hike! I chose the third way. Journey with me in your mind as I experience Machu Picchu!

Let's Think About...

What do you think was the author's purpose for writing this essay? What evidence supports your idea? **Personal Essay**

As the sun rises over Cusco's red tile rooftops, the train climbs through a series of steep switchback turns, out of the city and into the hillside.

We see tiny villages. People wave at the passing train. We see farmers atop the tin roofs of their cottages or in their fields, spreading corn for the sun to dry. Women and children tend animals nearby. We pass llamas and sheep grazing on grasses and wildflowers. Snaking its way through the Sacred Valley beside the train tracks is the fast-flowing Urubamba River. All around us are the beautiful mountains of the Andes.

Three hours after leaving Cusco, we reach the end of the rails, the train station called Puentes Ruinas. Looking up the mountain from the valley, I can see no evidence that Machu Picchu even exists. To get from the train station to the ruins, visitors can hike up a steep footpath or board buses that will take them to the entrance.

The town of Cusco

Let's Think About...

How does the map present factual information? How does this information help you understand the topic of the essay?
Personal Essay

From the entrance of the ruins, I follow a narrow dirt path and am stunned by what I see. I stop to feast my eyes on the stone city. Nearby a small lizard suns itself on an ancient rock. A large hummingbird sips nectar from a wildflower.

In my mind's eye, I picture Inca women filling ceramic jugs with water from one of the sixteen stone basins. I imagine Inca farmers harvesting crops from the terraces that look like giant steppingstones climbing the steep hillsides.

I walk up narrow flights of stone stairs to the highest point, the Intihuatana. I photograph the stunning sculpture called the Hitching Post of the Sun.

I climb steep steps and cross agricultural terraces to the Watchman's Hut. There I have a view of the entire city. It is spectacular and breathtaking!

In the middle of the afternoon, I must catch the train back to Cusco. I don't want to leave this amazing place. On the train, as I listen to Peruvian flute music, I think about my visit to mysterious Machu Picchu, lost city of the Incas. I remember the morning mist weaving its way through the steep hillsides of jungle. I dream of Inca cities that have not yet been discovered.

There are more adventures to be experienced!

Below: A shepherd tends his flock.

The Hitching Post of the Sun

Let's Think About...

How do you think the author feels about her experience at Machu Picchu? Provide evidence for your answer. **Personal Essay**

Let's Think About...

Reading Across Texts *Lost City* and "Riding the Rails" tell about people who traveled to Machu Picchu. Compare how the authors described these experiences.

Writing Across Texts Make a chart to compare and contrast the two explorers' journeys.

Objectives

- Read aloud grade-level texts and understand what is read.
- Determine the meaning of English words with roots from Greek, Latin, and other languages.
- Explain how the different methods used in media affect the message that is being communicated.
- Use and understand adverbs.

READING STREET ONLINE
ONLINE STUDENT EDITION
www.ReadingStreet.com

Vocabulary

Greek and Latin Roots

Word Structure Breaking a word into parts can help you figure out its meaning. Many English words have Greek or Latin word parts, or roots.

Practice It! The Latin root *terr* means "land." Turn to *Lost City: The Discovery of Machu Picchu*, pages 208 and 210. Look for words with the root *terr*. Write the words. Use the meaning of the Latin root to help you determine the meanings of the words. Then write a definition for each word. Check your definitions in a dictionary.

Fluency

Appropriate Phrasing

Reading aloud with proper phrasing shows that you understand what you are reading. Look for words that make sense together. Then read the phrase as a group of words.

Practice It! With your partner, practice reading aloud *Lost City: The Discovery of Machu Picchu*, page 212, paragraphs 3–6. As you read, look for words that go together in each sentence. Read the words in the phrase together as a group.

When you give a talk, speak clearly and provide details about your topic. Use adverbs correctly.

Media Literacy

Radio Announcement

In a radio announcement, an announcer broadcasts information about a certain topic. The purpose of an announcement is to inform listeners or to persuade them.

Practice It! Work with a partner to create a short radio announcement to recruit volunteers for an archaeology expedition. Speak as if you are at the site of Machu Picchu. Describe what the place looks like. Give instructions on how listeners can volunteer. Use persuasive words and expressive tones in your announcement. Record your announcement and play it for the class.

Tips

- When recording anything for radio, think about what kind of sound effects will attract the attention of your listeners.
- Consider creating sounds that remind listeners of the jungle. Birds chirping and monkeys chattering are sounds that will make listeners think it would be fun to join the expedition.
- Speak in short, quick sentences. Try to sound as if you are hiking up the mountain. You want to convince the audience to sign up.
- Use a tone of voice that will persuade listeners.

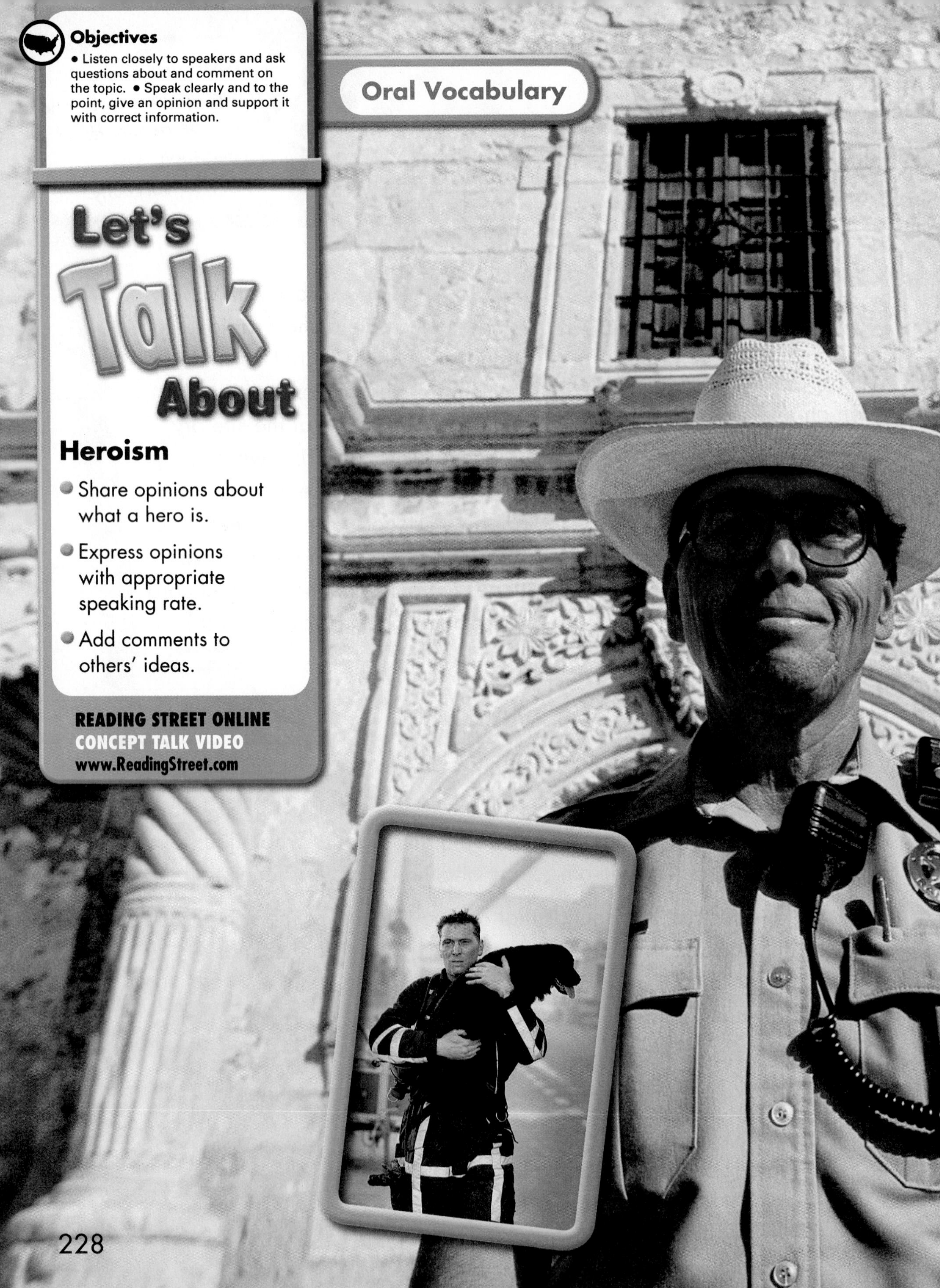

Objectives

- Listen closely to speakers and ask questions about and comment on the topic.
- Speak clearly and to the point, give an opinion and support it with correct information.

Oral Vocabulary

Let's Talk About

Heroism

- Share opinions about what a hero is.
- Express opinions with appropriate speaking rate.
- Add comments to others' ideas.

READING STREET ONLINE
CONCEPT TALK VIDEO
www.ReadingStreet.com

You've learned
2 2 0
Amazing Words
so far this year!

Objectives

- Understand that a story's theme is its central message or lesson.
- Tell the order of events in a story, summarize the events, and explain how they will influence future events in the story.

Envision It! Skill Strategy

Skill

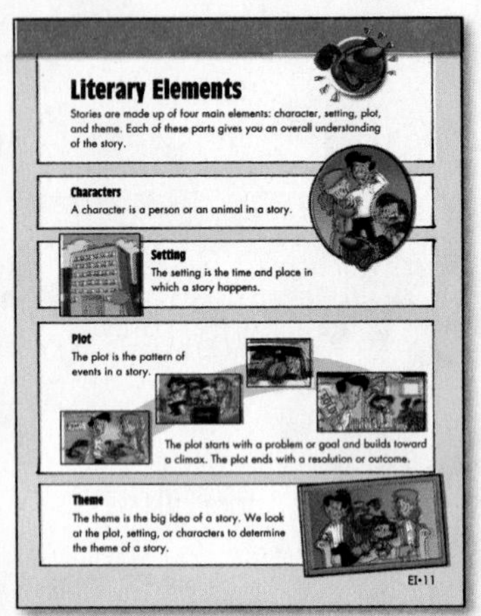

Literary Elements

Stories are made up of four main elements: character, setting, plot, and theme. Each of these parts gives you an overall understanding of the story.

Characters

A character is a person or an animal in a story.

Setting

The setting is the time and place in which a story happens.

Plot

The plot is the pattern of events in a story.

The plot starts with a problem or goal and builds toward a climax. The plot ends with a resolution or outcome.

Theme

The theme is the big idea of a story. We look at the plot, setting, or characters to determine the theme of a story.

EI•11

Strategy

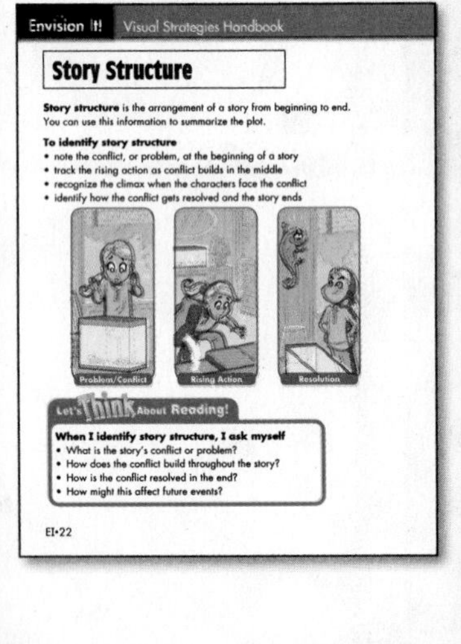

Envision It! Visual Strategies Handbook

Story Structure

Story structure is the arrangement of a story from beginning to end. You can use this information to summarize the plot.

To identify story structure

- note the conflict, or problem, at the beginning of a story
- track the rising action as conflict builds in the middle
- recognize the climax when the characters face the conflict
- identify how the conflict gets resolved and the story ends

Let's Think About Reading!

When I identify story structure, I ask myself

- What is the story's conflict or problem?
- How does the conflict build throughout the story?
- How is the conflict resolved in the end?
- How might this affect future events?

EI•22

READING STREET ONLINE
ENVISION IT! ANIMATIONS
www.ReadingStreet.com

Comprehension Skill

Literary Elements: Character, Plot, and Theme

- **Characters** are the people in a story. Readers learn about characters by what they say and how they act.
- A **plot** is the sequence of events in a story. Events that happen in the story move the plot forward.
- A story's **theme** is the most important idea. When you finish reading, ask yourself *What does this story mean? What is it all about?*
- Use the graphic to identify the characters, plot, and theme of "A Family Just Like Ours."

Character	Plot	Theme

Comprehension Strategy

Story Structure

Readers pay attention to story structure, or how a fictional story is put together. As you read, notice how the story begins, how it builds through the middle, and how it ends. Events that take place throughout the story move the plot to its logical conclusion.

A Family Just Like Ours

Madeline rolled over in her sleeping bag. Blinking, she looked at her mom, wide awake and curled up in a sleeping bag in their tent. "Good morning, Maddy."

"Morning, Mom."

Maddy and her mother left their tent in Grand Teton National Park, Wyoming. Maddy peeked into her dad and brother's tent. She could hear snoring.

"Let's let them sleep. How about a walk?" Mom whispered, handing Maddy a water bottle.

They trekked past the edge of the campsite. Suddenly, Mom stopped. She touched Maddy lightly on the shoulder, put her finger against her lips as a sign for quiet, and pointed toward the stream.

There stood a huge bull moose with a giant rack of antlers, a smaller female moose, and a baby moose. The mother moose walked into the stream, nudging the baby moose along with her. The baby moose splashed in the water, just like Maddy's little brother might have done.

The mother moose must have heard Maddy laugh. Turning her head, the moose looked in their direction. The father moose began herding his family away.

Skill Describe the interactions of the characters and their relationships.

Strategy What events have happened so far? Explain how the mother's sign for quiet results in the next event in the plot.

Skill What is this story about? Summarize the story's theme. Have the characters changed? Explain.

Your Turn!

Need a Review? See the *Envision It! Handbook* for help with literary elements and story structure.

Ready to Try It? To enhance your comprehension, establish your own purpose for reading *Cliff Hanger*.

Objectives

- Determine the meanings of unfamiliar words or multiple-meaning words by using the context of the sentence.

Envision It! Words to Know

coil

rappel

ridge

descent
foresaw
shaft
trekked
void

READING STREET ONLINE
VOCABULARY ACTIVITIES
www.ReadingStreet.com

Vocabulary Strategy for

Unfamiliar Words

Context Clues Sometimes you can use context clues, or the words in sentences around an unfamiliar word, to help you figure out its meaning.

1. Read the words and sentences around the unfamiliar word to see if the author has given you a definition of the word.
2. If not, say what the sentence means in your own words.
3. Predict a meaning for the unfamiliar word.
4. Try that meaning in the sentence to see if it makes sense.
5. If the context clues don't help, you can look up the word in a glossary or dictionary.

As you read "Climbing New Heights," use context clues to help you figure out the meanings of this week's *Words to Know.*

Words to Write Reread "Climbing New Heights." Imagine that Mr. Dunn is coming to speak to your class. Make a list of questions that you would like to ask him about his experiences mountain climbing. Use words from the *Words to Know* list in your questions.

George Dunn has trekked across flat glaciers and climbed steep mountains for more than thirty years. He grew up in an area around Seattle, Washington. George's parents foresaw their son's lifelong passion to climb up and rappel down mountains.

Dunn is never happier than when facing a ridge of mountains in the distance with a coil of rope over his shoulder. George has climbed to the top of Mount Rainier more times than any other human (480 summits and counting), and he has made a descent from some of the highest peaks in the world. Some of his favorite places to climb are the Swiss Alps and the peaks of Peru.

Dunn likes to share his knowledge and enjoyment of mountain climbing, rock climbing, rappelling, and ice climbing with others. He is an expert guide, and he helps train amateur climbers so that they can experience the feeling of sitting on top of the world. But climbing can be dangerous. Dunn teaches safety and responsibility too. He does not want his students falling into a void between two rocks or down a shaft of a glacier.

Your Turn!

Need a Review? For help with using context clues to determine the meanings of unfamiliar words, see *Words!*

Ready to Try It? Read *Cliff Hanger* on pp. 234–245.

JEAN CRAIGHEAD GEORGE

ILLUSTRATED BY WENDELL MINOR

Cliff Hanger

Realistic fiction tells about events that could really happen. To enhance your comprehension, think about your own desired outcome for reading this story and establish your purpose for reading it.

Question of the Week
What does it take to be a hero?

Axel washed his tin cup at the hand pump outside the Teton Mountains Climbing School hut and looked up. A storm cloud darkened Death Canyon. Lightning flashed. Axel was glad he wasn't rock climbing now.

"Axel!"

Two mountain climbers ran down the trail. "Your dog followed us up the mountain," one of the women said. "We had to leave him at the top of Cathedral Wall."

"You left Grits?" Axel was upset.

"That storm's bad," she said looking over her shoulder. "We had to get out of there."

Axel's father, Dag, the leader of the school, heard the news. He closed the registration book and stepped outside.

Lightning exploded.

Dag counted slowly.

". . . thirty-eight, thirty-nine, forty. . . ."

"A mile for every five counts," Dag said. "The storm's eight miles away. We've got enough time to get Grits."

Dag put on his belt, which jangled with climbing nuts and carabiners, and shouldered his rope and backpack.

Axel looked at his dad. "Thanks," he said, and put on his own mountain-climbing gear.

Axel and Dag trekked steadily up the wooded trails, climbed over rock avalanches, and finally arrived at the bottom of the shaft of rock that is Cathedral Wall. A lightning bolt split open the black cloud.

"One, two, three ..."

Kaboom.

"The storm's only a half mile away," Dag said. "Too close. We'd better wait it out here."

From high on the wall came a howl. Axel looked up.

"Look! Grits got down to Monkey Ledge. If he tries to come on down, he'll fall. Let's go."

"No," said Dag. "We can't make that climb. It's too difficult. We'll go back to the trail split and up the ridge."

"That'll take too long," Axel said. "I can do it." He tied the rope to his belt and placed his foot in a crack. He reached up.

Dag had no choice. His son was climbing. He picked up the top coil of Axel's rope and took a deep breath.

"Think out your moves," he said, wrapping the rope around his waist and bracing his foot against a rock.

"On belay," he called out.

"Climbing!" Axel answered.

Axel climbed slowly, from crack to crack to ledge to crack, moving like a ballet dancer. His father let out rope as he climbed.

When Axel was fifteen feet up, he jammed a climber's nut securely into a crack. He clipped a carabiner into the nut, and his rope in the carabiner. He relaxed. If he fell now, the nut, the carabiner, and his dad would stop him from plunging to his death. He climbed on.

Axel looked up. Grits was crouched on the ledge, about to jump to him. "Stay!" Axel yelled.

Splats of rain hit the wall. Axel climbed very carefully. Using the tips of his fingers and the edges of his climbing shoes, he pulled himself upward until his hand found the rim of Monkey Ledge. The next move was dangerous. Climbers had fallen here.

Thinking clearly, Axel placed both hands firmly on the ledge and concentrated. Slowly he pressed on them. His body rose. When his arms were straight, he placed his right foot beside his right hand, then his left foot beside his left hand.

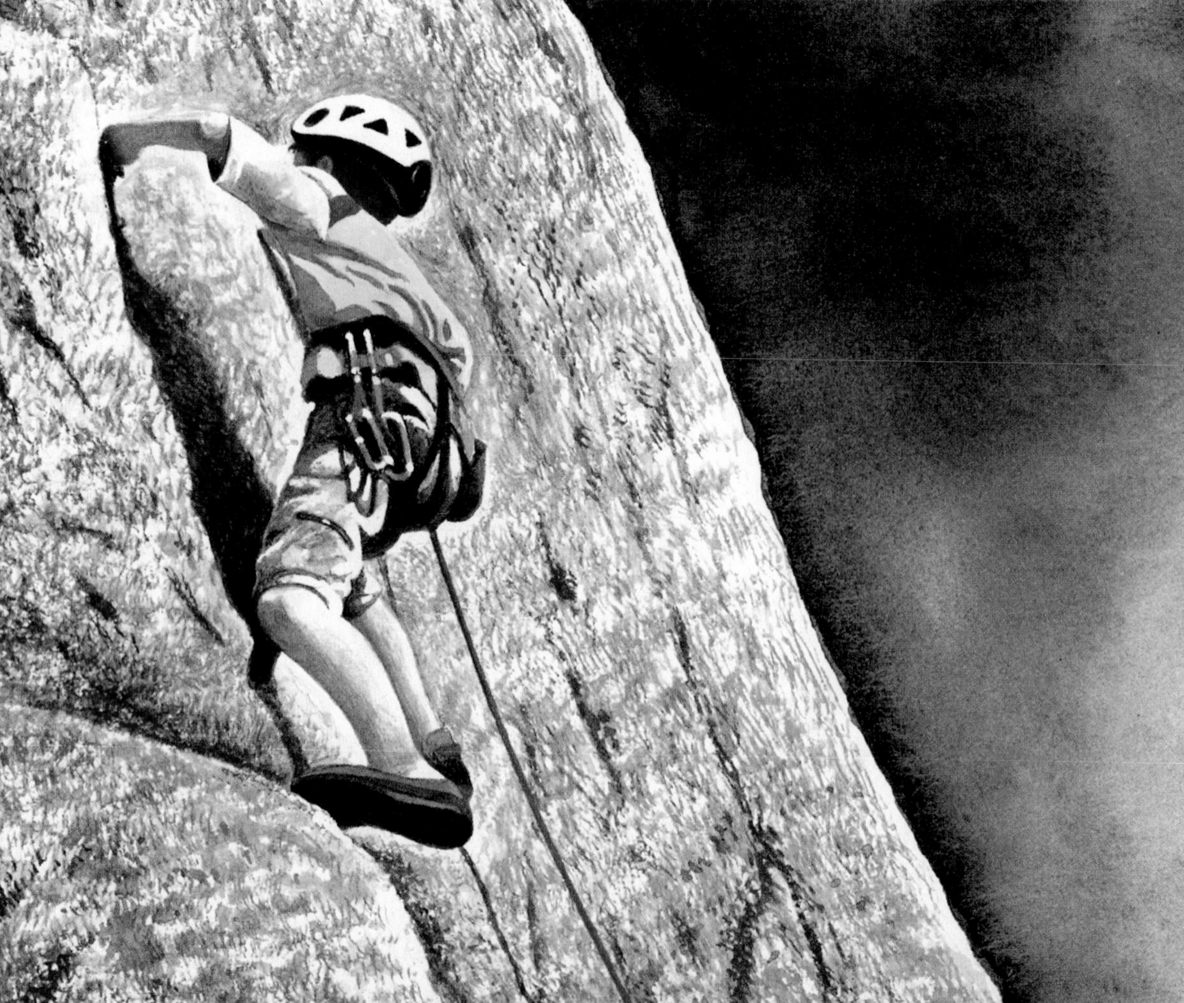

Bent like a hairpin, he found his balance and stood up. Grits wagged his tail but did not move. He was scared.

Lightning buzzed across the sky.

"One . . ."

KABOOM. Grits shivered.

"A quarter mile away."

Axel put a nut and carabiner in the wall and roped himself to them. He sat down beside Grits and breathed a sigh of relief. Grits was safe.

Axel picked up his little dog and hugged him.

The cloud opened, and rain poured down. Grits whimpered.

"It's all right," Axel whispered into his fur. "It's all right."

The sky flashed. *KABOOM!*

"No count," said Axel. "It's here, Grits. We're right in the center of the storm." Crackling electricity lifted the hair straight up on Axel's head and arms. The air hummed. Sparks snapped from his ears to the rocks.

He hugged Grits closer.

Flash.

". . . seven, eight, nine, ten . . ."

Kaboom.

"Two miles," said Axel. "The storm's going away."

Axel took a dog harness from his pocket and slipped it over Grits's head and shoulders.

The rain stopped. The sun came out. Axel picked up Grits and eased him over the edge of the ledge. Grits clawed the air.

"Dog on belay!" he called to his dad. Slowly Axel let out the rope, lowering Grits down through space.

"Got him!" Dag finally shouted, and looked up. "Axel," he shouted, "when you double your rope to rappel, you'll only have enough rope to get halfway down."

"I know it, but it's OK. I see a good ledge where the rope will end."

Axel wrapped the rope around an outcrop and clipped it to his harness. Then he put his back to the void and leaned out. Holding one end of the rope, letting out the other, he jumped out, dropped, caught himself, jumped out, dropped, caught himself.

And then he came to the end of the rope.

The planned route was still ten feet below.

Dag saw the problem. He studied the wall.

"If you can swing out to your left," he said quietly, "you'll find a good route."

Axel swung across the face of the wall. He reached but could not find a handhold near the route. He swung back. Dag foresaw a disaster.

"Stay where you are," he said. "I'm going for help."

"It'll be too dark," Axel answered. "I'll try again."

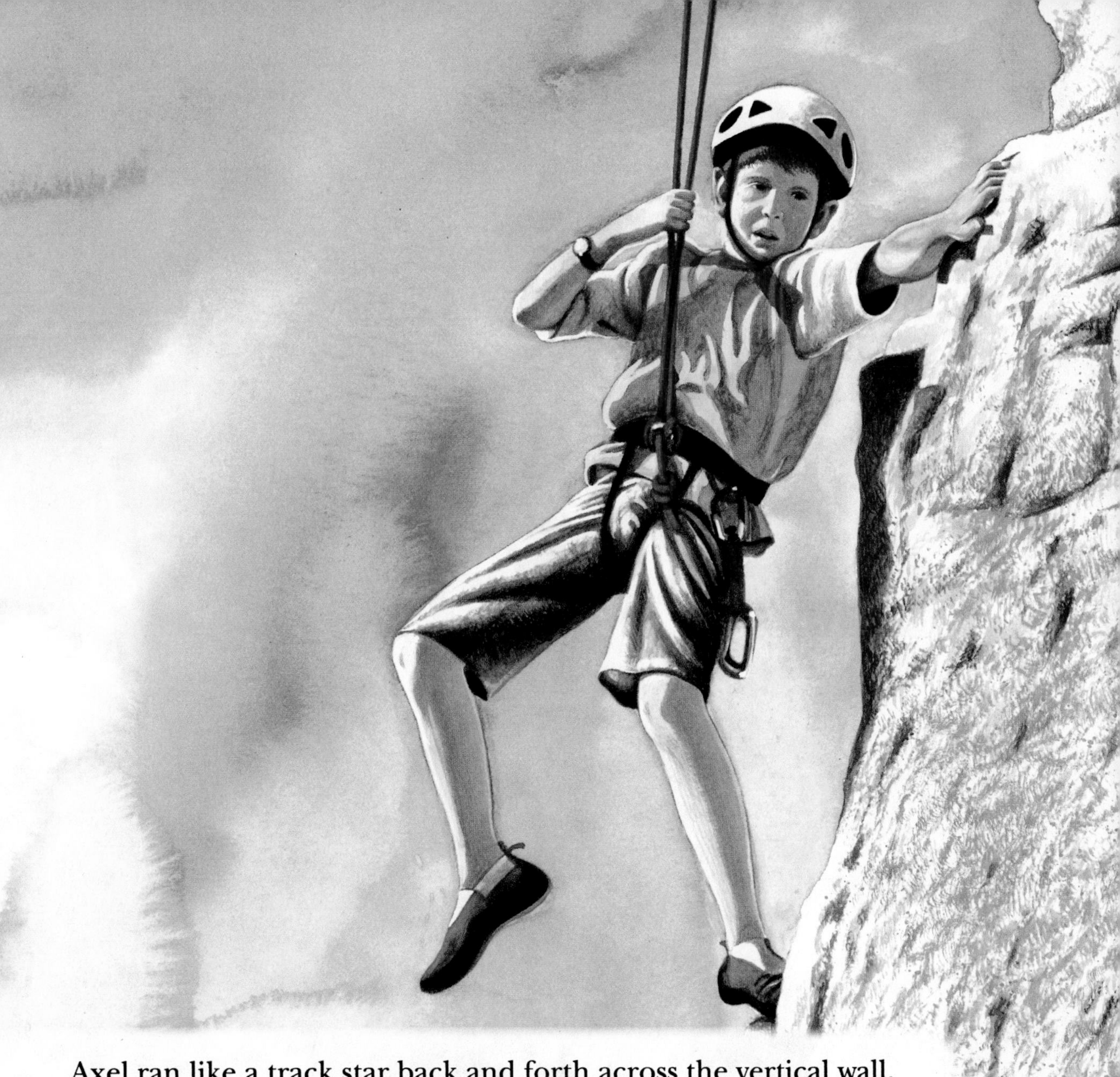

Axel ran like a track star back and forth across the vertical wall, back and forth. He swung wider and wider. When he was over Dag's route, he jammed his fist in a crack. He did not swing back.

Axel forced his toes into another crack. When he was secure and firmly balanced, he untied the rope from his waist, pulled it from the boulder on Monkey Ledge, and let it fall to his dad.

No nut, carabiner, or rope was there to save him if he made a mistake. From this moment on, he must free climb.

He began his descent.

Dag watched. The old pro said not one word, for fear of breaking his son's concentration.

When Axel was three feet from the ground, he whooped and jumped down to his father.

"Did it!"

"That was so close, I can't talk about it," Dag said. There was a flash in the canyon. Axel hugged Grits.

". . . twenty-one, twenty-two, twenty-thr—" *Kaboom!*

"The storm's at the hut," Dag said. "Let's wait it out here. I'm beat." He lit his small gas stove and made soup with clear stream water and instant mix. He poured some into a cup for Axel.

"I'll bet Grits sleeps well tonight," Dag said when he finally relaxed. "He was one scared dog."

"I don't know about Grits," Axel answered. "But I was sure scared. I thought I had lost my friend forever."

Objectives

- Read independently for long periods of time and paraphrase the reading, including the order in which events occur.
- Write responses to texts using details to show understanding.

Envision It! Retell

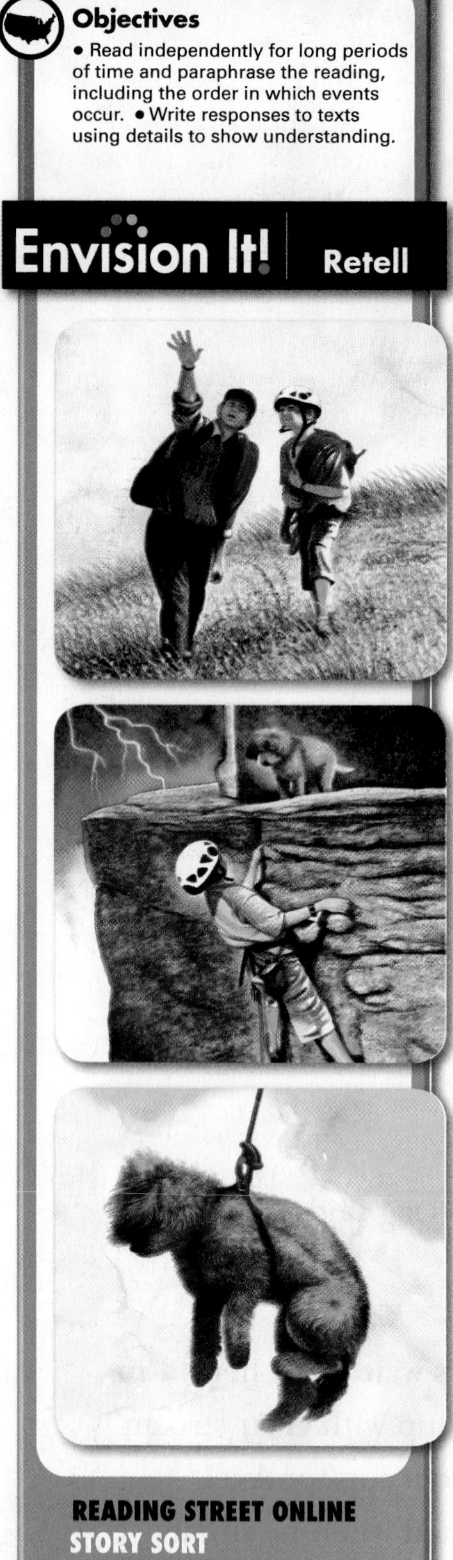

READING STREET ONLINE
STORY SORT
www.ReadingStreet.com

Think Critically

1. The willingness to take risks is an important quality of heroic people. Think of a real-life hero you've seen interviewed on TV or read about in a newspaper. What qualities does that person have that make him or her a hero? Explain. **Text to World**

2. On pages 240–241, the author tries to give readers a sense of how dangerous mountain climbing can be, particularly during a storm. How does the author make you feel like you are with Axel on his adventure? Find sample sentences that made you feel this way. **Think Like an Author**

3. What do the actions and words of Axel and his dad tell you about their relationship? **Literary Elements**

4. In this story, one event leads to the next event. Why do you think that this type of structure is important in the telling of Axel's adventure? **Story Structure**

5. **Look Back and Write** Look back at pages 238–239. How can you tell that Axel is an experienced mountain climber? Provide evidence to support your answer. **TEST PRACTICE Extended Response**

Meet the Author

Jean Craighead George

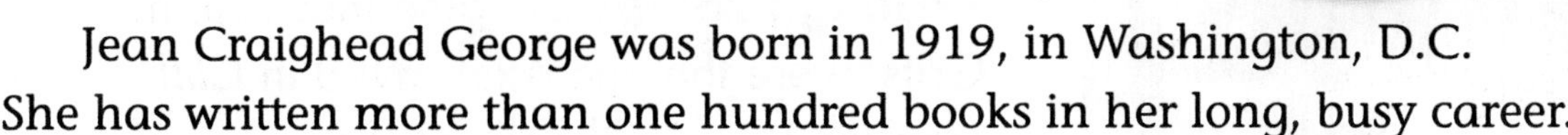

Jean Craighead George was born in 1919, in Washington, D.C. She has written more than one hundred books in her long, busy career.

When Ms. George was a young girl, her father would take her to the Potomac River to learn about plants and animals. Her father, an entomologist and ecologist, taught her how to identify the edible plants along the river and how to make homemade fish-hooks and lean-tos to sleep in. Ms. George cherished these trips with her father. She says she had "a glorious childhood."

Her trips with her father into the wilderness inspired many of her books, including the award-winning *My Side of the Mountain* and *Julie of the Wolves*. She says, "Children are still in love with nature, and I am too." Ms. George's advice to young writers is to "read, write, and talk to people, hear their knowledge, hear their problems. Be a good listener. The rest will come."

Here are other books by Jean Craighead George.

Choose a book from the library and read independently for a sustained period of time. Record your reading by paraphrasing in a logical order what you have read. Be sure what you write maintains meaning.

Objectives

- Write letters for a specific reader and reason using a style that is suited to the situation.
- Use and understand adjectives and their special forms.
- Use and understand adverbs.

Key Features of a Thank-You Note

- uses letter format
- has a friendly tone
- explains why the writer feels grateful

READING STREET ONLINE
GRAMMAR JAMMER
www.ReadingStreet.com

Expository

Thank-You Note

A **thank-you note** is a friendly letter that expresses thanks for a thoughtful act or gift. The student model on the next page is an example of a thank-you note.

Writing Prompt Imagine that you, not Grits, were the one Axel saved in *Cliff Hanger.* Write a thank-you note to your friend for his help.

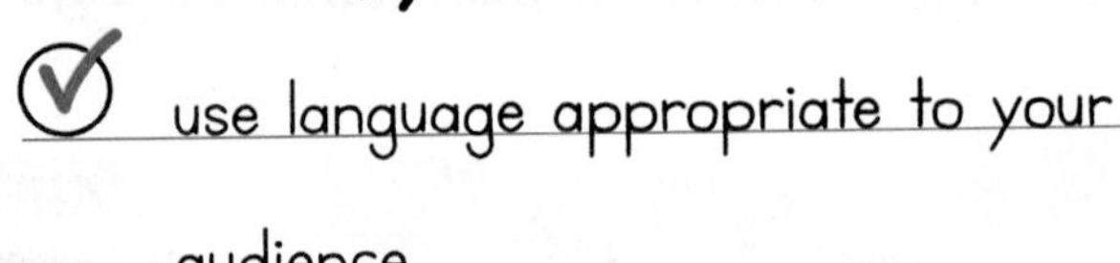

Remember, you should ...

- ✓ use language appropriate to your audience.
- ✓ include a date, salutation, body, closing, and signature.
- ✓ describe the event and how you feel about your friend's actions.
- ✓ use comparative and superlative adjectives and adverbs correctly.

Student Model

August 20, 20_ _

Dear Axel,

Getting stuck on that rock ledge was the **scariest** moment of my life! I was so relieved when you began to climb up to help me, but then I got even **more scared** as I worried about the dangerous climb you were making for me. I knew that the climb was even **more difficult** because of the stormy weather. I was so happy to see that goofy grin of yours when you pulled yourself up onto my ledge—that was the **most welcoming** sight I had ever seen. You were so calm and assured that my crippling fears immediately started to fade.

Your skill and tireless bravery completely carried the day. You saved my life, Axel, and I'll never forget your courage.

Your friend for life,
Tim

Genre Thank-you notes include a date and salutation.

Comparative and superlative adjectives and adverbs are used correctly.

Writing Trait Word Choice Exact words paint a visual picture.

Conventions

Comparatives and Superlatives

Remember Comparative adjectives compare two nouns. **Comparative adverbs** compare two verbs. **Superlatives** compare three or more nouns or verbs.

Objectives

- Compare how different writing styles are used to communicate different kinds of information on the Internet.

21st Century Skills
INTERNET GUY

Online Sources What is the first thing to do at a new Web site? Find out who wrote the information. Use the "About This Site" button. Is the site reliable?

- Online sources, such as Web sites, can be found on the Internet. Some sources are more reliable than others.
- Web addresses that end in *.gov* (government), *.edu* (education), or *.org* (organization) are usually reliable. Sites that end in *.com* (commercial) may be less so.
- Compare the language in a Web-based article to language written in an e-mail.
- Read "Rock Climbing." Think of the steps you must follow to find reliable Web sites.

ROCK CLIMBING

by Ron Fridell

Some rocks are easier to climb than others. Learning more about the different types of rocks can improve your rock-climbing technique. Suppose you are searching the Internet for information on different types of rocks. Which of the following Web sites might be useful for your report? As you examine the sites, note the source of the information as well as the description.

When you look at this link, you see that it is a *.com* Web site. The letters *com* are short for *commercial*. A *.com* site often sells things or contains ads. It may or may not be reliable. Right away you see that this site is about a different kind of "rock," so it will not be useful to you.

File Edit View Favorites Tools Help
http://www.url.here
Search Engine
different types of rocks
Search
Music that Rocks
These great albums will make you glad you love real rockin' music like we do!
www.website_here.com
The Art Museum: Painting on Rocks
This lively art project starts with a field trip to collect unusual-looking rocks to turn into colorful art objects.
www.website_here.org
Leedburg University – All About Rocks and Minerals
Rocks are divided into three types, depending on how they were formed.
www.website_here.edu

This is a *.org* Web site. The letters *org* are short for *organization*. A *.org* site is usually reliable. After reading the description, you decide that this site is not useful because you are not doing an art project about rocks.

This is a *.edu* Web site, short for *education*. A *.edu* site is usually a school or university and is often reliable. Both the source and description tell you that this site should be useful.

You click on the Leedburg University link to connect to the Web site. The following information appears on your screen:

ALL ABOUT ROCKS AND MINERALS

The entire Earth is made of rocks and minerals, inside and out. Inside is a super-hot core of liquid rock. Outside is a hard crust made of rocks and minerals. Rocks are divided into three types, depending on how they were formed: igneous, sedimentary, and metamorphic. Learn more here:

Igneous Rocks
Sedimentary Rocks
Metamorphic Rocks
The Earth's Crust
The Rock Cycle
Identifying Minerals
Rock Collecting Tools
Collecting Locations
Famous Rock Formations
Links to Rock & Mineral Web Sites

A mountain you want to climb is made of granite (igneous rock), so you click on that link. A new window opens with the following information on p. 253.

You take notes on igneous rocks for your climbing report. Then you go to the links on sedimentary and metamorphic rocks. After that you search other sources for more information on types of rocks, taking notes as you go. During your search, you take care to evaluate the sources of information you find.

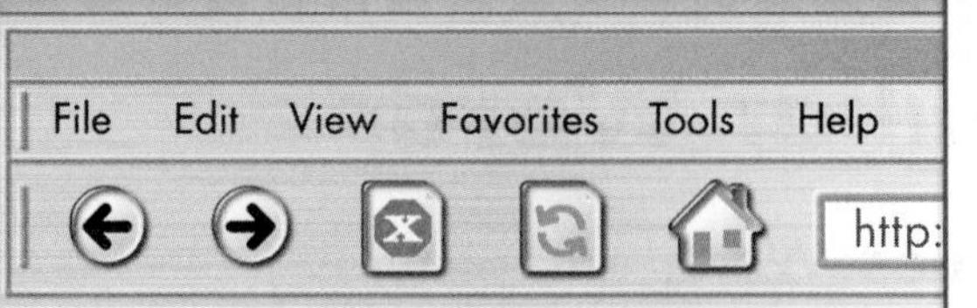

IGNEOUS ROCKS

Igneous rocks form when molten lava, also known as magma, cools and becomes solid rock. This magma comes from deep within Earth's core.

When magma cools and hardens inside the crust, it turns into hard rock called granite. Most mountains are made of granite.

When magma reaches Earth's surface and flows out, it becomes lava, a fiery liquid that flows down the sides of volcanoes. When this lava cools quickly, it becomes a smooth, glassy rock called obsidian.

for more practice

Evaluate online sources about rocks.

21st Century Skills Online Activity

Log on and follow the step-by-step directions for evaluating reliable Web sites about different types of rocks.

Objectives

- Determine the meanings of unfamiliar words or multiple-meaning words by using the context of the sentence.
- Follow and give instructions and state instructions in your own words.
- Read aloud grade-level texts and understand what is read.
- Use and understand adjectives and their special forms.
- Listen closely to speakers and ask questions about and comment on the topic.

READING STREET ONLINE
ONLINE STUDENT EDITION
www.ReadingStreet.com

Vocabulary

Unfamiliar Words

Context Clues Words and pictures near an unfamiliar word can give clues to its meaning. Use these context clues to understand the meaning of unfamiliar words.

Practice It! Find the word *harness* in the first sentence on page 242 in *Cliff Hanger*. Use the picture to help you understand what a *harness* is. Rewrite the sentence using another word to replace *harness*.

Fluency

Expression

Partner Reading
Change the volume of your voice as you read. It makes a story more interesting. Reading a character's shouted dialogue in a loud voice and a character's whispered dialogue in a soft voice adds to the story's excitement.

Practice It! With a partner, read aloud page 238 in *Cliff Hanger*. Take turns reading the dialogue, with one partner reading Dag's words and the other reading Axel's words. Read loudly or softly to match the action in the story.

Listening and Speaking

When you listen to a presentation, ask thoughtful questions.

How-to Demonstration

A how-to demonstration uses words and pictures to describe how to make an item or how to do an activity. The purpose of a how-to demonstration is to teach others how to complete an activity or perform a task.

Practice It! With a partner, design a demonstration on how to rock climb based on *Cliff Hanger*. List the steps to follow and equipment to use. Create drawings or diagrams to support your demonstration. Present your demonstration to the class. Ask your listeners to restate the oral instructions. Restate any steps if necessary.

Tips

Listening . . .

- Ask the speaker to restate any oral instructions that are unclear, such as "Please restate the sequence of action for rappeling."
- Be ready to ask relevant questions that are about the topic, such as "How much does the equipment weigh?"

Speaking . . .

- Give clear instructions in each step.
- Restate any oral instructions that are unclear.
- Use comparative and superlative adjectives correctly.

Teamwork . . .

- Ask and answer questions with detail.

Objectives

- Take part in discussions led by teachers or other students, ask and answer questions, and offer ideas that build on the ideas of other people.

Oral Vocabulary

Let's Talk About

Adaptations to Harsh Climates

- Describe an extreme climate with detail. Tell as much as you can about what you can see, hear, and feel.
- Ask questions with appropriate detail about ideas on how to survive there. Be specific about what you want to know. For example, "Is water available?"

READING STREET ONLINE
CONCEPT TALK VIDEO
www.ReadingStreet.com

You've learned
2 3 0
Amazing Words
so far this year!

Objectives

• Summarize the main idea and supporting details. • Use text features to understand the text and to locate information.

Envision It! | **Skill Strategy**

Skill

Envision It! Visual Skills Handbook

Main Idea and Details

Main idea is the most important idea about a topic. Details support the main idea.

EI•12

Strategy

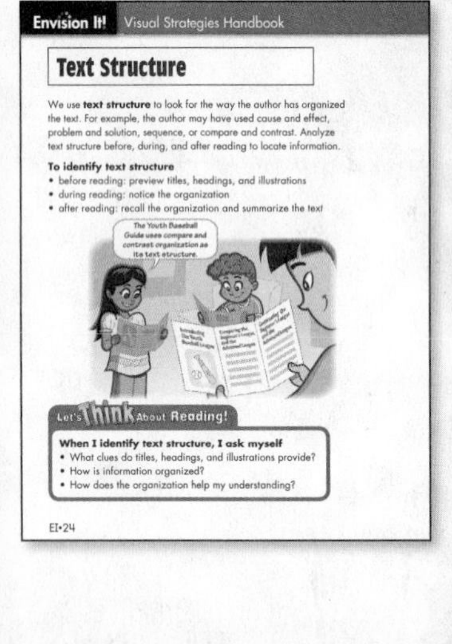

Envision It! Visual Strategies Handbook

Text Structure

We use **text structure** to look for the way the author has organized the text. For example, the author may have used cause and effect, problem and solution, sequence, or compare and contrast. Analyze text structure before, during, and after reading to locate information.

To identify text structure

- before reading: preview titles, headings, and illustrations
- during reading: notice the organization
- after reading: recall the organization and summarize the text

The Youth Baseball Guide uses compare and contrast organization as its text structure.

Let's Think About Reading!

When I identify text structure, I ask myself

- What clues do titles, headings, and illustrations provide?
- How is information organized?
- How does the organization help my understanding?

EI•24

READING STREET ONLINE
ENVISION IT! ANIMATIONS
www.ReadingStreet.com

Comprehension Skill

Main Idea and Details

- A topic is what a piece of writing is about.
- The main idea is the most important idea about the topic.
- Supporting details give information about the main idea.
- Use the graphic organizer to summarize both main ideas and supporting details as you read "Glaciers and Icebergs."

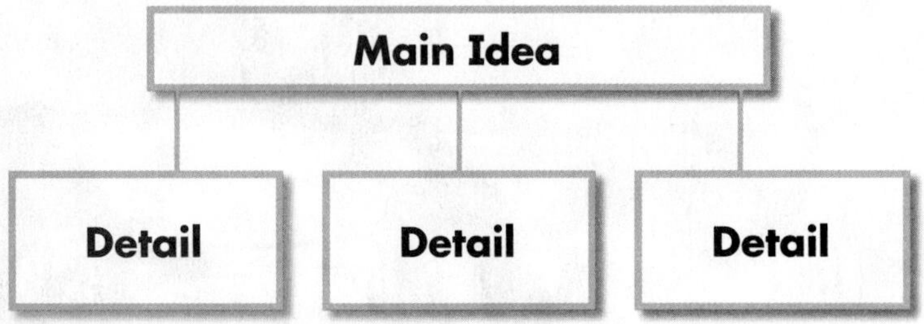
Main Idea
Detail
Detail
Detail

Comprehension Strategy

Text Structure

Text structure helps readers understand what they read. For example, a nonfiction article may compare and contrast two things, put events in sequence, or be a series of main ideas. When you preview, look for text features such as headings, guide words in bold print, and underlined words to help you know what to expect.

Glaciers and Icebergs

Glaciers and icebergs are both made of ice and are both very large.

Glaciers Glaciers are huge pieces of ice that are on land. They are found in areas where there is steady snowfall. Glaciers form when more snow falls than melts away over the years. The leftover snow slowly recrystallizes to form ice.

Skill Summarize the main idea of this paragraph. Summarize the details that support that idea.

Types of Glaciers There are two types of glaciers. Mountain glaciers move down the sides of mountains. Ice sheets, on the other hand, form on level ground and spread out in all directions. The continent of Antarctica is covered by a huge ice sheet.

Strategy Which text structure is used in this paragraph? How can you tell?
A. sequence
B. compare and contrast
C. main ideas

Icebergs Some glaciers or ice sheets go all the way to the seashore. As the ice reaches the shore, a part of it may break off and fall into the sea. This huge piece of ice, now floating in the ocean, is called an iceberg. About 10,000 icebergs each year come from the glaciers that cover Greenland.

Strategy Explain where you would find information about kinds of glaciers. What text feature tells you?

Your Turn!

Need a Review? See the *Envision It! Handbook* for help with main idea and details and text structure.

Ready to Try It? Use what you've learned about main ideas and details as you read *Antarctic Journal.*

Objectives

- Determine the meaning of English words with prefixes from Greek, Latin, and other languages.

Envision It! Words to Know

continent

depart

icebergs

anticipation

convergence

forbidding

heaves

READING STREET ONLINE
VOCABULARY ACTIVITIES
www.ReadingStreet.com

Vocabulary Strategy for

Greek and Latin Prefixes

Word Structure Many English academic vocabulary words have Latin or Greek prefixes. The Latin prefix *de-* means "away from" and appears in words such as *defrost.* The prefix *con-* means "with" or "together," as in *connect.* The Greek prefix *geo-* means "of the earth's surface" and *pan-* means "all." You can use what you know about prefixes to help you figure out the meaning of an unknown word.

1. Look at the unknown word. Does it have a Latin or Greek prefix that you know?
2. Think about whether or not the prefix affects the meaning of the unknown word.
3. Try the meaning in the sentence to be sure it makes sense.

As you read "The Hunger to Know," use what you know about Greek and Latin prefixes to figure out the meanings of *depart, continent, geography, panorama,* and other academic words.

Words to Write Reread "The Hunger to Know." Imagine that you are part of a team that has spent two years exploring space. You've returned to Earth and are talking to reporters about your trip. Someone asks, "What made you decide to travel to space?" Use words from the *Words to Know* list in your answer.

THE HUNGER TO KNOW

There is something in us that yearns to explore new places. Often these places are dangerous, even forbidding. That doesn't stop us from going there, though. In fact, risk may be part of what calls to us.

Five hundred years ago, the continent of North America lay waiting. Explorers from Europe sailed the Atlantic. Filled with anticipation, they couldn't wait to depart. These adventurers had no idea what the geography of this new land would be. Would they find treasure or be killed by monsters? They were ready for the new, the strange, the unexpected.

Today men and women still wonder, plan, and go. They travel to the ocean floor. There they see fantastic forms of life. They view wild panoramas of mountains and canyons formed when the stuff of Earth heaves and twists. They sail through fields of icebergs to the frozen poles. They blast into space, leaving the only home humans have ever known.

What drives people so? It may be the convergence of two needs: the hunger to know and the desire to be the first. Whatever makes it so, we gain from it. As long as we keep seeking and learning, our world keeps growing.

Your Turn!

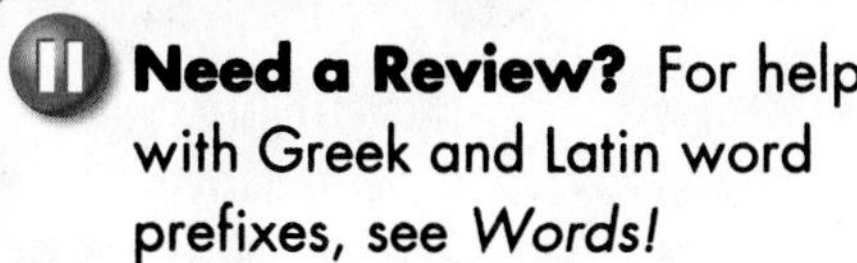

Need a Review? For help with Greek and Latin word prefixes, see *Words!*

Ready to Try It? Read *Antarctic Journal: Four Months at the Bottom of the World* on pp. 262–277.

Antarctic Journal

Four Months at the Bottom of the World

by Jennifer Owings Dewey

Genre

A **journal** is a record of thoughts and events that are important to the writer. It is a kind of autobiography. Think about what is important to Jennifer Owings Dewey as you read her journal.

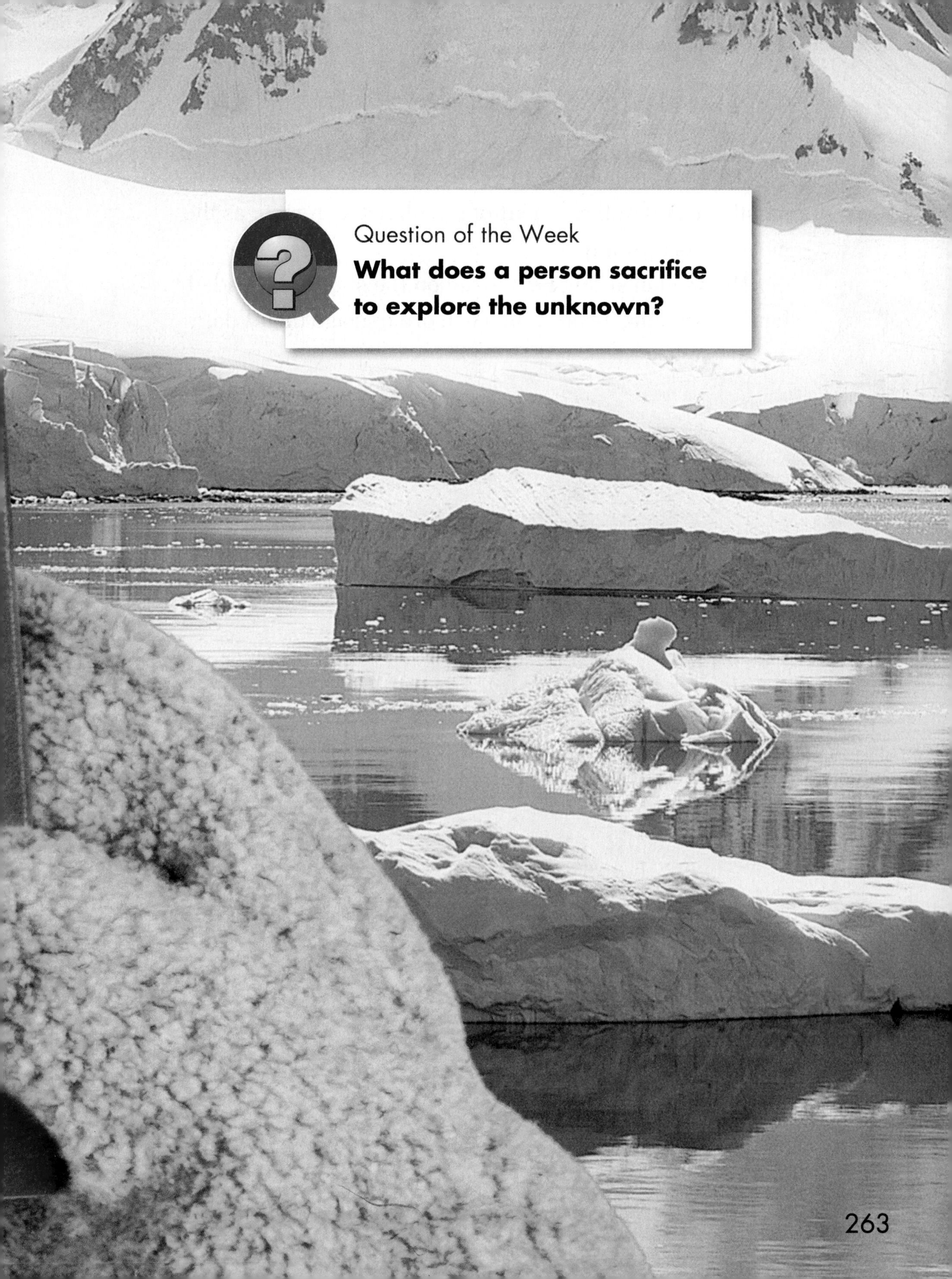

Question of the Week

What does a person sacrifice to explore the unknown?

November 12th

Depart from home in the early morning, to be gone four months to Antarctica, a part of the planet as remote as the moon in its own way.

The woman sitting next to me on the shuttle is headed for San Antonio, Texas. She has more luggage than I do.

For millions of years Antarctica, the fifth largest continent, has been in the grip of an ice age. It is the windiest, coldest, most forbidding region on Earth, and I am heading straight for it.

"Good-bye, America," I whisper as the airplane heaves off the ground with a shuddering roar. "See you later."

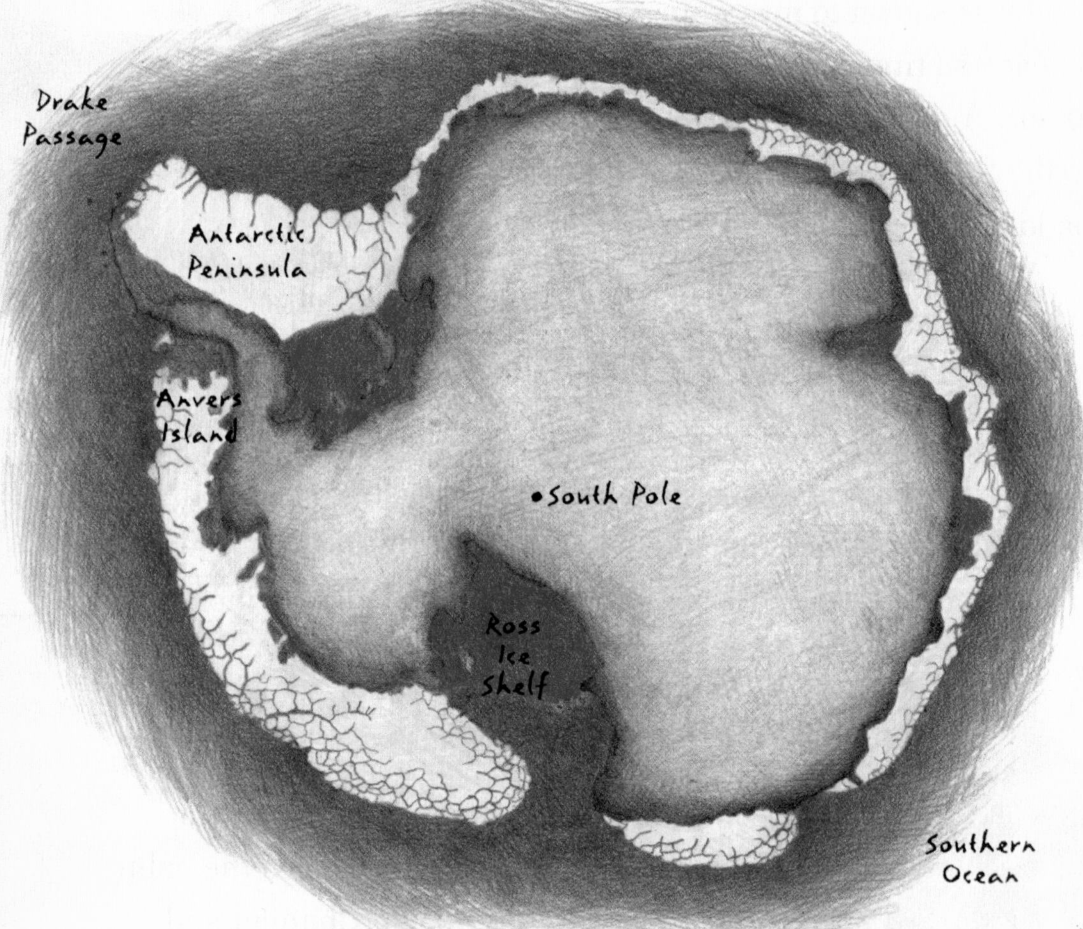

November 17th

We flew from Miami to Santiago, Chile. Early the next morning we boarded a plane bound for Punta Arenas, a town at the southern tip of Chile.

We landed and were driven to a hangarlike building, where we received our Antarctic clothing issue, on loan for the length of our stay, to be returned when we head back.

Our next stop was the pier where the *Polar Duke,* our ship, was tied up.

I was shown to my cabin—a space so tiny, I wished I were an elf. A desk and chair are bolted to the floor. The bedding is a well-padded sleeping bag.

We're off this morning. Clear skies, cool breeze, and no chop. The ship heaves and rolls like the smallish, sturdy seaworthy vessel it is.

I make a nest in one of the boats tied on deck, a cozy spot to spend hours drawing or just looking. I resist going below to sleep or eat. There is too much to take in—rolling seas, salt spray, broad-winged seabirds soaring inches above the wave tops.

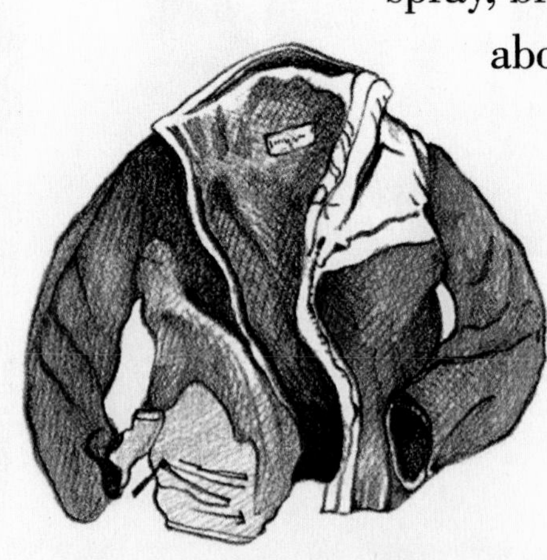

The sun never sets. It lowers and rolls lazily along the northern horizon before rising again. I shiver with anticipation when we leave the calm waters of the Beagle Channel and enter Drake Passage.

sooty albatross

Two days pass and we cross the Antarctic Convergence. Along this invisible line warm northern water meets cold southern water. The layering of warm and cold, and the upwelling that results, creates ideal conditions for an abundance of life in the seas.

From the convergence on, we are *in* Antarctica.

A day later the ship's motor stops humming. From the bridge I look out over the bow. A group of whales breaks the surface of the sea, spy hopping, heads pointing straight up out of the water. They slap their flukes and roll playfully.

"Humpbacks," one of the crew says. "Whales have the right of way in these waters. We stop when we see them, turn the engines off, and let them pass before we start up again."

It's good to know an ocean exists where whales have the right of way over ships.

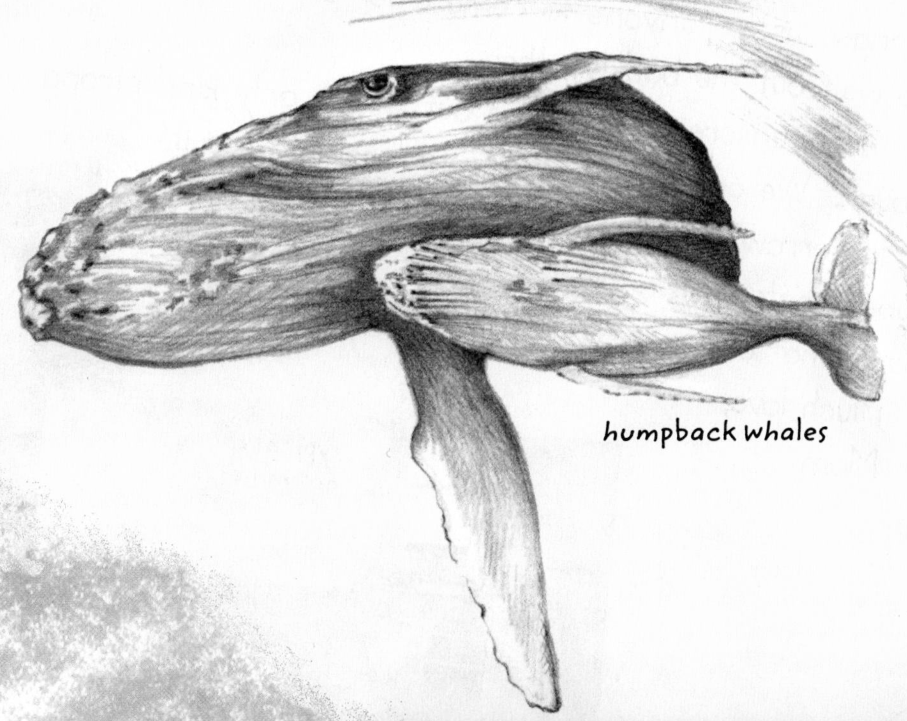

humpback whales

November 18th
Palmer Station

Palmer Station

Dear T.,

Palmer Station is a group of insulated metal buildings, housing fifty people comfortably. The station was built on Anvers Island. You don't know you're on an island because permanent ice fills the gap between Anvers and the mainland.

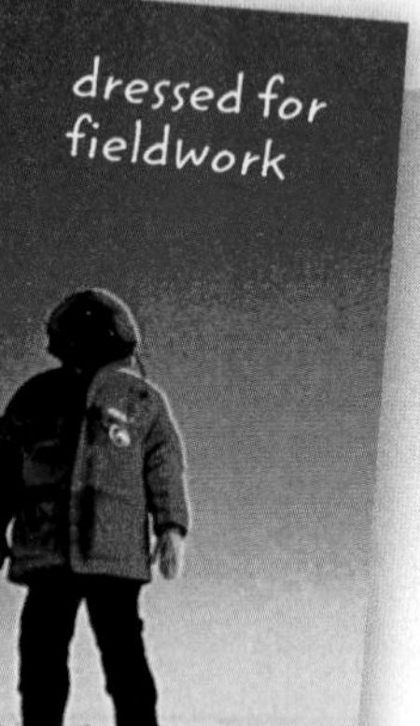
dressed for fieldwork

We learn the rules the first night: no travel alone, except to climb the glacier behind Palmer, flagged with poles to show the safest way up. We sign out when leaving, giving a departure hour and an estimated time of return. We are given walkie-talkies and check with "base" every hour. If we're half an hour off schedule, someone comes looking, unless a storm blows in. If it's too dangerous for anyone to come after us, we are expected to wait out the bad weather.

The sunscreen they pass out is "the only kind strong enough." We are ordered never to forget to use it.

Tomorrow we learn about the zodiacs, small rubber boats with outboard motors. I'm excited about what comes next, and sleepy.

Much love,

Mom

view looking away from Palmer

typical room, not mine!

November 27th
Litchfield Island

In fair weather I go to Litchfield Island and spend the day, sometimes the night. Litchfield is three miles from Palmer by zodiac, a protected island visited by two or three people a year. Before going to Litchfield, I'm shown how to walk on open ground in Antarctica. An inch of moss takes one hundred years to grow. The careless scuff of a boot heel could rip out two hundred years of growth in seconds.

I pack my food and extra clothes in a waterproof sea bag. A daypack holds pencils, pens, and paper for drawing and writing. There is no fresh water on the island. I carry two one-gallon canteens.

gray gull chick

Each island has an emergency cache of food and supplies, marked with a flag, available if a person gets stranded during a storm.

Alone after being dropped on the island, I hear birds call, the whine of the wind, the waves pounding gravel shores, and no human sounds except my breathing.

Twilight falls and I crawl into my tent, alert and unable to sleep for a long time, listening to the sounds of the Antarctic night.

The emergency cache on Litchfield contained a tarp, blankets, rope, candles, matches, anchovy paste, crackers, and chocolate.

December 15th
Visiting Old Palmer

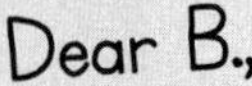

gentoo parent feeding chicks

Dear B.,

I am in a tiny office behind the kitchen. Supper is over. I came to find quiet time and write you. It's strange to write at night by the light of the sun.

Today I went with a penguin scientist to Old Palmer, twenty minutes by zodiac from New Palmer. Not used for years, the base is empty of life except for a small colony of gentoo penguins. A few of the birds have built stone nests on top of abandoned oil drums and other debris left behind. The chicks have orange spots on their bills and are identical to the parents, only smaller. They sit half squashed under a parent's white belly, black-billed faces poking out, eyes blinking.

A sunny day, thirty-two degrees, dangerously hot for the chicks. I've seen some keel over dead on days like this, their blubber-rich bodies unable to tolerate temperatures above freezing. A parent penguin suffering heat stroke will not abandon a nest. It will fall dead in a heap first.

traveling by zodiac

gentoos on nests

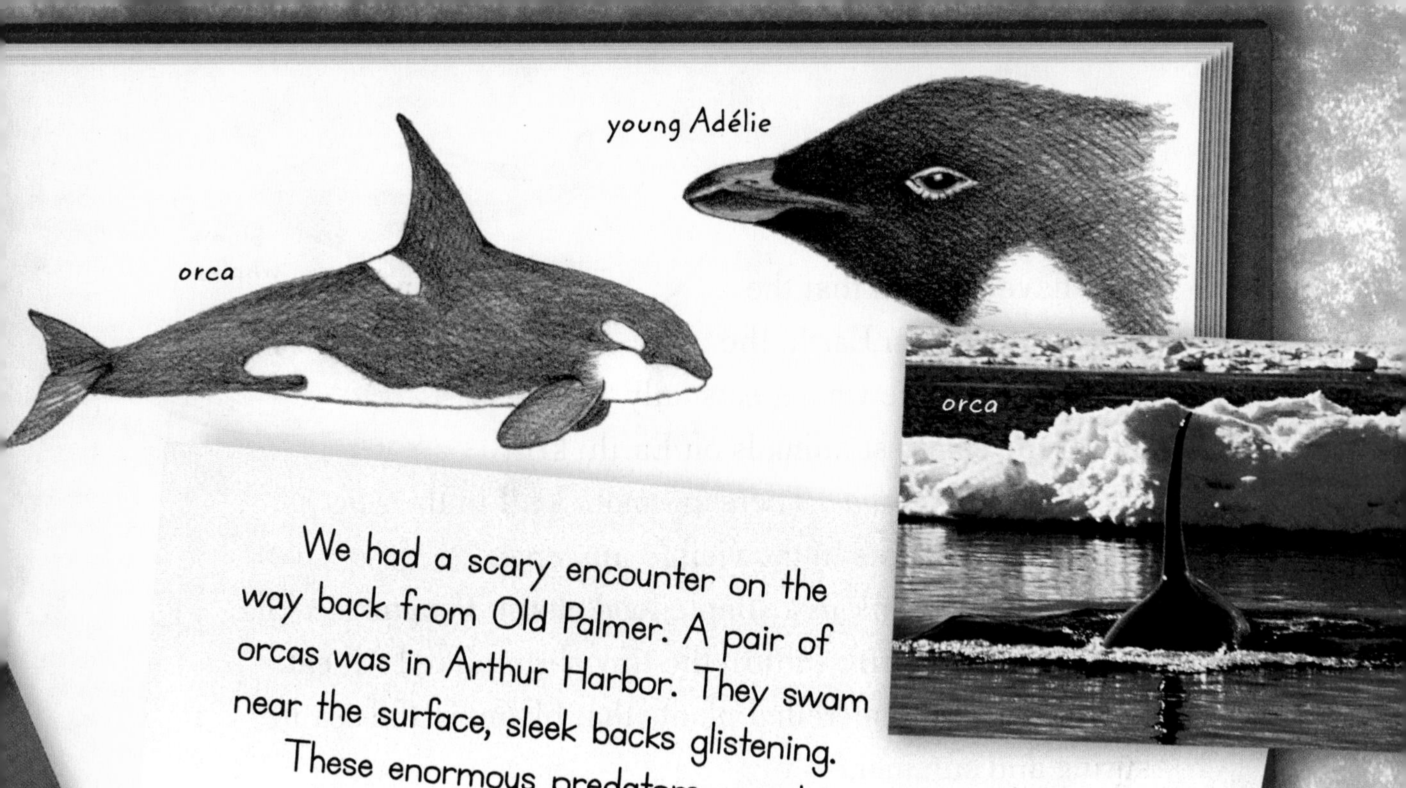

We had a scary encounter on the way back from Old Palmer. A pair of orcas was in Arthur Harbor. They swam near the surface, sleek backs glistening.

These enormous predators sometimes take bites out of boats, mistaking a zodiac for a seal or a penguin. We slowed the engine and held back.

A small group of Adélies was porpoising in the water. In a quick stroke one orca grabbed a penguin in its huge mouth and whirled the helpless bird in the air. Teeth gripped penguin flesh, penguin wings flailed. The skin of the penguin flew away and landed with a plop on the sea. The bird was stripped of its hide as easily as we remove a sweater.

The second orca took a penguin before the pair surged out of the harbor, leaving a swirling wake behind.

We sped back to Palmer, aware that what we'd seen was a reminder that we are in a wilderness where a delicate balance exists between predator and prey.

I'm tired, although I have the BIG EYE. This is when we can't sleep because it's never dark. We get silly and wide-eyed, peculiar in our behavior, until a friend says, "Time for bed," and sees that we get there.

Love and hugs,
J.

December 20th
Palmer Station

blue whales

krill

I have learned that the largest animal on Earth, the hundred-ton blue whale, eats only one of the smallest animals on Earth: krill *(Euphausia supurba).* There are more krill in the seas than there are stars in the visible universe.

Krill is one link in a simple food chain. Penguins, seals, and whales eat krill. In turn the tiny shrimplike krill eat phytoplankton, one-celled plants that bloom in the sea in spring and summer.

My new friend, Carl, an oceanographer, said, "We ought to try eating krill since so many animals thrive on it."

In the bio lab we scooped krill into a jar.

We got a small fry pan, then melted butter and cooked up the krill.

Someone said, "Add garlic."

Somebody said, "How about pepper and salt?"

These were added. When the mixture looked ready, we ate it.

"Tastes like butter," one person said.

"More like garlic," another said.

"Tastes like butter *and* garlic," Carl said.

"Krill don't have their own taste," I concluded.

December 21st
Palmer Station

A storm has raged for three days. A blast of wind smacked the main window with such force, we thought a bomb had gone off. The storm rose in intensity in minutes. Looking out the big window, we see a solid wall of sleet and blowing snow.

A friend and I checked the wind-speed monitor a few hours ago. It was clocking eighty knots. We decided to sneak outside and see what eighty-knot winds feel like. It's against the rules to leave the protection of the station in such high winds. Nobody saw us leave.

We were barely able to force the door open against the gale. Head down, face stung with driven sleet, I leaned with all my weight on the wind and did not fall over.

Fearing I'd be blown away, I pressed my mittened hands on the side of the building.

We crawled on hands and knees, lashed by pellets of frozen rain. In five minutes we were back inside.

Thinking of the penguins and their chicks on Litchfield, I can't help wondering how many will die of exposure to the cold and wet.

after the storm

Christmas Eve, December 24th
Palmer Station

It was three in the morning, bright outside, and I couldn't sleep. I crept downstairs, signed out, and took the flagged trail up the glacier.

Dressed in a watchman's cap, three layers under my parka, and Sorel boots, I climbed in a stillness broken only by the noise of snow crunching under my soles. Greenish-purple clouds covered the sky from edge to edge. The sea was the color of pewter.

Near the top I heard a cracking sound, a slap magnified a million times in my ear. Another followed, then another. Echoes of sound, aftershocks, sizzled in the air. The sky began to glow with an eerie luminescence, as if someone in the heavens had switched on a neon light in place of the sun.

front of glacier

I felt myself dropping straight down. A crack had appeared under me, a crevasse in the glacier. Summer softening of the ice had thrown the pole settings off.

I'm alive because the crack was narrow. I fell to my shoulders, my boot soles too wide to fit through the bottom of the crack. I stared below into a blue-green hole cut with facets like a diamond.

After a few deep breaths, I began to scramble out. Terrified the crack would keep growing, I moved slowly. It was an hour before I was on firm ice.

young tern

The color of the sky shifted to blue-gray with streaks of yellow along the western horizon. To my horror, I saw a pattern of cracks zig-zagging, like fractured window glass, across the glacier surface.

I checked my watch. I'd been gone three hours. I don't know why, but I didn't want anyone rescuing me. I decided to crawl down the glacier on hands and knees.

I felt my way inch by inch, rubbing the surface of the snow with my palms before making a move.

Back before the hour someone would have come looking for me, I told the station manager what happened. Trained in glaciology, he went up the glacier to reset the flags.

I have a new weariness tonight, born of having been frightened out of my wits while watching one of the most beautiful skies I'll ever see.

February 16th
On the *Polar Duke*

I am along on a trip of the *Polar Duke*, north of Palmer in Gerlache Strait. The crew and scientists trawl for krill using fine-mesh nets dropped off the stern.

Coming back we see icebergs drifting south out of the Weddell Sea. The bergs originate hundreds of miles away and ride ocean currents.

We sail close, but not too close, for beneath the waves is where the bulk of an iceberg is.

Weddell seal under the ice

Seawater splashes up on iceberg shores shaped by years of wave action. Sunlight strikes gleaming ramparts that shine with rainbow colors. Erosion works at the ice, creating caves and hollows, coves, and inlets.

Penguins and seals hitch rides on icebergs. Gulls and other seabirds rest on high points.

One iceberg collides in slow motion with another. The smaller one topples, rolls, and heaves like a dying rhinoceros, emerald seawater mixed with spray drenching its surfaces.

I yearn to ride an iceberg like a penguin or a gull, touching its frozen sides, drifting slowly on the waves. I draw them, but I can't capture their splendor.

March 12th
Winging Home

penguin egg

Before leaving, I collected (with permission) a sterile penguin egg that would never hatch. I made room for it in my suitcase by giving a lot of my clothes away.

The airline lost my bag in Miami. I told the airline people that I had to have it back, pleading, begging. "It has a penguin egg in it," I said. They glanced at each other and eyed me funny.

Fortunately for me, and them, they found the bag.

The egg reminds me of my trip to the place where penguins raise downy chicks, krill swarm in numbers greater than stars in the sky, whales have rights, and icebergs drift in graceful arcs across Southern Ocean swells. At home, I'll look out at the desert landscape and remember the Antarctic desert, the last great wilderness on Earth.

Objectives

- Read independently for long periods of time and paraphrase the reading, including the order in which events occur.
- Write responses to texts using details to show understanding.

Envision It! | **Retell**

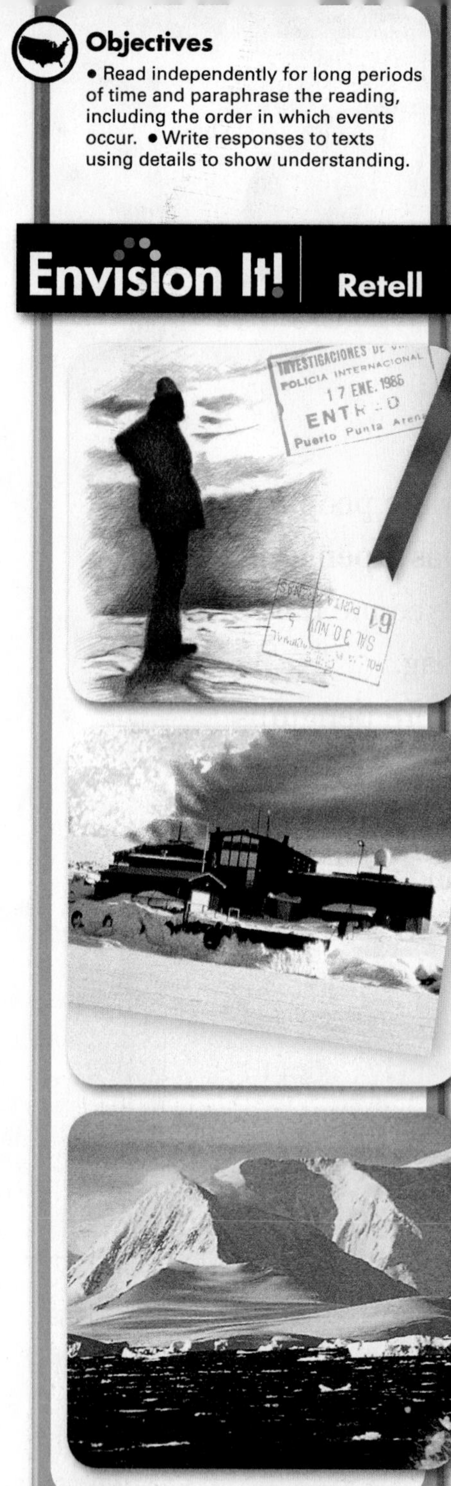

READING STREET ONLINE
STORY SORT
www.ReadingStreet.com

Think Critically

1. Hiram Bingham in *Lost City: The Discovery of Machu Picchu* and Jennifer Owings Dewey both sacrificed their personal safety to explore unknown places. Why do you think these two people put themselves in dangerous situations to explore new places? **Text to Text**

2. The author describes her experiences in Antarctica in a way that will help readers feel as if they were there with her. Did you feel as if you were with her on her journey? Why or why not? **Think Like an Author**

3. The author describes Antarctica as the "most forbidding region on Earth." What details in her letter on page 268 support this opinion? **Main Idea and Details**

4. What text structure does the author use in writing the December 24th entry on pages 274–275? Explain why the author chose this method. Would another text structure be more effective? Explain. **Text Structure**

5. **Look Back and Write** Look back at page 272. The author and her friends thought they had discovered a new food for humans. What was this food, and why did they think it would be good to eat? What did they think after they tasted it? Provide evidence to support your answer. **TEST PRACTICE** **Extended Response**

Jennifer Owings Dewey

Jennifer Owings Dewey loves to study and write about animals and nature. She says, "I enjoy traveling to remote or wild places to do research." For *Antarctic Journal*, she traveled to Antarctica. During her four months there, she drew the animals and landscape, took photographs, and wrote in her journal. Friends and family saved the letters she wrote home. All these went into her book.

Ms. Dewey lives in Santa Fe, New Mexico. She has written more than twenty nonfiction books for children. She says, "I like writing about extreme environments—cold and hot, dry and wet." She also writes about the amazing variety of animals on Earth. "Writing about the world we live in prevents running out of ideas," she says.

Here are other books about Antarctica.

***An Extreme Dive Under the Antarctic Ice* by Brad Matsen**

***Antarctic Ice* by Jim Mastro and Norbert Wu**

Reading Log

Use the Reading Log in the *Reader's and Writer's Notebook* to record your independent reading.

Objectives
• Write essays that persuade readers about certain issues and include opinions and details to support your points. • Use and understand words that show a change in time or order or that indicate an ending.

Let's Write It!

Key Features of a Persuasive Advertisement

- grabs readers' attention
- takes a position about a product, service, or idea
- uses details to urge readers to take action or make a purchase

READING STREET ONLINE
GRAMMAR JAMMER
www.ReadingStreet.com

Persuasive Advertisement

A **persuasive ad** tries to influence readers' ideas about a product, service, or idea. The student model on the next page is an example of a persuasive ad.

Writing Prompt Write an advertisement encouraging readers to take a trip to Antarctica.

Writer's Checklist

Remember, you should ...

- ✓ begin with an attention-grabbing statement.
- ✓ establish a position to appeal to the emotions of a specific audience.
- ✓ use supporting details to influence the audience.
- ✓ use time-order transition words effectively.

Student Model

Would you like to take your family on an unforgettable trip where you can get away from all the hassles of everyday life? Take a fun, educational trip to Antarctica! As your journey unfolds, you will experience nature as you never have before!

- **Start** your adventure even before your ship arrives at your Antarctic destination. On the ship, enjoy the opportunity to study a wide variety of wildlife, from terns to humpback whales, to orcas, to penguins.
- **Then,** once you land, let your inner artist become inspired by Antarctica's amazing neon skies and the incredible landscape of gigantic, fantastically shaped icebergs.
- **Finally,** end your trip with a lesson in climbing glaciers. Adventurers of all ages won't be able to pass up this unusual challenge.

Don't wait, space is limited! Sign up now!

Writing Trait Focus Shows a clear purpose.

Genre Persuasive ads attempt to influence readers' choices.

Time-order words are used correctly.

Conventions

Time-Order Words

Remember Time-order words help to explain the order in which things happen. Examples of time-order words include *first, second, third, then, next,* and *finally.*

Objectives

• Explain information that is shown in graphics. • Make connections between literary and informational texts with similar ideas and support your ideas with details from the texts.

Science in Reading

Genre

Biography

- A biography is the story of a person's life written by another person. Biographies are based on facts, so they are examples of literary nonfiction.
- Biographies are written in the third person, using words such as *he, she, him,* and *her.*
- Biographies might include graphics to explain some facts.
- Read "Swimming Towards Ice." Look for elements that make this article a biography.

Swimming Towards Ice

by Claire Daniel

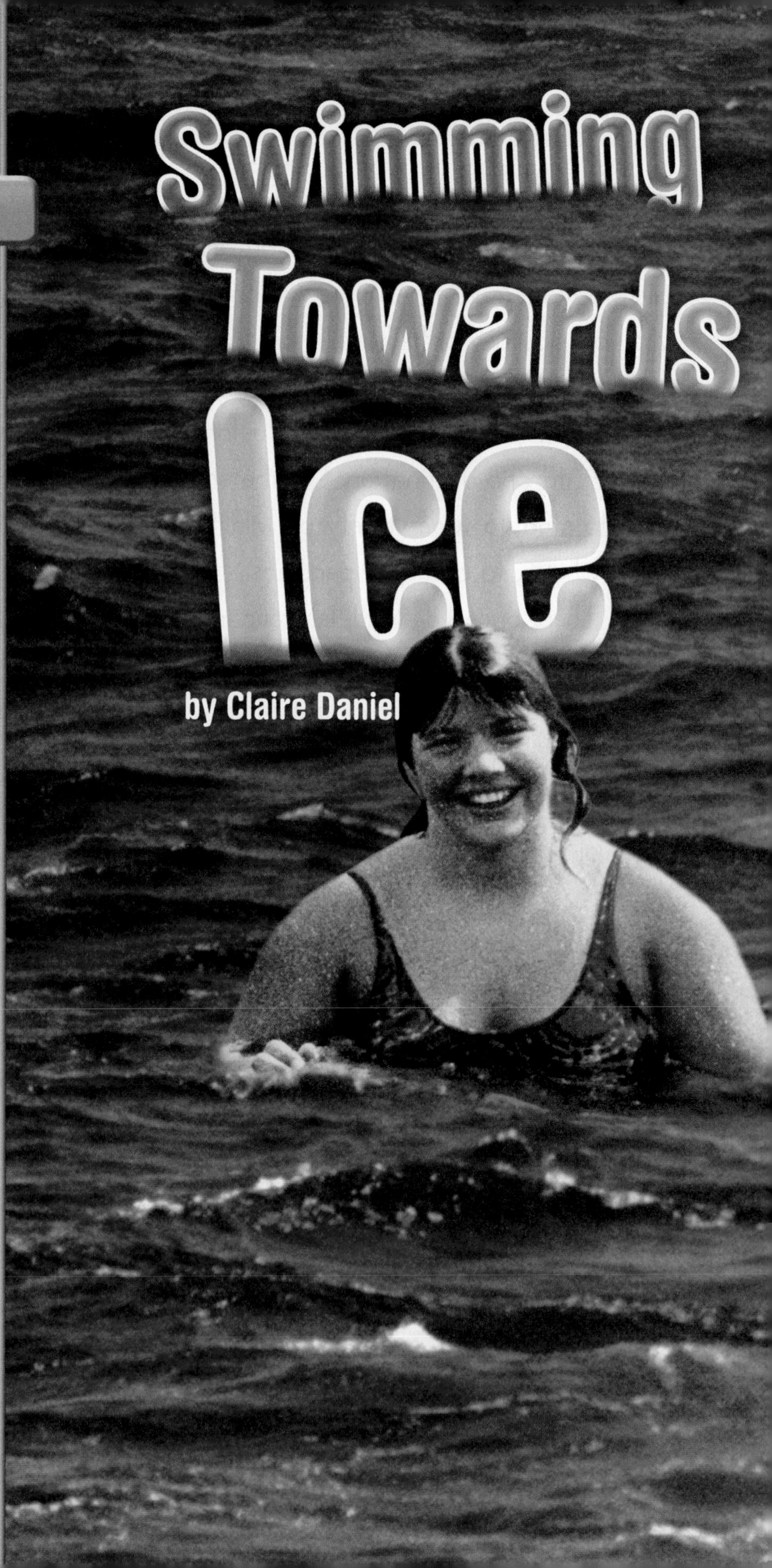

Unlike the usual visitor to Antarctica, who is bundled from head to toe, Lynne Cox approached the continent a bit differently. Dressed in only a swimsuit, swim cap, and goggles, she lowered herself from a boat into the freezing 32°F water and swam more than a mile to Antarctica's shore.

Lynne Cox is among the best cold-water, long-distance swimmers in the world. But she wasn't born that way.

Lynne Cox makes a test swim in the chilly waters (33°F) north of Antarctica.

A Swimmer Is Born

When Lynne was 14 years old, she became bored with swimming laps in a pool. Encouraged by her coach, she entered a series of rough-water swims near her home in California. She loved the cold water, the chopping of the waves, the quiet of the ocean, and the feeling of freedom. Lynne Cox became hooked on long-distance, cold-water swimming.

Let's Think About...

Which words on this page tell you that the selection is written in the third person? **Biography**

Preparing for the Icy Plunge

To prepare for her swim to Antarctica, Lynne trained hard for two years. Each day, for an hour, she worked out in a gym, using weights and other equipment to strengthen her muscles. Five- to six-mile walks were also part of her daily training, and for one hour each day, she swam as hard and as fast as she could in a pool.

Lynne also borrowed ideas from sea animals that survive in cold water. She added 12 pounds of body fat to help keep her body temperature from falling in the icy water. And she grew her hair long to trap warm air inside her swim cap.

Let's Think About...

Why does the author include these life events on this page? What do these events tell you about Lynne? **Biography**

A Swimmer's Hope

For most of her life, Lynne Cox has braved the elements to swim in the world's major bodies of water. Often she has been the first woman to do so. While it is always her hope to have successful swims, it is also Lynne's wish to bring people of the world together to show how closely they live to each other and to work for peace and understanding.

Now in her forties, Lynne looks forward to her next swimming challenge. While she won't say where it will be, she has said that it will be "[in] an area I've never seen, some place that captures my imagination, something that's never been tried before." To be sure, it will be amazing.

Lynne Cox's Record-Breaking Swims

Year	Age	Location	Swimming Distance*	Time	Sea Temp. (°F)
1971	14	First crossing of Catalina Channel (CA)	27 miles	12 hours 36 min.	65°– 70°
1972	15	English Channel	27 miles	9 hours 57 min.	55°– 60°
1973	16	English Channel	27 miles	9 hours 36 min.	55°– 60°
1976	19	Strait of Magellan (Chile)	3.0 miles	1 hour 2 min.	44°
1987	30	Bering Strait (between the former Soviet Union and the United States)	5.0 miles	2 hours 6 min.	38°– 42°
2002	45	Swim to Antarctica	1.2 miles	25 min.	32°

*This number reflects the miles Lynne swam, not the actual distance between two points.

Let's Think About...

How does the chart on this page present Lynne's accomplishments? **Biography**

Let's Think About...

Reading Across Texts Connect what you know about Jennifer Owings Dewey and Lynne Cox. How are they alike? How are they different?

Writing Across Texts Make a compare-and-contrast chart to show how these women prepared for their adventures.

Objectives

• Read aloud grade-level texts and understand what is read. • Determine the meaning of English words with affixes from Greek, Latin, and other languages. • Speak clearly and to the point, give an opinion and support it with correct information. Make eye contact, change how fast, loud, and clearly you speak, and get your ideas across clearly. • Take part in discussions led by teachers or other students, ask and answer questions, and offer ideas that build on the ideas of other people.

READING STREET ONLINE
ONLINE STUDENT EDITION
www.ReadingStreet.com

Vocabulary

Greek and Latin

Word Structure If you know the meaning of a Greek or Latin root or affix, you can use the meaning to help you understand an unknown word. Look for roots and affixes in words whose meaning you are unsure of.

Practice It! The Greek prefix *ant-* means "opposite." Find Antarctica on a globe. What is "opposite" of this continent? Is Antarctica a good name for this continent? Explain.

Fluency

Expression

Partner Reading When you change the pitch of your voice as you read, you are reading with expression. Speaking in higher and lower tones adds interest to what you are reading.

Practice It! With a partner, read aloud *Antarctic Journal,* page 268, paragraph 2. Read the rules in this paragraph once in a regular speaking voice. Then read them with intonation. Which way is more interesting? Why?

Listening and Speaking

Get Ready For Middle School

In a good discussion, speakers provide suggestions that build upon the ideas of others.

Panel Discussion

In a panel discussion, a group of people talk about a topic in front of an audience. The purpose of a panel discussion is to share ideas and information. At times you need to use your background knowledge to understand implicit, or unstated, ideas and information.

Practice It! Work with a small group to present a panel discussion about Antarctica to your class. Discuss and share opinions about the importance of this continent. Use information from *Antarctic Journal* in your discussion. Talk about the landforms, the climate, and the wildlife of Antarctica.

Tips

Listening . . .

- Be prepared to ask relevant questions related to the topic, such as "What is the lowest recorded temperature in Antarctica?"
- Use your background knowledge as you listen for implicit ideas and information.

Speaking . . .

- Use time-order transition words correctly.
- Share implicit ideas and information.

Teamwork . . .

- Make suggestions that build upon others' ideas. For example, if someone talks about the climate, you can tell what you know about the climate in Antarctica.

Objectives

- Listen closely to speakers and ask questions about and comment on the topic.

Oral Vocabulary

Let's Talk About

The Moon

- Share facts about the moon.
- Listen to others' information.
- Ask relevant questions.

READING STREET ONLINE
CONCEPT TALK VIDEO
www.ReadingStreet.com

You've
2 4 0
Amazing
so far this

Objectives

- Monitor your comprehension of a text and adjust your reading based on how well you understand what you are reading.

Skill

Strategy

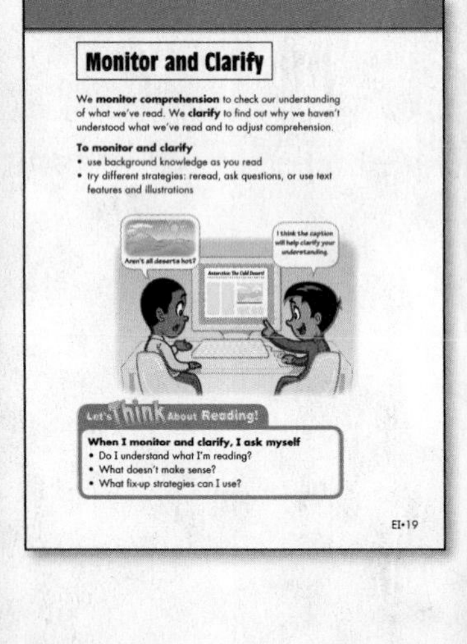

READING STREET ONLINE
ENVISION IT! ANIMATIONS
www.ReadingStreet.com

Comprehension Skill

Draw Conclusions

- The small pieces of information in a selection are called the facts and details.
- When you put facts and details together to form an opinion, you are drawing a conclusion. When you draw a conclusion, be sure it is supported by what you have read.
- Use the graphic organizer to draw conclusions as you read "The Man in the Moon."

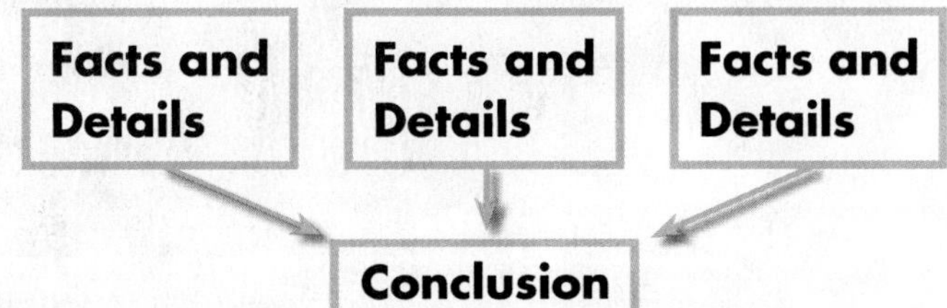

Comprehension Strategy

Monitor and Clarify

While you are reading, it's important to know when you don't understand something. If you are confused, stop and reread the selection aloud. Looking back and rereading is one way to clarify, or "adjust," your understanding. You might also read on to look for an explanation of what you don't understand.

The Man in the Moon

When we look up and see (with the help of our imaginations) a face in the moon, the question is not whom we see, but what we see. For when we gaze at the moon, we are seeing craters, mountains, deep narrow valleys, and wide-open plains.

Skill Draw a conclusion from the first sentence. Is this piece going to be science or fantasy? (It's a little tricky!)

The moon is a dry and airless place made up of rocks and dust. But when the telescope was first invented—about 400 years ago—people had no way of knowing that there was no water on the moon. So when they looked through the telescope and saw the open plains, they assumed they were looking at bodies of water. They named these places mares (MAH-rees), which is Latin for "seas."

Today, we know there is no water on the moon, but the names have stuck. That is why these dry and dusty places have such lovely names as Bay of Rainbows, Lake of Dreams, and Sea of Tranquillity.

Skill If you read these names without knowing what the moon is like, what conclusion might you draw?

Will you travel to the moon someday? Maybe. And maybe you'll come back and say, "It's a nice place to visit, but I wouldn't want to live there!"

Strategy Is there something about the article you don't understand? Rereading can help.

Your Turn!

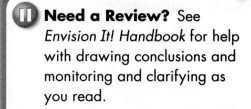

Need a Review? See *Envision It! Handbook* for help with drawing conclusions and monitoring and clarifying as you read.

Ready to Try It? Use what you've learned about drawing conclusions as you read *Moonwalk*.

Objectives

- Determine the meanings of unfamiliar words or multiple-meaning words by using the context of the sentence.
- Complete analogies based on knowledge of synonyms and antonyms.

Envision It! Words to Know

rille

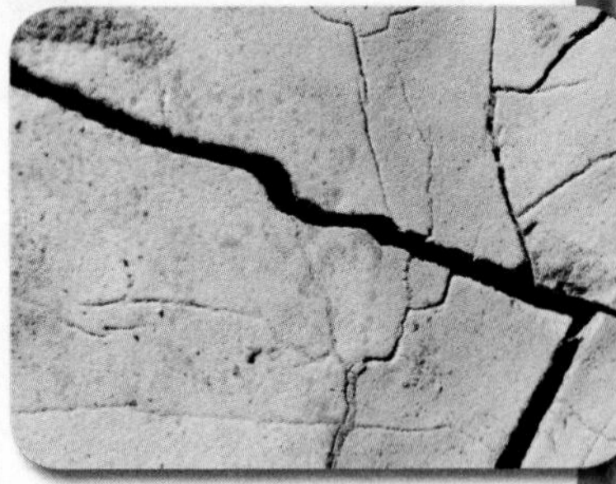

runt

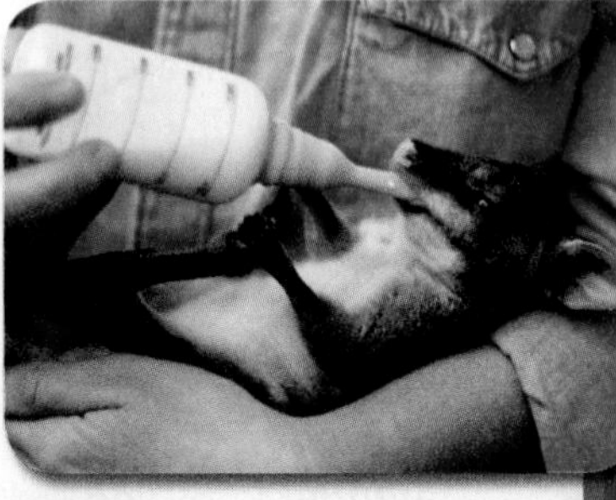

trench

loomed
staggered
summoning
taunted
trudged

READING STREET ONLINE
VOCABULARY ACTIVITIES
www.ReadingStreet.com

Vocabulary Strategy for

Synonyms

Context Clues Sometimes a synonym can be a clue to help you figure out the meaning of a word. Look at the sentence: *The tiny spider was so miniscule I almost stepped on it.* You can use the synonym *tiny* to help you figure out the meaning of *miniscule.*

1. Use what you know about synonyms to complete this analogy with a word from *Words to Know: marched* is to *hiked* as *tramped* is to ______.
2. When you read a word you don't know, read the words and sentences around it. Look for a synonym.
3. If you find a synonym, try using it in place of the unfamiliar word. Then see if it makes sense.

As you read "Gone to the Moon," check the context of words you don't know. Look for a synonym to help you figure out the unfamiliar word.

Words to Write Reread "Gone to the Moon." Imagine that you are the first fourth grader to travel to the moon. Your job is to send back messages describing what you see and how you feel as you walk on the moon. Use words from the *Words to Know* list in your message.

Gone to the Moon

People have long dreamed of going to the moon. Maybe this is because the moon circles so close by. No other thing in space is closer to Earth. How could we not conquer this small thing, this runt?

When the machine age arrived, the moon still taunted us. "I'm so close," it teased. "Why don't you come on up?" In 1969, three people did. Summoning all our knowledge and technology, we sent them into space and guided them to the moon. They had to call on all their bravery to blast off into the unknown.

Imagine how their hearts raced as the moon loomed before them. Imagine their awe as two of them stepped where no person had ever set foot. They saw craters and a rille, a narrow valley that looks like a trench.

With every step, they leaped rather than trudged. (On Earth, because of gravity, we plod along.) It was easy to pick up moon rocks under whose weight they would have staggered and stumbled on Earth.

Was it worth it to go to the moon? Yes!

Your Turn!

Need a Review? For help with using context clues to determine the meanings of synonyms, see *Words!*

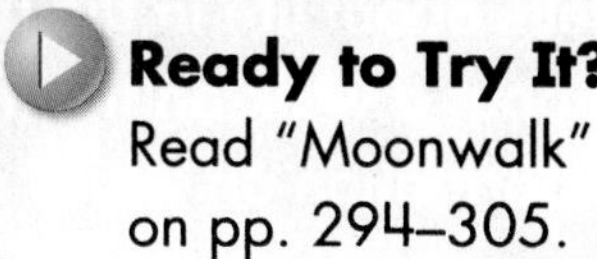

Ready to Try It? Read "Moonwalk" on pp. 294–305.

Moonwalk

by Ben Bova illustrated by Peter Bollinger

Genre

Science fiction is a story based on science. It often tells about life in the future. As you read this story about a walk on the moon, look for the scientific information on which it is based.

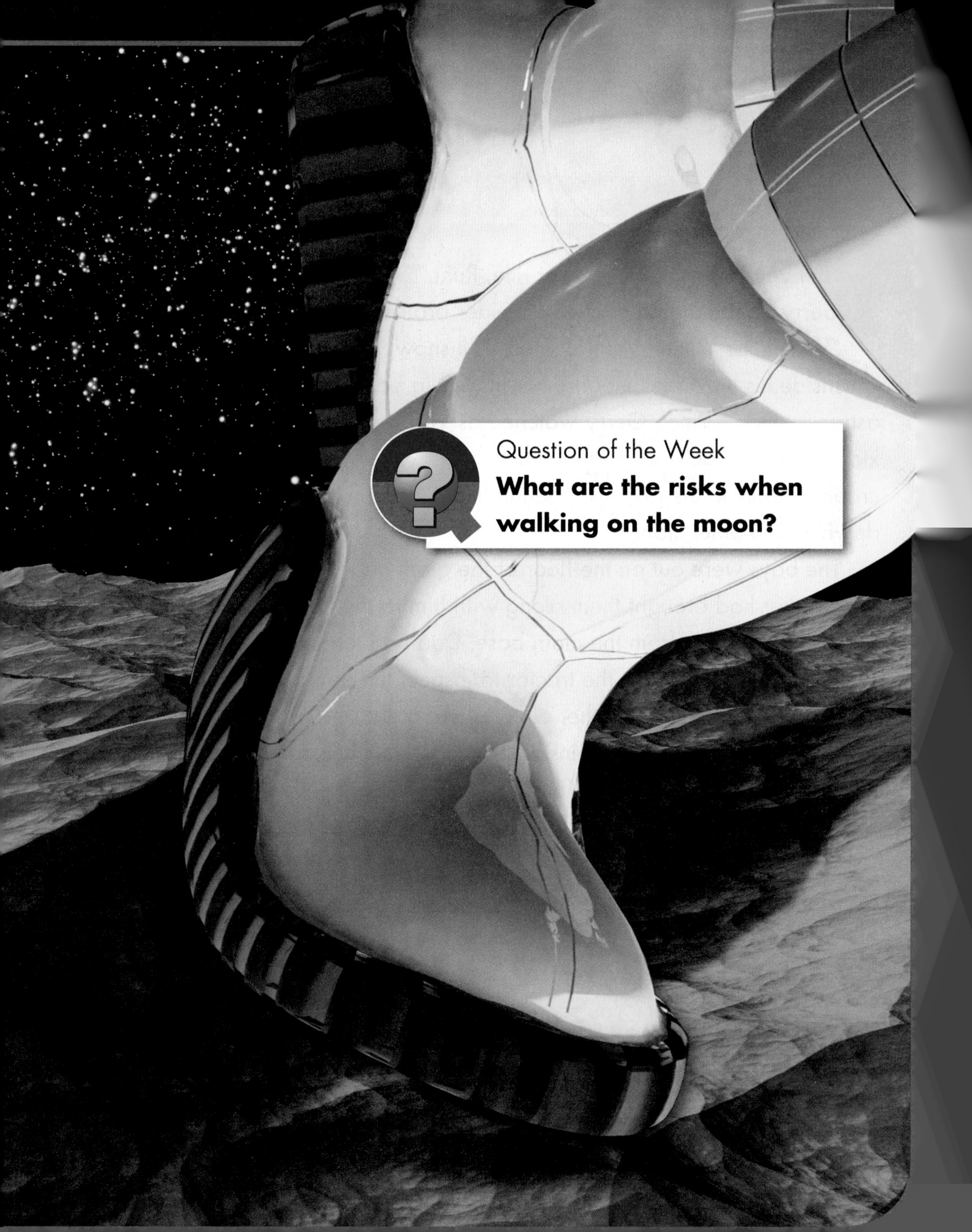
Question of the Week
What are the risks when walking on the moon?

"Bet you can't jump over that rille, Runt," Vern challenged.

Gerry Kandel hated it when his older brother called him Runt.

"Watch me, Runt," Vern taunted. "I'll show you how to do it."

Inside his hard-shell moonsuit, with its big backpack and astronaut-type helmet, Gerry watched as Vern got a running start, kicking up lazy puffs of dust with each step. He sailed over the crooked crack in the ground, floating like a cloud until he touched down on the other side.

The boys were out on the floor of the giant crater Alphonsus. Their father had brought them along with him to the half-buried shelter fifteen miles from the main base. Dad had left them at the shelter and gone off with the tractor to inspect the new telescope that was being built still farther out on the crater floor.

Dad had told them to stay inside the shelter until he came back. But Vern wanted to go outside for a moonwalk. Now he was jumping over gullies in the bare, dark ground.

"Come on, Runt," Vern called from the other side of the rille. "Let's see you do it!"

Gerry glanced at the thermometer on the wrist of his moonsuit. It was 214 degrees below zero. Yet he was sweating inside his suit.

"What's the matter? You scared?"

Even though it was nighttime, it wasn't really dark. A big, blue and white Earth hung in the starry sky, shining beautifully. Gerry could see the rough uneven ground, the rocks and boulders scattered everywhere on the moon's surface.

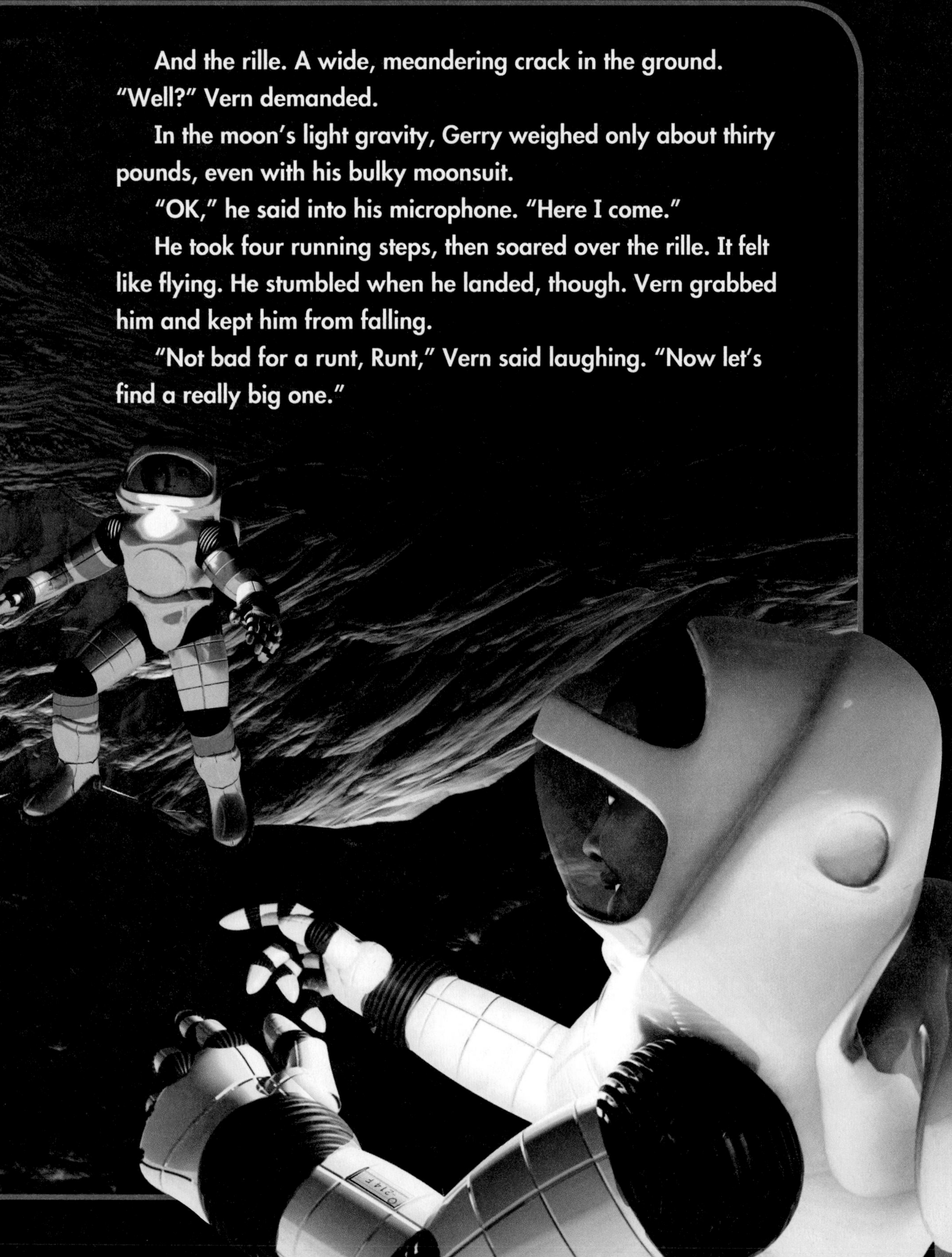

And the rille. A wide, meandering crack in the ground.

"Well?" Vern demanded.

In the moon's light gravity, Gerry weighed only about thirty pounds, even with his bulky moonsuit.

"OK," he said into his microphone. "Here I come."

He took four running steps, then soared over the rille. It felt like flying. He stumbled when he landed, though. Vern grabbed him and kept him from falling.

"Not bad for a runt, Runt," Vern said laughing. "Now let's find a really big one."

"We shouldn't be doing this," Gerry said. "Dad told us to stay inside the shelter. If he finds out. . . ."

"Who's going to tell him?" Vern demanded.

"Um . . . nobody, I guess."

"That's right. We'll be back in the shelter by the time Dad gets back. And you'll keep your mouth shut. Right?"

"Right," Gerry said reluctantly.

He followed Vern along the rille they had just crossed, their boots kicking up dust that settled slowly in the low gravity.

They trudged along for nearly an hour, leaving boot prints in the dust. Off on the other side of the crater, sunlight was bathing the top of the ringwall mountains with harsh, brilliant light. It would soon be daytime.

"Hey, there's one," Vern called out, pointing with a gloved hand at a broad gully up ahead. It was much wider than the one they'd jumped across. It looked deep, too, like a trench.

"Bet you can't jump over that one, Runt."

Gerry peered at the rille. "It's pretty wide," he said.

Gerry was, but he didn't want to admit it. He shook his head inside his helmet, then realized that Vern couldn't see it.

"Well? Want me to go first?"

Summoning up his courage, Gerry said, "Naw, I'll try it."

Gerry backed up several paces, then started running. In the light gravity, every step was a leap. The edge of the rille loomed up like the rim of the Grand Canyon. Gerry jumped as hard as he could.

He soared, sailing up and over the yawning trench, and landed almost perfectly. He hardly staggered.

Turning to look back across the rille at Vern, he called, "Nothing to it! Piece of cake!"

"OK," Vern answered. "Here I come."

Vern started running, each stride a long hop across the uneven ground. With his last step, though, he stumbled on a small rock. When he took off for the jump across, Gerry saw that he wasn't going to make it.

"Watch out!" he yelled uselessly.

Vern soared, arms and legs flailing, and landed hard—just short of the rille's rim. Gerry heard him go "Oof!" as he hit the side of the rift and tumbled down, out of sight.

Gerry rushed to the edge of the gully and saw his brother halfway down the rille, lying motionless.

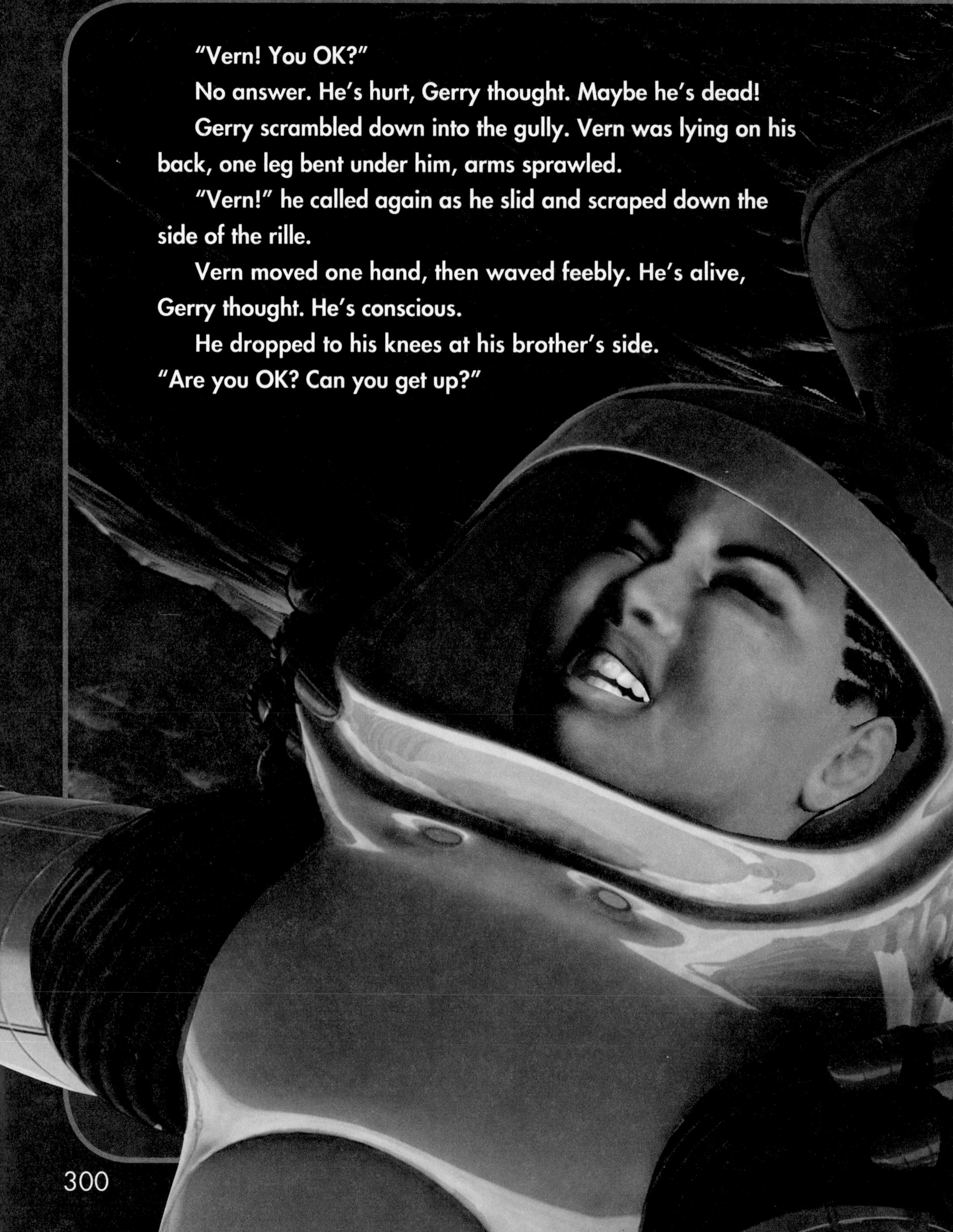

"Vern! You OK?"

No answer. He's hurt, Gerry thought. Maybe he's dead!

Gerry scrambled down into the gully. Vern was lying on his back, one leg bent under him, arms sprawled.

"Vern!" he called again as he slid and scraped down the side of the rille.

Vern moved one hand, then waved feebly. He's alive, Gerry thought. He's conscious.

He dropped to his knees at his brother's side. "Are you OK? Can you get up?"

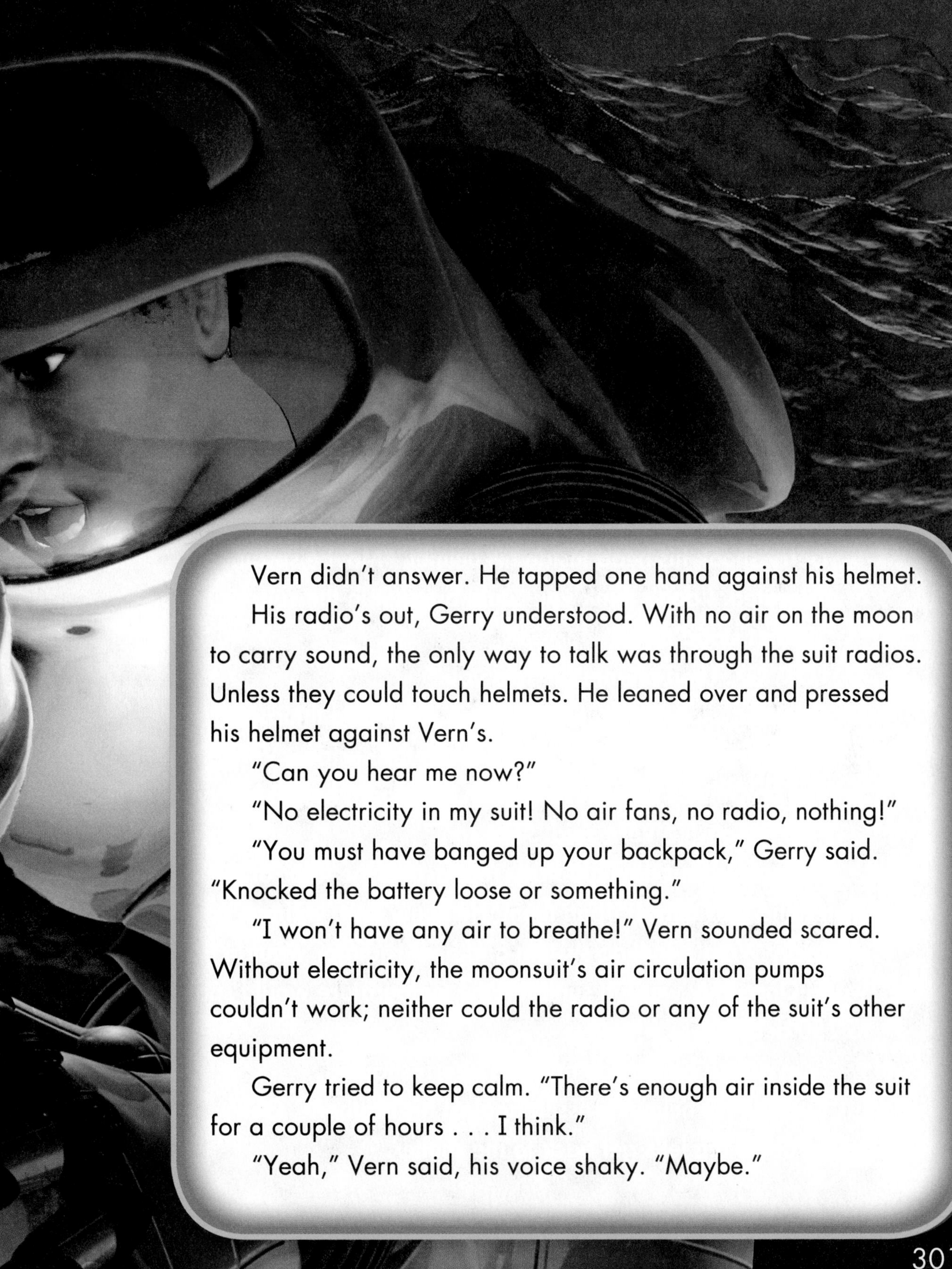

Vern didn't answer. He tapped one hand against his helmet.

His radio's out, Gerry understood. With no air on the moon to carry sound, the only way to talk was through the suit radios. Unless they could touch helmets. He leaned over and pressed his helmet against Vern's.

"Can you hear me now?"

"No electricity in my suit! No air fans, no radio, nothing!"

"You must have banged up your backpack," Gerry said. "Knocked the battery loose or something."

"I won't have any air to breathe!" Vern sounded scared. Without electricity, the moonsuit's air circulation pumps couldn't work; neither could the radio or any of the suit's other equipment.

Gerry tried to keep calm. "There's enough air inside the suit for a couple of hours . . . I think."

"Yeah," Vern said, his voice shaky. "Maybe."

"Come on, get up."

Vern started to push himself to his feet. "Oow!" he cried, sinking back to the dusty ground again.

"What's the matter?"

"My knee! It must be broken!"

Gerry shook his head inside his helmet. "Maybe sprained or dislocated. I don't think you could break it in the suit."

"I can't stand on it!"

"OK, OK. Lean on me. I'll help you."

Grunting, staggering, the two boys scrabbled their way across the bottom of the rille and back to the surface, Vern leaning on Gerry's shoulder. Even on the moon, he felt heavy.

"Oh my gosh," Vern said. "The sun."

Gerry saw that daylight had crept across the floor of the crater and was almost upon them. He knew that, without electricity, Vern's cooling system and heat radiator wouldn't work. Once they were in sunlight, the temperature would soar to 250 degrees.

"I'm gonna boil inside my suit!" Vern shouted.

Keeping his helmet pressed against his brother's, Gerry said, "Come on, let's get back to the shelter."

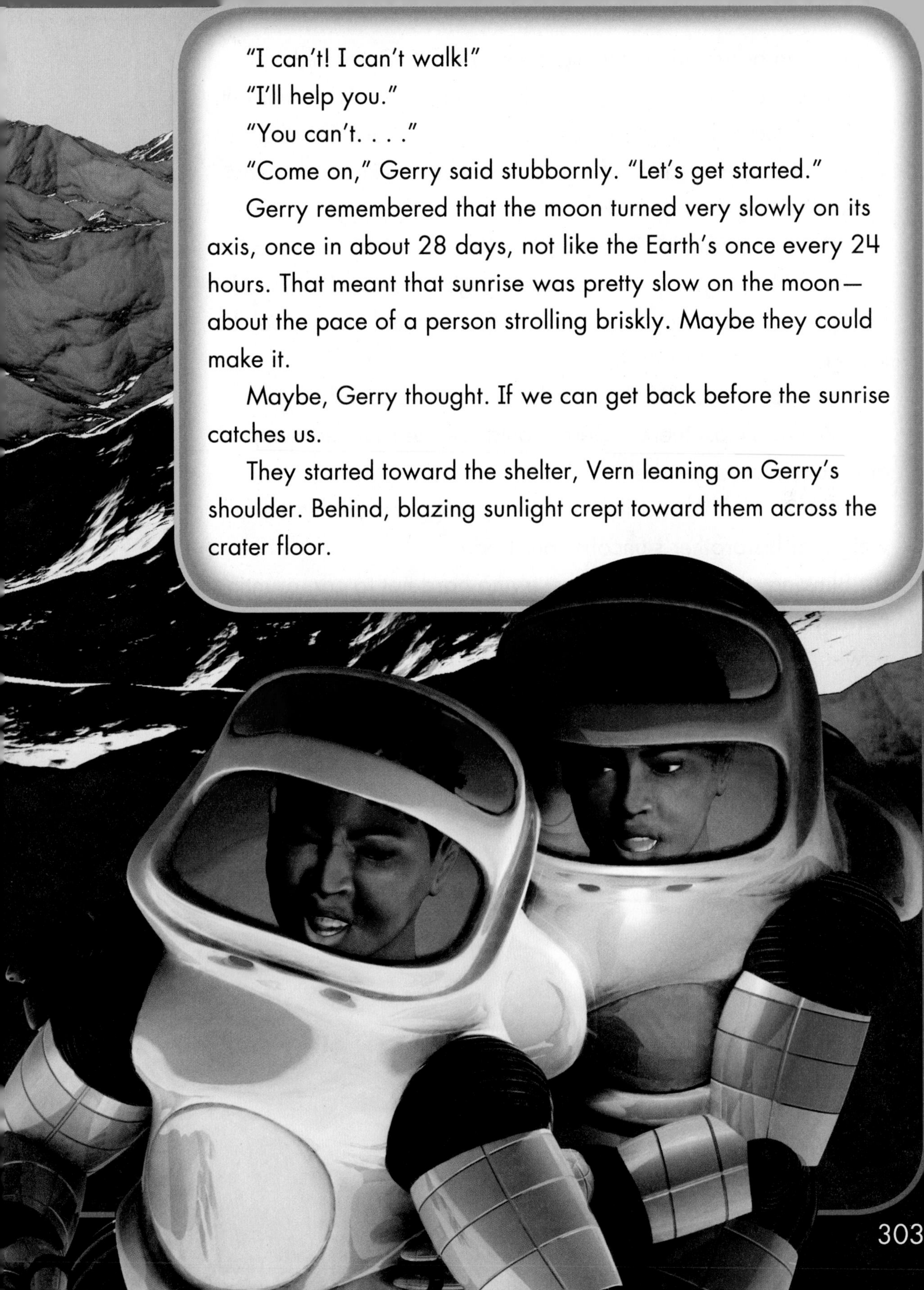

"I can't! I can't walk!"

"I'll help you."

"You can't. . . ."

"Come on," Gerry said stubbornly. "Let's get started."

Gerry remembered that the moon turned very slowly on its axis, once in about 28 days, not like the Earth's once every 24 hours. That meant that sunrise was pretty slow on the moon—about the pace of a person strolling briskly. Maybe they could make it.

Maybe, Gerry thought. If we can get back before the sunrise catches us.

They started toward the shelter, Vern leaning on Gerry's shoulder. Behind, blazing sunlight crept toward them across the crater floor.

As long as we stay in the night we'll be OK, Gerry told himself. If we can get back to the shelter before Vern's air runs out.

They trudged along for what seemed like hours. The sky was spangled with thousands of stars; they seemed like hard, solemn eyes watching the two boys.

"We can make it," Gerry kept muttering. "We can make it."

But with every step Vern seemed to get heavier. The line of daylight was catching up with them. Gerry could almost feel the sun's blazing heat roasting him.

Vern coughed. "Hard . . . to breathe," he gasped.

"We're almost there." Gerry could see the rounded hump of dirt that covered the shelter.

"Can't. . . ." Vern collapsed. Gerry staggered under the full weight of his brother's unconscious body.

Blinking sweat from his eyes, trying hard not to cry, grunting, puffing hard, Gerry dragged Vern to the shelter. The tractor was nowhere in sight. Dad's not back yet, he realized, not knowing if he should be glad or sorry.

As he pulled his brother into the airlock, he saw the tractor coming slowly over the horizon, kicking up a lazy roostertail of dust.

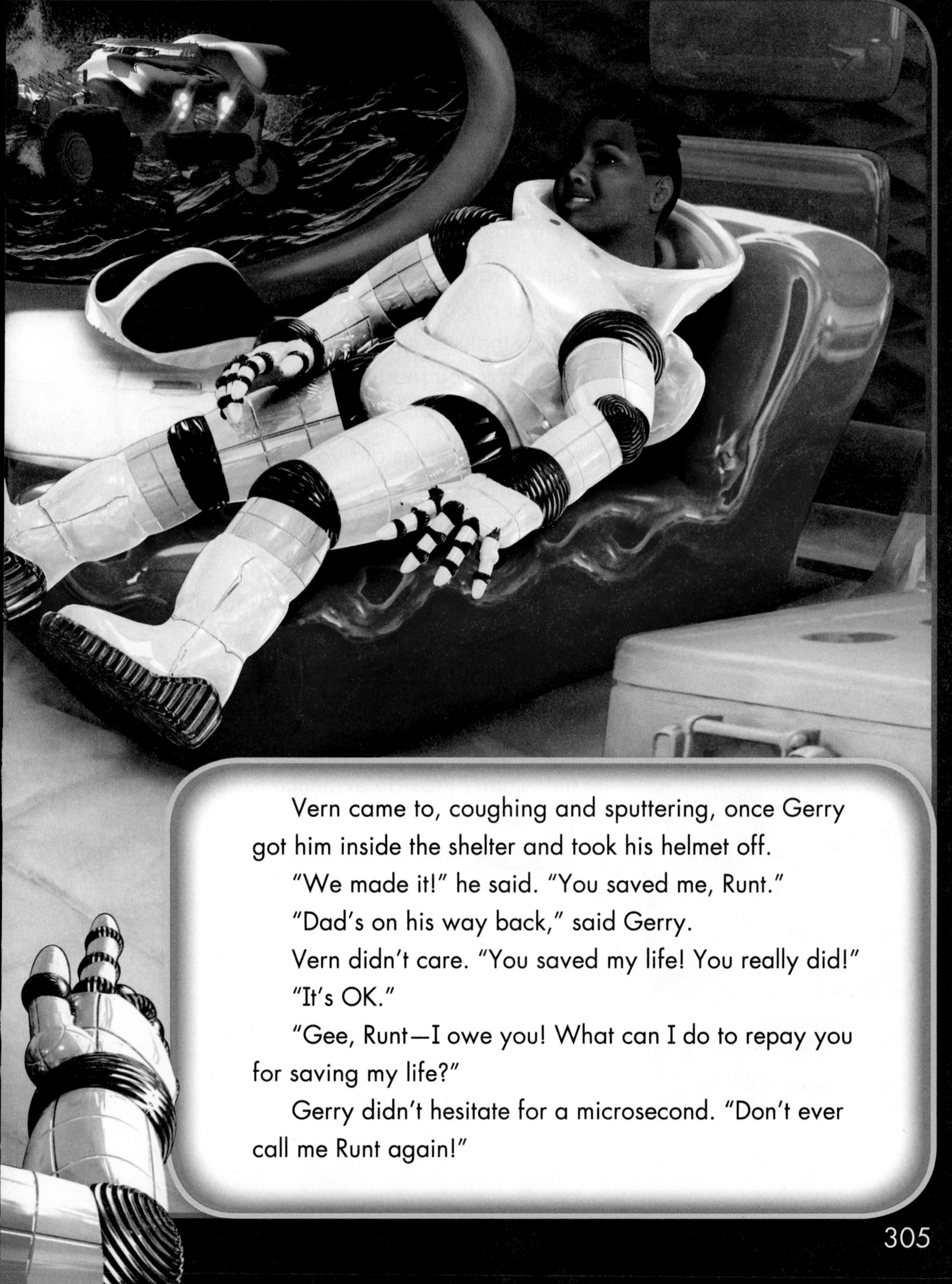

Vern came to, coughing and sputtering, once Gerry got him inside the shelter and took his helmet off.

"We made it!" he said. "You saved me, Runt."

"Dad's on his way back," said Gerry.

Vern didn't care. "You saved my life! You really did!"

"It's OK."

"Gee, Runt—I owe you! What can I do to repay you for saving my life?"

Gerry didn't hesitate for a microsecond. "Don't ever call me Runt again!"

Objectives

- Read independently for long periods of time and paraphrase the reading, including the order in which events occur.
- Write responses to texts using details to show understanding.

Envision It! **Retell**

READING STREET ONLINE
STORY SORT
www.ReadingStreet.com

Think Critically

1. Gerry reluctantly agrees to accompany his brother on a moonwalk. Why do you think Gerry goes with his brother? If you were Gerry, what would you have done? Why? **Text to Self**

2. Ben Bova's science fiction stories contain a careful mix of things that are familiar and things that are unfamiliar. What was familiar to you as you read "Moonwalk"? What was unfamiliar? **Think Like an Author**

3. What conclusions did you draw about the relationship between Gerry and Vern after reading the first line of the story? **Draw Conclusions**

4. What is a *rille*? How did you figure out what it is? **Monitor and Clarify**

5. **Look Back and Write** Look back at pages 303–304. How do Gerry's actions and thoughts show that he is both brave and smart? Provide evidence to support your answer. **TEST PRACTICE** **Extended Response**

Meet the Author

Ben Bova

Ben Bova has been writing science fiction for more than fifty years. He combines an understanding of science with the ability to tell great stories. His popular Grand Tour series of books for older readers tells of humans who explore and colonize the solar system in the future.

As a scientist, Mr. Bova has worked on major research projects. (For example, he helped prepare Apollo 11 for flight.) He calls upon the latest in scientific knowledge to write his books about the future. In the past, he predicted the first U.S. trip to the moon, virtual reality, video games, and possible life on Mars. Now, he predicts that we will one day enjoy tours in space and the discovery of extraterrestrial life. We'll see—he's been right so far!

Here are other science fiction books.

The Wonderful Flight to the Mushroom Planet
by Eleanor Cameron

The Forgotten Door
by Alexander Key

Use the Reading Log in the *Reader's and Writer's Notebook* to record your independent reading.

Objectives
- Write about important experiences in your life.
- Use and understand prepositions and prepositional phrases.

Key Features of a Personal Narrative

- tells about a personal experience
- recounts true events
- usually organized by sequence of events
- first-person narrator

READING STREET ONLINE
GRAMMAR JAMMER
www.ReadingStreet.com

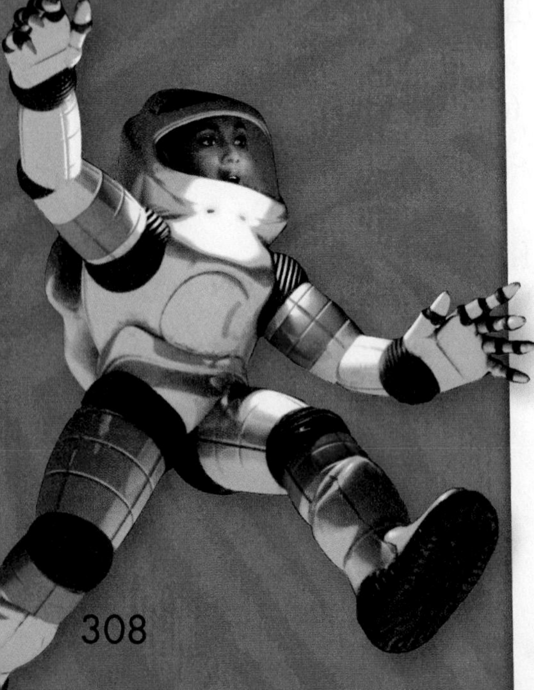

Personal Narrative

A **personal narrative** is a true story about a personal experience. The student model on the next page is an example of a personal narrative.

Writing Prompt Write about a time you took a risk that paid off.

Writer's Checklist

Remember, you should ...

- ✓ tell events in order.
- ✓ describe your thoughts and feelings about a real event.
- ✓ include interesting details.
- ✓ make your writing clear and organized.
- ✓ use prepositions and prepositional phrases correctly.

Student Model

Last year, I entered the school talent show. The prize for first place was a laptop computer, and I really wanted that computer. I wasn't worried about performing in front of an audience because I am a soloist in a local choral group. What I was worried about was choosing the right song to perform.

I know lots of songs, but I wanted to sing a song that I had written myself. My family said this would be a mistake. They thought the judges would respond best to a popular song. I wasn't sure what to do, so I practiced two songs—a popular song and my own song.

On the day of the talent show, I decided to take the risk. I was nervous when I went out onto the stage, faced the audience, and launched into the song I had written. When I finished, there was silence, and my heart sank. My family was right, I thought. The audience wanted to hear a familiar song. But suddenly the audience erupted into thunderous applause. They loved it! I won first place.

Writing Trait Sentences Short sentences are combined for smooth flow.

Genre A **personal narrative** describes the narrator's thoughts and feelings.

Prepositions and prepositional phrases are used correctly.

Conventions

Prepositions

Remember A **preposition** connects a noun or a pronoun to another word in the sentence. A **prepositional phrase** begins with a preposition and often ends with a noun or pronoun.

Objectives

- Explain the difference between a stated purpose and an implied purpose in expository texts.
- Describe how ideas are related in texts and whether the ideas are directly stated or not.
- Explain information that is shown in graphics.

Science in Reading

Genre

Expository Text

- Expository text contains facts about a subject.
- Some authors of expository texts state their purpose for writing. When an author does not state what it is, the reader has to infer, or figure it out.
- Some expository texts organize information by explicit comparisons and explain information with charts.
- Read "A Walk on the Moon." Look for elements that make this article an expository text. Does the author state her purpose for writing this article or do you have to figure it out?

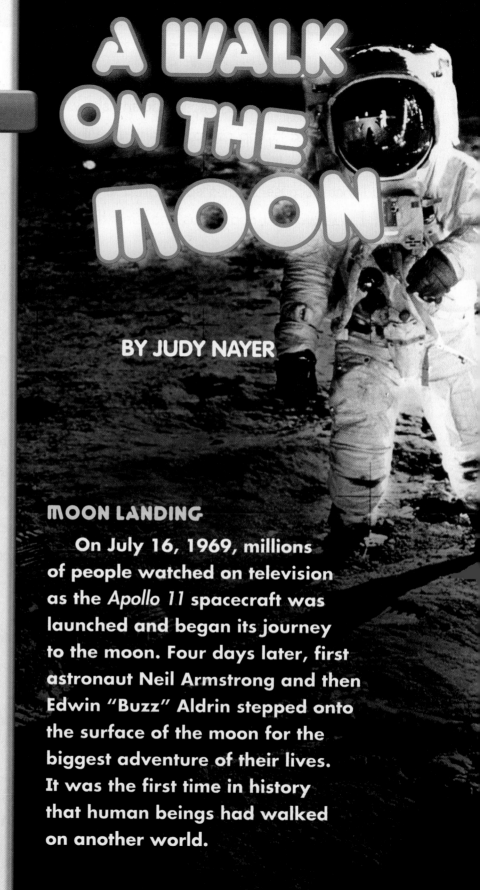

A WALK ON THE MOON

BY JUDY NAYER

MOON LANDING

On July 16, 1969, millions of people watched on television as the *Apollo 11* spacecraft was launched and began its journey to the moon. Four days later, first astronaut Neil Armstrong and then Edwin "Buzz" Aldrin stepped onto the surface of the moon for the biggest adventure of their lives. It was the first time in history that human beings had walked on another world.

MOON SUITING

The astronauts could not have walked on the moon without wearing special spacesuits. Unlike Earth, the moon has no air, so a backpack supplies oxygen for the astronaut to breathe. The spacesuit's many layers protect the astronaut from extreme temperatures (+250°F in the sun and –250°F in the shade) and cool water pumped through tubes inside the suit keeps the astronaut's body temperature constant. The suit and helmet protect the astronaut from the sun's harmful rays and from flying particles hurtling through space. There is also a headset and a microphone in the helmet so that astronauts can talk to one another.

MOON WALKING

What was it like for Neil Armstrong and Buzz Aldrin to walk on the moon? The moon's lower gravity had a big effect. Gravity is the force that pulls things toward the center of the Earth and keeps them from floating away. The Earth's metallic core has a lot to do with gravity. The moon, however, is only one quarter the size of the Earth, and it has only a tiny metallic core, about 15 times smaller than the Earth's. The result is that the moon has only one-sixth the gravity of Earth. The moon's weaker gravity means that the astronauts feel lighter—and they can float!

When the astronauts walked on the moon, each step was a leap that threw off clouds of fine dust. In order to land in the right place, they had to think a few steps ahead instead of just putting one foot in front of the other. They also had to be careful not to lose their balance.

Let's Think About...

How does walking on the moon compare to walking on Earth? **Expository Text**

The astronauts experimented with different ways of moving on the moon. When Aldrin tried running, he made giant strides and felt as though he were running in slow motion! The astronauts found that the easiest way to get around was to hop on two feet and bound like a kangaroo. They also discovered that they could effortlessly jump several feet off the ground and float gently down!

Let's Think About...

Describe how the moon's surface compares to the Earth's surface. How do "seas" on the moon compare to seas on Earth? **Expository Text**

MOON SIGHTINGS

What did Armstrong and Aldrin see on the moon? With no atmosphere to protect it, objects that hit the moon make a deep impact. Most of the moon's surface is covered with thousands of craters caused by rocks from space crashing into it. The craters range in size from small holes to basins more than a hundred miles across. The smoother areas on the moon are called maria, or "seas," which are not really seas but large, dark plains. Armstrong and Aldrin touched down at the Sea of Tranquility.

MOON COLLECTING

Besides walking around, what did the astronauts do on the moon? Armstrong and Aldrin's moonwalk lasted two and a half hours. During this time, they collected 48 pounds of rock and soil, took photographs, and planted an American flag. They also set up experiments to find out more about the moon.

THE APOLLO MISSIONS

Between 1969 and 1972, the Apollo space program landed twelve astronauts on the surface of the moon in six separate missions. In all, they spent 300 hours on the moon's surface, including 80 hours outside the landing craft.

MANNED MOON MISSIONS

Mission*	Date	Landing Site on Moon	Astronauts Who Walked on the Moon
Apollo 11	July 1969	Sea of Tranquility	Neil A. Armstrong Edwin E. "Buzz" Aldrin Jr.
Apollo 12	Nov. 1969	Ocean of Storms	Charles P. "Pete" Conrad Alan L. Bean
Apollo 14	Feb. 1971	Fra Mauro crater region	Alan B. Shepard Jr. Edgar D. Mitchell
Apollo 15	July 1971	Hadley Rille-Apennine mountain region	David Scott James Irwin
Apollo 16	April 1972	Descartes highlands	John W. Young Charles W. Duke
Apollo 17	Dec. 1972	Between the Taurus mountains and Littrow crater	Eugene A. Cernan Harrison H. Schmitt

* In April 1970, the *Apollo 13* mission was abandoned after an explosion in the spacecraft.

Let's Think About...

Describe how the chart helps you compare the information in the article. What is the author's purpose? Is it implied or stated? **Expository Text**

Let's Think About...

Reading Across Texts "Moonwalk" and "A Walk on the Moon" both deal with science. How do the authors treat science differently? Use evidence from the texts to explain.

Writing Across Texts Compare and contrast science fiction with nonfiction. Which genre would you rather read when reading about space travel? Why?

Objectives

• Read aloud grade-level texts and understand what is read. • Determine the meanings of unfamiliar words or multiple-meaning words by using the context of the sentence.
• Explain how the different methods used in media affect the message that is being communicated. • Use and understand prepositions and prepositional phrases. • Listen closely to speakers and ask questions about and comment on the topic.

READING STREET ONLINE
ONLINE STUDENT EDITION
www.ReadingStreet.com

Vocabulary

Synonyms

Context Clues Context clues give hints about a word's meaning. These clues might include other sentences that contain synonyms of the unfamiliar word. They should help you determine the meaning of the unfamiliar word.

Practice It! Find the word *rille* on pages 296 and 297 in *Moonwalk*. Look at nearby words and phrases to help figure out its meaning. Explain its meaning and how you figured it out to a partner. Have your partner do the same for the word *trench* on page 298.

Fluency

Rate and Accuracy

Partner Reading Reading at a steady pace can help you read accurately. If you read a word you are unsure of, slow down. Then read the sentence again at your original pace.

Practice It! With a partner, take turns reading aloud "Moonwalk," page 296, paragraphs 1–5. Slow down when you come to an unfamiliar word. Then reread the paragraphs, all at the same pace after you have mastered the unfamiliar words.

Media Literacy

When you participate in a discussion, maintain eye contact with others.

Talk Show

On a TV talk show, a host chats informally with guests who know about a subject or who have done something noteworthy. The camera will focus on the face of the speaker. Will the camera angle affect how you view the speaker and what he or she says?

Practice It! With a partner, conduct a TV talk show in front of the class. Take turns acting as host and guest. Choose to portray Gerry or Vern from *Moonwalk* as the guest. Use personality traits to play your roles.

Tips

Listening . . .

- Listen attentively to speakers.
- Be prepared to ask relevant questions. For questions to be relevant be sure to include appropriate details, such as "How does it feel to walk on the moon?"

Speaking . . .

- Use prepositions and prepositional phrases to show location, time, direction, or details correctly.
- Make eye contact when you speak.

Teamwork . . .

- Ask and answer questions with detail.
- Build upon others' ideas.

Objectives

- Explain how different poems use elements of poetry, such as rhyme and meter.

Poetry

- Lines of poems can be grouped together into **stanzas.** Stanzas share the same meter and rhyme.
- Paying attention to the stanzas helps you understand the poem's meaning.
- Poets create sounds with words. **Onomatopoeia** is a word that sounds the same as what it means. "Bang" is an example.
- Read "The Best Paths" and "Roller Coasters." Explain how the poems' stanzas help you understand the poems' meanings. Listen for onomatopoeia.

The Best Paths

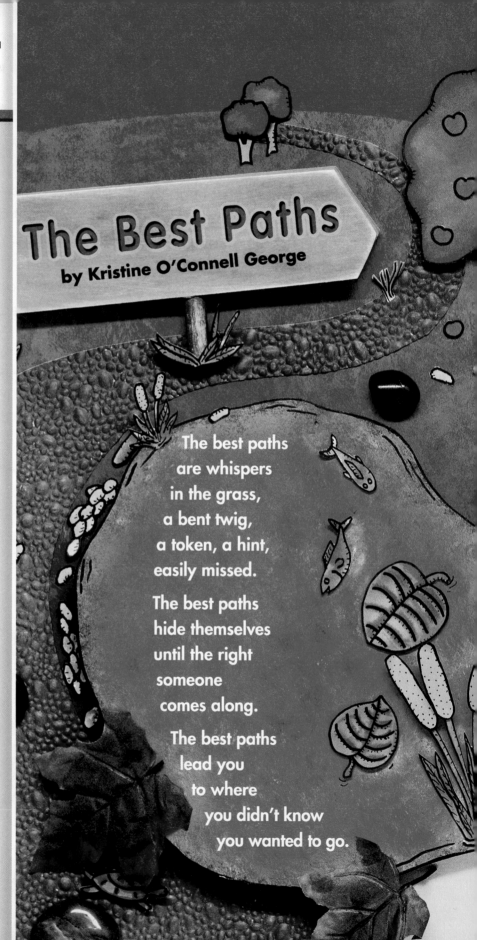

by Kristine O'Connell George

The best paths
are whispers
in the grass,
a bent twig,
a token, a hint,
easily missed.

The best paths
hide themselves
until the right
someone
comes along.

The best paths
lead you
to where
you didn't know
you wanted to go.

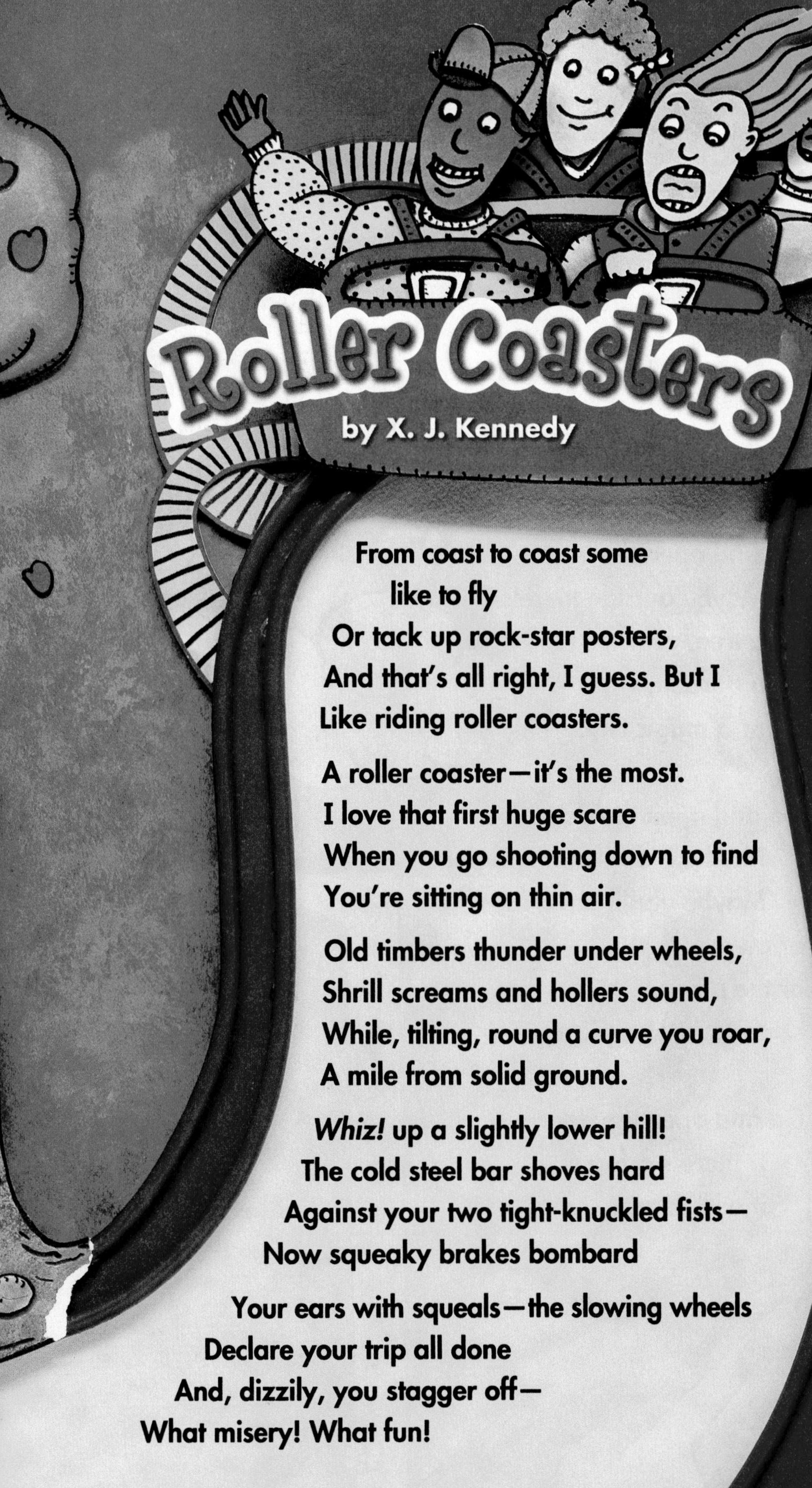

Roller Coasters

by X. J. Kennedy

From coast to coast some
like to fly
Or tack up rock-star posters,
And that's all right, I guess. But I
Like riding roller coasters.

A roller coaster—it's the most.
I love that first huge scare
When you go shooting down to find
You're sitting on thin air.

Old timbers thunder under wheels,
Shrill screams and hollers sound,
While, tilting, round a curve you roar,
A mile from solid ground.

Whiz! up a slightly lower hill!
The cold steel bar shoves hard
Against your two tight-knuckled fists—
Now squeaky brakes bombard

Your ears with squeals—the slowing wheels
Declare your trip all done
And, dizzily, you stagger off—
What misery! What fun!

Let's Think About...

Explain how the lines are grouped into stanzas in "The Best Paths." What does each stanza say? How are stanzas different in "Roller Coasters"?

Let's Think About...

Find an example of onomatopoeia in "Roller Coaster." Explain how the poet's use of it tells you how she feels about roller coasters.

The Door

by Miroslav Holub

Go and open the door.
Maybe outside there's
a tree, or a wood,
a garden,
or a magic city.

Go and open the door.
Maybe a dog's rummaging.
Maybe you'll see a face,
or an eye,
or the picture
of a picture.

Go and open the door.
If there's a fog
it will clear.

Go and open the door.
Even if there's only
the darkness ticking,
even if there's only
the hollow wind,
even if
nothing
is there,
go and open the door.

At least
there'll be
a draft.

Unit 6

Reaching for Goals

What does it take to achieve our goals and dreams?

Reading Street Online

www.ReadingStreet.com

- Big Question Video
- eSelections
- Envision It! Animations
- Story Sort

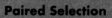

Let's Think About Reading!

Objectives

- Listen closely to speakers and ask questions about and comment on the topic. • Take part in discussions led by teachers or other students, ask and answer questions, and offer ideas that build on the ideas of other people.

Oral Vocabulary

Let's Talk About

Equal Opportunities

- Share opinions about what *equal opportunity* means.
- Express ideas about how equal opportunities help people reach goals.
- Answer questions with appropriate detail.

READING STREET ONLINE
SOUND-SPELLING CARDS
www.ReadingStreet.com

You've learned
250
Amazing Words
so far this year!

Objectives
- Ask different types of questions about a text.
- Describe how ideas are related in texts whether the ideas are directly stated or not.

Envision It! Skill Strategy

Skill

Strategy

Questioning

Questioning is asking good questions about important text information. Questioning takes place before, during, and after reading.

To question
- read with a question in mind
- stop, think, and record your questions as you read
- make notes when you find information
- check your understanding and ask questions to clarify

Let's Think About Reading!

When I question, I ask myself
- Have I asked a good question with a question word?
- What questions help me make sense of my reading?
- What does the author mean?

EI•21

READING STREET ONLINE
ENVISION IT! ANIMATIONS
www.ReadingStreet.com

Comprehension Skill

Cause and Effect

- The *effect* is what happens. The *cause* is why it happens.
- Clue words such as *because, so, therefore,* and *as a result* signal explicit causes and effects. When there aren't any clue words, the relationship will be implicit. You will have to figure out the relationship for yourself.
- Sometimes one effect becomes the cause of another effect, which causes another, and so on. This is called a chain of events.
- Use the graphic organizer to identify the chain of events Rosa Parks set in motion as you read "Rosa Parks Started Something Big."

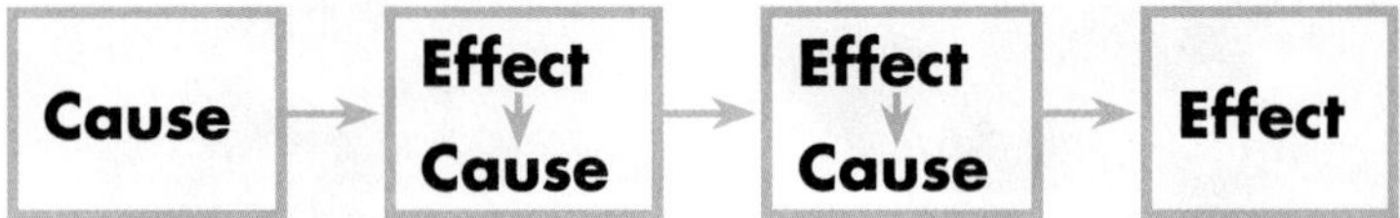

Comprehension Strategy

Questioning

Good readers ask different types of questions as they read. When you ask a literal question, the answer can be found "right there" in the text. An interpretive question is answered by using other information in the text to figure out an answer on your own. An evaluative question is answered by making a judgment. You will go beyond the text to answer the question.

Rosa Parks Started Something Big

Rosa Parks was tired. She had worked hard all day. To ride home, she took a seat on the Cleveland Avenue bus in Montgomery, Alabama.

On that evening of December 1, 1955, segregation was the law. That meant white people could ride in the front of the bus, but black people had to ride in the back. Black people could sit in the middle rows—as long as no white people wanted those seats.

Skill What effect did the law regarding segregation on buses have on black people in Montgomery, Alabama, in 1955?

Rosa Parks, an African American, was settled in the first row of the section for black people when a white man demanded her seat. She refused to get up.

Because she refused, the bus driver called the police. Rosa Parks was arrested. Black people throughout the city protested by refusing to ride the buses. This action, called a boycott, was organized by a minister name Martin Luther King Jr. After more than a year, the law was changed. Segregation on buses was no longer allowed.

Skill What was the final effect in the chain of events that started with Rosa's action?

Because of Martin Luther King Jr.'s work, he became widely known. He went on to lead the struggle for African Americans' rights throughout the country.

Strategy •Ask a literal question about what you have read. •Ask a question that can be answered by interpreting what you have read. •Ask a question that can be answered by making a judgment about what you have read.

Your Turn!

Need a Review? See *Envision It! Handbook* for help with cause and effect and questioning.

Let's Think About...

Ready to Try It? Describe implicit cause-and-effect relationships as you read *My Brother Martin*.

Objectives

- Determine the meaning of English words with roots from Greek, Latin, and other languages.

Envision It! Words to Know

generations

pulpit

shielding

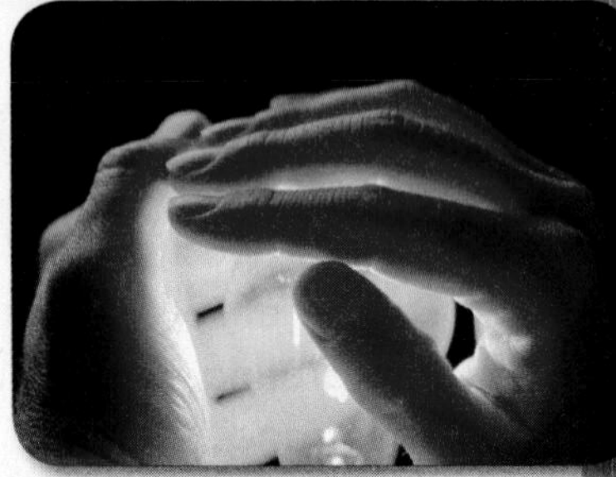

avoided
ancestors
minister
numerous

READING STREET ONLINE
VOCABULARY ACTIVITIES
www.ReadingStreet.com

Vocabulary Strategy for

Root Words

Word Structure A root word is a word that other words are made from. The academic word *numerous* contains the Middle English root *numerus*, which means "number." If you know the root of a word, it can help you figure out the word's meaning.

1. Look at the word *avoided*. Does it have a root word you know?
2. How does the meaning of the prefix, suffix, or ending affect the meaning of the root?
3. Put together the root and the meaning of the prefix, suffix, or ending. The root word *avoid* means "to keep away from," and the ending *-ed* indicates past tense. *Avoided* means "to have kept away from."
4. Check to see that the meaning makes sense in the sentence.

As you read "Out of Slavery," use what you know about root words to figure out the academic words *courageous* and *nourishment*, and the *Words to Know*.

Words to Write Reread "Out of Slavery." Think about one of your ancestors. Write about what makes you proud of your ancestor. Use words from *Words to Know* in your article.

OUT OF SLAVERY

Slavery caused great hardship and sorrow in the United States. Africans were forced to come here as slaves. For generations slaves lived without freedom, and many white masters were cruel to them. All along, some white people said it was wrong to keep slaves. Over the years, more and more believed and said this. Often these voices came from the pulpit. It took a courageous minister to speak out and work for change. The number of people who wanted to free all slaves slowly grew.

Some very brave white and free black people helped slaves escape to freedom. They found numerous ways of shielding the runaway slaves. For example, helpers hid them in safe houses to sleep and gave them nourishment and clothes. Slaves who had run away avoided being seen by staying off roads and traveling at night.

Many people helped slaves escape, but it took a long, terrible war to bring an end to slavery. Today African Americans remember their ancestors and are proud and thankful for the sacrifices they made.

Your Turn!

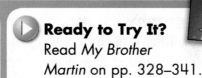

Need a Review? For help with root words, see *Words!*

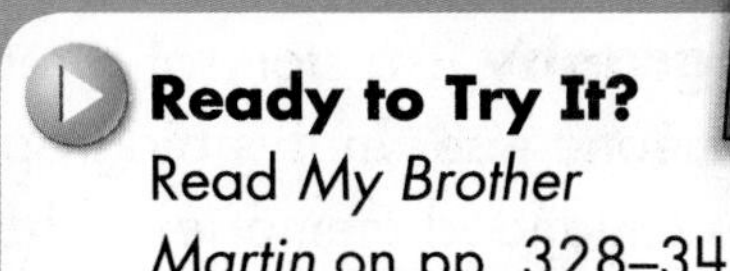

Ready to Try It? Read *My Brother Martin* on pp. 328–341.

Genre

A **biography** is a story of a real person told by someone else. In this biography, a sister shares childhood memories of her younger brother. Why do you think she chose to tell about these experiences?

MY BROTHER MARTIN

A Sister Remembers Growing Up with the Rev. Dr. Martin Luther King Jr.

by Christine King Farris
illustrated by Chris Soentpiet

Question of the Week

How can words change people's lives?

Let's Think About...

Can you predict whether you will find out what the dream was by the end of this biography? **Predict**

Gather around and listen as I share the childhood memories of my brother, the Reverend Dr. Martin Luther King Jr. I am his older sister, and I've known him longer than anyone else. I knew him long before the speeches he gave and the marches he led and the prizes he won. I even knew him before *he first dreamed* the *dream that would change the world.*

We were born in the same room, my brother Martin and I. I was an early baby, born sooner than expected. Mother Dear and Daddy placed me in the chifforobe drawer that stood in the corner of their upstairs bedroom. I got a crib a few days afterward. A year and a half later, Martin spent his first night in that hand-me-down crib in the very same room.

The house where we were born belonged to Mother Dear's parents, our grandparents, the Reverend and Mrs. A. D. Williams. We lived there with them and our Aunt Ida, our grandmother's sister. And not long after my brother Martin—who we called M. L. because he and Daddy had the same name—our baby brother was born. His name was Alfred Daniel, but we called him A. D., after our grandfather.

They called me Christine, and like three peas in one pod, we grew together. Our days and rooms were filled with adventure stories and Tinkertoys, with dolls and Monopoly and Chinese checkers.

And although Daddy, who was an important minister, and Mother Dear, who was known far and wide as a musician, often had work that took them away from home, our grandmother was always there to take care of us. I remember days sitting at her feet, as she and Aunt Ida filled us with grand memories of their childhood and read to us about all the wonderful places in the world.

Let's Think About...

What kind of family were the Kings? What details tell you they lived in a happy home? **Inferring**

Let's **Think** About...

Identify the similarites and differences between the actual events and experiences described in this biography and the events and characters' experiences in a fictional work. **Inferring**

Let's **Think** About...

What can you do to help you understand what a "fur piece" is? **Monitor and Clarify**

And of course, my brothers and I had each other. We three stuck together like the pages in a brand-new book. And being normal young children, we were almost *always* up to something.

Our best prank involved a fur piece that belonged to our grandmother. It looked almost alive, with its tiny feet and little head and gleaming glass eyes. So, every once in a while, in the waning light of evening, we'd tie that fur piece to a stick, and, hiding behind the hedge in front of our house, we would dangle it in front of unsuspecting passersby. Boy! You could hear the screams of fright all across the neighborhood!

Then there was the time Mother Dear decided that her children should all learn to play piano. I didn't mind too much, but M. L. and A. D. preferred being outside to being stuck inside with our piano teacher, Mr. Mann, who would rap your knuckles with a ruler just for playing the wrong notes. Well, one morning, M. L. and A. D. decided to loosen the legs on the piano bench so we wouldn't have to practice. We didn't tell Mr. Mann, and when he sat ... *CRASH!* down he went.

But mostly we were good, obedient children, and M. L. did learn to play a few songs on the piano. He even went off to sing with our mother a time or two. Given his love for singing and music, I'm sure he could have become as good a musician as our mother had his life not called him down a different path.

But that's just what his life did.

Let's Think About...

What different path was M. L. called on to take?

Questioning

My brothers and I grew up a long time ago. Back in a time when certain places in our country had unfair laws that said it was right to keep black people separate because our skin was darker and our ancestors had been captured in far-off Africa and brought to America as slaves.

Atlanta, Georgia, the city in which we were growing up, had those laws. Because of those laws, my family rarely went to the picture shows or visited Grant Park with its famous Cyclorama. In fact, to this very day I don't recall ever seeing my father on a streetcar. Because of those laws, and the indignity that went with them, Daddy preferred keeping M. L., A. D., and me close to home, where we'd be protected.

We lived in a neighborhood in Atlanta that's now called Sweet Auburn. It was named for Auburn Avenue, the street that ran in front of our house. On our side of the street stood two-story frame houses similar to the one we lived in. Across it crouched a line of one-story row houses and a store owned by a white family.

Let's Think About...

Can you use clues in the text to infer that Christine, M. L., and A. D. would not be safe if they rode on a streetcar? **Inferring**

When we were young all the children along Auburn Avenue played together, even the two boys whose parents owned the store.

And since our house was a favorite gathering place, those boys played with us in our backyard . . .

. . . and ran with M. L. and A. D. to the firehouse on the corner where they watched the engines and the firemen.

The thought of *not* playing with those kids because they were different, because they were white and we were black, never entered our minds.

Let's Think About...

Describe one or two implicit cause-and-effect relationships in this text. **Inferring**

Let's Think About...

Why did the author mention the idea that the kids might not play together? **Questioning**

Well, one day, M. L. and A. D. went to get their playmates from across the street just as they had done a hundred times before. But they came home alone. The boys had told my brothers that they couldn't play together anymore because A. D. and M. L. were Negroes.

And that was it. Shortly afterward the family sold the store and moved away. We never saw or heard from them again.

Looking back, I realize that it was only a matter of time before the generations of cruelty and injustice that Daddy and Mother Dear and Mama and Aunt Ida had been shielding us from finally broke through. But back then it was a crushing blow that seemed to come out of nowhere.

"Why do white people treat colored people so mean?" M. L. asked Mother Dear afterward. And with me and M. L. and A. D. standing in front of her trying our best to understand, Mother Dear gave the reason behind it all.

Let's Think About...

How do the illustration on this page and M. L.'s question to his mother help you understand how M. L. and A. D. felt? **Inferring**

Her words explained the streetcars our family avoided and the WHITES ONLY sign that kept us off the elevator at City Hall. Her words told why there were parks and museums that black people could not visit and why some restaurants refused to serve us and why hotels wouldn't give us rooms and why theaters would only allow us to watch their picture shows from the balcony.

But her words also gave us hope.

She answered simply, "Because they just don't understand that everyone is the same, but someday, it will be better."

And my brother M. L. looked up into our mother's face and said the words I remember to this day.

He said, "Mother Dear, one day I'm going to turn this world upside down."

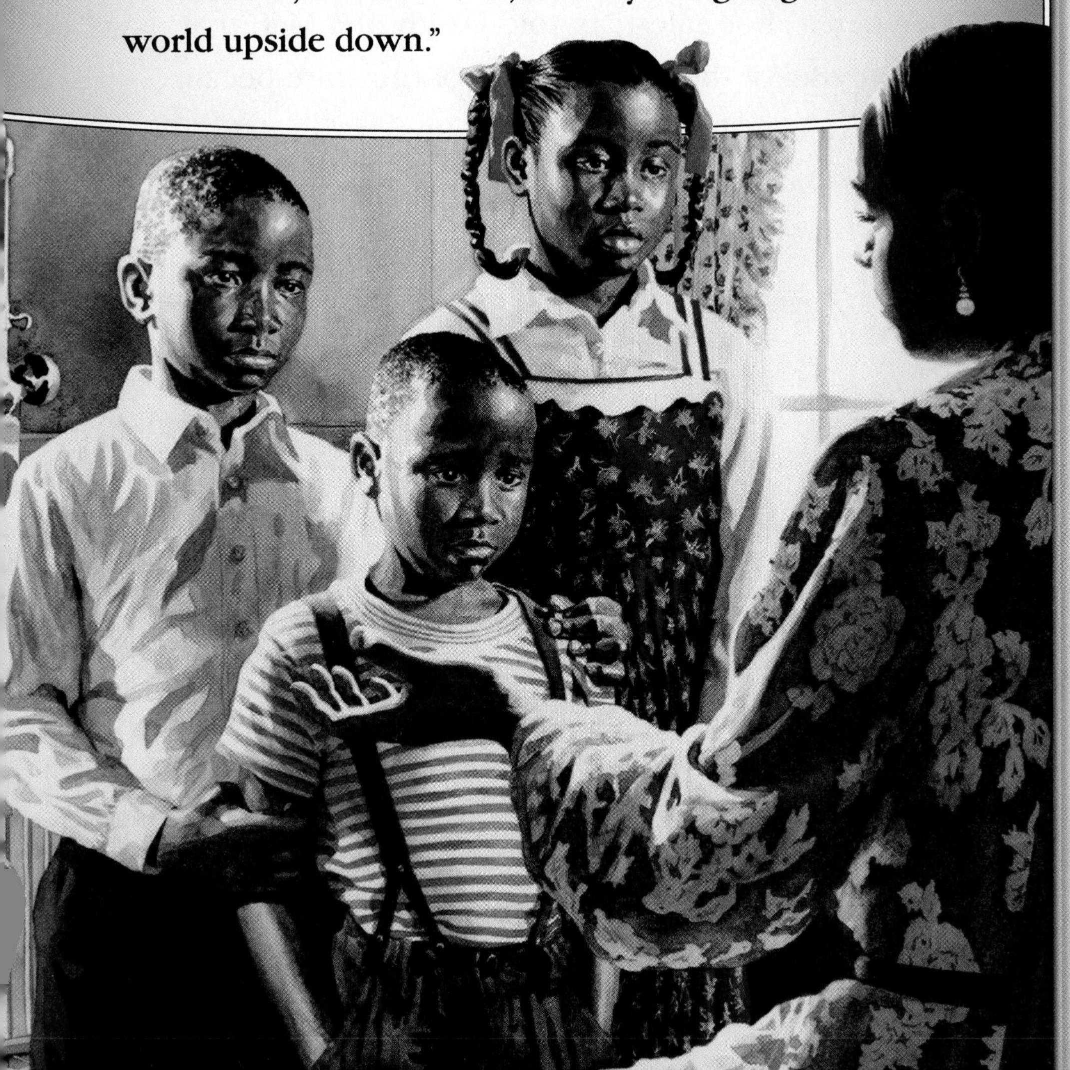

In the coming years there would be other reminders of the cruel system called segregation that sought to keep black people down. But it was Daddy who showed M. L. and A. D. and me how to speak out against hatred and bigotry and stand up for what's right. Daddy was the minister at Ebenezer Baptist Church. And after losing our playmates, when M. L., A. D., and I heard our father speak from his pulpit, his words held new meaning.

And Daddy practiced what he preached. He always stood up for himself when confronted with hatred and bigotry, and each day he shared his encounters at the dinner table.

When a shoe salesman told Daddy and M. L. that he'd only serve them in the back of the store because they were black, Daddy took M. L. somewhere else to buy new shoes.

Let's **Think** About...

Can you figure out what segregation is? What can you do to help you understand what the word means? **Monitor and Clarify**

Another time, a police officer pulled Daddy over and called him "boy." Daddy pointed to M. L. sitting next to him in the car and said, "This is a boy. I am a man, and until you call me one, I will not listen to you."

These stories were as nourishing as the food that was set before us.

Years would pass, and many new lessons would be learned. There would be numerous speeches and marches and prizes. But my brother never forgot the example of our father, or the promise he had made to our mother on the day his friends turned him away.

And when he was much older, my brother M. L. dreamed a dream. . . .

Let's Think About...

Does the illustration help you answer the question about how Dr. Martin Luther King would change the world?

Questioning

. . . that turned the world upside down.

I Have a Dream

Speech delivered by Martin Luther King Jr.

28 August 1963, at the Lincoln Memorial, Washington, D.C.

. . . And if America is to be a great nation, this must become true.
And so let freedom ring from the prodigious hilltops of New Hampshire.
Let freedom ring from the mighty mountains of New York.
Let freedom ring from the heightening Alleghenies of Pennsylvania.
Let freedom ring from the snow-capped Rockies of Colorado.
Let freedom ring from the curvaceous slopes of California.
But not only that:
Let freedom ring from Stone Mountain of Georgia.
Let freedom ring from Lookout Mountain of Tennessee.
Let freedom ring from every hill and molehill of Mississippi.
From every mountainside, let freedom ring. . . .

Objectives

- Identify how an author uses similes and metaphors to create imagery.
- Write responses to texts using details to show understanding.

Envision It! | **Retell**

READING STREET ONLINE
STORY SORT
www.ReadingStreet.com

Think Critically

1. The three King children had to live through the injustice of segregation. Think about a time when you felt like you were treated unfairly. How did you feel? What did you do? Why? **Text to Self**

2. On page 331, the author says that the three King children were "like three peas in one pod." What image does this simile bring to mind? On page 332 she uses another simile to describe the children's relationship. What simile would you use to describe them? **Think Like an Author**

3. Why did young Martin promise his mother that he would turn the world upside down one day? **Cause and Effect**

4. Do you think that Martin's parents should have told their children about the many injustices they would have to face in the world? Why or why not? **Questioning**

5. **Look Back and Write** Look back at pages 338 and 339. Find an example of how Martin's father "practiced what he preached." Then write what that example meant to the King family. Provide evidence to support your answer.
   TEST PRACTICE **Extended Response**

Meet the Author and the Illustrator

Christine King Farris

Christine King Farris was close in age to her brother Martin Luther King Jr. The two of them played together a lot as they were growing up. Ms. Farris's main goal in writing *My Brother Martin* was to let children know that her brother was an ordinary child. Many youngsters seem to think he "came from outer space," she says.

Ms. Farris thinks her brother can be a role model for all children. "I want children to understand as they are growing up that they, too, can become great individuals." Even as a child, her brother seemed to have known that. "It all goes back to what Martin said to my mother. He said, 'You know, Mother dear, one day I'm going to turn this world upside down.' And that is exactly what he did."

Ms. Farris is an Associate Professor of Education at Spelman College.

Chris Soentpiet

Chris Soentpiet, a native Korean, was orphaned before he was eight and adopted by the Soentpiets, an American family who lived in Hawaii.

Mr. Soentpiet says, "It was exciting to work with the sister of Dr. King. When I was in school, we celebrated his birthday every year. Dr. King is one of my heroes. I hope this book will tell boys and girls that Dr. King was just like them when he was their age."

Here are other books about Martin Luther King Jr. and the Civil Rights movement.

Martin's Big Words
by Doreen Rappaport

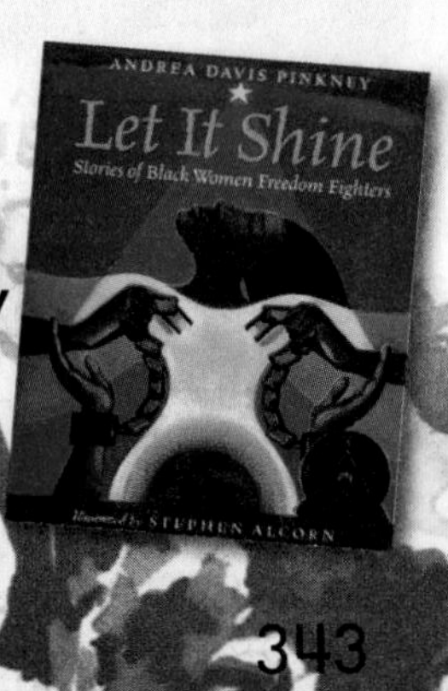

Let It Shine
by Andrea Davis Pinkney

Reading Log

Use the Reading Log in the *Reader's and Writer's Notebook* to record your independent reading.

Objectives
- Write brief texts that establish a main idea in a topic sentence.
- Write brief texts that contain a conclusion.
- Write responses to texts using details to show understanding.
- Use and understand the function of correlative conjunctions.

Key Features of a Cause-and-Effect Essay
- describes events or outcomes
- details explain why the events or outcomes happened
- uses words that signal cause-and-effect relationships

READING STREET ONLINE
GRAMMAR JAMMER
www.ReadingStreet.com

Expository

Cause-and-Effect Essay

A **cause-and-effect essay** explains something that happens and why it happens. The student model on the next page is an example of a cause-and-effect essay.

Writing Prompt Write a cause-and-effect essay about the influences in Reverend Dr. Martin Luther King Jr.'s life.

Writer's Checklist

Remember, you should ...
- ✓ have a topic sentence with a clear cause-and-effect focus.
- ✓ provide evidence to show the cause and its effects.
- ✓ end with a concluding statement about the cause and its effects.
- ✓ use correlative conjunctions correctly.

Student Model

Changing the World

Dr. Martin Luther King Jr. grew up in a time when African Americans were subject to discrimination, or unfair treatment. How, you might ask, did he manage to rise above those obstacles to become such a great leader? The answer can be traced to lessons from his parents.

Writing Trait Focus/Ideas New terms are defined.

Both King's mother **and** father tried to protect their children from experiencing the cruelty of discrimination. When King was hurt by the sudden end of his friendship with some neighborhood children, his mother didn't get angry with them. Instead, she told him that some people "just don't understand that everyone is the same."

Correlative conjunctions are used correctly.

King's father simply chose not to buy shoes from the salesman who, because King was black, would only serve him in the back of the store.

Genre Cause-and-effect essays use evidence as support.

Because of these experiences, and others like them, Martin Luther King Jr. grew up with a sense of dignity and the knowledge that he was equal to all men. His parents gave him the determination to change this world.

Conventions

Conjunctions

Remember A conjunction joins words or groups of words in a sentence. **Correlative conjunctions** are pairs of words such as *either/or, neither/nor,* and *both/and.* Correlative conjunctions can join either single words or groups of words.

Objectives

- Identify how an author uses similes and metaphors to create imagery.
- Make connections between literary and informational texts with similar ideas and support your ideas with details from the texts.

Poetry

Genre
Poetry

- Poetry expresses ideas, thoughts, and feelings.
- A poet may use rhyme and line breaks to emphasize the ideas of a poem.
- Poets also use similes and metaphors to create images in a poem. A simile is a comparison of two unlike things or ideas, using the word *like* or *as*. A metaphor also compares unlike things, but it does not use *like* or *as*.
- Read these poems. Look for similes and metaphors as you read.

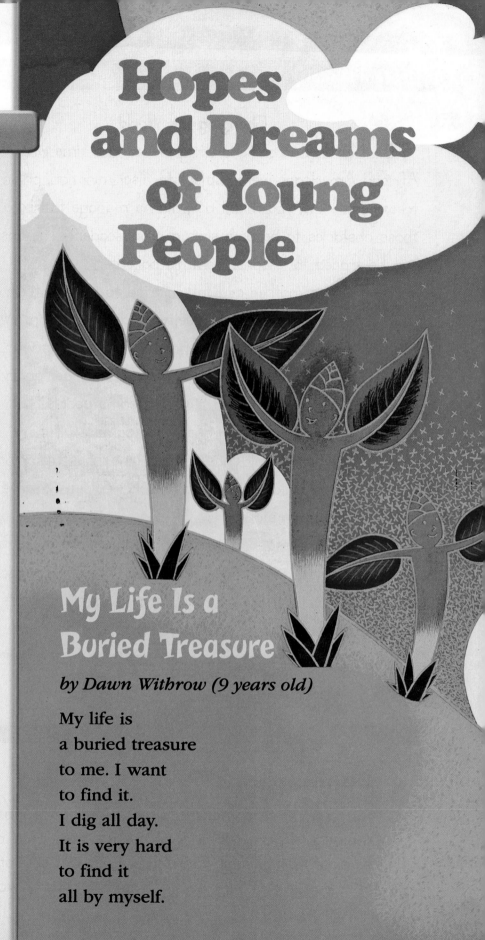

Hopes and Dreams of Young People

My Life Is a Buried Treasure

by Dawn Withrow (9 years old)

My life is
a buried treasure
to me. I want
to find it.
I dig all day.
It is very hard
to find it
all by myself.

When You Hope, Wish, and Trust

by Ek Ongkar K. Khalsa
(10 years old)

There was something that kept
me on a path,
like a strong steady rope,
but what really kept me there,
was nothing more than hope.

You cannot let yourself fail,
when you hope, wish, and trust,
when you give up your dream,
it's like letting your wish rust.

Like Martin Luther King Jr.,
he made his dream come true,
so I know if you don't give up,
your dream will come to you.

Sometimes the words we speak,
became real and near,
so when we hope,
wish and trust,
our dreams will
really appear.

Haiku

by Cristina Beecham (9 years old)

Just a small seedling
Can make a big difference
Could you be that seed?

Does the poet of "My Life Is a Buried Treasure" use metaphors or similes? Find a simile in "When You Hope."

Let's Think About...

Reading Across Texts Connect one of these poems with *My Brother Martin.* Which one expresses the same ideas that he believed in?

Writing Across Texts Explain your choice.

Objectives

- Read aloud grade-level texts and understand what is read.
- Determine the meaning of English words with roots from Greek, Latin, and other languages.
- Take part in discussions led by teachers or other students, ask and answer questions, and offer ideas that build on the ideas of other people.
- Use and understand the function of correlative conjunctions.
- Listen closely to speakers and ask questions about and comment on the topic.

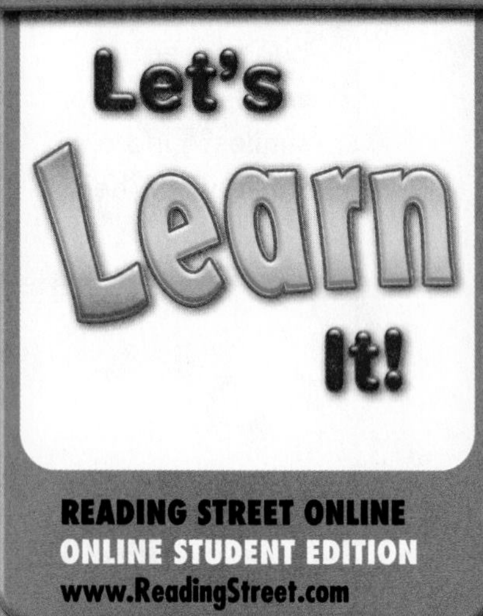

READING STREET ONLINE
ONLINE STUDENT EDITION
www.ReadingStreet.com

Vocabulary

Root Words

Word Structure Many academic words in the English language contain roots, or word parts, from other languages. When you read a word whose meaning you are unsure of, look for a root word that can help you figure out the word's meaning.

Practice It! Look at the word *chifforobe* on page 330 in *My Brother Martin*. The root *chiffo* comes from the French word *chiffonier*, which means "a tall chest of drawers." Use the root's meaning to figure out the meaning of *chifforobe*. Check to see that the meaning makes sense in the sentence.

Fluency

Appropriate Phrasing

Partner Reading Keeping related words grouped together as you read makes sentences easier to understand.

Practice It! With a partner, practice reading aloud *My Brother Martin*, page 331, paragraphs 1–3. Read with careful phrasing, paying attention to the commas and dashes that set off clauses. Then listen as your partner reads.

Listening and Speaking

Get Ready For Middle School

When you express an opinion, employ eye contact, speaking rate, volume, and enunciation, and the conventions of language to communicate ideas effectively.

Panel Discussion

In a panel discussion, a group of people talks about a certain subject in front of an audience.

Practice It! With a group, present a panel discussion in front of the class on whether school should be open twelve months. Form small groups based on differing opinions. Try to convince others to agree with your views. Respond to opinions you disagree with.

Tips

Listening . . .

- Listen to the main points of the panel discussion to help you understand the language that you are familiar with and that you are unfamiliar with.

Speaking . . .

- Make eye contact to express an opinion.
- Speak at an even rate, appropriate volume, and enunciate, or speak clearly.
- Employ the conventions of language. Use correct grammar.

Teamwork . . .

- Answer questions with examples that support your opinion.
- Talk about familiar and unfamiliar language you heard used in the panel discussion.

Objectives

- Take part in discussions led by teachers or other students, ask and answer questions, and offer ideas that build on the ideas of other people.

Oral Vocabulary

Let's Talk About

Challenges

- Ask questions about how to meet a physical challenge.
- Answer questions with appropriate detail.
- Express opinions with conventions of language.

READING STREET ONLINE
CONCEPT TALK VIDEO
www.ReadingStreet.com

You've learned
2 6 0
Amazing Words
so far this year!

Objectives

- Explain the difference between a fact and an opinion in a text and tell why a fact is true.
- Summarize information in a text.
- Summarize the main idea and supporting details.

Envision It! Skill Strategy

Skill

Fact and Opinion

A fact is something that can be proved true or false. An opinion can't be proved.

Fact

Wow, you blew the tuba for 45 seconds straight!

Opinion

But I think it sounds HORRIBLE!

Generalize

To generalize is to make a broad statement or rule that applies to many examples.

Batteries never last very long.

EI•7

Strategy

Summarize

We **summarize**, or retell, to check our understanding of what we've read. A summary is a brief statement—no more than a few sentences—and maintains a logical order.

To summarize fiction
- tell what happens in the story
- include the goals of the characters, how they try to reach them, and whether or not they succeed

To summarize nonfiction
- tell the main idea
- think about text structure and how the selection is organized

Let's Think About Reading!

When I summarize, I ask myself
- What is the story or selection mainly about?
- In fiction, what are the characters' goals? Are they successful?
- In nonfiction, how is the information organized?

EI•23

READING STREET ONLINE
ENVISION IT! ANIMATIONS
www.ReadingStreet.com

Comprehension Skill

Fact and Opinion

- Statements of fact can be proved true or false. Statements of opinion are judgments, beliefs, or ways of thinking about something.
- Evaluate statements of opinion by using the text, your prior knowledge, and logic. Ask: Is the statement of opinion valid? Is it supported well? Or is it faulty, without support?
- Use the graphic organizer to distinguish facts from opinions as you read "Are You Ready for Some Football?"

Statement of Fact or Opinion	How to Check Statement of Fact/ Support for Statement of Opinion	Valid or Faulty?

Comprehension Strategy

Summarize

Good readers summarize information in texts. As you read, decide what are the main ideas. Then put these ideas together in logical order into a short statement, or summary, that maintains the meaning of the text. As you summarize, does your thinking change?

ARE YOU READY FOR SOME FOOTBALL?

WHEN DID THE GAME BEGIN?

American football wasn't invented all at once. It evolved at colleges in the late 1800s from two other games: soccer and rugby. Football was like soccer in that you could move the ball toward a goal by kicking it. Football was like rugby in that you could run with the ball and tackle players.

Skill Even in this text, there can be statements of opinion. Ask: Will this statement be supported by facts or logic? Will it be valid or faulty?

PLAY NICE!

By 1900, football had become rough! A team could have as many as 25 to 30 players on the field at one time. That's a lot of people running, blocking, and tackling. Often the "game" was more like a brawl! To make matters worse, players didn't wear pads or helmets. Not a good idea! Finally, President Theodore Roosevelt said the sport must have rules for safety.

Skill Is this sentence a statement of fact or opinion? If opinion, explain if it is valid or faulty.

FOOTBALL TODAY

Over the years, the game of football has continued to change. New rules have been added, and while college football is still popular, sports fans have also grown to love professional football. In fact, do you know what the most watched American TV sports event is? The Super Bowl! It is also the best American sports event.

Strategy What is the main idea of this article? What details would you include in a summary of this article?

Your Turn!

Need a Review? See the *Envision It! Handbook* for help with fact and opinion and summarizing.

Ready to Try It? Use what you have learned about fact and opinion as you read *Jim Thorpe's Bright Path.*

Objectives

- Use a dictionary or glossary to find the meanings of unknown words, the syllable rules for these words, and how to pronounce them.

Envision It! Words to Know

dormitory

endurance

manual

boarding school

reservation

society

READING STREET ONLINE
VOCABULARY ACTIVITIES
www.ReadingStreet.com

Vocabulary Strategy for

Multiple-Meaning Words

Dictionary/Glossary Sometimes you may read a word whose meaning you know, but that meaning doesn't make sense. The word may have more than one meaning. Use a dictionary or glossary to find the correct meaning.

Choose one of the *Words to Know* and follow these steps.

1. Try the meaning that you know to see if it makes sense in the sentence.
2. If it doesn't, look up the word in a dictionary or glossary.
3. Find the entry for the word. The entries are in alphabetical order.
4. Read all the meanings given for the word. Try each meaning in the sentence.
5. Choose the meaning that makes the best sense in the sentence.

Read "Dreaming of Home." Use a dictionary or glossary to figure out the meanings of *reservation* and *manual* and other words with multiple meanings.

Words to Write Reread "Dreaming of Home." Imagine you went to school far away. Write about your feelings. Use words from the *Words to Know* list.

DREAMING OF HOME

Annie gazed out the window of the dormitory and longed to go outside. She knew that being outside would make her feel less homesick. But the students were required to do three hours of manual labor every day.

Annie's task was to wash the windows. While her hands were busy, her mind was back home on the reservation. There, she was talking to her mother and playing games with her sisters. Here, she lived in the dormitory with a hundred other girls. There, she was riding her pony and listening to her grandfather tell stories. Here, she sat in a classroom reciting English verbs.

Annie had not wanted to go away to boarding school, but that was the policy for Indian children in 1895. The school was supposed to teach them how to live in white society. Annie thought about what her father had said to her: "Akikta, remember the meaning of your name. You have determination. This experience will teach you patience and endurance."

Your Turn!

Need a Review? For help with using a dictionary or glossary to determine the meaning of multiple-meaning words, see *Words!*

Ready to Try It? Read *Jim Thorpe's Bright Path* on pp. 356–371.

Jim Thorpe's Bright Path

by Joseph Bruchac
illustrated by S. D. Nelson

A **biography** is the story of a real person's life as told by someone else. As you read this biography, think about why the author chose to write about this athlete.

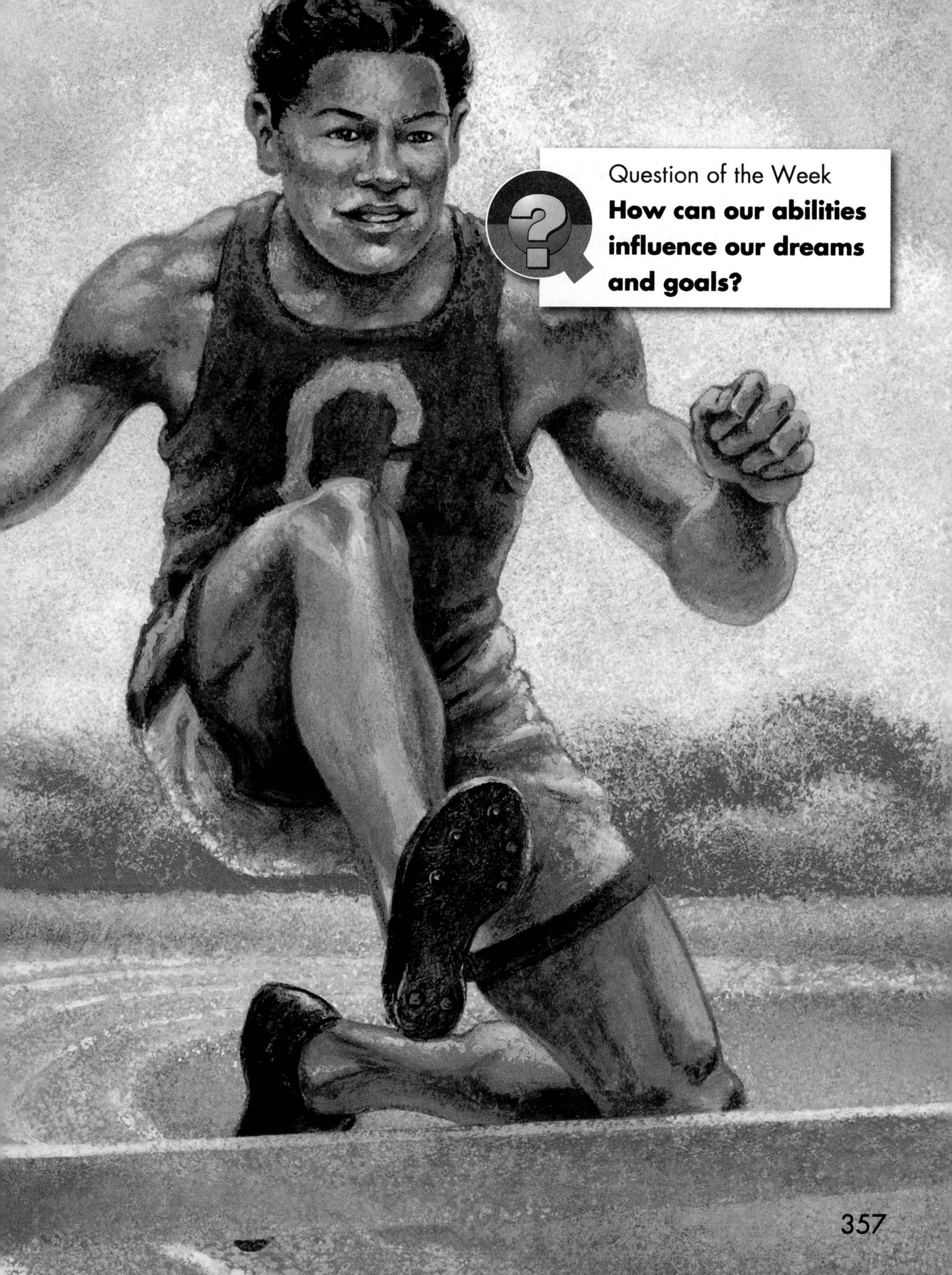

Question of the Week

How can our abilities influence our dreams and goals?

They say Jim Thorpe's story began in May of 1887 in a small log cabin on the North Canadian River. There in the Indian Territory that became the state of Oklahoma, Charlotte Vieux Thorpe, a Pottowatomie woman, gave birth to twin boys. Her husband, Hiram, a mixed-blood Indian of the Sac and Fox nation, stood close by on that spring day.

The sun was in Hiram Thorpe's heart as he looked down at the sons he named Charles and James. Jim's mother gave him another name.

"Wa-tho-huck," she said, thinking of how the light shone on the road to their cabin. "Bright Path."

As good as that name was, neither of them knew just how far that path would lead their son.

Like most twins, Jim and Charlie were close, even though they were not exactly the same. Charlie had darker skin and brown hair, while Jim's skin was light and his hair dark black. When they raced or wrestled, Jim was always a little ahead of Charlie, his best friend. Whenever Jim got too far ahead, he would stop and wait.

"Come on, Charlie," he would say with a grin.

Then, when his brother caught up, they would be off again.

Summer or winter, Jim and Charlie's favorite place was outdoors. They roamed the prairies, swam, and played together. By the time they were three, Pa Thorpe had taught his boys to ride a horse. He showed them how to shoot a bow, set a trap, and hunt. Jim took to it all like a catfish takes to a creek. Although small, he was quick and tough. He was so fast and had so much endurance that he could run down a rabbit on foot. When it came to the old ways, those skills that made the men of the Sac and Fox great providers for their families, Jim was a great learner. By the time the twins were six, Pa Thorpe said Jim knew more about the woods than many men.

Their sixth year also brought a big change for Jim and Charlie. The Indian Agency that oversaw the reservation said that when Sac and Fox children reached age six, they had to go to the Agency Boarding School. Indian boarding schools did not provide the same education offered to whites. In addition the boarding schools were designed to cut them off from everything that made them Indians—their language, their traditions, even their families.

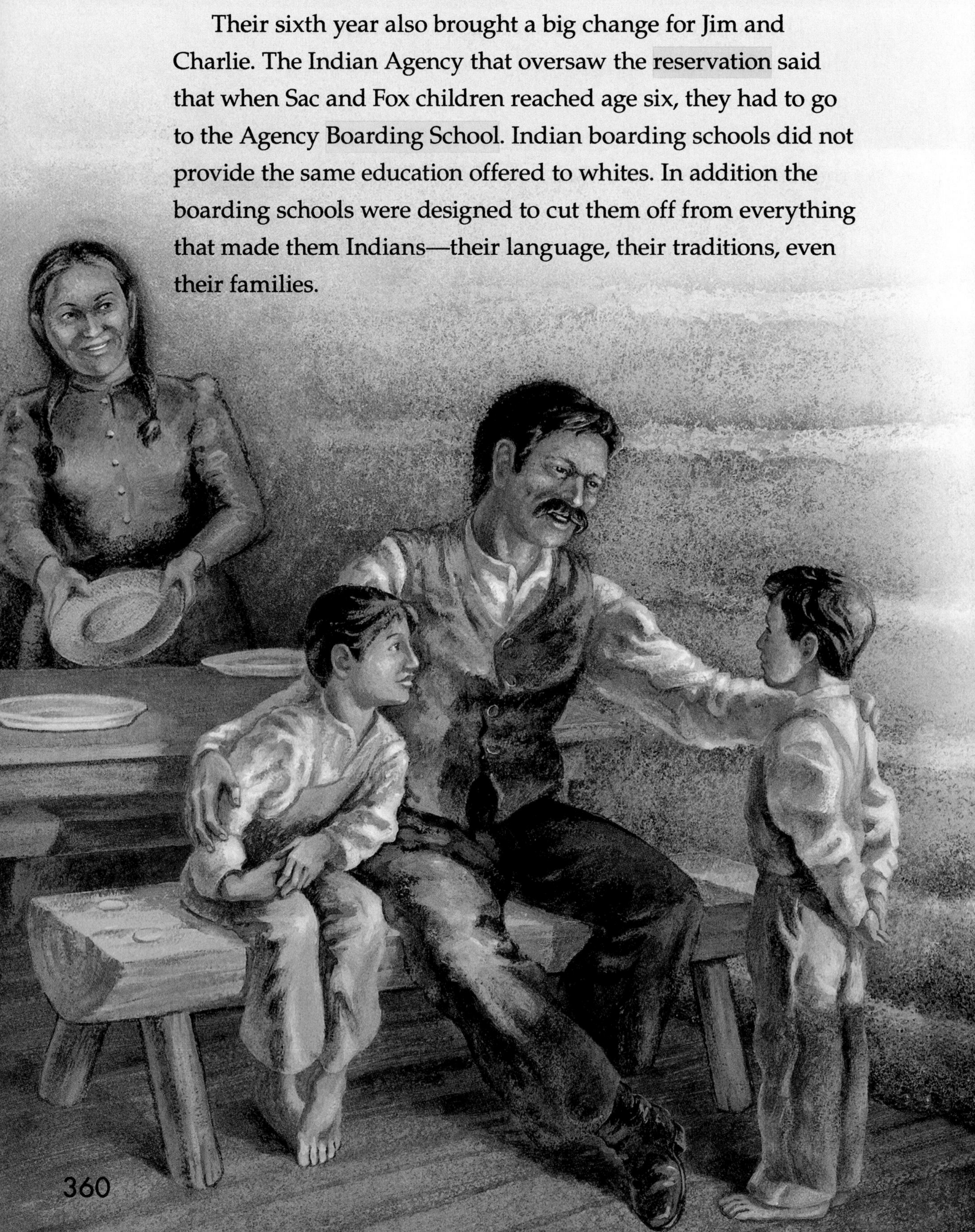

Jim's father had become one of the few Sac and Fox men who could read and write English. He'd seen uneducated Indians cheated out of everything by dishonest men who tricked the Indians into signing papers they could not read.

"My sons," he said to Jim and Charlie, "you need white man's knowledge to survive."

It was no surprise that Jim hated school. He had to wear awful clothes—a heavy wool suit, a felt cap, tight shoes, a shirt and necktie that strangled him. He also got smacked hard across his knuckles with a wooden ruler whenever he spoke a word of Sac. He missed Ma's cooking and Pa's stories about their clan ancestor, Chief Black Hawk, the famous warrior who had fought the whites to defend his people. Worst of all, school kept Jim inside all day and locked him up all night in a cold dormitory away from the forest and prairies. It made him feel like a fox caught in an iron trap. Jim didn't care about what school might do for him or his people. He just wanted to get away from it.

Charlie was better at his studies than Jim. He didn't seem to mind the military discipline or being stuck at a desk. Solving an arithmetic problem was a challenge to Charlie the way winning a race was to Jim. Now it was Charlie who was waiting for his brother to catch up.

"Come on, Jim," Charlie said. "Don't give up. You can do it."

So, Jim tried to master basic arithmetic, reading, and writing. Then, in his third year of school, something happened that broke his heart.

Sickness often struck the crowded, unheated dormitories of the Indian boarding schools. Sanitation was poor, and there were no real doctors to tend the sick. Epidemics of influenza swept through like prairie fires. Even common childhood diseases such as measles and whooping cough could be fatal to the Indian children jammed together in those schools.

Charlie was one of those who became sick. He caught pneumonia and died. Jim felt as if the sunlight had gone from his life. His twin brother had been his best friend.

Jim's mother tried to comfort her son, but he was inconsolable. He would never hear Charlie's encouraging voice again. The thought of going back to school without his brother tore at Jim's heart.

"Let me work around the farm, Pa," Jim begged.

His father, though, was sure he knew what was best.

"Son," he said, "you have to get an education. Charlie would have wanted you to keep learning."

Jim tried to listen to his father, but when he returned to school and saw the empty cot where Charlie had slept, it was too much for him. As soon as the teacher's back was turned, Jim ran the twenty-three miles back home, straight as an arrow.

Pa Thorpe had no choice but to send his stubborn son even farther away. So young Jim, at age eleven, was sent to Haskell Institute in Lawrence, Kansas, almost three hundred miles away.

Haskell was stricter than the Agency Boarding School. There children from more than eighty tribes were dressed in military uniforms and were awakened before dawn with a bugle call. Manual training was mixed with classroom studies to teach them trades useful to white society. Hard work was the rule, and the students of Haskell did it all—growing corn, making bread, building wagons, and sewing their own uniforms.

Jim did better at Haskell. He worked in the engineering shop. Learning how things were made was more interesting than being cooped up in a classroom.

Plus Haskell had something the Agency Boarding School didn't have—football. For the first time in his life, Jim saw a football game. The cheers of the crowd and the athleticism of the players wakened something deep inside Jim, the same emotions that had been stirred by Pa's stories of Black Hawk and the other warriors who had fought for their people. Jim knew right away that football was something he wanted to play.

But Jim was too small for the sport. He was less than five feet tall and weighed just one hundred pounds. He joined the track team instead and became one of the fastest runners. Meanwhile, he watched every football game he could. Jim also met Chauncy Archiquette, Haskell's best football player, who taught him about the game. Chauncy even helped Jim make a little football out of scrap leather stuffed with rags. With that football Jim organized games with other boys too small for the school team.

Near the end of his second year at Haskell, Jim got word that his father had been shot in a hunting accident and was dying. Jim's only thought was that he had to get home. He ran off and headed south. It took him two weeks to reach their farm. To his surprise, Pa was there, recovered from his wound and waiting.

"We knew you were coming home," his father said, embracing him.

Jim never went back to Haskell. Shortly after he returned home, his mother died of a sudden illness. Jim grieved over the loss of his mother, and Pa Thorpe finally agreed that his son did not have to go back to boarding school.

Jim's father believed his son still needed education, so Jim began attending school nearby in Garden Grove. At Garden Grove, students were learning about a new thing called electricity. Electricity could make it seem as if the sun were still shining, even at night. The thought of that appealed to Jim. Electrical sunlight could be brought to Indian homes too. Pa Thorpe had always told Jim that education would give him the ability to help his people. Maybe becoming an electrician was the bright path he was supposed to follow.

One day a recruiter from the Carlisle Indian School in Pennsylvania came to Garden Grove. Carlisle was always looking for Indian students who were good athletes, and the recruiter had heard of Jim's success as a runner at Haskell.

"Would you like to be a Carlisle man?" the recruiter asked.

"Can I study electricity there?" Jim said.

"Of course," the recruiter replied, even though Carlisle offered no such course.

Something else also attracted Jim to Carlisle—sports. Carlisle was one of the most well-known of the Indian boarding schools. Everyone knew about the school and its amazing record of winning sports teams. The Carlisle Indians even beat teams from the big, famous colleges. At Carlisle, Jim thought, he could play football.

Pa Thorpe urged Jim to seize the opportunity. Somehow he knew Carlisle would be the first step on a trail that would lead his son to greatness.

"Son," he said, "you are an Indian. I want you to show other races what an Indian can do."

Soon after Jim arrived at Carlisle, he received bad news. His father had been bitten by a snake while working in his fields and had died of blood poisoning. The man who had fought so hard to force his son to get an education was gone.

Already a quiet person, Jim retreated further into silence after his father's death. But he did not desert Carlisle. Perhaps, Jim felt the best way to remember his father was to live the dream Pa Thorpe had for him. It was now up to Jim to push himself.

The Carlisle system of sending new students off campus for work experience helped. Jim ended up at a farm in New Jersey. The farm labor reminded him of the many hours he had spent working by Pa's side in Oklahoma. Jim worked so hard and with such quiet confidence that everyone saw him as a man they could like and trust. To his delight, Jim was made foreman, head of all the workers.

When Jim came back to Carlisle in the fall, he was no longer a boy. He had grown taller, stronger, more self-assured. He was ready to play football, but he knew it would not be easy. Carlisle's famous coach Pop Warner would only allow the best to join his track squad or his football team as one of his "Athletic Boys."

One day Jim's big chance came. He was on his way to play a game of scrub football with some of his friends who were too small for the school team. As Jim crossed the field, he saw a group of varsity athletes practicing the high jump.

Jim asked if he could have a try, even though he was wearing overalls and an old pair of work shoes. The Athletic Boys snickered as they reset the bar for him. They placed it higher than anyone at Carlisle had ever jumped. Even in his work clothes, Jim cleared the bar on his first jump. No one could believe it. People stood around with their mouths wide open, staring. Jim just grinned and walked off to play football with his friends.

The next day Jim was told to report to the office of Coach Warner. Everyone knew Pop Warner was a great coach, but he was also a man with a bad temper. Jim wondered if Pop was going to yell at him for interrupting track practice.

"Do you know what you've done?" Pop Warner growled.

"Nothing bad, I hope," Jim said.

"Bad?" Pop Warner said. His face broke into a smile. "Boy, you've just broken the school record. Go down to the clubhouse and exchange those overalls for a track outfit. You're on my track team now."

Before long Jim Thorpe was Carlisle's best track athlete. He competed in the high jump, hurdles, and dashes, winning or placing in all of them. Still, Jim wanted to play football. Reluctantly Pop Warner told him he could give it a try.

Pop Warner didn't like the idea of his slender high jumper being injured in a football game, so he decided to discourage Jim by beginning his first practice with a tackling drill. Jim, the newcomer, had to take the ball and try to run from one end to the other, through the whole varsity team.

"Is that all?" Jim said. He looked at the football in his hands. It was the first time he'd ever held a real football, but he believed in himself. Then he took off down the field like a deer. He was past half the team before the players even saw him coming. At the other end Jim looked back. Behind him was the whole Carlisle team, the players holding nothing in their hands but air.

There was a grin on Jim's face when he handed Coach Warner the ball.

"Doggone it," Pop Warner said. "You're supposed to give the first team tackling practice, not run through them." Pop Warner slammed the ball back into Jim's belly. "Do it again."

Jim's jaw was set as he ran the Carlisle gauntlet a second time. He was carrying not just a football, but the hopes and dreams of his family, his people, and all the Indians who had been told they could never compete with the white man. Tacklers bounced off Jim as he lowered his shoulders. No one stopped him. The sun shone around him as he stood in the end zone.

For years Jim had fought against his education. He had run away from it so many times. This time Jim used all he had learned from his mother's wisdom, his brother's encouragement, and his father's fierce determination that his son show what an Indian could do. From now on Jim Thorpe would run forward, toward the finish line, toward the goal. He didn't know how far he would go, but he believed in his journey. His education had put his feet on the bright path.

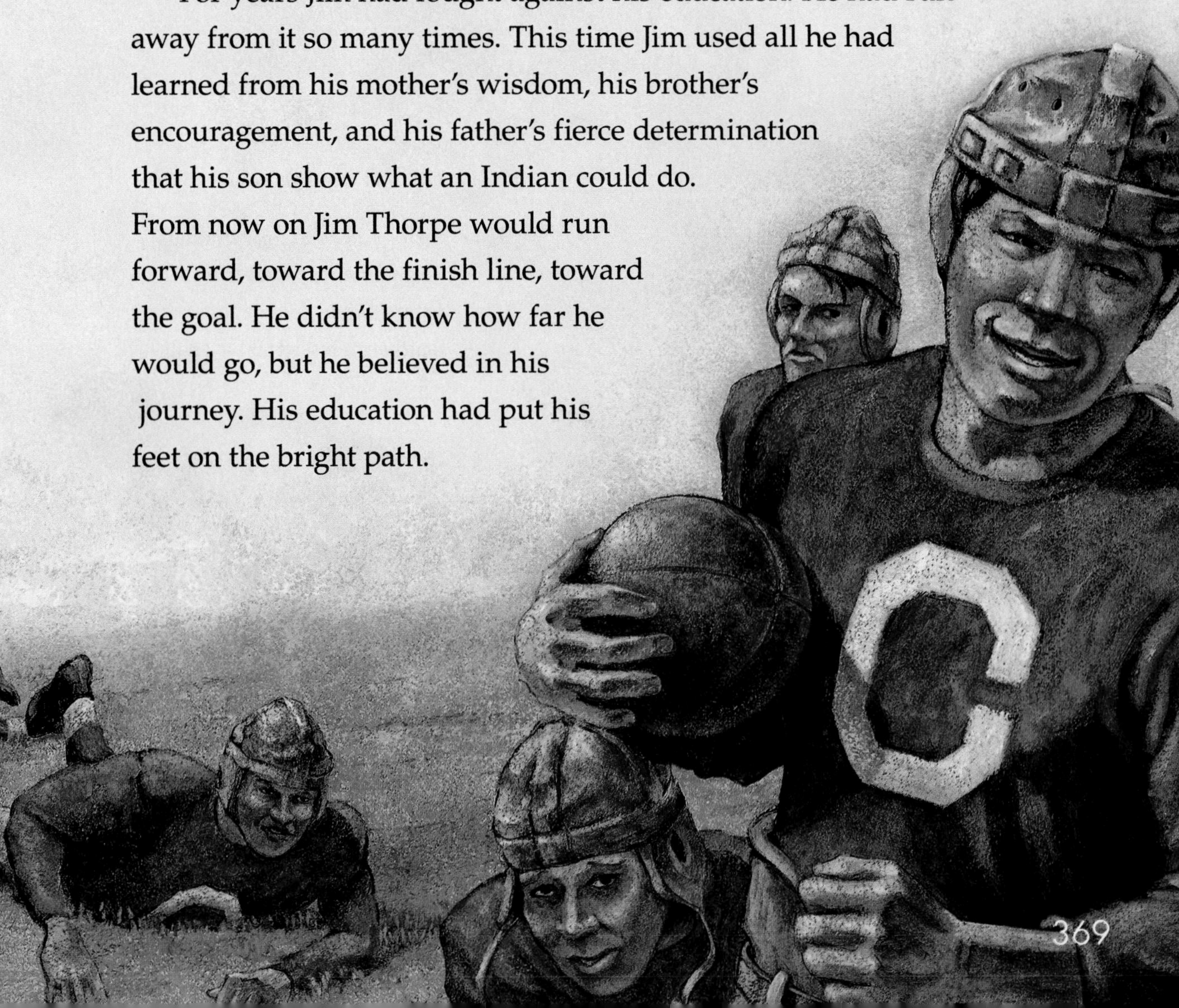

Important Dates in Jim Thorpe's Life and Legacy

1887* James Francis Thorpe and twin brother, Charles, born on Sac and Fox Indian Reservation along North Canadian River in Oklahoma, May 28

Jim, left, and Charlie, age 3

1893 Enters Agency Boarding School with Charlie

1896 Charlie dies of pneumonia

1898 Arrives at Haskell Institute in Lawrence, Kansas

1902* Charlotte Thorpe (mother) dies; begins attending school in Garden Grove, Oklahoma

1904 Enters United States Indian Industrial School in Carlisle, Pennsylvania; Hiram Thorpe (father) dies

***Date cited obtained from Thorpe family or most reliable sources**

1907–1912 Plays college football

1909–1910 Plays minor league baseball

1911, 1912 Named First Team All American Halfback at Carlisle

1912 Wins gold medals in Pentathlon and Decathlon at Summer Olympic Games in Stockholm, Sweden

Original Olympic gold medals

1913 Stripped of Olympic medals and name removed from record books for playing minor league professional baseball

1913–1919 Plays major league baseball

1915–1929 Plays professional football

1917 Becomes a United States citizen

1920 Elected first president of American Professional Football Association (now National Football League)

1922 Forms Oorang Indians, an all-Indian professional football team

1929 Retires from professional football at age forty-two

1953 Dies March 28; buried in Mauch Chunk, Pennsylvania, which is renamed Jim Thorpe, Pennsylvania

1963 Inducted into Pro Football Hall of Fame as part of original class

1982 International Olympic Committee restores Thorpe's name to record books

1983 Duplicate Olympic gold medals given to Thorpe family; inducted into U.S. Olympic Hall of Fame

1998 U.S. Postal Service issues Jim Thorpe commemorative stamp as part of its Celebrate the Century program

Thorpe statue in Pro Football Hall of Fame

Objectives

- Read independently for long periods of time and paraphrase the reading, including the order in which events occur.
- Write responses to texts using details to show understanding.

Envision It! | **Retell**

READING STREET ONLINE
STORY SORT
www.ReadingStreet.com

Think Critically

1. Jim Thorpe became so famous that a movie was made about his life. Why do you think it was important to share Jim Thorpe's story with the world? **Text to World**

2. Biographers usually write about grown-ups. Why do you think this biographer wrote about the early life of Jim Thorpe, before he became famous? Would you have done the same thing? Explain. **Think Like an Author**

3. Look back at page 365. Find three facts and one opinion. How can you tell the difference between the facts and the opinion? **Fact and Opinion**

4. Coach Pop Warner met Jim Thorpe when he was a student at the Carlisle Indian School. Skim pages 368 and 369. Then summarize the role Pop played in Jim's journey toward becoming a world-famous athlete. **Summarize**

5. **Look Back and Write** Reread pages 370 and 371. During his life, many people believed that Jim Thorpe was the greatest athlete in the world. Provide evidence from the time line on these pages to find examples of Jim Thorpe's athletic greatness. **TEST PRACTICE** **Extended Response**

Meet the Author and the Illustrator

Joseph Bruchac and S. D. Nelson

Joseph Bruchac, who is of Abenaki Indian descent, grew up admiring Jim Thorpe. He says, "Jim Thorpe struck me as a true American hero. The fact that part of my own heritage was American Indian made Jim even more special to me."

Mr. Bruchac learned more about Jim Thorpe from a friend. "One of my dearest friends was a Pueblo/Apache elder named Swift Eagle. For many years, Swift Eagle told me stories about Jim Thorpe, who had been a personal friend of his when both of them were living in California and working in the movies. It made me feel even closer to Jim and his story." He adds, "I think that all of us, whatever our backgrounds, can find inspiration from our unique heritages."

S. D. Nelson creates illustrations, often in the style of his Lakota ancestors. He was eager to illustrate a story about Thorpe, whom he also admired as a boy. He says, "Jim Thorpe is a wonderful example of someone who struggled against many difficulties in order to make his dream come true. I hope young people today will be inspired by his true life story."

Here are other books by Joseph Bruchac.

A Boy Called Slow: The True Story of Sitting Bull

The Arrow Over the Door

Use the Reading Log in the *Reader's and Writer's Notebook* to record your independent reading.

Objectives

- Write responses to texts using details to show understanding.
- Use correct capitalization for titles of books, stories, and essays.
- Use correct capitalization for languages, races, and nationalities.

Key Features of a Book Review

- tells what a book is about
- discusses the book's theme or message
- gives an opinion about the book

READING STREET ONLINE
GRAMMAR JAMMER
www.ReadingStreet.com

Narrative

Review

A **book review** tells what a book is about and gives opinions about its quality. The student model on the next page is an example of a review.

Writing Prompt Write a review of *Jim Thorpe's Bright Path.*

Writer's Checklist

Remember, you should . . .

- ✓ include the title and author of the book in the first paragraph.
- ✓ tell what the book is about and what you like about it.
- ✓ capitalize the title of the book.
- ✓ also capitalize proper nouns such as races, languages, nationalities, states, and people's names.

Student Model

Education: A Path to a Better Life

Jim Thorpe's Bright Path by Joseph Bruchac is about how a young boy named Jim Thorpe grew up to become a world-famous athlete. Jim Thorpe's Native American name was "Bright Path." Jim and his twin, Charlie, loved running, riding, and hunting in the outdoors. When they were six, the Indian Agency sent the boys to boarding school.

Later, Jim attended the Carlisle Indian School in Pennsylvania, which was famous for its winning sports teams. It was there that Jim's amazing athletic ability was recognized. He decided to show the world "what an Indian could do," just as his father had wanted him to.

The message that the author, Mr. Bruchac, gives readers is that getting an education can help you to find your best path in life. Jim Thorpe's father knew this. Jim didn't always agree, but he followed his father's advice and it paid off. I liked this book because it showed what life was like for many Native American boys in the late 1800s. Also, I think Jim Thorpe was someone I would have liked.

Writing Trait Sentences Sentence beginnings are varied.

Capitalizations and abbreviations are used correctly.

Genre A **book review** gives an opinion about a book.

Conventions

Capitalization and Abbreviations

Remember A proper noun, or name of a particular person, place, or thing, should always be **capitalized. Abbreviated** titles that come before people's names should also be capitalized.

• Use text features to understand the text and to locate information. • Make connections between literary and informational texts with similar ideas and support your ideas with details from the texts.

Social Studies in Reading

Genre
Expository Text

- An expository text contains information about a subject.
- Topic and concluding sentences give you an overview of the text and help you locate information.
- Read "Special Olympics, Spectacular Athletes." Look for elements that make this article an expository text. Look for topic and concluding sentences as you read.

Special

Athletes from all over the world have made their dreams come true at the Special Olympics World Games. The Games are a place for mentally disabled athletes to compete in twenty-six different sports.

How did the Special Olympics Games get started? In 1962, a woman named Eunice Kennedy Shriver had an idea. She wanted to start a sports day camp for mentally disabled children. Her sister Rosemary was mentally disabled. She wanted to help mentally disabled children like her sister succeed as athletes. Mrs. Shriver was part of a famous family. Her brother was U.S. President John F. Kennedy.

Eunice Kennedy Shriver

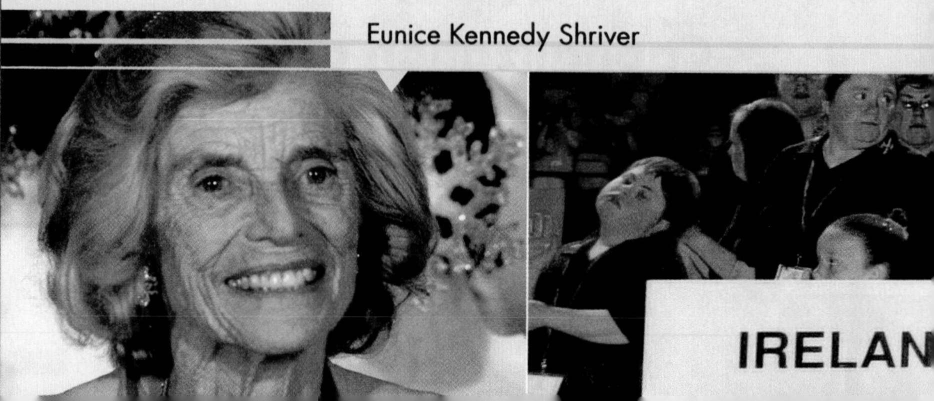

Olympics, Spectacular Athletes

by Marlene Perez

Thirty-five mentally disabled boys and girls attended the first camp at the Shriver home in Maryland. It was called Camp Shriver. The camp grew and soon became what is now known as Special Olympics.

In 1968, the first International Special Olympics Games were held in Chicago. Eunice Kennedy Shriver opened the Games with a quote from Roman gladiators. She said, "Let me win. But if I cannot win, let me be brave in the attempt." This quote became the motto of Special Olympics. A thousand athletes took part in the first Games, and the number has grown ever since.

Athletes compete at local Special Olympics events. The athletes who do well move on to the next level. Finally, the top athletes go to the World Games.

Let's Think About...

The first sentence of the first paragraph is a topic sentence. What overview of the paragraph does this sentence give you? **Expository Text**

The current leader of Special Olympics is Chairman Timothy Shriver. He says that Special Olympics athletes are the true leaders. In his words, "They have taught me what it is to lead without fear, to succeed without ego, and to approach challenges with a positive attitude."

The Special Olympics Summer and Winter Games are each held every four years. The 2005 Special Olympics World Winter Games were held in Nagano, Japan. The Winter Games featured contests in several sports, including figure skating, hockey, skiing, and snowboarding.

In 2007, Special Olympics held its Summer Games in Shanghai, China. The Summer Games had contests in twenty different sports, including basketball, judo, tennis, and volleyball.

Let's Think About...

Summarize the topic of the first paragraph. Summarize the details that tell you about the topic. **Expository Text**

Alisa Harding

Who are some of the athletes of Special Olympics?

The athletes are people like Alisa Harding. Harding, from Michigan, competed in the snowshoe competition at the 2005 Winter Games. She has an impressive collection of medals from past Special Olympics Games.

Dane Waites ran in the half marathon and the 10,000-meter event in the 2003 Summer Games. His small town in Australia raised money to get him to the Games.

Special Olympics athletes often find new challenges after experiencing Special Olympics. Special Olympics athlete Kester Edwards was in a fashion shoot with a professional tennis player. Paula Sage, a Special Olympics athlete from Great Britain, had a starring role in a major motion picture.

Special Olympics provide a way for mentally disabled athletes to achieve their dreams, as athletes and beyond.

Let's Think About...

Why is the last sentence on this page a good concluding sentence? What overview does it provide? How could it help you locate information? **Expository Text**

Let's Think About...

Reading Across Texts Connect what you have learned about Jim Thorpe and Special Olympics athletes. List the accomplishments of both.

Writing Across Texts Look at the list you made. Write a brief article about the accomplishments of one of the athletes.

Objectives

• Use a dictionary or glossary to find the meanings of unknown words, the syllable rules for these words, and how to pronounce them. • Determine the sequence needed to follow a procedure. • Explain how the different methods used in media affect the message that is being communicated. • Follow and give instructions and state instructions in your own words. • Read aloud grade-level texts and understand what is read.

READING STREET ONLINE
ONLINE STUDENT EDITION
www.ReadingStreet.com

Vocabulary

Multiple-Meaning Words

Dictionary/Glossary Some words have more than one meaning. Remember that when you look up a word in a glossary or dictionary, you can find all the meanings of a word.

Practice It! Find the word *trades* on page 363 of *Jim Thorpe's Bright Path*. Use a dictionary to find all the meanings of the word *trade*. Decide which meaning fits the sentence. Repeat for the word *drill* on page 368.

Fluency

Expression

Partner Reading Change the volume of your voice as you read to bring more drama to a story. Reading in a soft or a loud voice adds excitement to the story.

Practice It! With a partner, practice reading aloud *Jim Thorpe's Bright Path*, page 368. Adjust the volume of your voice as you read. Then have your partner read the same section without using volume. Which reading is more exciting?

When you plan a presentation, keep your purpose and your audience in mind.

Media Literacy

How-to

A how-to demonstration uses words and pictures to describe how to make an item or how to do an activity. The purpose is to teach the skill to others. Make sure steps are clear before you record. Ask your partner to restate any series of related sequences of action so that they are clear.

Practice It! With a partner, create a how-to demonstration for TV about playing a football running-back position. Describe the steps needed to practice the skill. One of you states the directions as the other one follows the oral directions. If directions are unclear, ask your partner to restate the oral instructions that involve a series of related sequences of actions. Restate directions as needed, such as "The quarterback hands the ball to the running back. Then, he runs with the ball."

Tips

- TV sports directors use different camera angles to show the game and make the viewers feel as if they are experiencing it in person.
- A close-up is when the camera shows only the face or any small area of who or what is being filmed. This shot focuses the viewer's attention on the subject.
- A wide-angle view shows a landscape. You may want to show a football field or the running back in motion on the field.

Objectives

- Speak clearly and to the point, give an opinion and support it with correct information.
- Take part in discussions led by teachers or other students, ask and answer questions, and offer ideas that build on the ideas of other people.

Oral Vocabulary

Let's Talk About

Coming to a New Culture

- Express opinions about what foods, sports, and music make up our culture.
- Share ideas or experiences about being in a new culture.
- Discuss how it might feel to move to a new place. Use words, short phrases, and sentences to express your feelings.
- Speak clearly when describing ideas.

READING STREET ONLINE
CONCEPT TALK VIDEO
www.ReadingStreet.com

You've learned
270
Amazing Words
so far this year!

Objectives

- Tell the order of events in a story, summarize the events, and explain how they will influence future events in the story.
- Use your prior knowledge and details from a text to make inferences and support them with evidence from the text.

Envision It! | **Skill Strategy**

Skill

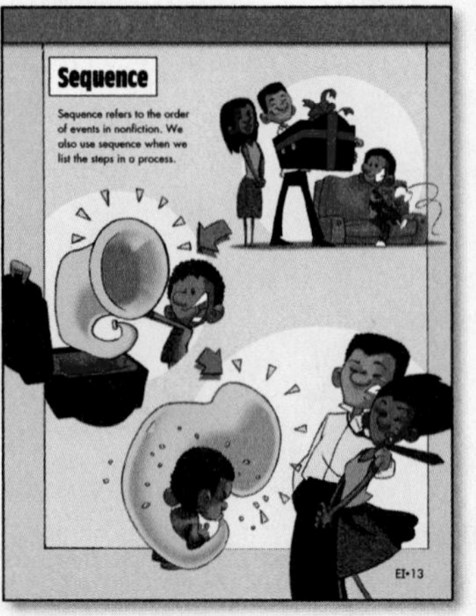

Sequence

Sequence refers to the order of events in nonfiction. We also use sequence when we list the steps in a process.

EI•13

Strategy

Envision It! Visual Strategies Handbook

Inferring

When we **infer** we use background knowledge with clues in the text to come up with our own ideas about what the author is trying to present.

To infer
- identify what you already know
- combine what you know with text clues to come up with your own ideas

Brianna wore herself out before she reached the finish line.
Since you said Brianna wore herself out, that must mean you won the race!

Let's Think About Reading!

When I infer, I ask myself
- What do I already know?
- Which text clues are important?
- What is the author trying to present?

EI•18

READING STREET ONLINE
ENVISION IT! ANIMATIONS
www.ReadingStreet.com

Comprehension Skill

Sequence

- Sequence is the order in which events happen in a story. The order of events may be explicit, and clue words such as *first*, *before*, and *after* signal the sequence. Or the sequence may be implicit, and there are no clue words. The reader has to figure out which events came first, next, and last.
- A story's plot has a sequence of main events. Sometimes main events are told out of sequence. Something that happened earlier might be told after something that happened later.
- Use the graphic organizer to sequence the main events of the plot and to describe explicit and implicit relationships among the ideas in "Dare to Dream," a text organized by sequence. Then summarize the story.

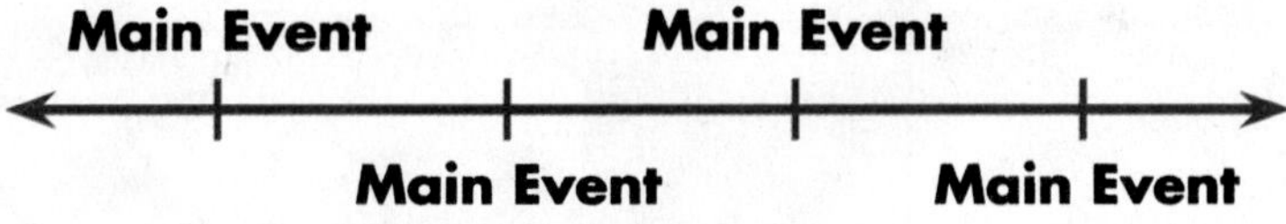

Main Event
Main Event
Main Event
Main Event

Comprehension Strategy

Inferring

When you infer, you combine your background knowledge with evidence in the text to come up with your own idea about what the author is trying to present. Active readers infer the ideas, morals, lessons, and themes of a written work.

Dare to Dream

Ever since he was a little boy, Rico was one of the best young baseball players in the Dominican Republic. Carlos was sure that one day his big brother would play for a major league team.

Though Rico was eighteen and Carlos was ten, they were best buddies. For the past four years, Carlos had gone to every one of Rico's games. But today there was no game—there was something much more important. Rico was trying out for one of the baseball training camps that are run by major league teams from the United States.

Skill What is the story's first main event?

The weeks before the tryouts, Rico worked harder than usual. "If you want to make it," Rico told Carlos, "don't give up. Always dare to dream."

Finally, the big day arrived. Rico was nervous, and so was Carlos. But Carlos knew that his brother was ready. He had worked too hard. This was going to be his brother's next big step.

Strategy What can you infer about Carlos and his relationship with his brother? How does Carlos feel about his big brother?

The very next day, Carlos was the first to hear the happy news from Rico. He was going to training camp! Dreams *can* come true, thought Carlos—especially if you help them along with hard work.

Skill What is the story's last main event? Explain whether the sequence was explicit or implicit.

Your Turn!

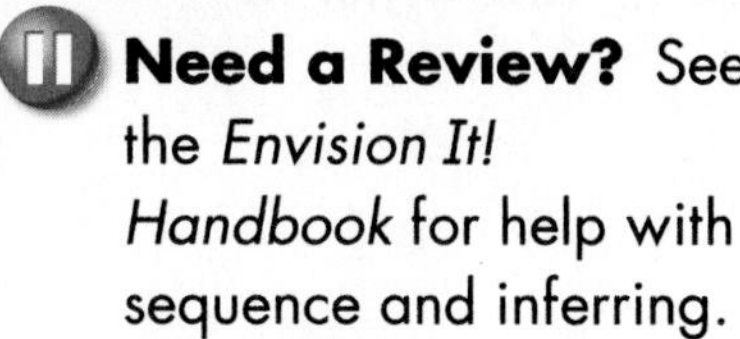

Need a Review? See the *Envision It! Handbook* for help with sequence and inferring.

Ready to Try It? Establish your own purpose for reading *How Tía Lola Came to ~~Visit~~ Stay* based on your desired outcome to enhance comprehension.

Objectives

- Determine the meanings of unfamiliar words or multiple-meaning words by using the context of the sentence.

colonel

lurking

palettes

affords
glint
quaint
resemblance

READING STREET ONLINE
VOCABULARY ACTIVITIES
www.ReadingStreet.com

Vocabulary Strategy for

Unfamiliar Words

Context Clues When you read, you may come across a word you are not familiar with. The context of the sentence—the words and sentences around the unfamiliar word—may give you clues to the word's meaning.

Choose one of the *Words to Know* and follow these steps.

1. Read the words and sentences around the unfamiliar word. See if the author has put an example or a definition of the word in parentheses or between commas or dashes in the sentence.
2. If not, say what the sentence means in your own words.
3. Think of a meaning for the unfamiliar word.
4. Try that meaning in the sentence. Determine whether or not it makes sense.

As you read "An Officer and an Artist," use context clues to help you figure out the meanings of *affords* and *glint* and other unfamiliar words.

Words to Write Reread "An Officer and an Artist." Write a description of an interesting person you know. Describe what the person does and why the person is interesting to you. Use words from the *Words to Know* list in your writing.

An Officer and *an Artist*

My great-uncle Bob is an artist who has never sold a painting. In fact, he had a career that has nothing to do with art. He was a colonel in the army. Bob doesn't look like an artist. He doesn't wear a quaint beret or paint-stained clothes. His face has no resemblance to a wild-eyed dreamer, such as the Dutch painter Van Gogh. No, Colonel Bob stands at attention, and he does everything precisely.

Ever since he retired from the army, Colonel Bob spends hours every day painting. Having been an officer affords, or gives, him the income to pursue his dream.

You may see Colonel Bob lurking and waiting for the right light, as though to surprise an enemy. He knows just when the sun should produce a glint, or shine, on a pond or a barn roof. He takes many pictures of a scene. Then he draws it on canvas and begins to paint. Nothing is simply green, blue, or yellow. One flower contains enough colors to fill two palettes. Colonel Bob says he sees everything with different eyes now.

Your Turn!

Need a Review? For help with using context clues to determine the meanings of unfamiliar words, see *Words!*

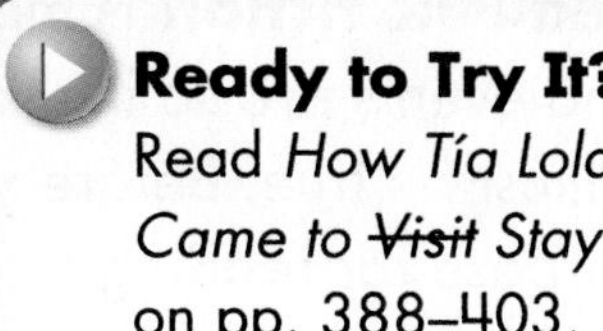

Ready to Try It? Read *How Tía Lola Came to ~~Visit~~ Stay* on pp. 388–403.

How Tía Lola Came to ~~Visit~~ Stay

by Julia Alvarez
illustrated by Macky Pamintuan

Realistic fiction is made up, but the characters and events are so lifelike that the story seems as if it must be true. Before you read, establish your own purpose for reading to enhance your comprehension.

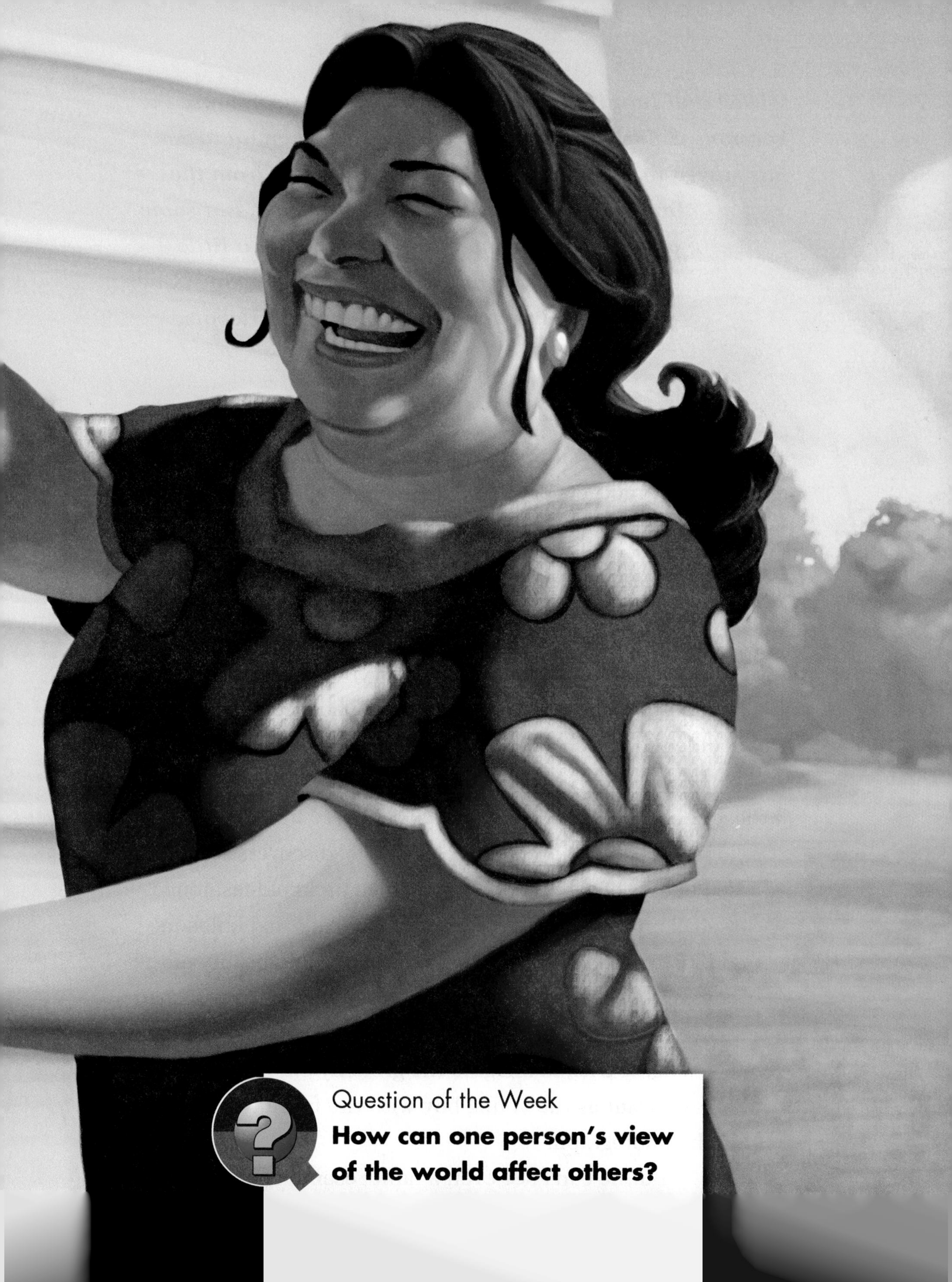

Question of the Week

How can one person's view of the world affect others?

Miguel and Juanita have moved to a rented farmhouse in Vermont with their mother, Mami. Their father, an artist, has stayed in New York. Tía Lola, Mami's aunt from the Dominican Republic, has come to visit. But some of the ideas she has brought along are a little "different" and not always to the liking of Miguel or the family's landlord, Colonel Charlebois.

The long, sweet, sunny days of summer come one after another after another. Each one is like a piece of fancy candy in a gold-and-blue wrapper.

Most nights, now that school is out, Tía Lola tells stories, sometimes until very late. The uncle who fell in love with a *ciguapa* and never married. The beautiful cousin who never cut her hair and carried it around in a wheelbarrow. The grandfather whose eyes turned blue when he saw his first grandchild.

Some nights, for a break, they explore the old house. In the attic, behind their own boxes, they find dusty trunks full of yellowing letters and photographs. Miguel discovers several faded photos of a group of boys all lined up in old-fashioned baseball uniforms. Except for the funny caps and knickers and knee socks, the boys in the photos could be any of the boys on Miguel's team. One photo of a boy with a baseball glove in his hand is inscribed, *Charlebois, '34.*

Miguel tries to imagine the grouchy old man at Rudy's Restaurant as the young boy with the friendly smile in the photograph.

But he can't see even a faint resemblance.

Since the team doesn't have a good place for daily practice, Miguel's mother suggests they use the back pasture behind the house. "But let me write Colonel Charlebois first, just in case."

Their landlord lives in a big white house in the center of town. He has already written them once this summer, complaining about "the unseemly shape of the vegetation," after Tía Lola trimmed the hedges in front of the house in the shapes of pineapples and parrots and palm trees.

"Can't you just call him and ask him, Mami?" Miguel asks. After all, the team is impatient to get started with practice. A letter will take several days to be answered.

"You try calling him," Miguel's mother says, holding out the phone. Miguel dials the number his mother reads from a card tacked on the kitchen bulletin board. The phone rings once, twice. A machine clicks on, and a cranky old voice speaks up: "This is Colonel Charles Charlebois. I can't be bothered coming to the phone every time it rings. If you have a message, you can write me at 27 Main Street, Middlebury, Vermont 05753."

"Let's write that letter, shall we?" Mami says, taking the phone back from Miguel.

Two days later, Colonel Charlebois's answer is in their mailbox. It has not been postmarked. He must have driven out and delivered it himself.

"I would be honored to have the team practice in my back pasture," he replies in a shaky hand as if he'd written the letter while riding in a car over a bumpy road.

"Honored!" Miguel's mother says, lifting her eyebrows. She translates the letter for Tía Lola, who merely nods as if she'd known all along that Colonel Charlebois is really a nice man.

And so every day Miguel's friends come over, and the team plays ball in the back field where only six months ago, Miguel (or maybe it was the *ciguapas?*) wrote a great big welcome to Tía Lola. Twice a week, Rudy drops by to coach. They play all afternoon, and afterward, when they are hot and sweaty, Tía Lola invites them inside for cool, refreshing smoothies, which she calls *frío-fríos.* As they slurp and lick, she practices her English by telling them wonderful stories about Dominican baseball players like Sammy Sosa and the Alou brothers and Juan Marichal and Pedro and Ramón Martínez. The way she tells the stories, it's as if she knows these players personally. Miguel and his friends are enthralled.

After a couple of weeks of practice, the team votes to make Miguel the captain. José, who is visiting from New York, substitutes for whoever is missing that day. Tía Lola is named manager.

"*¿Y qué hace el manager?*" Tía Lola wants to know what a manager does.

"A manager makes us *frío-fríos,*" Captain Miguel says.

Every day, after practice, there are *frío-fríos* in a tall pitcher in the icebox.

It is a happy summer—

Until Tía Lola decides to paint the house purple.

Miguel and his friends have been playing ball in the back field—their view of the house shielded by the ample trees. As they walk back from practice, they look up.

"Holy cow!" Miguel cries out.

The front porch is the color of a bright bruise. Miguel can't help thinking of the deep, rich purple whose name he recently learned from his father in New York. "Dioxazine," he mutters to himself. The rest of the house is still the same color as almost every other house in town. "Regulation white," Papi calls it whenever he comes up to visit and drives through town.

In her high heels and a dress with flowers whose petals match the color of the porch stands Tía Lola, painting broad purple strokes.

For a brief second, Miguel feels a flash of that old embarrassment he used to feel about his crazy aunt.

"Awesome," his friend Dean is saying.

"Cool!" Sam agrees.

"*¡Qué* cool!" José echoes.

They wave at Tía Lola, who waves back.

"*¡Frío-fríos!*" she calls out. Today she has chosen grape flavor in honor of the new color of the house.

By the time Miguel's mother comes home from work, he and his friends look like they have helped Tía Lola paint the house: their mouths are purple smudges. When they open their mouths to say hello, their tongues are a pinkish purple.

"Okay, what is going on?" Mami asks, glancing from Miguel to Tía Lola. She looks as if she is about to cry, something she has not done in a long time.

Tía Lola speaks up. Don't the colors remind her of the island? *"La casita de tu niñez."* The house where Mami spent her childhood.

Miguel can see his mother's face softening. Her eyes have a faraway look. Suddenly, Mami is shaking her head and trying not to laugh. "Colonel Charlebois is going to throw a fit. Actually, he's going to throw us out."

"El coronel, no hay problema," Tía Lola says, pointing to herself and Miguel and his friends. Miguel's mother looks from face to face as if she doesn't understand. Miguel and his friends nod as if they understand exactly what Tía Lola is up to.

The next afternoon, when Miguel's friends come inside from practice, Tía Lola takes their measurements. She has bought fabric with the money the team has collected and is making them their uniforms.

When it is Miguel's turn, he stands next to the mark that his mother made on the door frame back in January. He is already an inch taller!

"Tía Lola, what are you up to?" the team keeps asking. "Are we going to lose our playing field if Colonel Charlebois takes back his house?"

"No hay problema," Tía Lola keeps saying. Her mouth curls up like a fish hook that has caught a big smile.

"Are you going to work magic on him?" Miguel asks his aunt that night.

"The magic of understanding," Tía Lola says, winking. She can look into a face and see straight to the heart.

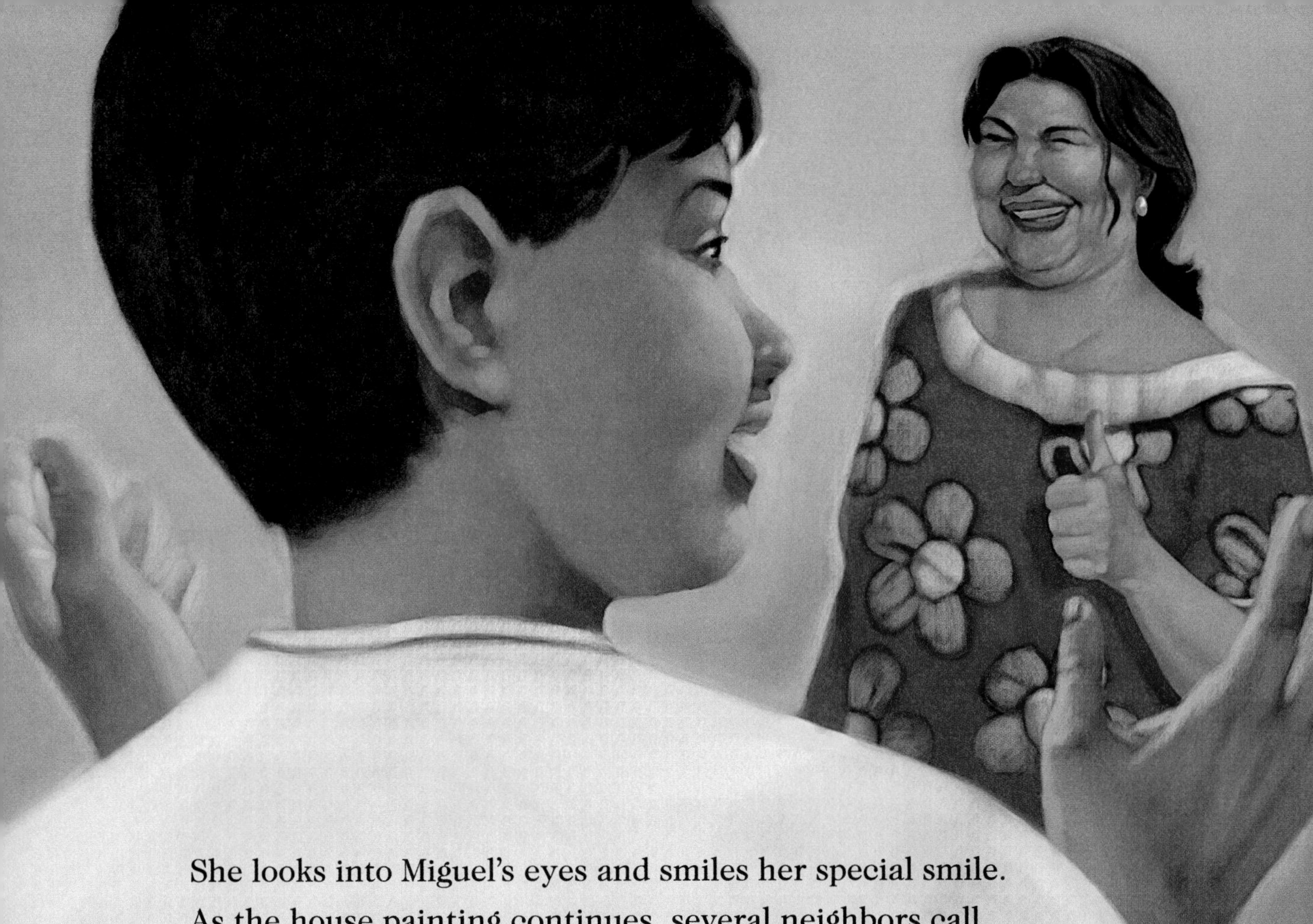

She looks into Miguel's eyes and smiles her special smile.

As the house painting continues, several neighbors call. "What's happening to your house?" farmer Tom asks Miguel. "I don't believe I've ever seen a purple house. Is that a New York style or something?"

Their farming neighbors think of New York as a foreign country. Whenever Miguel and his family do something odd, Tom and Becky believe it is due to their having come from "the city."

"I've never seen a purple house in my life," Miguel admits.

"Neither have I," José adds, "and I live in the city!"

"I've seen one!" Juanita speaks up, showing off.

"Where?" Miguel challenges.

"In my imagination." She grins.

Miguel has been trying to imitate Tía Lola, looking for the best in people. He stares straight into Juanita's eyes, but all he can see is his smart-alecky little sister.

One afternoon, soon after José has returned to the city, Miguel is coming down the stairs to join his teammates in the back field. He pauses at the landing. The large window affords a view of the surrounding farms and the quaint New England town beyond.

A silver car Miguel doesn't recognize is coming down the dirt road to their house. Just before arriving at the farmhouse, it turns in to an old logging road at the back of the property. Behind a clump of ash trees, the car stops and the door opens.

Later, as he stands to bat, Miguel can make out a glint of silver among the trees. Who could it be? he wonders. He thinks of telling his mother about the stranger, but decides against it.

She would probably think an escaped convict was lurking in the woods and not allow the team to practice in the back field anymore.

The next afternoon, Miguel watches from behind the curtain as the same silver car he saw in the woods yesterday comes slowly up the drive. His friends have already left after their baseball practice, and his mother is not home from work yet. He can hear Tía Lola's sewing machine humming away upstairs.

"Who is it?" Juanita is standing beside him, holding on to her brother's arm. All her smart-alecky confidence is gone.

"I think it's him—Colonel Charlebois," Miguel whispers. Now that the car is so close, he can make out the old man behind the wheel. The hood has a striking ornament: a little silver batter, crouched, ready to swing. "I'm going to pretend no one is home," Miguel adds.

But Colonel Charlebois doesn't come up to the door. He sits in his car, gazing up at the purple-and-white house for a few minutes, and then he drives away. Later that day, a letter appears in the mailbox. "Unless the house is back to its original white by the end of the month, you are welcome to move out."

"*Welcome* to move out?" Miguel repeats. He wrote *¡BIENVENIDA!* to his Tía Lola when she moved in. It doesn't sound right to *welcome* someone to move out.

"We've got three weeks to paint the house back or move," their mother says in a teary voice at dinner. "I'm disappointed too," she admits to Tía Lola. After all, she really loves the new color. That flaking white paint made the place look so blah and run-down. "But still, I don't want to have to move again," Mami sighs.

Tía Lola pats her niece's hand. There is something else they can try first.

"What's that?" her niece asks.

They can invite *el coronel* over on Saturday.

"But that's the day of our big game," Miguel reminds his aunt. They'll be playing against another local team from the next county over.

Tía Lola winks. She knows. *"Pero tengo un plan."* She has a plan. Miguel should tell his friends to come a little early so they can change.

"Change what?" Miguel's mother asks. "Change the color of the house?"

Tía Lola shakes her head. Change a hard heart. She'll need more grape juice from the store.

The day dawns sunny and warm. The cloudless sky stretches on and on and on, endlessly blue with the glint of an airplane, like a needle sewing a tiny tear in it. Every tree seems filled to capacity with dark green rustling leaves. On the neighboring farms, the corn is as tall as the boys who play baseball in the fallow field nearby. Tía Lola's garden looks like one of Papi's palettes. But now, after living in the country for seven months, Miguel has his own new names for colors: zucchini green, squash yellow, chili-pepper red, raspberry crimson. The eggplants are as purple as the newly painted house. It is the full of summer. In a few weeks, up in the mountains, the maples will begin to turn.

Miguel's friends and their parents arrive early. The boys head upstairs behind Tía Lola and Rudy. Their parents stay downstairs, drinking grape smoothies and talking about how their gardens are doing. At last, the silver car rolls into the driveway.

Slowly, Colonel Charlebois climbs out. He stands, a cane in one hand, looking up at the house. One quarter of the house is purple. The other three-quarters is still white. Which color will the whole house end up being?

Miguel looks down at the old man from an upstairs window. Suddenly, he feels a sense of panic. What if Tía Lola's plan doesn't work? He doesn't want to move from the house that has finally become a home to him.

He feels his aunt's hand on his shoulder. *"No hay problema, Miguelito,"* she reassures him as if she can read his thoughts even without looking into his eyes.

CHARLIE'S
BOYS

Colonel Charlebois is still staring up at the house when the front door opens. Out file nine boys in purple-and-white striped uniforms and purple baseball caps. They look as if the house itself has sprouted them! Miguel leads the way, a baseball in his hand. Behind them, Tía Lola and Rudy each hold the corner of a pennant that reads: CHARLIE'S BOYS.

Colonel Charlebois gazes at each boy. It is difficult to tell what is going through his mind. Suddenly, he drops his cane on the front lawn and calls out, "Let's play ball!" He stands, wobbly and waiting and smiling. Miguel looks into the old man's eyes and sees a boy, legs apart, body bent forward, a gloved hand held out in front of him.

He lifts his arm and throws the ball at that young boy—and the old man catches it.

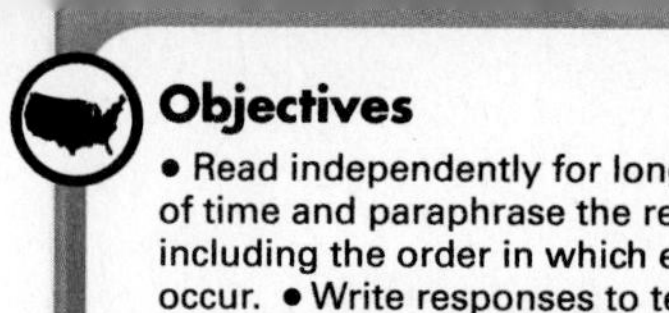

Objectives

- Read independently for long periods of time and paraphrase the reading, including the order in which events occur.
- Write responses to texts using details to show understanding.

Envision It! Retell

READING STREET ONLINE
STORY SORT
www.ReadingStreet.com

Think Critically

1. This story is set in a small farm town, but the family had moved there from a big city. What would be different about living in a small town and living in a large city? Which would you prefer? Why? **Text to Self**

2. Describe Tía Lola as the author portrays her in the story. Think about her actions, appearance, and thoughts. **Think Like an Author**

3. Think about the relationship between Colonel Charlebois and Miguel's family at the start of the story and at the story's end. What events bring about the change in this relationship? **Sequence**

4. Look at the illustration on pages 388–389. What can you infer about Tía Lola's personality from it? Explain your thinking. After reading the selection, do you still feel this way? Why? **Inferring**

5. **Look Back and Write** Look back at page 390. Miguel finds something that helps him learn about Colonel Charlebois's past. Write about what Miguel finds and why it is important to understanding the colonel's change of heart at the end of the story. How do you think the colonel and Miguel's family will get along in the future?

TEST PRACTICE **Extended Response**

Meet the Author

Julia Alvarez

Julia Alvarez wrote *How Tía Lola Came to ~~Visit~~ Stay* for her nephew when he was ten. He kept asking when he was going to get to read one of her books. Ms. Alvarez decided to write a story about an aunt like the ones she had in the Dominican Republic. She says Tía Lola is "a kind of Mary Poppins with a Spanish accent."

Julia Alvarez grew up in the Dominican Republic, a beautiful tropical island. When she was ten, her family moved to the United States. It was difficult starting over in a New York City school. Ms. Alvarez says, "Not understanding the language, I had to pay close attention to each word—great training for a writer."

Ms. Alvarez became a teacher. Her first novel, *How the Garcia Girls Lost Their Accents*, was successful, and she was able to start writing full-time. She now lives on a farm in Vermont and writes novels, essays, and poetry.

Here are other books about children who are new to the United States.

***In the Year of the Boar and Jackie Robinson* by Bette Lord**

***The Magic Shell* by Nicholasa Mohr**

Choose a book from the library and read independently for a sustained period of time. Record your reading by paraphrasing in a logical order what you have read. Be sure what you write maintains meaning.

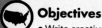

Objectives

- Write creative stories that build to an ending and contain details about the characters and setting.
- Write responses to texts using details to show understanding.
- Recognize and use commas in compound sentences.

Key Features of a Skit

- a scene, usually comic, in which characters interact
- uses dialogue and stage directions
- has a few characters and one setting
- written to be acted out, like a short play

READING STREET ONLINE
GRAMMAR JAMMER
www.ReadingStreet.com

Skit

A **skit** is a brief comic scene that is meant to be acted out. The student model on the next page is an example of a skit.

Writing Prompt There are a number of colorful characters in *How Tía Lola Came to ~~Visit~~ Stay*. Write a skit using at least three of the characters from the story.

Writer's Checklist

Remember, you should ...

- ✓ describe the setting, using stage directions.
- ✓ build the plot to a climax.
- ✓ give the scene a humorous tone.
- ✓ include details about the characters.
- ✓ use commas correctly in compound sentences.

Student Model

Tía Lola Brings the Outside Inside!

(Tía Lola is standing on a ladder in the living room of the rented farmhouse. She has a can of blue paint and a paintbrush. Miguel and Juanita enter the room.)

MIGUEL: What are you doing now, Tía Lola?

TIA LOLA: I'm bringing the outside inside. This will look like the beautiful Caribbean sky. I'll ask your father to paint lush green plants, and I want brilliant scarlet tropical flowers on the walls. It will remind me of my old home.

JUANITA: Cool—I like it!

MIGUEL: Oh, no! You know what the colonel will say when he sees this: "You are welcome to move out."

TIA LOLA: El coronel, no hay problema.

JUANITA: I know! We'll invite him over for another game of baseball, and he'll be so happy he won't care about the garden on the living room walls.

MIGUEL: Juanita, you're beginning to think like Tía Lola. That's frightening!

Genre
A **skit** includes stage directions.

Writing Trait
Word Choice
Vivid words make ideas come alive.

Commas are used correctly in compound sentences.

Conventions

Commas

Remember In a compound sentence, a **comma** usually comes before the conjunction that joins the two simple sentences.

Objectives

- Identify the language and devices used in biographies and autobiographies, including how authors present major events in a person's life.

Social Studies in Reading

Genre

Autobiography

- An autobiography is a form of literary nonfiction.
- An autobiography is the story of a person's life written by the person who lived it.
- Autobiographies are written in the first person, using *I, me,* and *my.*
- The events in an autobiography are actual events and experiences in a person's life. Events and characters' experiences in a fictional work did not actually happen.
- Read the selection. Notice the language the author uses to describe his excitement and nervousness when he meets Hiroshi Arakawa.

The Difficult Art of Hitting

by Sadaharu Oh and David Falkner

Sadaharu Oh was fourteen when this event took place. He would go on to become Japan's greatest home-run hitter, hitting a record 868 home runs in the Japanese Professional Baseball League. At the time of this event, however, Mr. Oh was still struggling to master the difficult art of hitting.

It was toward dusk. We were playing a practice game in Sumida Park in Asakusa. There was a good chill in the air. Winter was coming. You could feel it, but it didn't matter. I was pitching for our side; we were winning 5–0. Then, suddenly, there was a commotion on the field. One of the players recognized a man walking a dog nearby. The man was Hiroshi Arakawa, an outfielder for the Mainichi Orions, one of Japan's major league teams. We tried to continue with the game, but it was almost impossible. We watched the man following the dog—the dog pulling forward on the end of a taut leash—as they came closer and closer to our field. When he reached the area where we were playing, Arakawa-san stood behind the backstop at home plate and watched the action. All of us—players on both sides—became so keyed up! I felt my body fill with fighting spirit. I pitched as powerfully as I could. At bat, I swung from the heels, trying to send the ball clear across the river. Between innings, as I was about to leave the bench for the mound, my life changed. Arakawa-san left the backstop area and threaded his way between the players, who seemed to step aside before him in awe. He was making his way toward me! I felt myself freeze in place. I couldn't believe what was about to happen. He wanted to speak to me! He nodded to me and smiled, very gently. I very stiffly bowed to him.

"How come you pitch left-handed and bat right-handed?"

Sounds gurgled in my throat, but I had no words. I so badly wanted to make the best impression. I nodded my head, wanting to show that I accepted what he said—whatever he said.

"You know, you're probably wasting your talent that way. You look left-handed. Why don't you try to bat left-handed next time you come up?"

"Y— . . . yes, yes I will, of course, I will," I finally blurted out,

Let's Think About...

Which words on this page tell you that this selection is written in the first person? **Autobiography**

Let's Think About...

How did Sadaharu Oh feel talking to Arakawa? What language does he use to describe his feelings? **Autobiography** so ashamed of myself that I raced back out to the field at top speed. I expected Arakawa-san then to leave the area, to go on with his evening's stroll. But, no, he took a seat on a bleacher bench behind the plate!

It seemed like a year before my next turn at bat, and all the while I felt Arakawa-san's eyes on me. The game, the cold, the time of day, everything seemed to drop away. There was only this need to live within the cocoon of Arakawa-san's words. Finally, it was my turn to bat again. For the first time in my life I stepped to the plate to bat from the left side. I swung the bat back and forth. It felt easy, natural, as though I had done it always. I seemed now to come to my senses. I could feel everyone on the field watching me, as though in envy because a major league ballplayer had spoken only to me. I felt like a star! I knew I would hit! Nothing was going to stop me. If a building had fallen from the sky, I'm not sure I would have paid any attention to it, even if it had fallen on my head. I waited for the pitch I wanted. My bat met the ball squarely. For a moment, I watched the blur of the ball as it streaked out over the infield. Then I put my head down and ran. I looked up again at second base. I had lined a clean double to the fence in right-center field. I looked toward the bleacher bench behind the plate. Arakawa-san was still there. He gave

Let's Think About...

Could Sadaharu Oh turn this experience into a fictional story? What details should he include? **Autobiography**

Let's Think About...

What similarities and differences are there between the event described by Sadaharu Oh and the events in *How Tía Lola Came to ~~Visit~~ Stay?* **Autobiography** me a big nod of approval. My body filled with gooseflesh.

When the inning was over, he came up to me again.

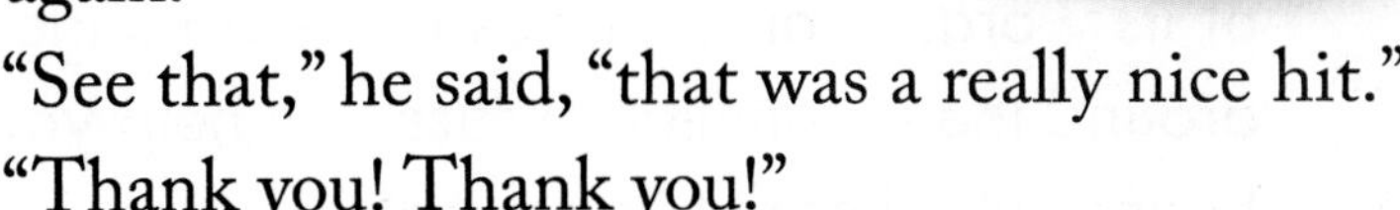

"See that," he said, "that was a really nice hit."

"Thank you! Thank you!"

"No reason to thank me. How old are you?"

I responded crisply, "I'm in the second year."

"Ah, good," he said, "then you'll be thinking of university next year. You might think of Waseda University. I went there. It has an excellent baseball program, and you will have a chance to develop your talents to the fullest."

I stood rigidly at attention.

"I am in the second year of junior high school," I said.

"Oh, I see. I thought . . . well, never mind what I thought. Perhaps you'll go to Waseda High School, then."

"Yes. Yes."

"You're a very good player, you know."

He smiled. We shook hands, and I bowed to him deeply. Then, with his dog, he turned and walked away. It seemed like only a few feet between where we were standing and the darkness surrounding the field. I tried to call to him. But I couldn't. Just like that, he was lost in the shadows as surely as if he had evaporated.

Let's Think About...

What differences are there between the actual experiences described in Sadaharu Oh's autobiography and the characters' experiences in the fictional work *How Tía Lola Came to ~~Visit~~ Stay?*
Autobiography

Let's Think About...

Reading Across Texts Both the colonel and Mr. Arakawa made contributions to baseball. Make a chart listing the contributions of both.

Writing Across Texts Use your chart to write a letter to the colonel or Mr. Arakawa thanking him for his support.

Objectives

• Read aloud grade-level texts and understand what is read. • Determine the meanings of unfamiliar words or multiple-meaning words by using the context of the sentence. • Identify the meaning of common idioms. • Take part in discussions led by teachers or other students, ask and answer questions, and offer ideas that build on the ideas of other people. • Listen closely to speakers and ask questions about and comment on the topic.

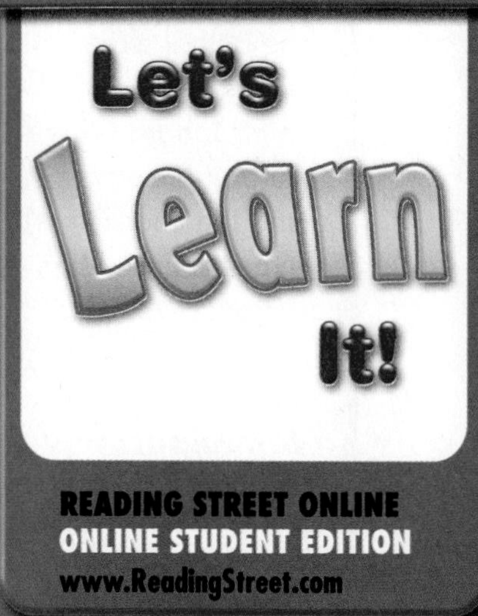

READING STREET ONLINE
ONLINE STUDENT EDITION
www.ReadingStreet.com

Vocabulary

Unfamiliar Words

Context Clues An idiom is a phrase whose meaning is different from the literal meaning of its words. Context clues in the passage around the unfamiliar phrase will help you figure out what the idiom means.

Practice It! On page 401, Tía Lola reassures Miguel as if she could "read his thoughts." What does this idiom mean? Do you know what the idiom "sleep tight" or "I'm broke" means? With a partner, think of other idioms that you use every day. Share them with the class.

Fluency

Expression

Partner Reading Reading with feeling, or expression, helps you better understand the characters in a story. Using expression helps you understand what the characters are thinking and feeling.

Practice It! With a partner, practice reading aloud page 396, paragraphs 7–10. Use what you know about the characters to read with feeling. Express how curious the boys are and how confident Tía Lola feels.

Listening and Speaking

Get Ready For Middle School

When you participate in a discussion, take turns speaking and listening.

Debate

A debate is a discussion between people who hold opposing views. The purpose of a debate is to persuade others to agree with an opinion.

Practice It! With a partner, conduct a debate between Colonel Charlebois and Tía Lola about painting the house purple. Each should take a position. Think of reasons supporting the opinion. Conduct your debate in front of the class. When you express an opinion, employ eye contact, speaking rate, volume, and enunciation, and use the conventions of language to communicate ideas effectively. Listeners will pay attention if you do these things.

Tips

Listening . . .

- Make comments that relate to the subject.

Speaking . . .

- Make eye contact with your partner to emphasize your opinion.
- Speak at an even rate, with enough volume and with enunciation to effectively communicate your ideas.
- You will communicate ideas more effectively if you follow the conventions of language. Speak in complete sentences, and avoid bad grammar.

Teamwork . . .

- Ask questions with detail.
- Answer questions with appropriate detail.

Objectives

- Take part in discussions led by teachers or other students, ask and answer questions, and offer ideas that build on the ideas of other people.

Oral Vocabulary

Let's Talk About

Achieving Goals

- Describe a goal you achieved.
- Discuss how it feels to achieve a goal. Use words, short phrases, and sentences to express your feelings.
- Answer questions with appropriate detail.
- Use conventions of language when you describe your achievement.

READING STREET ONLINE
CONCEPT TALK VIDEO
www.ReadingStreet.com

You've learned
2 8 0
Amazing Words
so far this year!

Objectives

- Set a purpose for reading a text based on what you hope to get from the text.

Envision It! Skill Strategy

Skill

Strategy

READING STREET ONLINE
ENVISION IT! ANIMATIONS
www.ReadingStreet.com

Comprehension Skill

Generalize

- A generalization is a broad statement or rule that applies to several examples.
- Authors sometimes use clue words such as *most, all, usually,* and *never* to help readers generalize.
- Some generalizations are valid, or supported by facts and details. Others are faulty, or not supported.
- Use the graphic organizer below to make generalizations as you read "Left in the Dust."

Generalization	Clue Word?

Comprehension Strategy

Predict and Set Purpose

As you read, it is important to make predictions. Your predictions will help you set your purpose for reading. Setting a purpose will guide your reading and help you understand what you read.

Left in the Dust

Sometimes a lot of rain can cause trouble, but not enough rain can cause trouble too. When an area has an extended dry spell, or period of time with an abnormally low amount of rainfall, it is called a drought.

In the 1930s, a severe drought hit Texas and other areas in the American Southwest. Winds that usually brought rain to these areas blew farther south than usual. As a result, not enough rain fell on the farm fields, so no crops could be grown and the dirt in the fields dried up.

The winds blew the dirt up into the air and created blizzardlike dust storms. These storms created dust clouds that blocked out the sun and darkened the skies. One farmer described a storm as being "like a black wall" that went over the area. It was so dry that a news reporter called the area the "Dust Bowl."

America still experiences droughts today, but the long, long dry spell that caused the Dust Bowl is believed to be the worst American drought in more than three hundred years!

Skill There are two generalizations in the first sentence. Identify them and tell whether you agree with them. Explain why or why not.

Skill What can you generalize about the amount of rain that usually falls in the American Southwest?

Strategy Reread the second paragraph. Predict what you will read about next and tell what your purpose for reading will be.

Your Turn!

Need a Review? See the *Envision It! Handbook* for additional help with generalizing and predicting and setting purpose.

Ready to Try It? Use what you learned about making generalizations as you read *A Gift from the Heart.*

Objectives

- Determine the meanings of unfamiliar words or multiple-meaning words by using the context of the sentence.

Envision It! Words to Know

abundance

backdrop

graze

ceremonial

drought

shock

READING STREET ONLINE
VOCABULARY ACTIVITIES
www.ReadingStreet.com

Vocabulary Strategy for

Unfamiliar Words

Context Clues Sometimes when you read, you come across a word you do not know. The context, or the words and sentences around the unknown word, may give you clues to the word's meaning.

1. Read the words and sentences around the unknown word. The author may have included a definition, synonym, or other clue to the word's meaning.
2. If not, say what the sentence means in your own words.
3. Think of a possible meaning for the unknown word.
4. Try that meaning in the sentence. Does it make sense?

As you read "Telling Stories," use context clues to help you figure out the meanings of *abundance, drought,* and other unfamiliar words.

Words to Write Reread "Telling Stories." Think of a traditional story you have heard from someone in your family or a friend. Write a short summary of the story. Use words from the *Words to Know* list in your summary.

Telling Stories

Everyone tells stories. Sometimes we tell stories to shock each other. Sometimes we tell stories to calm ourselves before we go to bed. Often we tell stories to entertain each other. Before the written word, storytelling was much more than just entertainment. It was the way people passed down their traditions and their culture's history.

Many cultures that didn't have access to the written word used storytelling to make sense of their world. They would tell their stories around ceremonial campfires against the backdrop of the night sky. Sometimes they would use art. The Greeks told stories about the origins of their gods through images painted on pottery.

Stories also passed on morals, or lessons, that offer a culture's advice on how to behave. One popular Sioux story is about a last ear of corn that cries to a woman not to be left in the field. This story teaches not to waste food, whether in times of abundance or drought.

Because the stories were spoken, and passed from one generation to the next, sometimes the details of the stories changed. For example, in one version of a legend, the animals might graze on corn instead of grass. It all depended on the speaker's choice (and desire to make things interesting!). The important thing was to keep the lesson of the story and the tradition alive.

Your Turn!

Need a Review? For help with using context clues to determine the meanings of unfamiliar words, see *Words!*

Ready to Try It? Read *A Gift from the Heart* on pp. 420–435.

A Gift From the Heart

by Katacha Díaz

illustrated by Erwin Madrid

Genre

Drama includes plays, which are stories written to be performed for an audience. As you read, think about how this story might appear if it were being acted out.

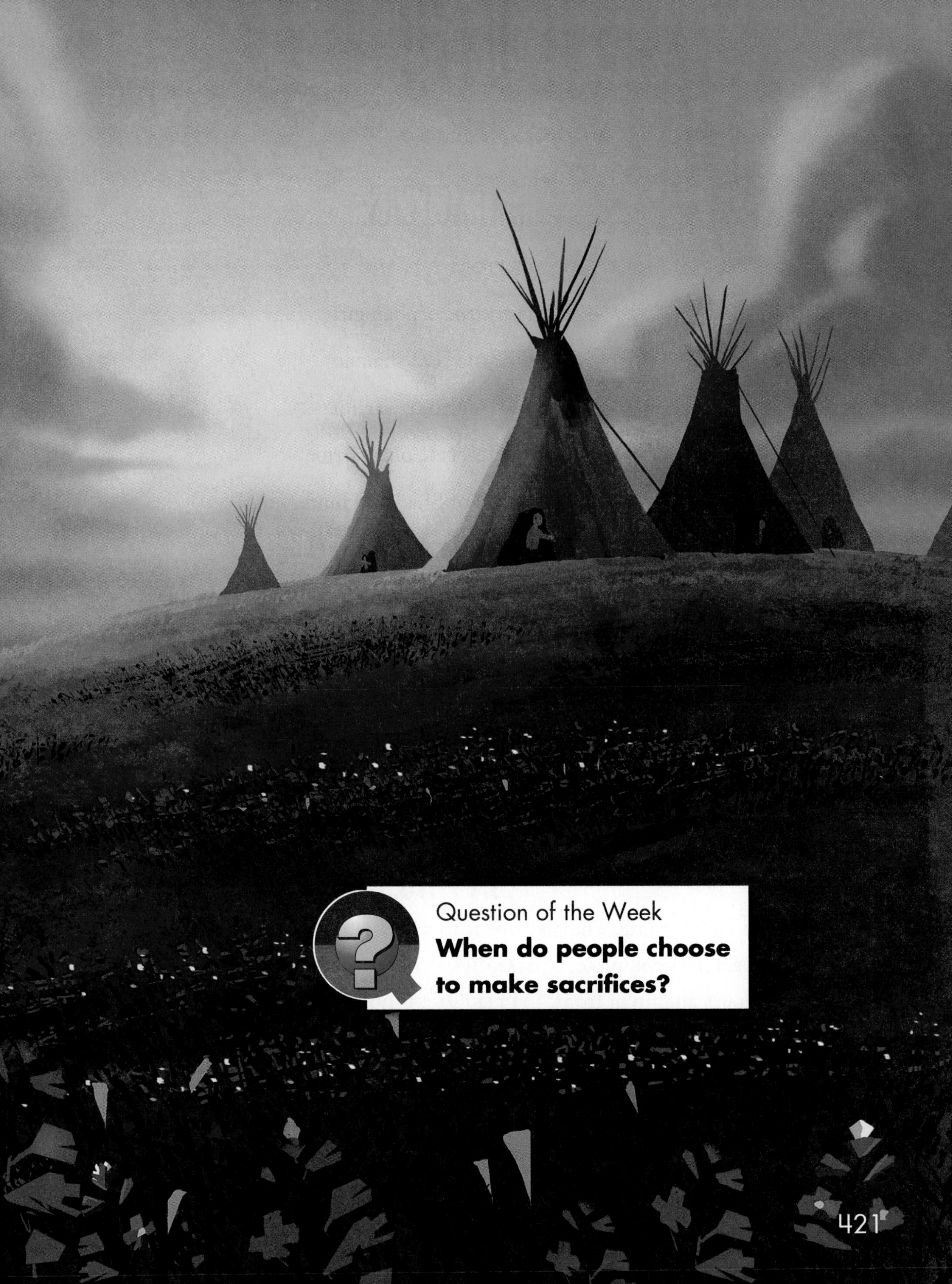

Question of the Week

When do people choose to make sacrifices?

CHARACTERS:

NARRATORS 1, 2, AND 3

LITTLE ONE, orphan girl

WISE EAGLE, old shaman

LITTLE BUFFALO, warrior

SHADOW HUNTER, old warrior

BLOSSOM, wife of Shadow Hunter

ONE-WHO-RUNS, son of Shadow Hunter

STARGAZER, old woman

HUMMINGBIRD, flute girl

BLUEBIRD, flute boy

COMANCHE PEOPLE

COMANCHE CHANTERS

SETTING:

The Texas prairie. The play opens to a backdrop of mountains. Tepees and actors are in place. COMANCHE PEOPLE stand on both sides of the tepees and up in front. LITTLE ONE is holding her treasured doll.

NARRATOR 1: This story takes place on the Texas prairie, where the COMANCHE PEOPLE make their home.

(COMANCHE CHANTERS *enter holding bluebonnet flowers and stand on both sides of the stage.)*

NARRATOR 2: The Great Spirit blessed the PEOPLE with rain and their crops grew tall. There was an abundance of food and wildlife.

NARRATOR 3: The buffalo roamed and grazed on prairie grasses. Eagles, hawks, and bluebirds flew in the sky, while hummingbirds went from flower to flower to get food.

NARRATOR 1 (COMANCHE PEOPLE *and* LITTLE ONE *all look up at the sky.*)*:* But this season was different. Winter now was over. The PEOPLE waited for the spring rains to come, but none came. Grass did not grow. Water did not fill the streams.

NARRATOR 2: The PEOPLE prayed and prayed to the Great Spirit to bless their land with rain, but none came. A drought fell over the land.

COMANCHE CHANTERS: Great Spirit, why are you so angry?

NARRATOR 3: Little One's mother and father became ill and died because of the drought. Now, she is an orphan. Stargazer, an old woman, and the People look after the little orphan girl.

LITTLE ONE *(Talks to her doll.)*: Wise Eagle will go to pray to the Great Spirit to end the drought and bring us rain. Without water, nothing will grow. And we will continue to starve. (Little One *hugs her doll and exits, as do the* Comanche People *and* Comanche Chanters.)

COMANCHE CHANTERS *(offstage)*: Great Spirit! Why do you ignore our calls for help?

(Wise Eagle *looks up at the sky and quietly prays.)*

NARRATOR 1: Wise Eagle, the old shaman, took his ceremonial stick and went off to the mountains to pray by himself. During the night, he heard the Great Spirit's words and thought about what he must say. Then he brought back this message for the People.

WISE EAGLE: I heard the Great Spirit's words. We took the many gifts Mother Earth gave us but did not give back. Mother Earth continued to sacrifice for us. But we never sacrificed for her. Now we must give the Great Spirit a special gift—something that is very dear to us. Who will be the first to sacrifice a gift and toss it in the campfire? (The PEOPLE *look at each other in shock and shake their heads.)*

(Enter COMANCHE CHANTERS; LITTLE ONE *clutching doll;* LITTLE BUFFALO *holds drum;* SHADOW HUNTER *holds a bow and arrow and stands next to his wife,* BLOSSOM, *and their son,* ONE-WHO-RUNS; STARGAZER *holds blanket; and* HUMMINGBIRD *and* BLUEBIRD *hold flutes.)*

LITTLE BUFFALO *(Looks down at his drum.)*: This is my favorite drum. It took me a very long time to carve and make it. I don't think Great Spirit wants me to toss my drum in the campfire. (LITTLE BUFFALO *bows his head and exits.)*

COMANCHE CHANTERS: Who will make a sacrifice to the Great Spirit?

SHADOW HUNTER *(Stands by his wife and son and looks at his bow and arrow.)*: Why, surely the Great Spirit doesn't want me to toss my bow and arrow in the campfire. How will I defend our PEOPLE or hunt for food? I will wait for someone else to make a sacrifice to the Great Spirit. (SHADOW HUNTER *bows his head. He exits followed by his wife and son.)*

STARGAZER *(Looks at the blanket she's carrying.)*: This is my favorite blanket. It keeps me warm during the cold winter months. I don't think Great Spirit wants an old woman like me to be cold and suffer. I will go to my tepee and think about the Great Spirit's message. (STARGAZER *bows her head and exits.)*

HUMMINGBIRD AND BLUEBIRD *(They look at the flutes they each hold and shake their heads.)*: The Great Spirit has blessed us with the gift of music. If we toss our flutes in the campfire, how will we play the Great Spirit's favorite songs during our special celebrations? Who will give our PEOPLE music? (HUMMINGBIRD *and* BLUEBIRD *bow their heads and exit.)*

COMANCHE CHANTERS: Who will make a sacrifice to the Great Spirit?

LITTLE ONE (*Hugging her doll.*): I know the Great Spirit wants a gift from the heart, but I can't bear to part with my favorite doll. It's all that is left from my family. (LITTLE ONE *holding her doll tightly to her heart bows her head and exits.*)

NARRATOR 2: The PEOPLE shook their heads and slowly walked away, taking their prized possessions with them, and leaving WISE EAGLE by himself. (The PEOPLE *bow their heads and exit.*)

WISE EAGLE *(Holding ceremonial stick.)*: Before I give up my ceremonial stick, I will go to my tepee and think about the Great Spirit's message and pray for guidance. (WISE EAGLE *bows head and exits.)*

COMANCHE CHANTERS: Who will make a sacrifice to the Great Spirit to end the drought?

(LITTLE ONE *goes inside her tepee and sits with the flap open; she's holding her doll tightly to her heart.)*

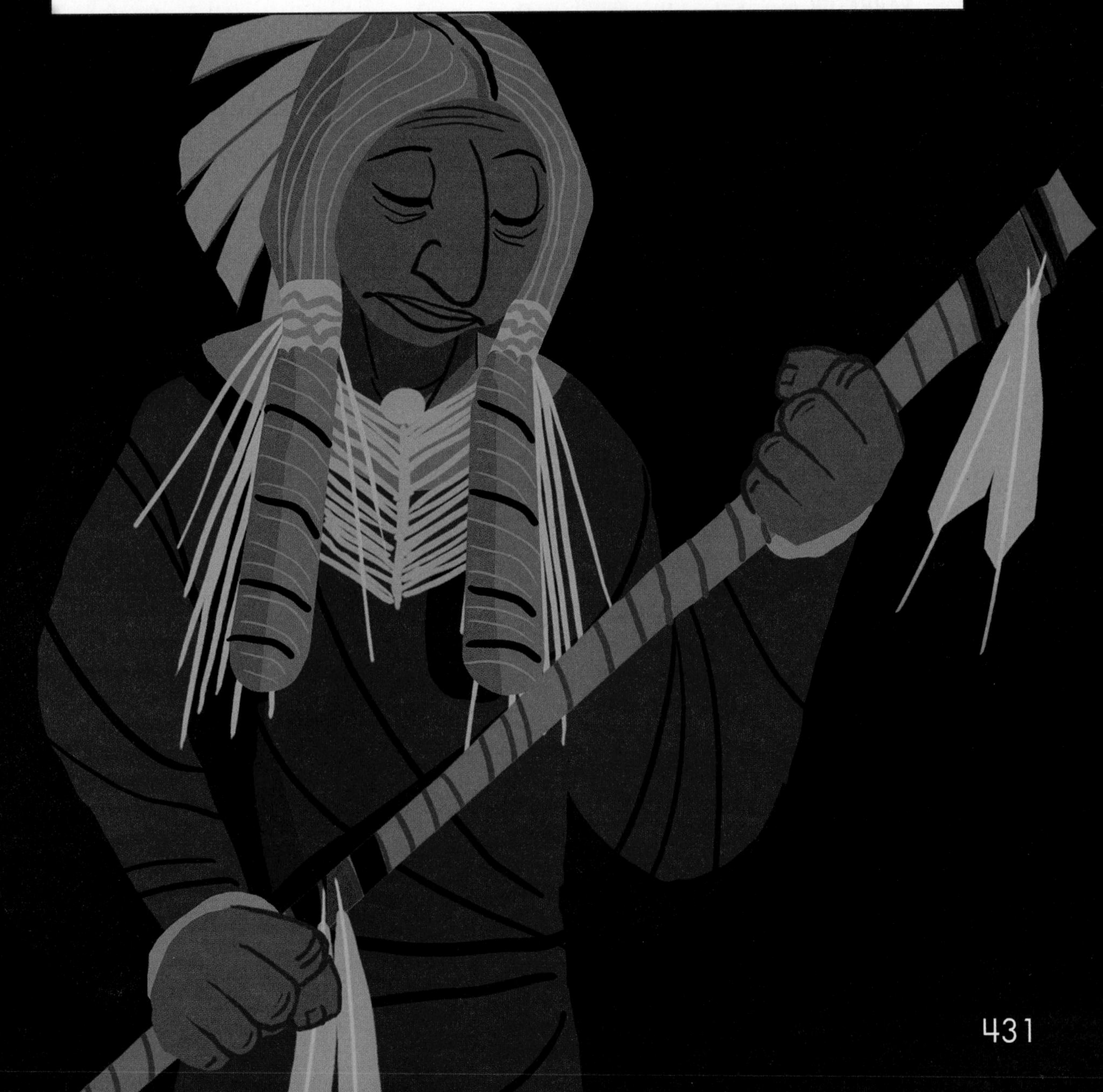

NARRATOR 3: The PEOPLE went inside their tepees and talked to each other about the Great Spirit's message.

NARRATOR 1: As darkness fell, the silvery moon and a million stars filled the night sky. The quiet was unearthly. Not a breath of air stirred. Not a leaf moved on a tree. Even the dogs that always barked and howled at the moon were deep asleep by the campfire.

NARRATOR 2: Like all the other PEOPLE, STARGAZER was asleep in the tepee that she and LITTLE ONE shared. But LITTLE ONE could not sleep. She tossed and turned. Round and round thoughts about the Great Spirit's message swirled in LITTLE ONE's head. She whispered to her doll in the dark.

LITTLE ONE (*Clutching her doll, quietly tiptoes out of the tepee and whispers to her doll.*): I love you more than anything else in this world.

NARRATOR 3: LITTLE ONE went to the same place where WISE EAGLE prayed to the Great Spirit.

LITTLE ONE (*Holding her doll tightly to her heart, stands in the very place where* WISE EAGLE *had prayed.*): Oh, Great Spirit, please accept my gift.

NARRATOR 1: LITTLE ONE kissed her doll good-bye. While she watched her most treasured possession burn, LITTLE ONE asked the Great Spirit to help the PEOPLE.

NARRATOR 2: The silvery moon and bright stars lit the trail back to camp. LITTLE ONE tiptoed inside her tepee and fell fast asleep.

NARRATOR 3: While STARGAZER and LITTLE ONE slept inside their tepee, heavy, dark clouds rolled over the mountains and filled the sky. Then the sound of light rain could be heard, softly at first. Soon the rains strengthened and the sound became deafening. But the People slept on. No one awakened.

NARRATOR 1: Finally, when the rains stopped and morning sunlight filled the sky, LITTLE ONE opened her eyes. She could hear the PEOPLE's voices outside her tepee.

[LITTLE ONE *comes out of her tepee. All the* PEOPLE *enter, look around, and smile.*]

NARRATOR 2: When LITTLE ONE opened the tepee flap and looked outside, she saw beautiful blue flowers covering the ground!

NARRATOR 3: The Earth was alive again! There was water in the stream for the PEOPLE, animals, and birds to drink. The hills and valleys were covered with the new blue wildflowers. It was WISE EAGLE who called the new flower "bluebonnets."

WISE EAGLE *(Puts his hand on* LITTLE ONE's *shoulder.)*: I saw the sacrifice you made last night, LITTLE ONE. It is because of your gift to the Great Spirit that the rains came and the drought ended. The beautiful blue flowers are a special gift sent by the Great Spirit. We shall call them "bluebonnets," and we shall now call you Bluebonnet Girl.

COMANCHE CHANTERS: And so when spring comes every year, bluebonnets blanket the earth. All are reminded of what the young girl gave up for the PEOPLE.

Curtain

Objectives

- Write responses to texts using details to show understanding.
- Read independently for long periods of time and paraphrase the reading, including the order in which events occur.

Envision It! | **Retell**

READING STREET ONLINE
STORY SORT
www.ReadingStreet.com

Think Critically

1. Think about someone in the world today who unselfishly did something for someone else. Do you think it was difficult for him or her to make this choice? Why? **Text to World**
2. Why do you think the author wanted the reader to know what things the other People refused to throw in the fire? **Think Like an Author**
3. With the exception of Little One, what general statement could you make about the actions of the People? **Generalize**
4. On page 432, Narrator 2 says: "Round and round thoughts about the Great Spirit's message swirled in Little One's head." Explain how this statement helped you predict what Little One would do next. **Predict and Set Purpose**
5. **Look Back and Write** Look back at pages 422–423. The structure of a play is very different from that of a story. What things does an author include in a play that would not be part of a story? Provide evidence to support your answer.

TEST PRACTICE **Extended Response**

Meet the Author

Katacha Díaz

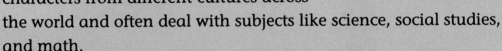

Katacha Díaz has written more than 40 fiction and nonfiction books for young readers. Her books feature characters from different cultures across the world and often deal with subjects like science, social studies, and math.

Her picture book *Badger at Sandy Ridge Road* was published as part of the Smithsonian Institute's Backyard Series. This series of books focuses on backyards and encourages children to explore all the animals and insects that might be hiding in them. Her book for young children, *Carolina's Gift: A Story of Peru*, introduces children to Spanish words through a story about a Peruvian girl looking for a gift for her grandmother.

Ms. Díaz graduated from the University of Washington with two degrees. She lives in Davis, California, with her Yorkshire terrier, Mister Keeper.

Here is another book by Katacha Díaz.

Carolina's Gift: A Story of Peru

Use the Reading Log in the *Reader's and Writer's Notebook* to record your independent reading.

Objectives

- Write creative stories that build to an ending and contain details about the characters and setting.
- Recognize and use quotation marks.

Key Features of a Play

- a story with plot, setting, and theme written to be performed
- includes dialogue labeled using characters' names
- may be divided into acts and scenes

READING STREET ONLINE
GRAMMAR JAMMER
www.ReadingStreet.com

Narrative

Play

A **play** is a story that is written to be acted out for an audience. The student model on the next page is an example of the beginning of a play.

Writing Prompt Write a short play about a legendary character or group of characters who are trying to achieve a goal.

Writer's Checklist

Remember, you should . . .

- ✓ write an imaginative story.
- ✓ include a cast of characters and a description of the setting.
- ✓ provide stage directions.
- ✓ create dialogue that fits each character.
- ✓ use quotation marks where appropriate.

Student Model

Johnny Appleseed's Grand Plan

Characters: Farmer Morgan, Tom Miller, John Chapman

(**Setting:** Ohio in the 1800s. Farmer Morgan and Tom Miller are standing near the edge of a field, talking.)

TOM: Have you met the fellow who is going around planting apple tree seedlings in the fields?

FARMER MORGAN: Yep—his name is John Chapman. He dresses in a strange way, but he sure does hold some interesting ideas. The first thing he said to me was, "You settlers in the West will need apples to eat and store for winter. So, I'm going to plant you some apple orchards that will grow all over the wilderness."

TOM: Here he comes now. It looks like he's carrying one of his seedlings.

(John Chapman enters carrying a small tree seedling.)

FARMER MORGAN: John, I'd like you to meet my neighbor, Tom Miller.

Genre A **play** includes a cast of characters.

Writing Trait Word Choice Avoid unnecessary words.

Quotations and quotation marks are used correctly.

Conventions

Quotations and Quotation Marks

Remember A speaker's exact words are called a **quotation.** In a play, **quotation marks** (" ") are used only when one speaker is quoting another speaker.

Objectives

- Explain the effects of an author's use of language on the reader.
- Explain how the different methods used in media affect the message that is being communicated.

Social Studies in Reading

Genre

Persuasive Essay

- A persuasive essay is a type of persuasive text. The author's purpose for writing it is to persuade the reader to think a certain way or do something.
- The writer uses language to persuade the reader.
- Design techniques, such as illustrations or photographs, contribute to the message of a persuasive essay.
- Read "Vote for Bluebonnet Day." It is written in the form of a letter to the editor. Think about the language the writer uses to influence the reader to think or do something.

Dear Editor of the *4th Grade Times*:

I am a fourth grader with something important to say. I am writing to convince you to make May 1 a school holiday. We should call this holiday Bluebonnet Day.

There are many reasons why we should celebrate the bluebonnet. First of all, the bluebonnet is the official flower of our state. Each and every year, we Texans look for the first bluebonnets to appear. These beautiful wildflowers tell us that winter is over. They tell us that spring is here. The arrival of the bluebonnet means that summer is not far off. That means that summer vacation is coming soon. No wonder we love the bluebonnets so much!

Since the first bluebonnets appear around May 1, we should call that day Bluebonnet Day. We should spend the holiday picking bluebonnets. Many people think it is illegal to pick bluebonnets. In fact, it is perfectly legal. The state of Texas allows you do it, as long as you are not on private property. The best part is that it is a lot of fun!

Can you imagine our entire school walking through a huge field of bluebonnets? Look at the picture I included. Wouldn't you like to pick these bluebonnets under a clear blue sky? Then vote for Bluebonnet Day. Bluebonnet Day will remind us of how lucky we are to live in this beautiful state.

Now, I know what the teachers are thinking. They are thinking that this does not sound educational. But I disagree. Bluebonnet Day will be very educational. Our science teacher can tell us all about how the bluebonnet grows. Our art teacher can ask us to paint the bluebonnets we pick. Our English teacher can ask us to write a poem about bluebonnets. Our math teacher can ask us to count the buds in each flower. And we'll get plenty of exercise walking through the fields and picking flowers.

At the end of Bluebonnet Day, we can bring a bouquet of bluebonnets home. We can share the joy of Bluebonnet Day with our families. What a wonderful way to celebrate our state flower! Vote for Bluebonnet Day!

Yours truly,

Juanita Mason

Juanita Mason

Let's Think About...

Do the illustrations help persuade the reader that Bluebonnet Day is a good idea? How does this design element add to the writer's message?
Persuasive Essay

Let's Think About...

Reading Across Texts Look back at *A Gift from the Heart* and "Vote for Bluebonnet Day." Do you think the main character in *A Gift from the Heart* would agree with Juanita's letter? Why or why not?

Writing Across Texts Use details from *A Gift from the Heart* and "Vote for Bluebonnet Day" to write a poem about the bluebonnet.

Objectives

• Read aloud grade-level texts and understand what is read. • Determine the meanings of unfamiliar words or multiple-meaning words by using the context of the sentence. • Speak clearly and to the point, give an opinion and support it with correct information. Make eye contact, change how fast, loud, and clearly you speak, and get your ideas across clearly. • Take part in discussions led by teachers or other students, ask and answer questions, and offer ideas that build on the ideas of other people.

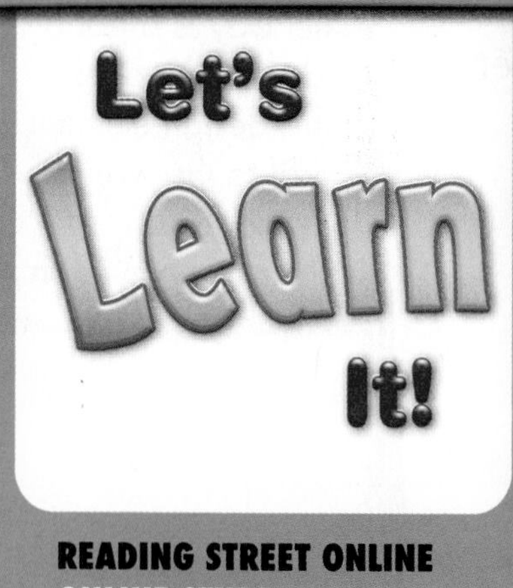

READING STREET ONLINE
ONLINE STUDENT EDITION
www.ReadingStreet.com

Vocabulary

Unfamiliar Words

Context Clues Sometimes words and sentences around an unfamiliar word can give you a clue to the word's meaning. Look at the surrounding words and sentences to help you figure out the meaning of an unfamiliar word.

Practice It! Choose an unfamiliar word from *A Gift from the Heart*, pages 420–435. Read the sentences that come before and after the unfamiliar word. How do they help you figure out its meaning? Make a list of other unfamiliar words in the story that you were able to figure out with context clues.

Fluency

Appropriate Phrasing

Partner Reading Punctuation cues help you know when to slow down, pause, or change the pitch of your voice as you read.

Practice It! With a partner, practice reading *A Gift from the Heart*, page 429. Slow down for commas. Stop for periods. Make your voice higher when you see a question mark. Help each other improve.

Listening and Speaking

Get Ready For Middle School

When you perform in front of an audience, speak clearly and loudly.

Readers' Theater

In Readers' Theater, you read from a script that illustrates a scene from a story. The idea is to bring the story to life.

Practice It! With a small group, choose a scene from *A Gift from the Heart.* Assign roles and characters' dialogue. Use details from the story to illustrate your character's personality. Perform your Readers' Theater for the class.

Tips

Listening . . .

- Listen attentively to the people who are speaking.
- Be ready to make relevant comments.

Speaking . . .

- Make eye contact with the other performers as you speak.
- Speak your character's dialogue quickly or slowly to match what's happening in the story.

Teamwork . . .

- Make suggestions about how to improve the performance.

Objectives

- Speak clearly and to the point, give an opinion and support it with correct information. Make eye contact, change how fast, loud, and clearly you speak, and get your ideas across clearly.

Oral Vocabulary

Let's Talk About

Space Exploration

- Share opinions about what it would be like to travel in space.
- Express ideas at an appropriate speaking rate.
- Add comments to others' ideas.

READING STREET ONLINE
CONCEPT TALK VIDEO
www.ReadingStreet.com

You've learned
290
Amazing Words
so far this year!

Objectives

• Monitor your comprehension of a text and adjust your reading based on how well you understand what you are reading. • Explain information that is shown in graphics.

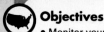

Envision It! | **Skill Strategy**

Skill

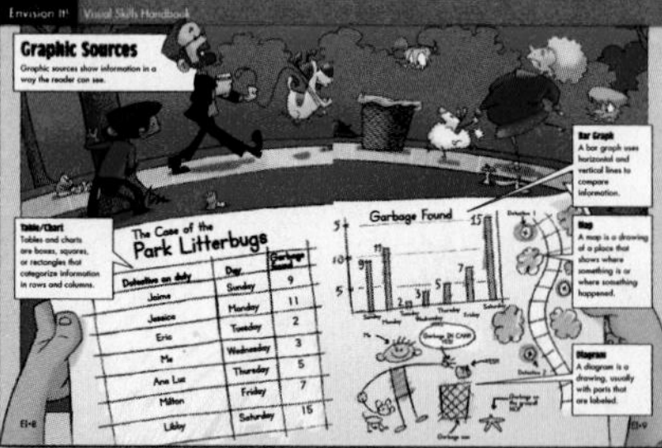

Envision It! Visual Skills Handbook

Graphic Sources

Graphic sources show information in a way the reader can see.

Table/Chart

Tables and charts are boxes, squares, or rectangles that categorize information in rows and columns.

The Case of the Park Litterbugs

Detective on duty	Day	Garbage found
Jaime	Sunday	9
Jessica	Monday	11
Eric	Tuesday	2
Me	Wednesday	3
Ana Luz	Thursday	5
Milton	Friday	7
Libby	Saturday	15

Garbage Found

Bar Graph

A bar graph uses horizontal and vertical lines to compare information.

Map

A map is a drawing of a place that shows where something is or where something happened.

Diagram

A diagram is a drawing, usually with parts that are labeled.

EI•8

EI•9

Strategy

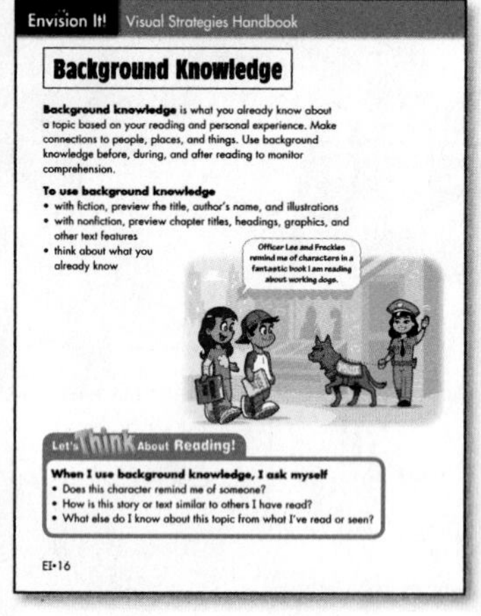

Envision It! Visual Strategies Handbook

Background Knowledge

Background knowledge is what you already know about a topic based on your reading and personal experience. Make connections to people, places, and things. Use background knowledge before, during, and after reading to monitor comprehension.

To use background knowledge

- with fiction, preview the title, author's name, and illustrations
- with nonfiction, preview chapter titles, headings, graphics, and other text features
- think about what you already know

Officer Lee and Freckles remind me of characters in a fantastic book I am reading about working dogs.

Let's Think About Reading!

When I use background knowledge, I ask myself

- Does this character remind me of someone?
- How is this story or text similar to others I have read?
- What else do I know about this topic from what I've read or seen?

EI•16

READING STREET ONLINE
ENVISION IT! ANIMATIONS
www.ReadingStreet.com

Comprehension Skill

Graphic Sources

- A graphic source, such as a chart, diagram, graph, or illustration, helps you organize information so it is easier to understand.
- Use graphic sources and text features as you read to help you understand and locate information. Compare information in the text with information in the graphic.
- Use the diagram on page 447 and the photograph below to organize the information presented in "The Other Side of the Moon."

Phases of the Moon

Comprehension Strategy

Background Knowledge

Background knowledge is what you already know about a topic or subject. Good readers use their background knowledge to monitor and adjust their reading. Previewing a selection will help you determine what knowledge you will bring to a selection. You can use background knowledge while you read, especially if you come across information you don't understand.

The Other Side of the Moon

There is one side of the moon—called the far side—that no one standing on the Earth has ever seen. Astronauts have gone behind the moon to see the other side. However, no one simply looking up at the sky has ever seen the back of the moon.

Why?

The answer lies in the way the moon moves. The moon orbits Earth, but it also turns once on its axis in the same amount of time. This is called synchronous rotation.

Study the diagram below.

Imagine you went to the moon and painted a crater red to serve as a marker. Then you came back to Earth and looked up at the moon night after night. If the moon did not rotate, your marker would seem to move across the moon and even disappear for a while as the moon orbited Earth. But your red crater stays in sight, which means that the moon rotates and shows us only one side.

Moon's rotation on its axis

Moon's orbit of Earth

Skill Preview the title and the diagram on this page. Explain how you think this diagram can help you to understand the passage.

Strategy What do you already know about this topic? How does this knowledge help you to understand the information in the passage?

Skill Do you think this sentence is important for the author to include in the passage? Explain why or why not.

Your Turn!

Need a Review? See the *Envision It! Handbook* for help with graphic sources and background knowledge.

Ready to Try It? Use multiple text features to locate information as you read *The Man Who Went to the Far Side of the Moon.*

Objectives

- Determine the meanings of unfamiliar or multiple-meaning words by using the context of the sentence.
- Use a dictionary or glossary to find the meanings of unknown words, the syllable rules for these words, and how to pronounce them.

Envision It! Words to Know

capsule

horizon

module

astronauts

hatch

lunar

quarantine

READING STREET ONLINE
VOCABULARY ACTIVITIES
www.ReadingStreet.com

Vocabulary Strategy for

Multiple-Meaning Words

Context Clues Sometimes the meaning of a word you know does not make sense in a sentence. This is because the word has multiple meanings. Look for context clues to help you decide which meaning the author is using. If context clues don't help you, use a dictionary.

1. Try the meaning you know. Does it make sense in the sentence?
2. If that meaning doesn't make sense reread the words and sentences around the word. Use the context to help you find the meaning for the unknown word.
3. If it still doesn't make sense, look up the word in a dictionary and choose the meaning that makes sense in the sentence.

As you read "Travelers in Space," use context clues to figure out the meanings of *capsule* and *hatch* and other multiple-meaning words.

Words to Write Reread "Travelers in Space." Imagine you are traveling in space. Describe your spaceship and what you can see. Use words from the *Words to Know* list.

TRAVELERS in SPACE

Astronauts are space workers. Since the 1960s, they have blasted off into space. Astronauts explore the unknown, which is exciting. But much of their time is spent working hard.

They may repair a space station or a satellite. To do this, they suit up, open the hatch, and float out into space. When they finish the job, they float back into the spacecraft through a small door. Astronauts also do many experiments and make calculations related to their flight.

Early in the space program, there were many lunar flights. The astronauts took off in a huge spaceship. Part of it fell away after they got into orbit. Then they rode in a capsule, or small space vehicle. By the time they landed on the moon, the astronauts were riding in a module. This tiny spacecraft fit into the larger ship and could fly on its own.

The astronauts stood on the moon's surface and saw the Earth on the horizon! When they got back to Earth, they were in quarantine. They had to stay away from everyone to be sure they had not brought back any diseases.

Your Turn!

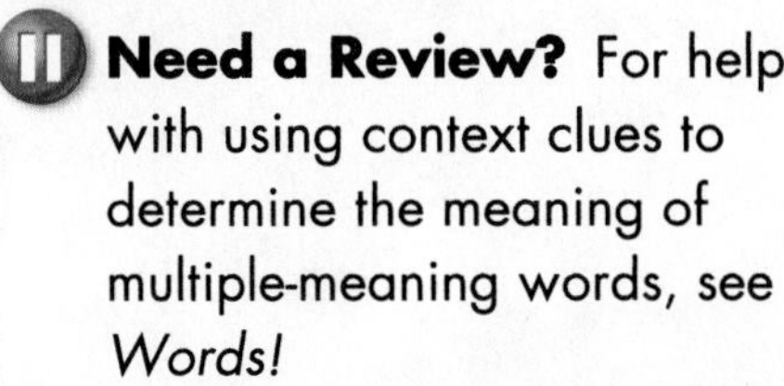

Need a Review? For help with using context clues to determine the meaning of multiple-meaning words, see *Words!*

Ready to Try It? Read *The Man Who Went to the Far Side of the Moon* on pp. 450–463.

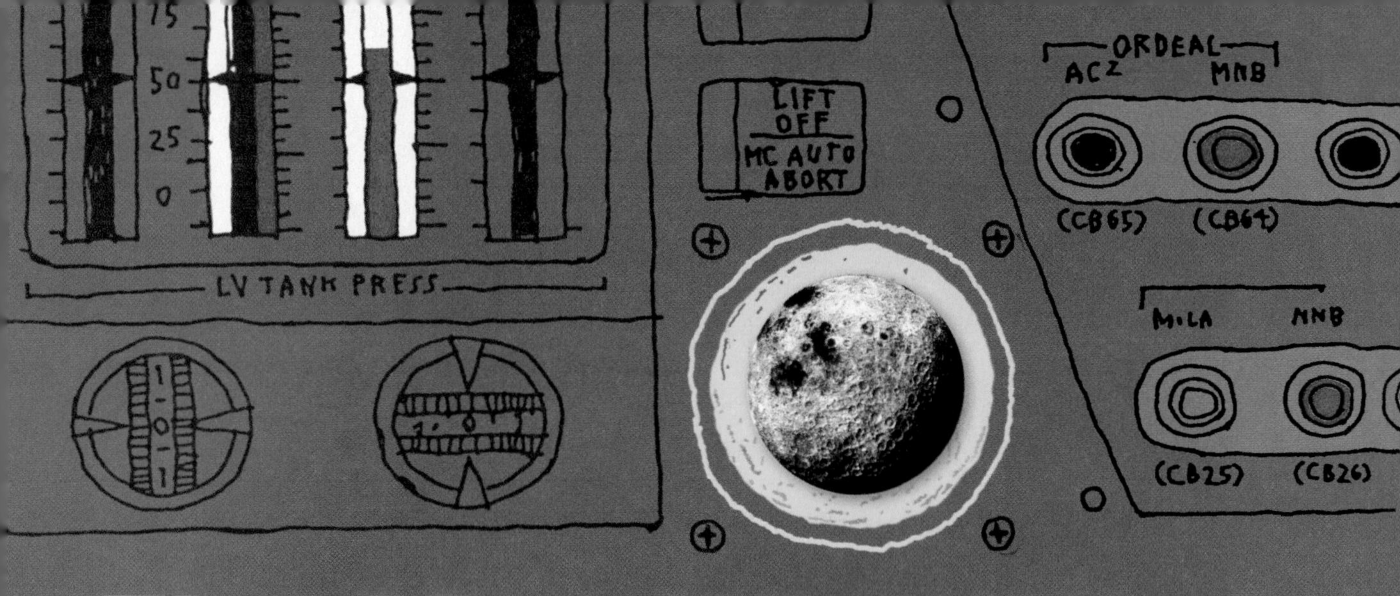

The Man Who Went to the Far Side of the Moon

The Story of Apollo 11 Astronaut Michael Collins

by Bea Uusma Schyffert

Genre

Expository Text can be an account of a historical event. As you read this selection about the historic *Apollo 11* space flight, imagine what it would have been like to have been part of the mission.

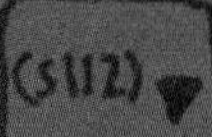
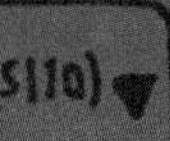

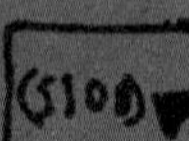
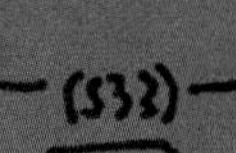
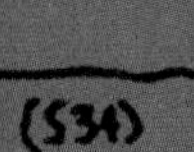

Question of the Week

How do the achievements of others influence our dreams?

On July 16, 1969, the United States launched the *Saturn 5* rocket into space. Aboard this spacecraft, the largest rocket ever built, were three men: astronauts Michael Collins, Buzz Aldrin, and Neil Armstrong. Their mission: to be the first to land on the moon. One of these men would not land on the moon, however. That man, Michael Collins, would circle the moon in the command module while Buzz Aldrin and Neil Armstrong landed the lunar module, *Eagle,* and explored the moon's surface.

It is July 20, 1969. A Sunday. It's four minutes to ten in the morning. It is –250°F (–180°C) in the shade and +250°F (+120°C) in the sun at the Sea of Tranquility, where Neil and Buzz have landed the *Eagle.* They are 242,000 miles (390,000 kilometers) from Launch Pad 39A at Kennedy Space Center in Florida.

In the earliest versions of the checklists, Buzz Aldrin would be the first man to step down onto the moon. But the lunar module hatch opens inward to the right, and Buzz, who stood right behind it, had difficulty climbing out. When the astronauts tried to switch places during practice, they damaged the cramped cabin. A few months before the launch, it was decided that Neil should go first. He crawls backward through a tiny hatch near the floor. As he looks toward the horizon, he can see that they have landed on a sphere: the horizon is a little bent since the moon is so small. His arms are covered with goosebumps. There is no air. No sound. No life. No footprints.

Wait: now there is one.

Neil Armstrong is the first man on the moon.

...I'M GOING TO STEP OFF THE LM NOW...

When you stand on the moon, you can cover the entire Earth with your hand.

242,000 miles (390,000 kilometers) from home, trapped inside a small vessel, two men are taking snapshots of each other.

Neil Armstrong's picture of Buzz Aldrin

Buzz Aldrin's picture of Neil Armstrong

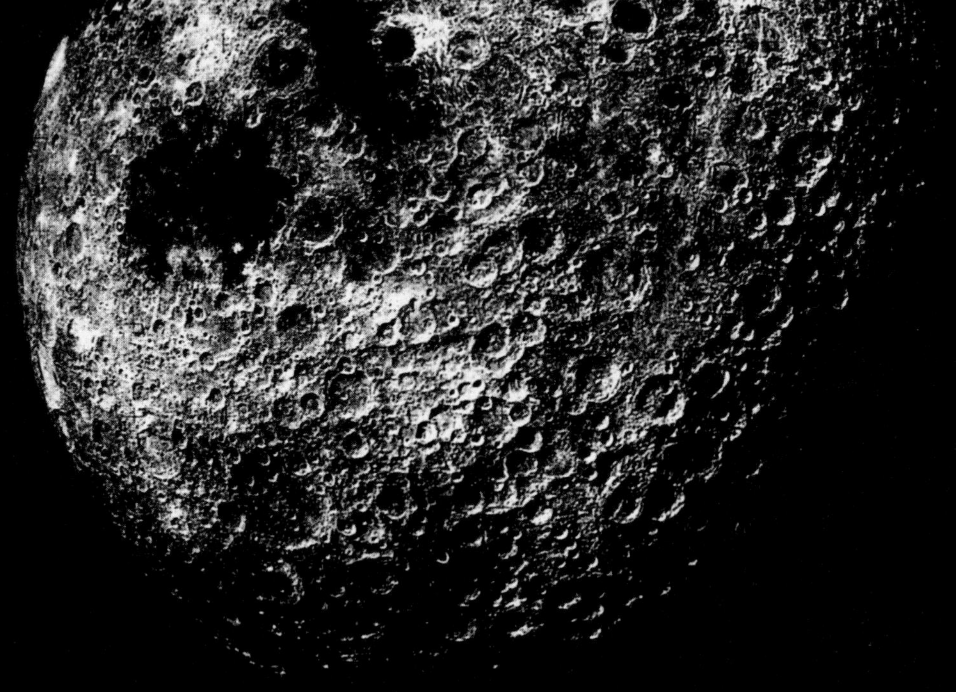

Neil and Buzz stay on the moon for 21 hours and 36 minutes, but only a little more than 2 hours of that time is spent outside the lunar module. They perform three minor experiments and load two aluminum suitcases with 48 pounds (22 kilograms) of moon dust and rocks.

The three minor experiments:

To measure solar particles
To measure the exact distance to Earth
To measure moonquakes and meteoritic impact

The major experiment:

To land on the moon

When they have climbed back into the lunar module and shut the hatch, they take their helmets off. They look at each other because they both sense a strong smell. Neil thinks it smells like wet ashes. Buzz says it smells like spent gunpowder. It is the moon. The moon has a smell.

OK, we copy you down, Eagle

Six hundred million people in 47 countries are watching the blurred TV transmission of the lunar landing. There is one person who has no chance of catching Neil and Buzz on TV. He is traveling at a height of 70 miles (110 kilometers) above the far side of the moon. All he can see is darkness and stars outside his window.

In case something unexpected should happen, the astronauts never bounce farther than 200 feet (60 meters) from the landing site.

Michael Collins has 28 hours to go, alone in the capsule. He has trained for so long. He has traveled so far. He is so close now and still he can't land on the moon. They did not choose him.

He was going for 99 percent of the trip and that was good enough for him, he has replied when people have asked. But he knew he didn't have the best seat on *Columbia.*

He thinks to himself that he never really got to know the astronauts who are now on the moon. Neil and Buzz trained together for many months in the lunar module simulator. Michael trained by himself in the capsule.

Once every two hours *Columbia* passes over the landing site. Michael Collins tries to locate the *Eagle.* He can't see it. He only sees crater after crater, cast with sharp shadows from the sun.

apollo 11, this is houston, we're three minutes away from loss of signal over

Every other hour, all radio communication with Earth is lost as the spacecraft skims over the far side of the moon. When Neil and Buzz are on the moon's surface, Michael Collins has to do three people's jobs. He has to make 850 computer commands. He has been taught just *how* to push the buttons—hard, right in the center, and to hold them pushed for a little over a second. They must be pushed in the right order, one after the other: VERB-88-ENTER. VERB-87-ENTER. If he loses track on the far side of the moon, there is no one to ask.

Michael turns up the light in the command module. It's almost cozy. He is used to flying alone. He has flown airplanes by himself for almost 20 years. He has even practiced how he should return home by himself if something should happen to Neil and Buzz down on the moon.

It's quiet in the capsule on the dark side of the moon. The only noises are the fans humming and a faint crackling from the radio. Michael Collins prepares his dinner. Looks out the windows. Every 120th minute he sees the Earth rise at the horizon.

MICHAEL COLLINS'S FOOD PACK ON THE FOURTH DAY OF THE TRIP

BREAKFAST:	LUNCH:	DINNER:
FROSTED FLAKES (FREEZE-DRIED) 4 PEANUT CUBES (BITE-SIZED) COCOA (POWDER) ORANGE AND GRAPEFRUIT DRINK (POWDER) CANADIAN BACON AND APPLESAUCE (FREEZE-DRIED)	SHRIMP COCKTAIL (FREEZE-DRIED) HAM AND POTATOES (WET-PACK) FRUIT COCKTAIL (FREEZE-DRIED) 4 DATE FRUITCAKE CUBES (BITE-SIZED) GRAPEFRUIT DRINK (POWDER)	BEEF STEW (SPOON-BOWL) 4 COCONUT CUBES (BITE-SIZED) BANANA PUDDING (POWDER) GRAPE PUNCH (POWDER)

ALL THE FOOD IS VACUUM PACKED AND MARKED WITH LABELS, SINCE IT IS DIFFICULT TO TELL WHAT EACH ITEM IS SUPPOSED TO BE. THE TRICKY THING ABOUT EATING IN WEIGHTLESSNESS IS MOVING THE FOOD FROM THE PACKAGE TO THE MOUTH, WITHOUT LETTING IT FLOAT AWAY. THE ASTRONAUTS EAT:

FREEZE-DRIED AND POWDERED FOOD:	WET-PACKED FOOD:	SPOON-BOWL FOOD:
THEY INJECT COLD OR HOT WATER INTO THE PACKAGE WITH A SPECIAL WATER GUN, SQUEEZE THE PACKAGE FOR ABOUT THREE MINUTES, THEN CUT OFF A CORNER AND SQUEEZE THE PASTE INTO THEIR MOUTHS.	THEY SUCK THE READY-MIXED WET-PACK FOOD, COLD, STRAIGHT OUT OF THE PACKAGE.	THEY INJECT COLD OR HOT WATER WITH THE WATER GUN AND SQUEEZE THE PACKAGE A LITTLE BEFORE THEY OPEN THE TOP. SPOON-BOWL FOOD IS EATEN WITH A SPOON. IT IS SO STICKY THAT IT EITHER STAYS IN THE PACKAGE OR CLINGS TO THE SPOON.

It is July 24, 1969. A Thursday. Ever since they left the moon, the astronauts have been eager to get back home. After 8 days, 3 hours, and 18 minutes in *Columbia* without washing, the entire body itches. It is hard to breathe in the spacecraft now. It smells like wet dogs and rotten swamp. Michael Collins has flown *Columbia* during reentry into the Earth's atmosphere. For 14 minutes, the astronauts have been pushed down into their seats. They have weighed seven times their weight on Earth. Now the capsule has splashed down in the ocean near Hawaii.

No one knows if the astronauts have been exposed to dangerous lunar germs that could potentially wipe out the human race. Because of this they are sent straight to a quarantine facility: a silver-colored mobile home. Inside, the astronauts write reports about their trip. Michael beats Neil in cards. As they sit there, bored as can be, they begin to understand just what they have experienced. During the trip itself they were so focused on their job that they didn't have time to think about what they have actually done. Everyone on Earth gathered together because of the moon landing. But the astronauts themselves have been far, far away.

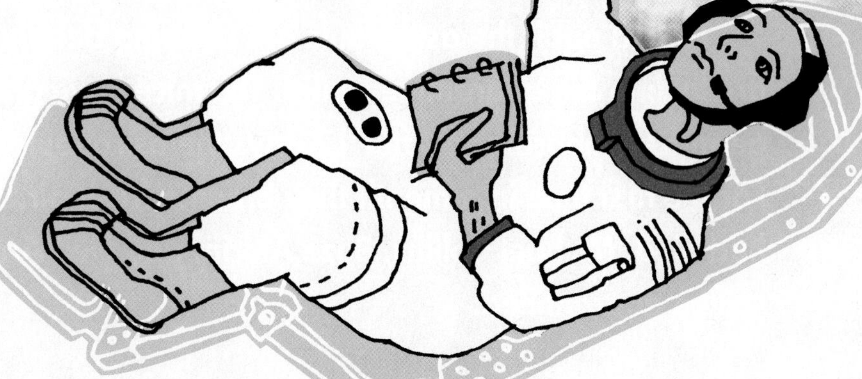

apollo 11, this is houston do you copy?

As they watch a taped recording of the moon landing, Buzz suddenly turns to Neil and says: "Neil, we missed the whole thing!"

In the past, Michael Collins never really cared about the machines he has flown, but this time it's different. On the second night of quarantine, he climbs back into *Columbia* and takes a seat. Then he leans over and scribbles a message in ballpoint pen on the capsule wall, in the tiniest handwriting imaginable:

Spacecraft 107—alias Apollo 11—alias Columbia
The best ship to come down the line
God bless her
Michael Collins, CMP

To find out if the astronauts are carrying deadly germs, mice are let into the quarantine trailer. The mice have grown up in a germ-free laboratory. After 17 days the astronauts are let out. For the first time in a month they breathe fresh air. If the mice had died, Michael Collins, Buzz Aldrin, and Neil Armstrong might still be quarantined.

This picture of *Apollo 16* astronaut Charlie Duke and his family, Dottie, Charles Jr., and Thomas, has been lying in the exact same place on the moon since 1972. ▼

LEFT ON THE MOON

SINCE *APOLLO 11*, THERE HAVE BEEN FIVE OTHER LUNAR MODULES ON THE MOON. THE LAST ONE LANDED IN 1972. EVERYTHING THE ASTRONAUTS LEFT BEHIND STAYS EXACTLY LIKE IT WAS WHEN IT WAS FIRST PUT THERE. THERE IS NO RUST. THERE IS NO WEAR AND TEAR. IN THE GRAY MOON DUST LIE THE TRACES OF SIX APOLLO MISSIONS:

2 GOLF BALLS HIT BY ASTRONAUT ALAN SHEPARD *(APOLLO 14)*

TO SAVE ON WEIGHT, THE ASTRONAUTS LEFT EVERYTHING THEY DIDN'T NEED BEFORE TAKING OFF IN THE LUNAR MODULE:

- SCIENTIFIC EXPERIMENTS
- TV CAMERAS AND CABLES
- HASSELBLAD CAMERAS
- EMPTY FOOD PACKAGES

PARTS OF THE SPACESUITS:

- BACKPACK, BOOTS

6 LUNAR MODULES

3 MOON BUGGIES (FROM *APOLLO 15, 16,* AND *17*)

MEMENTOS AND HONORARY OBJECTS:

- PLAQUES
- MEDALLIONS
- ASTRONAUT BADGES
- CRUCIFIXES
- A GOLD OLIVE BRANCH
- A COMPUTER DISC THE SIZE OF A SILVER DOLLAR WITH PEACEFUL GREETINGS FROM PRESIDENTS AND PRIME MINISTERS OF 73 COUNTRIES

A SCULPTURE OF A FALLEN ASTRONAUT, IN MEMORY OF ALL THOSE WHO HAVE DIED IN THE EFFORTS TO REACH THE MOON

ONE RED BIBLE

6 AMERICAN FLAGS

UNVERIFIED:

- LAS BRISAS HOTEL IN ACAPULCO, MEXICO, INSISTS THAT THE *APOLLO 11* ASTRONAUTS PLACED A PINK FLAG FROM THE HOTEL ON THE MOON IN GRATITUDE FOR THEIR COMPLIMENTARY STAY.

OVER FOUR HUNDRED SIXTY THOUSAND PEOPLE WORKED ON THE APOLLO PROJECT. THEY GOT 12 ASTRONAUTS TO THE MOON. ALTOGETHER, THE APOLLO ASTRONAUTS BROUGHT 840 POUNDS (380 KILOGRAMS) OF MOON MATERIAL BACK TO EARTH. ON THE MOON THERE ARE FOOTPRINTS FROM 12 PEOPLE, TRACES THAT WILL NEVER BE SWEPT AWAY BY ANY WIND.

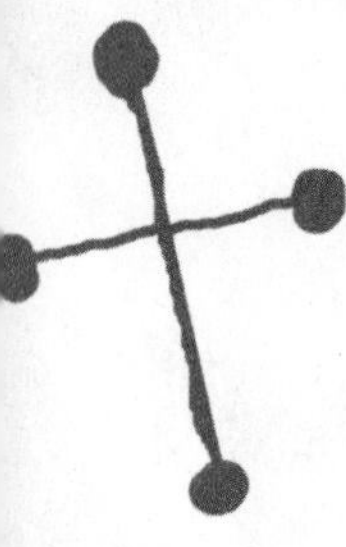

When Michael Collins returned from the moon, he made a decision to never travel again. He wanted to spend the rest of his life fishing, bringing up his children, taking care of his dogs, and sitting on the porch with his wife.

Sometimes, when he's talking to other people, the thought strikes him: *I have been to places and done things that no one can ever imagine. I will never be able to explain what it was like. I carry it inside, like a treasure.*

At night, Michael Collins tends to the roses in his garden at the back of his house. The soil smells good. The wind feels warm and humid against his face. He looks up at the yellow disk in the sky and thinks to himself: *I have been there. It was beautiful, but compared to Earth it was nothing.*

He never wants to go back to the moon.

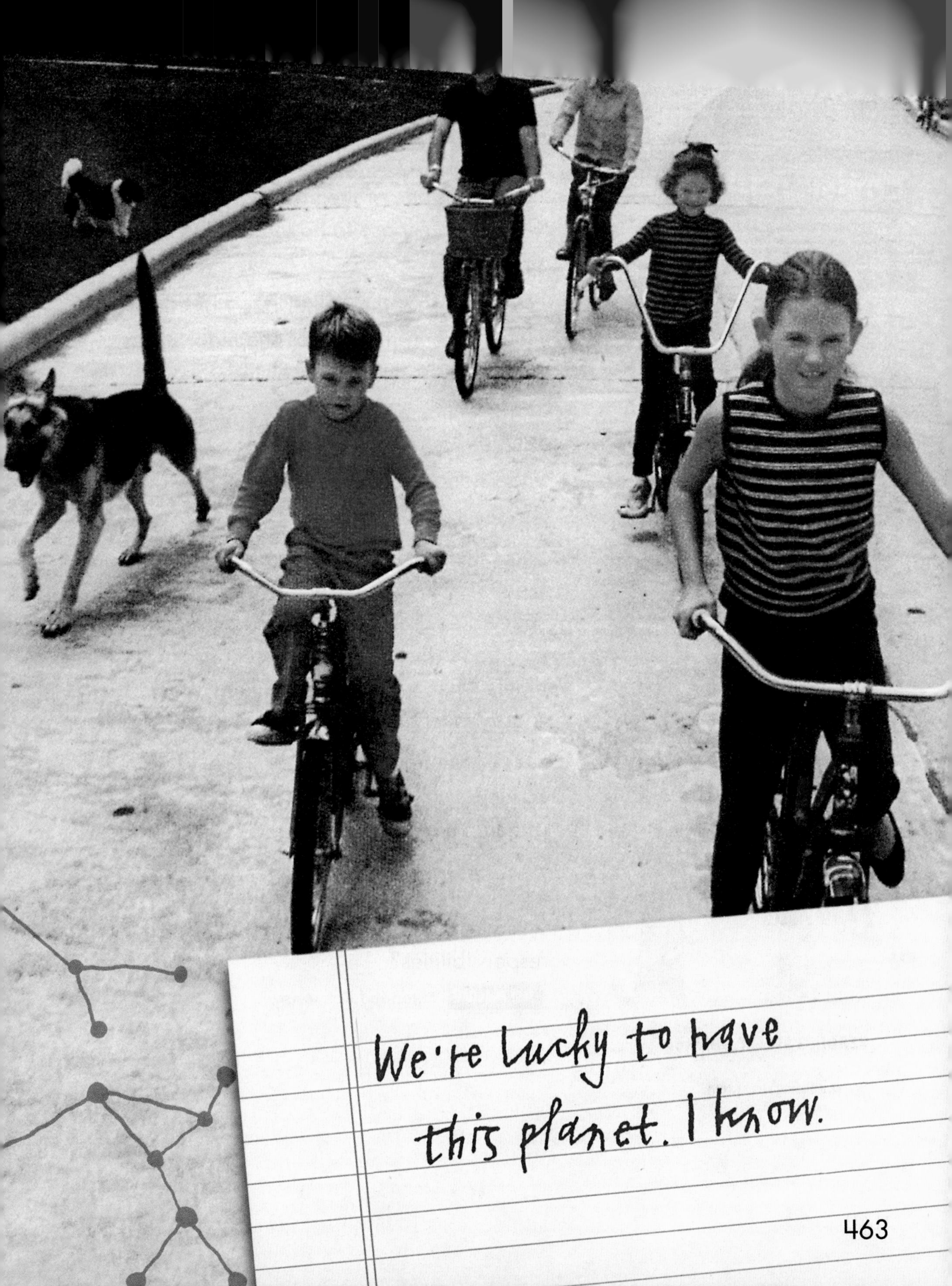
We're lucky to have
this planet. I know.

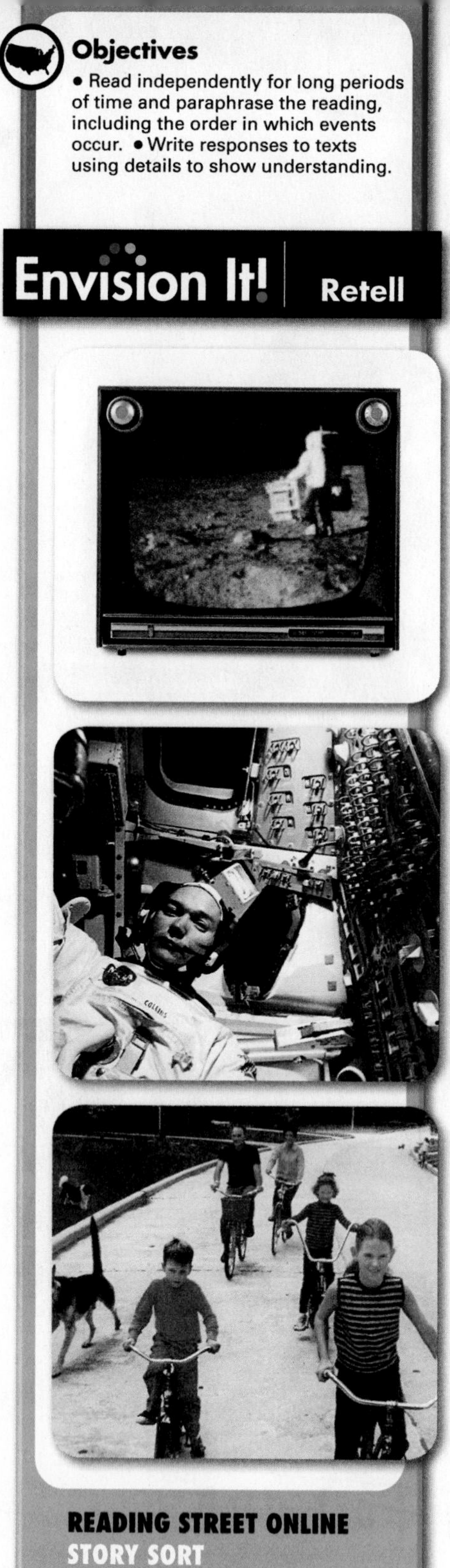

Objectives
- Read independently for long periods of time and paraphrase the reading, including the order in which events occur.
- Write responses to texts using details to show understanding.

Envision It! | **Retell**

READING STREET ONLINE
STORY SORT
www.ReadingStreet.com

Think Critically

1. Think about the three astronauts of *Apollo 11* and what they accomplished. If you could have been one of them, which of the three would you choose to have been? Why? **Text to Self**

2. On page 452, the author describes the moon landing. How does she make it suspenseful? **Think Like an Author**

3. The selection contains many graphic sources. Which one best helps you understand events in the selection? Why? **Graphic Sources**

4. Since the astronauts of *Apollo 11* set foot on the moon, there have been many flights into space. Recall TV news programs, movies, and books that tell about recent space flights. Then write what you know about space travel and astronauts. **Background Knowledge**

5. **Look Back and Write** Look back at page 456. Alone in the spacecraft, Michael Collins had many jobs to do. What were they? Why was it so important that he was well prepared to carry out these responsibilities? **TEST PRACTICE** **Extended Response**

Meet the Author

Bea Uusma Schyffert

Growing up in Sweden, Bea Uusma Schyffert didn't hear much about space travel. After spending time in the United States, however, she says she became "a space geek." She remembers, "I just had to learn everything there is about the Apollo program. The more I learned, the more questions I had."

Until recently, Ms. Schyffert illustrated books. With her strong interest in the Apollo missions, she was eager to both write and illustrate a book about Michael Collins. To uncover quirky facts about his mission, such as strange smells and foods, Ms. Schyffert visited NASA and "asked their space historians all kinds of odd questions."

For her next project, Ms. Schyffert will write a book about a Swedish polar expedition. She is going to the North Pole as part of her research! She lives with her husband and two sons in Stockholm, Sweden, and New York City.

Here are other books about *Apollo 11.*

Flying to the Moon: An Astronaut's Story **by Michael Collins**

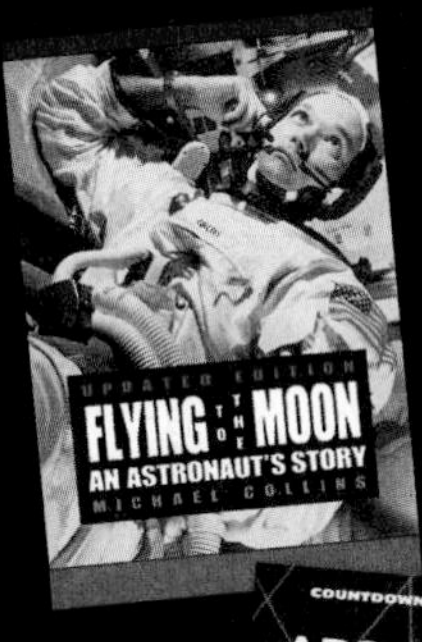

Apollo 11: First Moon Landing **by Michael D. Cole**

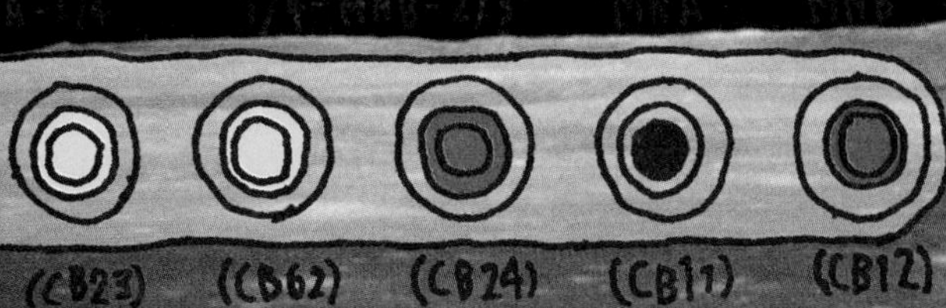

Use the Reading Log in the *Reader's and Writer's Notebook* to record your independent reading.

Objectives

- Write brief texts that include sentences that support your ideas with simple facts, details, and explanations.
- Use correct capitalization for historical events and documents.

Key Features of Narrative Nonfiction

- tells about a true event
- includes important details
- is often told in the order in which events occurred

READING STREET ONLINE
GRAMMAR JAMMER
www.ReadingStreet.com

Expository

Narrative Nonfiction

Narrative nonfiction is a description of a real event or series of events. The student model on the next page is an example of narrative nonfiction.

Writing Prompt Think about an exciting event in space or world exploration. Now write a narrative nonfiction account of that event and the people involved.

Writer's Checklist

Remember, you should ...

- ✓ tell events in sequential order.
- ✓ include all important information.
- ✓ include supporting sentences with facts, details, and explanations.
- ✓ capitalize historical events, documents, books, languages, nationalities, races, and other proper nouns.

Student Model

The First Teacher in Space

Barbara Morgan was one of five mission specialists to board the space shuttle Endeavor in 2007. She was chosen from the Educator Astronaut Project. Morgan had more than 24 years of teaching experience before she began working with NASA.

The mission lasted 11 days. The crew made repairs to the International Space Station. Morgan's job was to work the robotic arm of the shuttle and record the crew's task. She, like the commander, pilot, and other mission specialists, wanted to make sure they finished all the required tasks. During the mission, Morgan also participated in space education activities.

To complete their work, the crew was able to spend more time in space because they used power from the station. This was the first time any shuttle had done this. Space shuttle Endeavor landed safely, and the mission was a success!

Titles are capitalized.

Genre Narrative nonfiction tells about a real event.

Writing Trait Conventions Commas are used correctly in compound sentences.

Conventions

Titles

Remember Capitalize the official **titles** of people, organizations, and spacecraft, as well as the titles of books and stories.

Objectives

- Compare how different writing styles are used to communicate different kinds of information on the Internet.

21st Century Skills
INTERNET GUY

Directories have large amounts of information. They organize things for you. Look for the link to the category you need. Then follow the links. Bookmark useful directories.

- Online directories list links to different Web sites. Use them to find information on a topic.
- Topics in directories are listed as underlined links. Clicking on a link takes you to information on a topic.
- You can search for topics by keywords. Type a keyword into the search window and click the search button.
- Read "195 Days in Space." How does the writing on Web pages compare to other digital media, such as an online encyclopedia?

195 Days in Space

After reading *The Man Who Went to the Far Side of the Moon,* Mira wants to know more about the space program here on Earth. She wants to learn about the places where spacecraft are launched.

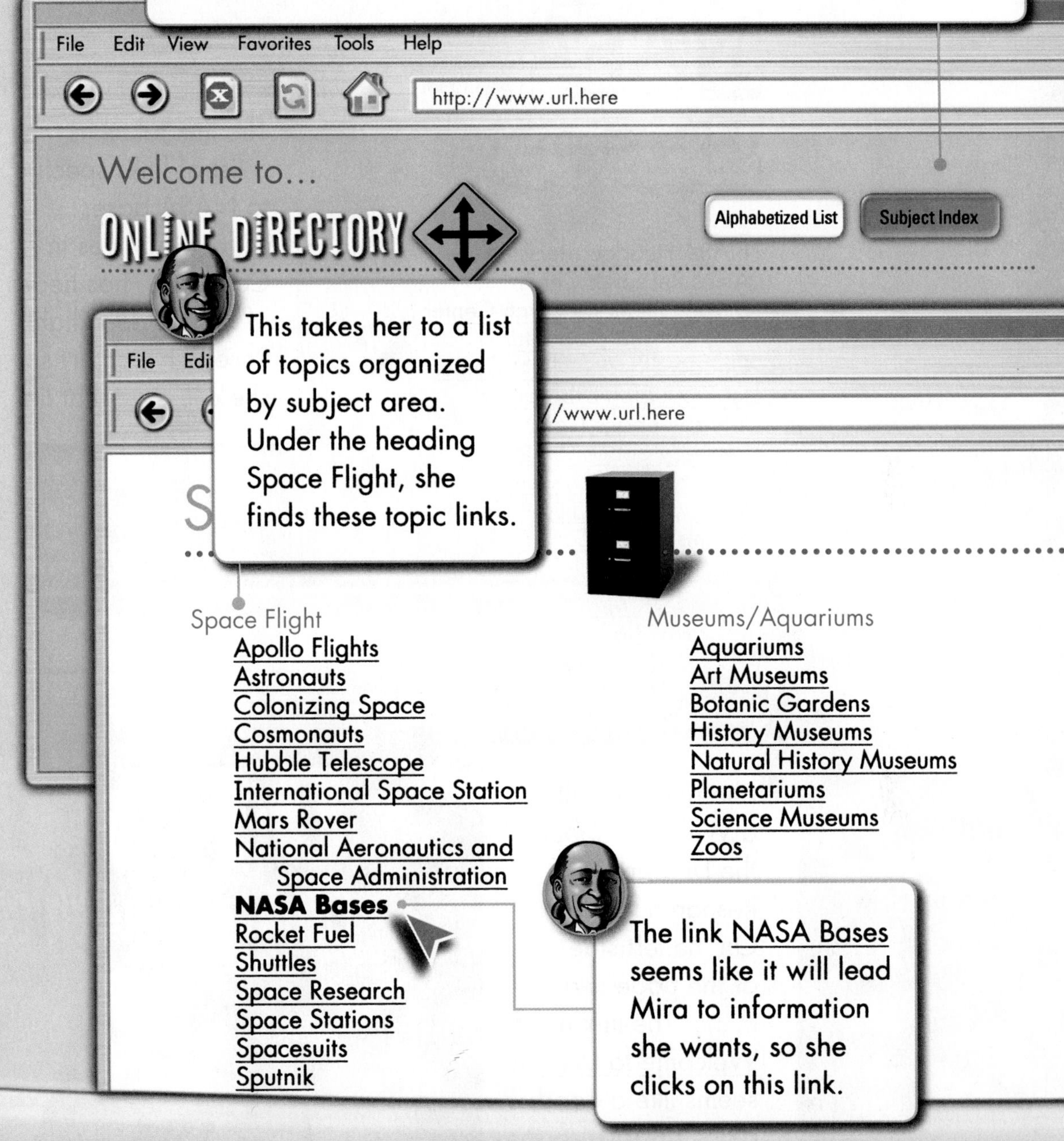
To find out more, Mira goes to an Internet online directory. She clicks on the Subject Index link on the home page.
File Edit View Favorites Tools Help
http://www.url.here
Welcome to...
ONLINE DIRECTORY
Alphabetized List
Subject Index
This takes her to a list of topics organized by subject area. Under the heading Space Flight, she finds these topic links.
File Edit
//www.url.here
Space Flight
Apollo Flights
Astronauts
Colonizing Space
Cosmonauts
Hubble Telescope
International Space Station
Mars Rover
National Aeronautics and Space Administration
NASA Bases
Rocket Fuel
Shuttles
Space Research
Space Stations
Spacesuits
Sputnik
Museums/Aquariums
Aquariums
Art Museums
Botanic Gardens
History Museums
Natural History Museums
Planetariums
Science Museums
Zoos
The link NASA Bases seems like it will lead Mira to information she wants, so she clicks on this link.

File Edit View Favorites Tools Help

http://www.url.here

NASA Bases

The link takes her to a list of links specific to NASA bases. Mira, who lives in California, has heard of the Dryden Flight Research Center, so she clicks on that link.

NASA Headquarters
Ames Research Center
Dryden Flight Research Center
Glenn Research Center
Goddard Space Flight Center
Jet Propulsion Laboratory
Johnson Space Center
Kennedy Space Center
Langley Research Center
Marshall Space Flight Center
Stennis Space Center

File Edit View Favorites Tools Help

http://www.url.here

She finds herself at a Web site about the Dryden Flight Research Center. On the left side of the page is a menu. The link titled Welcome to Dryden seems like a good place to start, so she clicks on it.

DRYDE
Flight Research Center

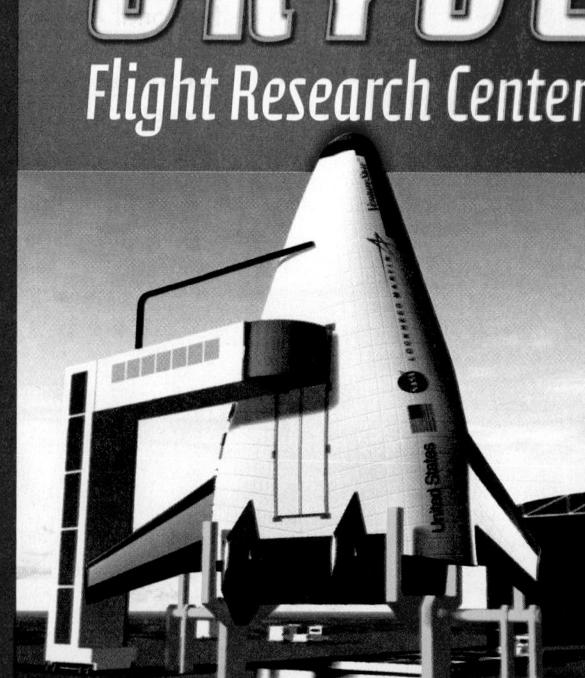

Home Page
Welcome to Dryden
Research
Education
History

File Edit View Favorites Tools Help

     http://www.url.here

DRYDEN Flight Research Center

Location

Welcome to the Dryden Flight Research Center. Dryden, a NASA base, is on the western edge of the Mojave Desert, about 90 miles north of Los Angeles.

Space Shuttle *Atlantis*

Edwards Air Force Base, where Dryden is located, served as the landing site for space shuttle *Atlantis* in 2007. The landing came after a visit to the International Space Station.

The *Atlantis* astronauts brought a space station crew member back with them. Their passenger was Sunita "Suni" Williams. She had been in space for 195 days, the longest single spaceflight by a woman. Suni said she would miss her six-month home in space. But she was glad to be back and was looking forward to eating pizza.

for more practice

Get Online!

www.ReadingStreet.com

Use online directories to find out more about the space program.

21st Century Skills Online Activity

Log on and follow the directions for using online directories to locate facts about the space program here on Earth.

Objectives

- Read aloud grade-level texts and understand what is read. • Determine the meanings of unfamiliar words or multiple-meaning words by using the context of the sentence. • Listen closely to speakers and ask questions about and comment on the topic.
- Speak clearly and to the point, give an opinion and support it with correct information. Make eye contact, change how fast, loud, and clearly you speak, and get your ideas across clearly.

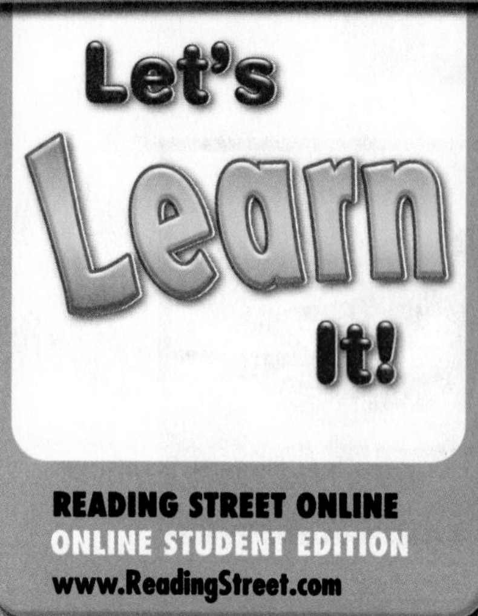

READING STREET ONLINE
ONLINE STUDENT EDITION
www.ReadingStreet.com

Vocabulary

Multiple-Meaning Words

Context Clues Some words have more than one meaning. Look for clues in nearby words and sentences to decide which meaning of a word fits in the story.

Practice It! Find the word *capsule* on page 455. The word has more than one meaning. Decide which meaning fits. Write two definitions for *capsule*. Explain to a partner how you figured out which meaning to use in the story. Do the same for the word *cast,* which appears on the same page.

Fluency

Rate and Accuracy

Partner Reading Stories may contain difficult terms, charts, and numbers. Slowing down as you read helps you understand the ideas and the story.

Practice It! With a partner, practice reading aloud page 455, paragraphs 1–3. Notice that there is a lot of information described with numbers. Read it slowly so you can read it accurately.

Listening and Speaking

Get Ready For Middle School

When you speak in front of a group, speak clearly and loudly to your audience.

Informational Speech

In an informational speech, a speaker tells an audience about people, ideas, or events. The purpose of an informational speech is to inform people.

Practice It! Use information from *The Man Who Went to the Far Side of the Moon* to give an informational speech about Michael Collins to the class. Include details about his training and his trip to the moon. Discuss his feelings when he returned.

Tips

Listening . . .

- Listen attentivley to the speaker.
- Be ready to ask relevant questions.

Speaking . . .

- Speak at a comfortable pace.
- Use proper grammar in your speech.

Teamwork . . .

- Ask questions with detail.
- Answer questions with appropriate details.

Objectives

- Explain how different poems use elements of poetry, such as rhyme and meter.

Poetry

- Poetry makes us see, feel, and think about things in a different way.
- Poets use words to create images and sounds. The words create a **meter,** or beat, in the poem.
- Poetry looks different from other kinds of writing. Its lines are arranged in **stanzas.**
- Read "Dream Dust," "Martin Luther King," and "Martin Luther King Day." Explain how the structure of the poems makes you think and feel about things in a new way.

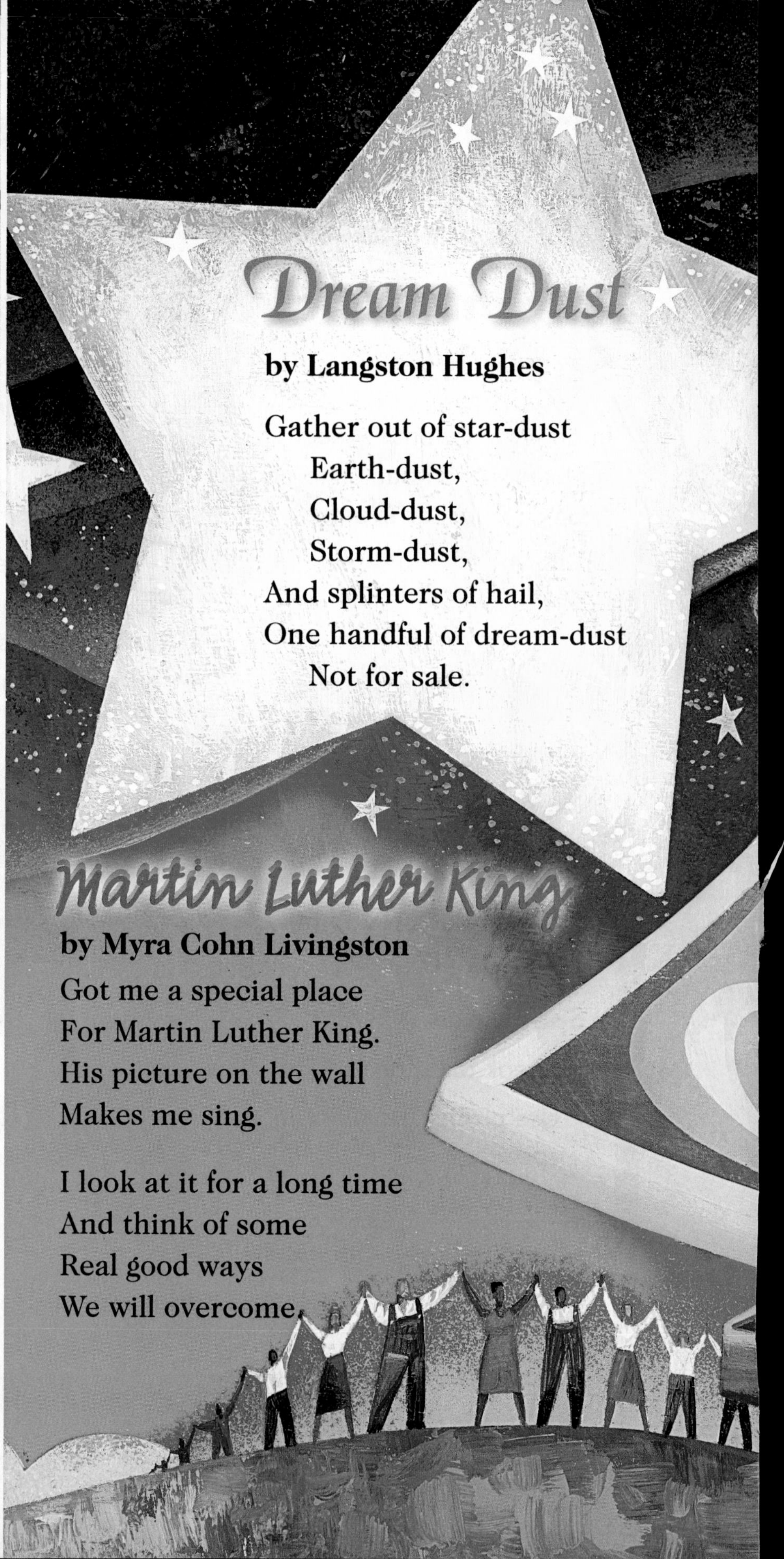

Dream Dust

by Langston Hughes

Gather out of star-dust
    Earth-dust,
    Cloud-dust,
    Storm-dust,
And splinters of hail,
One handful of dream-dust
    Not for sale.

Martin Luther King

by Myra Cohn Livingston

Got me a special place
For Martin Luther King.
His picture on the wall
Makes me sing.

I look at it for a long time
And think of some
Real good ways
We will overcome.

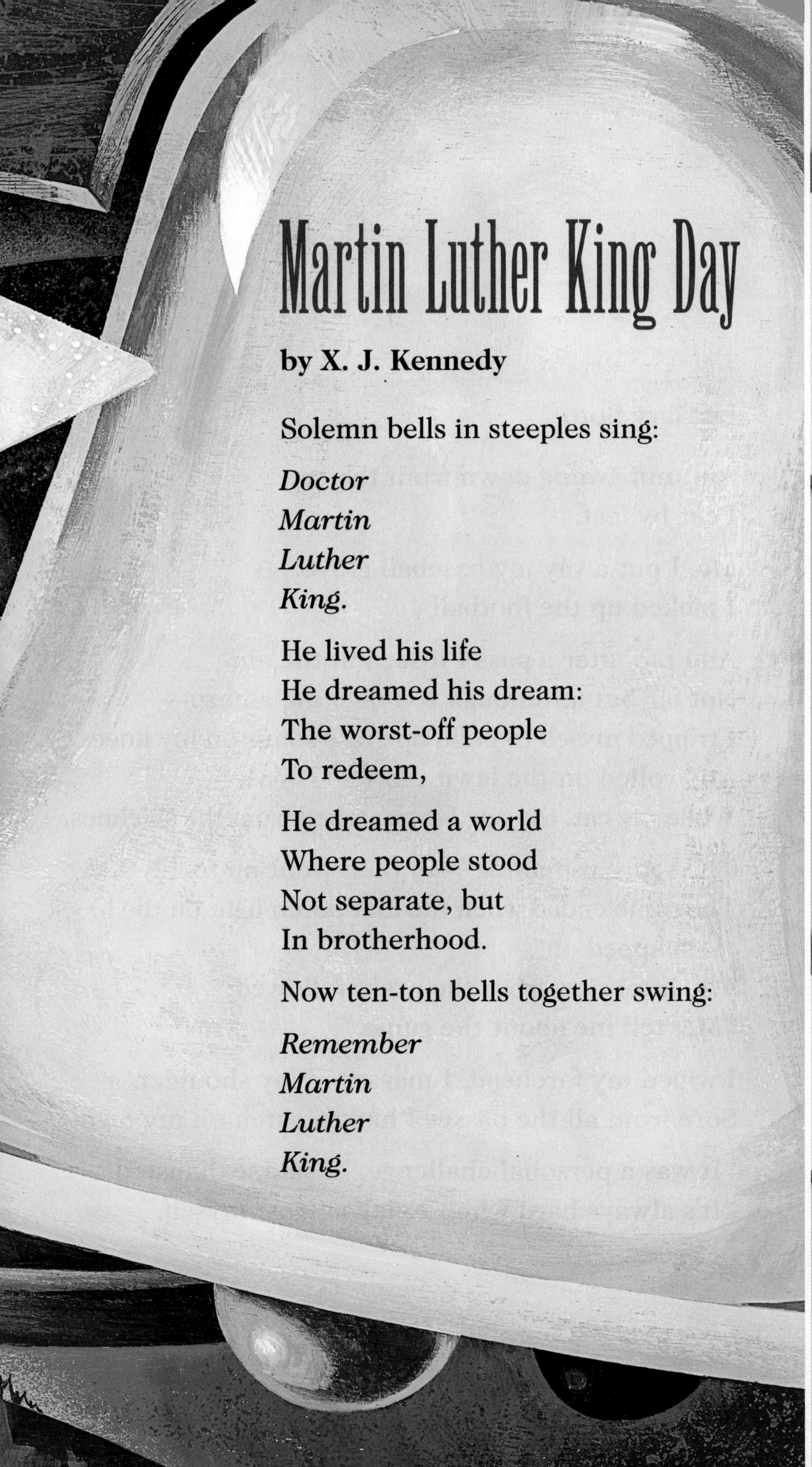

Martin Luther King Day

by X. J. Kennedy

Solemn bells in steeples sing:

Doctor
Martin
Luther
King.

He lived his life
He dreamed his dream:
The worst-off people
To redeem,

He dreamed a world
Where people stood
Not separate, but
In brotherhood.

Now ten-ton bells together swing:

Remember
Martin
Luther
King.

Let's Think About...

In which of the poems do you hear rhyming words? Do you hear words repeated in any of them? Explain how these elements convey the poets' ideas.

Let's Think About...

Can you hear the bells ringing in "Martin Luther King Day?" How did the poet make that sound?

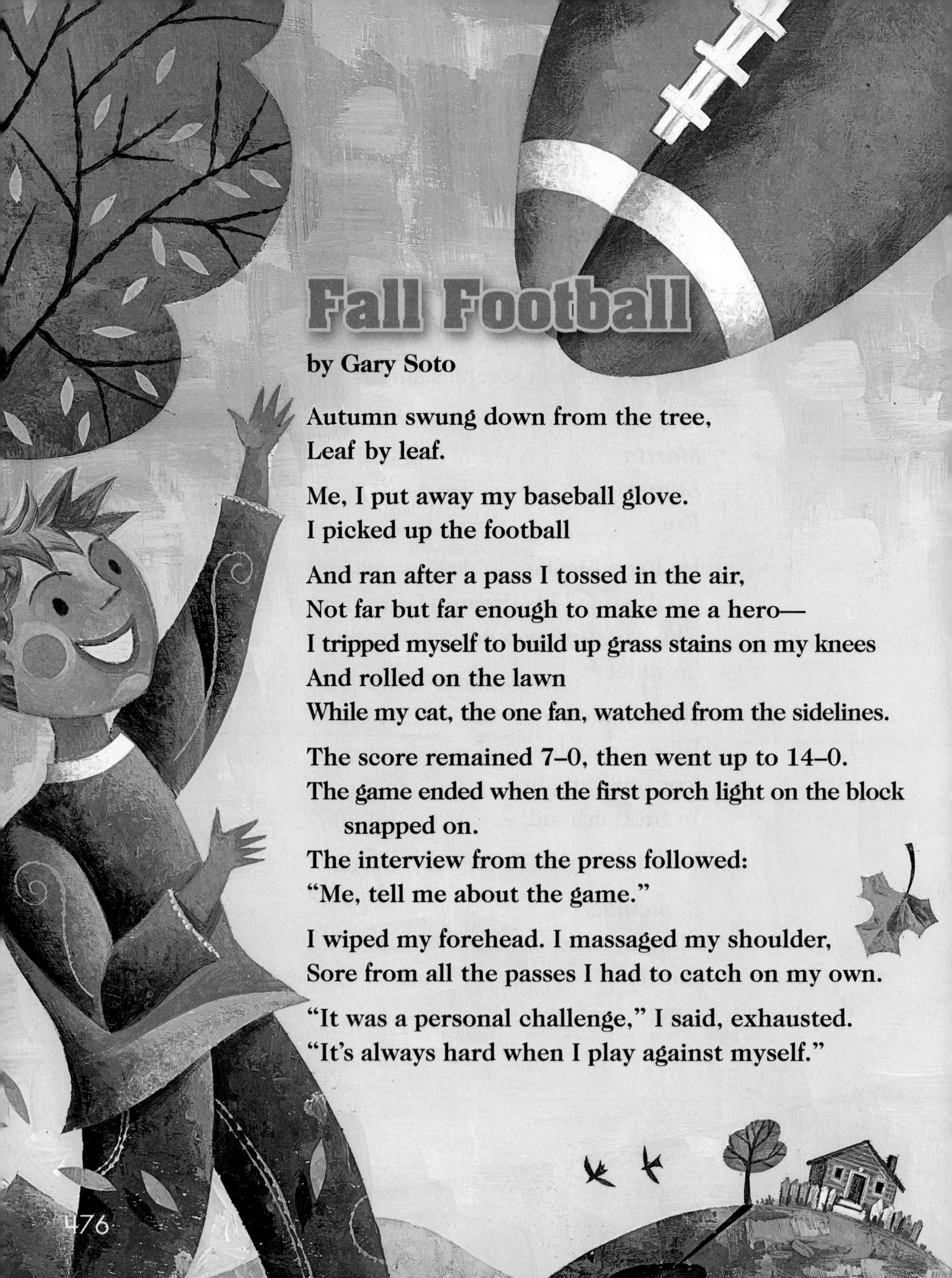

Fall Football

by Gary Soto

Autumn swung down from the tree,
Leaf by leaf.

Me, I put away my baseball glove.
I picked up the football

And ran after a pass I tossed in the air,
Not far but far enough to make me a hero—
I tripped myself to build up grass stains on my knees
And rolled on the lawn
While my cat, the one fan, watched from the sidelines.

The score remained 7–0, then went up to 14–0.
The game ended when the first porch light on the block
snapped on.
The interview from the press followed:
"Me, tell me about the game."

I wiped my forehead. I massaged my shoulder,
Sore from all the passes I had to catch on my own.

"It was a personal challenge," I said, exhausted.
"It's always hard when I play against myself."

First Men On the Moon

by J. Patrick Lewis

That afternoon in mid-July,
Two pilgrims watched from distant space
The Moon ballooning in the sky.
They rose to meet it face-to-face.

Their spidery spaceship *Eagle* dropped
Down gently on the lunar sand.
And when the module's engines stopped,
Cold silence fell across the land.

The first man down the ladder, Neil,
Spoke words that we remember now—
"Small step for man. . . ." It made us feel
As if we too were there somehow.

Then Neil planted the flag and Buzz
Collected lunar rocks and dust.
They hopped liked kangaroos because
Of gravity. Or wanderlust.

A quarter million miles away,
One small blue planet watched in awe.
And no one who was there that day
Will soon forget the Moon they saw.

How to Use This Glossary

This glossary can help you understand and pronounce some of the words in this book. The entries in this glossary are in alphabetical order. There are guide words at the top of each page to show you the first and last words on the page. A pronunciation key is at the bottom of page 479. Remember, if you can't find the word you are looking for, ask for help or check a dictionary.

The entry word is in dark type. It shows how the word is spelled and how the word is divided into syllables.

The pronunciation is in parentheses. It also shows which syllables are stressed.

Part-of-speech labels show the function or functions of an entry word and any listed form of that word.

an•ces•tor (an′ses′tər), NOUN. person from whom you are descended, such as your great-grandparents: *Their ancestors had come to the United States in 1812.* ❑ PLURAL **an•ces•tors.**

Sometimes, irregular and other special forms will be shown to help you use the word correctly.

The definition and example sentence show you what the word means and how it is used.

Aa

a•bun•dance (ə bun′dəns), NOUN. quantity that is a lot more than enough: *There is an abundance of apples this year.*

ad•vance (ad vans′), ADJECTIVE. in front of others; forward: *Our army received advance warning of the plan.*

af•ford (ə fôrd′), VERB. to give as an effect or a result; provide; yield: *Reading a good book affords real pleasure.* ❑ VERB **af•ford•ed, af•ford•ing.**

am•phib•i•an (am fib′ē ən), NOUN. any of many cold-blooded animals with backbones and moist, scaleless skins. Their young usually have gills and live in water until they develop lungs for living on land: *Frogs, toads, newts, and salamanders are amphibians.* ❑ PLURAL **am•phib•i•ans.**

amphibian

a•nal•y•sis (ə nal′ə sis), **1.** NOUN. separation of anything into its parts or elements to find out what it is made of. **2.** NOUN. an examination made carefully and in detail. ❑ PLURAL **a•nal•y•ses.**

an•ces•tor (an′ses′tər), NOUN. person from whom you are descended, such as your great-grandparents: *Their ancestors had come to the United States in 1812.* ❑ PLURAL **an•ces•tors.**

an•cient (ān′shənt), ADJECTIVE. of times long past: *In Egypt, we saw the ruins of an ancient temple built 6,000 years ago.* (*Ancient* comes from the Latin word *ante,* meaning "before.")

an•tic•i•pa•tion (an tis′ə pā′shən), *NOUN.* act of anticipating; looking forward to; expectation: *In anticipation of a cold winter, they cut extra firewood.*

a•quar•i•um (ə kwâr′ē əm), **1.** *NOUN.* tank or glass bowl in which fish or other water animals and water plants are kept in water. **2.** *NOUN.* building used for showing collections of live fish, water animals, and water plants.

aquarium (Definition 2)

as•tro•naut (as′trə nȯt), *NOUN.* pilot or member of the crew of a spacecraft. ❑ *PLURAL* **as•tro•nauts.**

a•void (ə void′), *VERB.* to keep away from; keep out of the way of: *We avoided driving through large cities on our trip.* ❑ *VERB* **a•void•ed, a•void•ing.**

Bb

back•drop (bak′drop′), *NOUN.* curtain at the back of a stage, often painted and used as part of the scenery.

beak•er (bē′kər), *NOUN.* thin glass or metal container with a flat bottom and small lip for pouring that is used in laboratories.

board•ing school (bôr′ding skül), *NOUN.* school with buildings where the pupils live during the school term.

Cc

cap•sule (kap′səl), **1.** *NOUN.* the enclosed front section of a rocket made to carry instruments, astronauts, etc., into space. In flight, the capsule can separate from the rest of the rocket and go into orbit or be directed back to Earth. **2.** *NOUN.* a tiny dose of medicine in a gelatin case.

cer•e•mon•i•al (ser′ə mō′nē əl), *ADJECTIVE.* of or used for a formal occasion or ceremony: *a ceremonial mask.*

coil (koil), **1.** *VERB.* to wind around and around in a circular or spiral shape. **2.** *NOUN.* anything that is coiled: *a coil of rope.*

colo•nel (kėr′nl), *NOUN.* military rank that is below the rank of general.

con•cen•trate (kon′sən trāt), *VERB.* to pay close attention; focus the mind: *He concentrated on his reading so that he would understand the story.* ❑ *VERB* **con•cen•trat•ing.**

con•ti•nent (kon′tə nənt), *NOUN.* one of the seven great masses of land on the earth. The continents are North America, South America, Europe, Africa, Asia, Australia, and Antarctica. (*Continent* comes from two Latin words, *com,* meaning "in" or "together," and *tenere,* meaning "to hold.")

a in *hat*	ėr in *term*	ô in *order*	ch in *child*	ə = a in *about*
ā in *age*	i in *it*	oi in *oil*	ng in *long*	ə = e in *taken*
â in *care*	ī in *ice*	ou in *out*	sh in *she*	ə = i in *pencil*
ä in *far*	o in *hot*	u in *cup*	th in *thin*	ə = o in *lemon*
e in *let*	ō in *open*	ů in *put*	ᴛʜ in *then*	ə = u in *circus*
ē in *equal*	ȯ in *all*	ü in *rule*	zh in *measure*	

convergence • foresee

con•ver•gence (kən vėr′jəns), *NOUN.* act or process of meeting at a point. (*Convergence* comes from two Latin words, *com,* meaning "in" or "together," and *vergere,* meaning "incline.")

crime (krīm), *NOUN.* activity of criminals; violation of law: *Police forces combat crime.*

cur•i•os•i•ty (kyůr′ē os′ə tē), *NOUN.* an eager desire to know: *She satisfied her curiosity about animals by visiting the zoo every week.* (*Curiosity* comes from the Latin word *cure,* meaning "care.")

Dd

ded•i•ca•tion (ded′ə kā′shən), *NOUN.* act of setting apart or condition of being set apart for a purpose; devotion: *The man was filled with dedication toward his family.*

de•part (di pärt′), *VERB.* to go away; leave: *Your flight departs at 6:15.* (*Depart* comes from the Latin word *departire,* meaning "to divide.") ❑ *VERB* **de•part•ed, de•part•ing.**

de•scent (di sent′), *NOUN.* act of coming or going down from a higher to a lower place: *the descent of a helicopter.*

de•vel•op (di vel′əp), *VERB.* to bring into being or activity: *Scientists have developed new drugs to fight disease.* ❑ *VERB* **de•vel•oped.**

dol•phin (dol′fən), *NOUN.* any of the numerous sea mammals related to the whale, but smaller: *Dolphins have beaklike snouts and remarkable intelligence.* ❑ *PLURAL* **dol•phins.**

dor•mi•to•ry (dôr′mə tôr′ē), *NOUN.* a building with many rooms in which people sleep: *Many college students live in dormitories on campus.* ❑ *PLURAL* **dor•mi•tor•ies.**

drought (drout), **1.** *NOUN.* a long period of dry weather; continued lack of rain: *The drought caused the fields to dry up.* **2.** *NOUN.* lack of moisture; dryness.

Ee

en•chant (en chant′), *VERB.* to delight greatly; charm: *The music enchanted us all.* ❑ *VERB* **en•chant•ed, en•chant•ing.** ❑ *ADJECTIVE* **en•chant•ing.**

en•dur•ance (en důr′əns), *NOUN.* power to last and to withstand hard wear: *It takes great endurance to run a marathon.*

es•sen•tial (ə sen′shəl), *ADJECTIVE.* absolutely necessary; extremely important: *Good food is essential to good health.*

ex•haust (eg zȯst′), *VERB.* to tire very much: *The long, hard climb up the hill exhausted us.* ❑ *VERB.* **ex•haust•ed, ex•haust•ing.** ❑ *ADJECTIVE.* **ex•haust•ed.**

ex•hib•it (eg zib′it), *NOUN.* display or public showing: *The village art exhibit drew 10,000 visitors.*

Ff

flex•i•ble (flek′sə bəl), **1.** *ADJECTIVE.* easily bent; not stiff; bending without breaking: *Leather, rubber, and wire are flexible.* **2.** *ADJECTIVE.* able to change easily to fit different conditions: *My mother works from our home, and her hours are very flexible.*

for•bid•ding (fər bid′ing), *ADJECTIVE.* causing fear or dislike; looking dangerous or unpleasant: *The coast was rocky and forbidding.*

fore•see (fôr sē′), *VERB.* to see or know beforehand: *We didn't take our bathing suits, because we could foresee that the water would be cold.* ❑*VERB.* **fore•saw.**

Gg

gen•e•ra•tion (jen′ə rā′shən), **1.** *NOUN.* all people born about the same time: *Your parents and their siblings and cousins belong to one generation; you and your siblings and cousins belong to the next generation.* **2.** *NOUN.* about thirty years, or the time from the birth of one generation to the birth of the next generation: *There are three generations in a century.* ❑ *PLURAL* **gen•e•ra•tions.**

glimpse (glimps), **1.** *NOUN.* a short, quick view or look: *I caught a glimpse of the falls as our train went by.* **2.** *NOUN.* a short, faint appearance: *There was a glimpse of truth in what they said.* ❑ *PLURAL* **glimp•ses.**

glint (glint), *NOUN.* a gleam; flash: *The glint in her eye showed that she was angry.*

glo•ri•ous (glôr′ē əs), *ADJECTIVE.* magnificent; splendid: *a glorious day.* (*Glorious* comes from the Latin word *gloria,* meaning "praise.")

gran•ite (gran′it), *ADJECTIVE.* made from a very hard gray or pink rock that is formed when lava cools slowly underground: *Mom chose a granite countertop for the kitchen.*

graze (grāz), *VERB.* to feed on growing grass: *Cattle were grazing in the field.* ❑ *VERB.* **grazed, graz•ing.**

Hh

hatch[1] (hach), **1.** *VERB.* to come out of an egg: *One of the chickens hatched today.* **2.** *VERB.* to keep an egg or eggs warm until the young come out: *The heat of the sun hatches turtles' eggs.*

hatch[2] (hach), *NOUN.* a trapdoor covering an opening in an aircraft's or ship's deck.

head•quar•ters (hed′kwôr′tərz), *NOUN, PLURAL OR SINGULAR.* place from which the chief or commanding officer of any army, police force, etc., sends out orders.

heave (hēv), **1.** *VERB.* to lift with force or effort: *The heavy cargo plane heaved off the runway.* **2.** *VERB.* to rise and fall alternately: *The waves heaved in the storm.* ❑ *VERB* **heaved, heav•ing.**

hol•low (hol′ō), **1.** *ADJECTIVE.* having nothing, or only air, inside; with a hole inside; not solid; empty: *A tube or pipe is hollow, and most rubber balls are hollow.*

ho•ri•zon (hə rī′zn), *NOUN.* line where the Earth and sky seem to meet; skyline. *You cannot see beyond the horizon.*

Ii

ice•berg (īs′bėrg′), *NOUN.* a large mass of ice, detached from a glacier and floating in the sea, which has about 90 percent of its mass below the surface of the water: *The* Titanic *hit an iceberg and sank.*

iceberg

i•den•ti•ty (ī den′tə tē), **1.** *NOUN.* who or what you are; what something is: *They learned the identity of the monster.* ❑ *PLURAL* **i•den•ti•ties.**

im•pos•si•ble (im pos′ə bəl), **1.** *ADJECTIVE.* not capable of being done or happening; not possible: *It is impossible for two and two to be six.* **2.** *ADJECTIVE.* not possible to use; not to be done: *He proposed an impossible plan.*

in•tense (in tens′), *ADJECTIVE.* very much; very great; very strong; extreme: *Intense heat melts iron. A bad burn causes intense pain.*

Ll

lec•ture (lek′chər), *NOUN.* a planned talk on a chosen subject given before an audience; a speech: *We went to a lecture on the history of space travel.*

link (lingk), *NOUN.* anything that joins or connects, as a loop of a chain does: *a link between the charms on her bracelet.*

liz•ard (liz′ərd), *NOUN.* any of many reptiles with long bodies and tails, movable eyelids, and usually four legs; some lizards that have no legs look much like snakes: *Iguanas, chameleons, and horned toads are lizards.* ❑ *PLURAL* **liz•ards.**

lizard

loom (lüm), *VERB.* to appear dimly or vaguely as a large, threatening shape: *A large shadow loomed across the doorway.* ❑ *VERB* **loomed, loom•ing.**

lu•nar (lü′nər), *ADJECTIVE.* of, like, or about the moon: *a lunar landscape.*

lurk (lėrk), *VERB.* to move about in a secret and sly manner: *Several people were seen lurking near the house before it was robbed.* ❑ *VERB* **lurked, lurk•ing.**

Mm

man•u•al (man′yü əl), **1.** *ADJECTIVE.* done with the hands: *Digging a trench with a shovel is manual labor.* **2.** *NOUN.* a small book that helps its readers understand and use something; a handbook: *An instruction manual came with my new telephone.*

mes•sage (mes′ij), *NOUN.* words sent or delivered from one person or group to another: *a telephone message.* ❑ *PLURAL* **mes•sag•es.**

meth•od (meth′əd), **1.** *NOUN.* way of doing something: *Roasting is one method of cooking meat.* **2.** *NOUN.* order or system in getting things done or in thinking: *If you followed a method, you wouldn't waste so much time.*

mi•cro•scope (mī′krə skōp), *NOUN.* device with a lens or combination of lenses for making small things look larger; often used to see bacteria, blood cells, and other objects not visible to the naked eye.

min•is•ter (min′ə stər), *NOUN.* member of the clergy; spiritual guide; pastor.

mod•ule (moj′ül), *NOUN.* a self-contained unit or system within a larger system, often designed for a particular function: *The lunar module circled the moon.*

murk•y (mėr′kē), *ADJECTIVE.* discolored with sediment: *the murky waters of the pond.*

Nn

nu•mer•ous (nü′mər əs), *ADJECTIVE.* very many: *The child asked numerous questions.*

Pp

pal•ette (pal′it), **1.** *NOUN.* a thin board, usually oval or oblong, with a thumb hole at one end, used by painters to lay and mix colors on. **2.** *NOUN.* set of colors used by a painter. ❑ *PLURAL* **pal•ettes.**

par•a•chute (par′ə shüt), *NOUN.* device shaped like an umbrella, made of nylon or silk, which allows people or objects to fall slowly after dropping out of an aircraft.

parachute

pre•cise (pri sīs′), **1.** *ADJECTIVE.* very definite or correct; exact; accurate: *Their measurements were absolutely precise.*

pul•pit (pu̇l′pit), *NOUN.* platform or raised structure in a church from which the pastor preaches or guests speak.

pulse (puls), **1.** *NOUN.* the regular beating of the arteries caused by the rush of blood into them after each contraction of the heart: *By feeling a person's pulse in the artery of the wrist, you can count the number of times the heart beats each minute.* **2.** *NOUN.* any regular, measured beat: *the pulse in music.* ❑ *PLURAL* **pul•ses.**

Qq

quaint (kwānt), *ADJECTIVE.* strange or odd in an interesting, pleasing, or amusing way: *Many old photographs seem quaint to us today.*

quar•an•tine (kwôr′ən tēn′ *or* kwär′ən tēn′), *NOUN.* detention, isolation, and other measures taken to prevent the spread of an infectious disease.

Rr

rap•pel (ra pel′), *VERB.* to lower yourself down the face of a cliff by means of a rope fastened at the top of the cliff and placed around your body so that the rope can gradually be lengthened.

ref•er•ence (ref′ər əns), *ADJECTIVE.* used for information or help: *The reference librarian can find the article that you need.*

re•lent•less (ri lent′lis), *ADJECTIVE.* without giving up; not relenting; unyielding: *They were relentless in their pursuit of the truth.* ❑ *ADVERB.* **re•lent•less•ly.**

rep•tile (rep′tīl), *NOUN.* any of many cold-blooded animals with backbones and lungs, usually covered with horny plates or scales. Snakes, lizards, turtles, alligators, and crocodiles are reptiles: *Dinosaurs were reptiles.* ❑ *PLURAL* **rep•tiles.**

re•sem•blance (ri zem′bləns), *NOUN.* similar appearance; likeness: *Twins often show great resemblance, even when they're not identical.*

res•er•va•tion (rez′ər vā′shən), **1.** *NOUN.* arrangement to have a room, a seat, etc., held in advance for your use later on: *make a reservation for a room in a hotel.* **2.** *NOUN.* land set aside by the government for a special purpose: *an Indian reservation.*

re•veal (ri vēl′), *VERB.* to make known: *Never reveal my secret.*

ridge (rij), **1.** *NOUN.* the long and narrow upper part of something: *the ridge of an animal's back.* **2.** *NOUN.* a long, narrow chain of hills or mountains: *the Blue Ridge of the Appalachian Mountains.*

rille (ril), *NOUN.* a long, narrow valley on the surface of the moon.

ruin (rü′ən), *NOUN.* [often *ruins, PL.*] what is left after a building, wall, etc., has fallen to pieces: *the ruins of an ancient city.* (*Ruin* comes from the Latin word *ruina,* meaning "a collapse.")

runt (runt), *NOUN.* animal, person, or plant that is smaller than the usual size. If used about a person, *runt* is sometimes considered offensive.

Ss

sal•a•man•der (sal′ə man′dər), *NOUN.* any of numerous animals shaped like lizards but related to frogs and toads: *Salamanders have moist, smooth skin and live in water or in damp places.* ❑ *PLURAL* **sal•a•man•ders.**

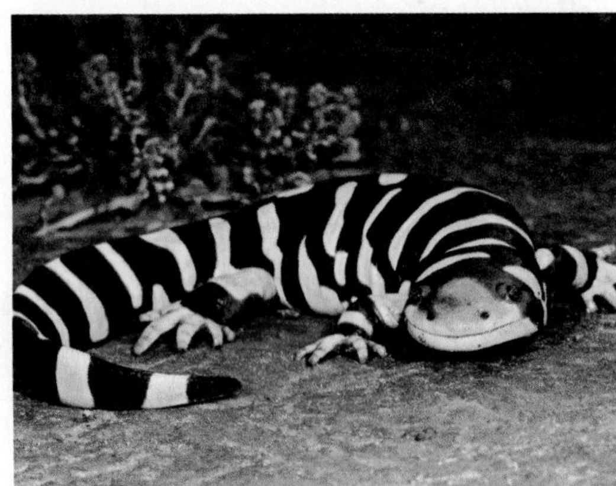

salamander

schol•ar (skol′ər), *NOUN.* a learned person; person having much knowledge: *The professor was a famous scholar.* (*Scholar* comes from the Greek word *schol,* meaning "discussion.") ❑ *PLURAL* **schol•ars.**

seek•er (sēk′ər), *NOUN.* one who tries to find; one who searches: *That judge is a seeker of truth.*

shaft (shaft), **1.** *NOUN.* the main part of a column or other structure. **2.** *NOUN.* a high, narrow space: *an elevator shaft.*

shield (shēld), *VERB.* to protect; defend: *They shielded me from unjust punishment.* ❑ *VERB* **shield•ed, shield•ing.**

shock (shok), **1.** *NOUN.* a sudden, violent, or upsetting disturbance: *Discovering their long-lost relative was a shock to her family.* **2.** *VERB.* to cause to feel surprise, horror, or disgust: *That child's bad language shocks everyone.*

so•ci•e•ty (sə sī′ə tē), **1.** *NOUN.* the people of any particular time or place: *twentieth-century society, American society.* **2.** *NOUN.* company; companionship: *The musicians belong to a special society that meets once a month.* ❑ *PLURAL* **so•ci•e•ties.**

stag•ger (stag′ ər), *VERB.* to become unsteady; waver: *The troops staggered because of their exhaustion.* ❑ *VERB* **stag•gered, stag•ger•ing.**

steer (stir), *VERB.* to guide the course of: *steer a ship, steer a car.*

stump (stump), *VERB.* to puzzle: *The riddle stumped me.* ❑ *VERB* **stumped, stump•ing.**

sum•mon (sum′ən), *VERB.* to stir to action; rouse: *We were summoning our courage before entering the deserted house.* ❑ *VERB* **sum•moned, sum•mon•ing.**

sur•face (sėr′fis), **1.** *NOUN.* the top of the ground or soil, or of a body of water or other liquid: *The stone sank beneath the surface of the water.* **2.** *NOUN.* the outward appearance: *He seems rough, but you will find him very kind below the surface.* **3.** *VERB.* to rise to the surface: *We were surprised to see the submarine surface.*

Tt

taunt (tȯnt), *VERB.* to jeer at; mock; reproach: *My classmates taunted me for being the teacher's pet.* ❑ *VERB* **taunt•ed, taunt•ing.**

tem•ple (tem′pəl), *NOUN.* building used for the service or worship of God or gods. (*Temple* comes from the Latin word *templum,* meaning "temple.") ❑ *PLURAL* **tem•ples.**

temple

ter•race (ter′is), *VERB.* to form into flat, level land with steep sides: *Terraces are often made in hilly areas to create more space for farming.* (*Terrace* comes from the Latin word *terra,* meaning "earth, land.") ❑ *VERB* **ter•raced, ter•rac•ing.**

thick•et (thik′it), *NOUN.* bushes or small trees growing close together: *We crawled into the thicket and hid.* ❑ *PLURAL* **thick•ets.**

tor•rent (tôr′ənt), *NOUN.* a violent, rushing stream of water: *The mountain torrent dashed over the rock.* (*Torrent* comes from the Latin word *torrentum,* meaning "boiling.")

trans•late (tran slāt′ *or* tranz lāt′), *VERB.* to change from one language into another: *translate a book from French into English.* (*Translate* comes from the Latin word *trans,* which means "across, through, or behind.") ❑ *VERB* **trans•lat•ed, trans•lat•ing.**

trek (trek), *VERB.* to travel slowly by any means: *The soldiers forced the Cherokee to trek from their homes in Georgia to Oklahoma.* ❑ *VERB* **trek•ked.**

trench (trench), *NOUN.* any ditch; deep furrow: *to dig a trench for a pipe.*

tri•umph (trī′umf), *NOUN.* victory; success: *The exploration of outer space is a great triumph of modern science.*

trudge (truj), *VERB.* to walk wearily or with effort: *We trudged up the hill.* ❑ *VERB* **trudged, trudg•ing.**

Uu

un•cov•er (un kuv′ər), *VERB.* to make known; reveal; expose: *The reporter uncovered a scandal.* ❑ *VERB* **un•cov•ered, un•cov•er•ing.**

un•der•brush (un′dər brush′), *NOUN.* bushes and small trees growing under large trees in woods or forests; undergrowth.

Vv

van•ish (van′ish), *VERB.* to disappear, especially suddenly: *The sun vanished behind a cloud.* ❑ *VERB* **van•ished, van•ish•ing.**

void (void), *NOUN.* an empty space.

Ww

wind[1] (wind), *NOUN.* air in motion: *The wind varies in force from a slight breeze to a strong gale.*

wind[2] (wīnd), *VERB.* to fold, wrap, or place around something or someone: *She likes to wind a ribbon around her ponytail.*

Unit 4

The Case of the Gasping Garbage

*analysis / análisis
beakers / vasos de precipitado
hollow / hueco
*identity / identidad
lecture / conferencia
*microscope / microscopio
precise / exacto
relentless / implacable

Encantado: Pink Dolphin of the Amazon

aquarium / acuario
*dolphins / delfines
enchanted / encantado
*flexible / flexibles
glimpses / vistazos fugaces
pulses / impulsos
surface / superficie

Navajo Code Talkers

advance / adelantar
developed / desarrolló
exhausting / agotando
headquarters / cuartel general
*impossible / imposible
*intense / intenso
messages / mensajes
*reveal / revelar

Seeker of Knowledge

ancient / antiguo
link / conexión
scholars / eruditos
seeker / buscador
*temple / templo
translate / traducir
*triumph / triunfo
uncover / descubrir

Encyclopedia Brown and the Case of the Slippery Salamander

amphibians / anfibios
*crime / crimen
exhibit / exposición
lizards / lagartos
*reference / referencia
*reptiles / reptiles
*salamanders / salamandras
stumped / perplejo

Unit 5

Smokejumpers

*concentrating / concentrando
*dedication / dedicación
*essential / esencial
method / método
parachute / paracaídas
steer / guiar
underbrush / maleza
wind / viento

Lost City: The Discovery of Machu Picchu

*curiosity / curiosidad
*glorious / gloriosa
*granite / granito
*ruins / ruinas
*terraced / en terrazas
thickets / matorrales
*torrent / torrente

* English/Spanish cognate: A **cognate** is a word that is similar in two languages and has the same meaning in both languages.

Cliff Hanger
coil / rollo
*descent / descenso
foresaw / previó
rappel / descender con cuerda
ridge / lomo
shaft / eje
trekked / caminó
void / vacío

Antarctic Journal
*anticipation / anticipación
*continent / continente
*convergence / convergencia
depart / salir
forbidding / inhóspita
heaves / sube
*icebergs / icebergs

Moonwalk
loomed / surgía
rille / valle lunar
runt / pequeño
staggered / se tambaleó
summoning / armándose
taunted / burló
trench / zanja
trudged / caminaron fatigosamente

Unit 6

My Brother Martin
*ancestors / ancestros
avoided / evitaba
*generations / generaciones
*minister / ministro
*numerous / numerosos
*pulpit / púlpito
shielding / protegiéndonos

Jim Thorpe's Bright Path
boarding school / internado
*dormitory / dormitorio
endurance / resistencia
*manual / manual
*reservation / reserva
*society / sociedad

How Tía Lola Came to ~~Visit~~ Stay
affords / ofrece
*colonel / coronel
glint / destello
lurking / acechando
*palettes / paletas
quaint / pintoresco
resemblance / semejanza

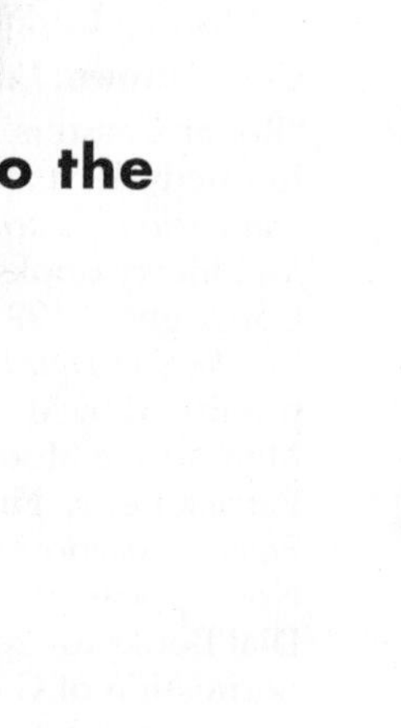

A Gift from the Heart
*abundance / abundancia
backdrop / de fondo
*ceremonial / ceremonial
drought / sequía
graze / pastar
shock / conmocionados

The Man Who Went to the Far Side of the Moon
*astronauts / astronautas
*capsule / cápsula
hatch / escotilla
*horizon / horizonte
*lunar / lunar
*module / módulo
quarantine / cuarentena

Acknowledgments

Text

Grateful acknowledgment is made to the following for copyrighted material:

A&C Black Publishers

"Who Knows" by Fatou Ndiaye Sow, translated by Véronique Tadjo from *Talking Drums: A Selection Of Poems From Africe South Of The Sahara* edited and illustrated by Véronique Tadjo. Used by permission of A & C Black Publishers.

Alfred A. Knopf a div of Random House & Harold Ober Associates

"Dream Dust" from *The Collected Poems Of Langston Hughes* by Langston Hughes edited by Arnold Rampersand with David Roessel, Associate Editor, copyright © 1994 by The Estate of Langston Hughes. Used by permission.

Ben Bova

"Moonwalk" by Ben Bova from *Boy's Life, November 2002. Pp 29-31.* Copyright © 2002 by Ben Bova. Reprinted by permission of Ben Bova.

Chronicle Books

From *The Man Who Went to the Far Side of the Moon,* copyright © 1999 by Bea Uusuma Schyffert. Used with permission of Chronicle Books LLC. San Francisco. Visit ChronicleBooks.com.

Clairon Books an imprint of Houghton Mifflin Harcourt Publishing Company

"The Best Paths" from *Toasting Marshmallows: Camping Poems* by Kristine O'Connell George. Text copyright © 2001 by Kristine O'Connell George. Reprinted by permission of Clarion Books, an imprint of Houghton Mifflin Harcourt Publishing Company. All rights reserved.

Curtis Brown, Ltd

"Roller Coasters", Copyright © 1991 by X.J. Kennedy. First appeared in *The Kite That Braved Old Orchard Beach,* published by Margaret K. McElderry Books. "Martin Luther King Day", Copyright © 1991 by X.J. Kennedy. First appeared in *The Kite That Braved Old Orchard Beach,* published by Margaret K. McElderry Books. "First Men on the Moon", Copyright (c) 1999 by J. Patrick Lewis. First appeared in *Lives: Poems About Famous Americans,* published by HarperCollins. Now appears in *A Burst of Firsts,* published by Dial Books for Young Readers. Reprinted by permission of Curtis Brown, Ltd.

Dutton Children's Books a div of Penguin Group (USA)

The Case of the Gasping Garbage by Michele Torrey, illustrated by Barbara Johansen Newman, copyright © 2001 by Michele Torrey, text. "Mr. Talberg's Famous Bread Recipe" from *The Case of the Gasping Garbage* by Michelle Torrey, illustrated by Barbara Johansen Newman, copyright © 2001 by Michele Torrey, text. Used by permission of Dutton Children's Books, A Division of Penguin Young Readers Group, A Member of Penguin Group (USA) Inc., 345 Hudson Street, New York, NY 10014. All rights reserved.

G.P. Putnam's Sons a div of Penguin Group (USA)

"Fall Football", from *Fearless Fernie: Hanging Out With Fernie & Me* by Gary Soto, copyright © 2002 by Gary Soto. Used by permission of G.P. Putnam's Sons, A Division of Penguin Young Readers Group, A Member of Penguin Group (USA) Inc., 345 Hudson Street, New York, NY 10014. All rights reserved.

Harold Ober Associates

"Poetry" from *Eleanor Farjeon's Poems For Children* by Eleanor Farjeon. Reprinted by permission of Harold Ober Associates Incorporated. Copyright 1938 by Eleanor Farjeon. Copyright renewed 1966 by Gervase Farjeon

HarperCollins Publishers

"Antarctic Journal: Four Months at the Bottom of the World" by Jennifer Owings Dewey. Text copyright © 2001 by Jennifer Dewey. Used by permission of HarperCollins Publishers.

HarperCollins Publishers & Curtis Brown, Ltd

"Cliff Hanger" by Jean Craighead George. Text copyright © 2004 by Jean Craighead George. First appeared in Cliff Hanger, published by HarperCollins. Used by permission.

Houghton Mifflin Harcourt Publishing Company

Abridged from *Encantado: Pink Dolphin Of The Amazon* by Sy Montgomery with photographs by Dianne Taylor-Snow. Text copyright © 2002 by Sy Montgomery. Photographs copyright © 2002 by Dianne Taylor-Snow. From *Seeker Of Knowledge: The Man Who Deciphered Egyptian Hieroglyphics* by James Rumford. Copyright © 2000 by James Rumford. Reprinted by permission of Houghton Mifflin Harcourt Company. All rights reserved.

Lee & Low Books

"Jim Thorpe's Bright Path". Text copyright © 2004 by Joseph Bruchac. Illustrations copyright © 2004 by S.D. Nelson. Permission arranged with Lee & Low Books, Inc. New York, NY 10016. Used by permission.

Marian Reiner Literary Agent

"The Seed" from *Always Wondering* by Aileen Fisher. Copyright © 1991 by Aileen Fisher. Inc. "Carolyn's Cat" from *When Whales Exhale and Other Poems* by Constance Levy. Copyright © 1996 by Constance Kling Levy. "Martin Luther King" from *No Way of Knowing Dallas Poems* by Myra Cohn Livingston. Copyright © 1980 by Myra Cohn Livingston. Used by permission of Marian Reiner.

Penguin Group, Ltd (UK)

"The Door" (26 lines) (p. 62) from *Miroslav Holub: Selected Poems,* translated by Ian Milner and George Theiner (Penguin Books, 1967) Copyright © Miroslav Holub 1967, Translation copyright © Penguin Books, 1967. Introduction Copyright © A Alvarez. Reproduced by permission by Penguin Books Ltd.

Philomel Books a div of Penguin Group (USA)

From *Lost City: The Discovery Of Machu Picchu* by Ted Lewin, copyright © 2003 by Ted Lewin. Used by permission of Philomel Books, A Division of Penguin Young Readers Group, A Member of Penguin Group (USA) Inc., 345 Hudson Street, New York, NY 10014. All rights reserved.

Picture Window/Compass Point Books

"Navajo Code Talkers" by Andrew Santella. Copyright © 2004 by Compass Point Books. Used by permission. All rights reserved.

Random House Children's Books a div of Random House

From *Encyclopedia Brown And The Case Of The Slippery Salamander* by Donald J. Sobol and illustrated by Warren Chong, copyright © 1999 by Donald J. Sobol. Illustration © 1999 by Warren Chang. Used by permission of Random House Children's Books, a division of Random House, Inc.

The Rosen Publishing Group

"Smokejumpers: Life Fighting Fires" by Mark Beyer, copyright 2001 by the Rosen Publishing Group, Inc. Used by permission.

Simon & Schuster Books for Young Readers an imprint of Simon & Schuster Publishing Div & The Jennifer Lyons Literary Agency, LLC

From *My Brother Martin: A Sister Remembers* by Christine King Farris. Copyright © 2003 by Christine King Farris. Used by permission.

Simon & Schuster Books for Young Readers & Sandford Lyne

"My Life Is a Buried Treasure" by Dawn Withrow, from *Ten Seconds Rainshowers: Poems for Young People, compiled* by Sandford Lyne, Simon & Schuster Books for Young Readers, 1996.

Skipping Stone Magazine

"Haiku" by Cristina Beecham. "When You Hope and Trust" by Ek Ongkar K. Khalsa. Reprinted with permission from Skipping Stones Magazine, Sept-Oct. 2003, Vol 15, No 4.

Susan Berholz Literary Services

Two Happy Months in Vermont" from *How Tia Lola Came To Visit/Stay.* Copyright © 2001 by Julia Alvarez. Published by Dell Yearling and in hardcover by Alfred A Knopf Children's Books, a division of Random House, New York. Reprinted with the permission of Susan Berholz Literary Services, New York and Lamy, NM. All rights reserved.

Times Books a div of Random House & Sanford J. Greenburger Associates

"Sadaharu Oh: a Zen Way of Baseball" from *Sadaharu Oh: A Zen Way Of Baseball* by Sadaharu Oh and David Falkner, copyright © 1984 by Sadaharu Oh and David Falkner. Used by permission.

Writer's House

"I Have a Dream" by Dr. Martin Luther King Jr. Copyright © 1963 Martin Luther King Jr., Copyright renewed © 1991 Coretta Scott King. Used by permission of The Estate of Martin Luther King, Jr.c/o Writer's House as agent for the proprietor New York, NY.

Note: Every effort has been made to locate the copyright owner of material reproduced on this component. Omissions brought to our attention will be corrected in subsequent editions.

Illustrations

Cover: Tim Jessel; **EI1–EI13** Bill McGuire; **EI16–EI25** Kenny Kiernan; **26–44** Barbara Johansen Newman; **146–154** Brett Helquist; **166–168** Joel Nakamura; **262–264** Jennifer Owings Dewey; **294–304** Peter Bollinger; **316–318** Franklin Hammond; **346** Stephen Daigle; **388–406** Macky Pamintuan; **408–410** SuLing Wang; **420–434** Erwin Madrid; **468, 476** Rafael Lopez; **W2–W15** Leslie Harrington.

Photographs

Every effort has been made to secure permission and provide appropriate credit for photographic material. The publisher deeply regrets any omission and pledges to correct errors called to its attention in subsequent editions.

Unless otherwise acknowledged, all photographs are the property of Pearson Education, Inc.

Photo locators denoted as follows: Top (T), Center (C), Bottom (B), Left (L), Right (R), Background (Bkgd)

18 (C) ©ChiselVision/Corbis; **20** (TL) ©Alistair Scott/Alamy, (B) ©Kathie Atkinson/PhotoLibrary Group, Ltd.; **23** (TR) ©DK Images, (BR) ©Lyn Balzer and Tony Perkins/Getty Images; **24** (CL) ©fStop/Alamy, (TL) ©Heinrich van den Berg/

Getty Images, (BL) Jupiter Images; **25** (B) Jupiter Images; **52** (BL) ©Erich Kuchling/Westend61/ Jupiter Images, (B) Jupiter Images; **53** (BR) ©Steve Kaufman/Corbis; **56** (CL) ©David Tipling/Getty Images, (BL) ©Ingo Wagner/ dpa/Corbis, (TL) ©mm-images/PhotoLibrary Group, Ltd.; **58** (C) ©Todd Pusser/Nature Picture Library; **60** (CR) ©Wolfgang Kaehler/ Corbis; **61** (CR) Getty Images; **62** (TL) Getty Images; **63** (TL) ©Dianne Taylor-Snow; **66** (CL) Jupiter Images; **67** (C) Andre Bartschi; **68** (TL) ©Royalty-Free/Corbis; **71** (B) ©Jay Dickinson/ Corbis; **76** (BR) ©Darek Karp/Animals Animals/ Earth Scenes, (TR) ©Dr. Morley Read/Photo Researchers, Inc.; **77** (CR) Andy Crawford/©DK Images, (TR, BR) Getty Images; **78** (B) ©William Grenfell/Visuals Unlimited; **79** (T) ©Manfred Klindwort GDT/Visuals Unlimited; **82** (TL) ©Bettmann/Corbis, (BC) ©Cindy Miller Hopkins/Danita Delimont/Alamy Images; **86** (CL) ©Enigma/Alamy, (BL) ©Gray Mortimore/ Getty Images, (TL) ©Pat Doyle/Corbis; **88** Marine Corps/Department of Defense; **90** (TR) ©Hulton Archive/Getty Images, (B) National Archives; **91** Courtesy of FDR Library, Hyde Park, NY; **92** (CL) ©Underwood & Underwood/Corbis, (TL) Marine Corps/Department of Defense; **93** (BL) Cline Library, Northern Arizona University; **94** (B) National Archives; **95** National Archives; **98** Museum of Northern Arizona; **99** Cline Library, Northern Arizona University; **100** ©Bettmann/ Corbis; **101** J. L. Burns/Marine Corps/U.S. Department of Defense; **102** (TR) ©AFP/Getty Images, (TL) Joe Rosenthal, Associated Press/ Navy/U.S. Department of Defense; **105** (BR) ©DK Images, (TR, CR) Library of Congress; **108** (Bkgd) ©Dennis Hallinan/Alamy Images, (BR) ©Jose Luis Palaez, Inc./Corbis; **112** (B) ©Bettmann/Corbis, (CL) ©Stefan Sollfors/Alamy Images; **113** (BR) ©Myrleen Ferguson Cate/ PhotoEdit; **116** (CL) ©Jim Sugar/Corbis, (TL) ©Jon Arnold Images Ltd/Alamy, (BL) ©Phil Boorman/Getty Images; **120** (CL) Getty Images; **123** Getty Images; **132** (TL) ©Kenneth Garrett/ National Geographic Image Collection; **134** (BR) ©The Print Collector/Alamy Images; **135** (TR) ©Mike Nelson/epa/Corbis, (CR) ©Ron Watts/Corbis; **140** (B) ©Dirk Anschutz/Getty Images, (CL) ©Corbis/Jupiter Images, (TL) Getty Images; **144** (CL) ©Juniors Bildarchiv/ Alamy, (TL) ©Phil Degginger/Alamy Images, (CL) ©Westend61/Alamy; **161** (TCR) ©Royalty-Free/Corbis; **162** (TL) ©Becky Shink/Lansing State Journal, (BC) Getty Images; **163** (CC) Getty Images; **165** (BR) ©Michael Krasowitz/Getty Images; **170** (C) Corbis; **172** (BL) ©Reuters/ Corbis, (B) Getty Images; **173** (TR) USDA Forest Service, Missoula, MT; **176** (TL) ©Alex Mares-Manton/Getty Images, (CL) ©Matthias Clamer/ Getty Images, (BL) ©Panoramic Images/Getty Images; **178** ©Kevin R. Morris/Corbis; **180** ©Mike McMillan/Spotfire Images; **181** (TR) ©Mike McMillan/Spotfire Images; **182** (T) ©Mike McMillan/Spotfire Images; **185** ©Mike McMillan/Spotfire Images; **186** (T) ©Mike McMillan/Spotfire Images; **187** (B) ©Mike McMillan/Spotfire Images; **188** (T) ©Mike McMillan/Spotfire Images; **189** (B) ©Mike McMillan/Spotfire Images; **191** (B) ©Kevin R. Morris/Corbis; **193** (CC) ©Rainer Holz/zefa/ Corbis; **200** (BL) ©ImageGap/Alamy; **201** (BR) ©Ron Levine/Getty Images; **204** (CL) ©Angelo Cavalli/zefa/Corbis, (BL) ©Helene Rogers/ Alamy Images, (CL) ©Travelshots/Alamy Images; **222** (C) ©Jim Erickson/Corbis; **224** (B) ©Dave Wilhelm, (CR) ©Roman Soumar/Corbis; **225** (TR) ©Francesco Venturi/Corbis, (CL) ©Kevin Schafer/Corbis; **228** (B) ©Bo Zaunders/ Corbis, (BL) ©Marcel Antonisse/epa/Corbis; **229** (TR) ©Image Source Limited; **232** (TL) ©david sanger photography/Alamy Images; **247** (CR) Ian O'Leary/©DK Images; **250** ©Ant Strack/Corbis; **252** ©Christophe Boisvieux/ Corbis; **253** ©Hoberman Collection/Corbis, **(Inset)** ©Jim Arbogast/Corbis; **256** (CL) ©Bill Hatcher/National Geographic Image Collection, (B) ©Patrick Robert/Corbis, (BC) National Science Foundation; **260** (BL) ©ImageState/ Alamy Images; **264** (Bkgd) Getty Images; **266** (CR) Jennifer Owings Dewey; **268** (BR) Jennifer Owings Dewey, (TR, CL, BC) National Science Foundation; **270** (BL, BC) Jennifer Owings Dewey; **271** (TR) National Science Foundation; **273** (TR) National Science Foundation; **274** (TR) National Science Foundation; **275** (BR) National Science Foundation; **276** (CL) National Science Foundation; **277** (B) National Science Foundation; **282** (Bkgd) Corbis; **283** (CR) ©Gabriella Miotto; **284** (TL) ©Gabriella Miotto, (BR) AP/Wide World Photos; **285** (Bkgd) Corbis; **288** (B) ©Bloomimage/Corbis, (TL) Corbis; **289** (BR) ©NASA/Roger Ressmeyer/Corbis; **292** (TL) ©Kari Marttila/Alamy Images, (CL) ©Michael Coyne/Getty Images, (BL) ©Nigel Cattlin/Alamy Images; **310** (Bkgd) Getty Images; **311** (CR) Getty Images; **312** (CL) Getty Images, (B) Original image courtesy of NASA/Corbis; **313** (TL) Getty Images, (CR) NASA/Corbis; **320** (C) ©Michael Wong/Corbis; **322** (B) ©Bob E. Daemmrich/ Sygma/Corbis, (CC) ©Enigma/Alamy; **326** (BL)

©ImageState/Alamy Images, (CL) ©Roger Day/ Alamy Images, (TL) Jupiter Images; **350** (BC) ©LWA-Dann Tardif/Corbis, (B) Corbis/Jupiter Images; **351** (BC) Jupiter Images; **354** (TL) ©David Joel/Getty Images, (B) ©Paul Doyle/ Alamy Images, (CL) ©Tim Tadder/Corbis; **370** (CR, CL, BR) Cumberland County Historical Society, Carlisle, PA, (TL) Getty Images; **371** (TL, CC, BR) Cumberland County Historical Society, Carlisle, PA, (BC) Getty Images; **376** (T) ©Joseph Sohm/ChromoSohm Inc/Corbis, (BC) ©Reuters/Corbis; **377** (B) ©Stephane Cardinale/ Corbis; **378** (BL, B) ©Jonathan Nourok/ PhotoEdit, (TR) ©Kathleen Kliskey-Geraghty/ Index Stock Imagery, (TL) ©Robert W. Ginn/ PhotoEdit; **379** (TR) ©The Daily Oakland Press/ AP/Wide World Photos, (TR) ©The Times/ AP/Wide World Photos; **381** (BR) ©PCN Photography/Alamy; **382** (BL) ©Bettmann/ Corbis, (B) ©Mickael Parpet/Sygma/Corbis; **383** (BR) ©Chuck Place/Alamy Images; **386** (TL) ©Robert W. Ginn/Alamy Images, (BL) ©Corbis/Jupiter Images, (CL) ©Image100/ Jupiter Images; **414** (BC) ©Colin Underhill/ Alamy Images, (B) ©Sean Justice/Corbis, (BL) Corbis; **417** (TR) George E. Marsh Album/ NOAA; **418** (TL) ©Oote Boe Photography/Alamy Images, (BL) ©ScotStock/Alamy Images, (CL) ©Thom Lang/Corbis; **419** (TR) ©Bananastock/ Jupiter Images; **437** (BR) Neil Fletcher/©DK Images; **444** (B) ©Roger Ressmeyer/Corbis, (BL) Jupiter Images; **445** (TR) NASA; **448** (TL) ©Jon Arnold Images Ltd/Alamy Images, (CL) ©Nik Keevil/Alamy, (BL) STS-122 Shuttle Crew/ NASA; **451** (R) NASA; **453** (CR, BL) NASA; **454** (TC) NASA; **455** (CC) NASA; **457** (C) NASA; **459** (BR) NASA; **460** (TR) N.ASA; **461** NASA; 462 (BC) ©Time Life Pictures/Getty Images; **463** (C) ©Time Life Pictures/Getty Images; **473** Original image courtesy of Buzz Aldrin/NASA/ Corbis; **478** ©Corbis/Jupiter Images; **479** Digital Vision; **480** (L) ©FogStock/Index Open, (R) Getty Images; **481** ©Matthew Mawson/Alamy; **482** (R) ©FogStock/Index Open, (L) ©Kitt Cooper-Smith/Alamy; **483** (L) ©Keith Levit Photography/Index Open, (R) Getty Images; **484** (L) Index Open; **485** (R) Corbis/Jupiter Images, Getty Images; **486** (R) NASA; **488** (BR) DFRC/ NASA; **489** (TR) ©Mark J. Terrill/AP Images, (CR) ©Tim Johnson/AP Images.